# THEORY IN LANDSCAPE ARCHITE[]

12

PENN STUDIES IN
LANDSCAPE ARCHITECTURE

John Dixon Hunt, Series Editor

*This series is dedicated to the study and promotion of a wide variety of approaches to landscape architecture, with special emphasis on connections between theory and practice. It includes monographs on key topics in history and theory, descriptions of projects by both established and rising designers, translations of major foreign-language texts, anthologies of theoretical and historical writings on classic issues, and critical writing by members of the profession of landscape architecture.*

# Theory in Landscape Architecture

A Reader

Edited by
SIMON SWAFFIELD

**PENN**

UNIVERSITY OF PENNSYLVANIA PRESS

Philadelphia

10   9   8   7

Published by
University of Pennsylvania Press
Philadelphia, Pennsylvania 19104-4011

Library of Congress Cataloging-in-Publication Data

Theory in landscape architecture : a reader / edited by Simon Swaffield.
    p.   cm. — (Penn studies in landscape architecture)
  Includes bibliographical references.
  ISBN 0-8122-1821-3 (paper : alk. paper)
  1. Landscape architecture.  I. Swaffield, Simon R.  II. Series.
SB472 .T44   2002
712.2—dc21                                         2002019461

# CONTENTS

# ILLUSTRATIONS

# PREFACE

This volume has two complementary objectives, the first educational, the second scholarly. The educational objective is to provide a teaching resource for undergraduate and graduate courses in landscape architecture and related disciplines which have a theoretical orientation. The collection of readings is intended to provide students with insight into many of the key theoretical concepts that underpin contemporary landscape architecture.

This collection comprises published English-language material from the period 1950–1999, drawn from conventional sources. Most of the authors are North American landscape architects, although a few examples from non-landscape architects are included, to indicate connections to a broader literature. Those selected are frequently cited within the discipline. Several British authors and one French author are included to expose students to the field of landscape architecture beyond North America.

The selection aims to provide insight into a range of important theoretical concepts, influential authors, and types of theory in landscape architecture. The concepts and the themes by which they are organized are discussed further in the Introduction. The choice of texts provides examples of *instrumental, interpretive,* and *critical* theory, of *particular* and more *general* application. The selections from outside the discipline serve to illustrate the *mediating* and *reconciling* roles of theory highlighted by Meyer, linking landscape architectural concerns to the wider society. Several of the readings provide a synthetic perspective, *bridging* across the discipline.

The readings range from a few hundred words to a seven-thousand-word article. The inclusion of a significant number of extracts reflects a desire to ensure that a wide range of writers and ideas is accessible to students within a single text. To balance the extracts, however, several complete articles are included to provide examples of how theoretical arguments are laid out and presented in the discipline. The selection of readings is a form of map, which offers an overview of the theoretical terrain of landscape architecture, and includes some important landmarks by which students can navigate through potentially confusing territory. Like all maps it is a selective account, and expresses a particular view. It is also backed up by more detailed maps—the articles from which the extracts are drawn—and the notes for each reading provide references to which teaching faculty and students may refer for further elaboration of the terrain.

The selection is focused upon design theory rather than planning or management, and excludes important bodies of theory in environmental perception and behavior and landscape ecology. The reason for this narrowing of focus is partly pragmatic, but also respects the availability of a number of excellent collections in those areas.[1] It reflects a view that has been expressed by others, and which I share, that "design" captures best the distinctive activity of configuring landscape which lies at the heart of landscape architecture.

The time span of the selected readings is fifty years. It is a fortunate coincidence that this takes us back to the publication of Eckbo's *Landscape for Living,*[2] which drew together a number of theoretical trends from the preceding couple of decades, and has subsequently underpinned education and practice for much of the latter part of the twentieth century. Lest students take this to imply that there was no theory before 1950, an essay by Elizabeth Meyer[3] uses a historical review of key writers on the picturesque to illustrate an approach to teaching contemporary theory. This is intended to reinforce an understanding of the necessity for a historical frame of analysis.

The collection draws almost entirely upon writings by recognized landscape architectural scholars. This has both advantages and disadvantages. The main advantage is that it provides an overview of the "core" of the discipline, if, indeed, one exists (I discuss this question further in the Introduction).

The disadvantage is that it can lead to a presentation of theory as something which is autonomous and somewhat detached from wider culture and society. Addition of a range of work from related disciplines, to highlight the social and cultural context for landscape architectural theory, is impractical owing to space limitations. Several extracts from widely cited authors "outside" the discipline are included, but in other cases, extracts from "landscape architecture" writing have been selected to show how these links have been made. For example, the diagram from Rosalind Krauss's seminal article on "Sculpture in the Expanded Field"[4] is featured in Peter Jacobs's reinterpretation of her work within the extract from "De/Re/In[form]ing Landscape"[5] and again in Meyer's "Expanded Field of Landscape Architecture."[6]

By going back half a century, the collection is clearly not a presentation of the "state of the art." There are several recent publications which review contemporary thinking and set a future theoretical agenda.[7] This collection instead consolidates. Indeed, in all the sections, a significant proportion of the readings date from the 1970s and 1980s. This reflects my judgment of their continuing salience as theoretical sources for landscape architecture.

The educational objective links to the second, scholarly, objective for this volume, which is more reflective in intent. A number of recent commentators have argued that landscape architecture lacks an adequate theoretical underpinning. The implication is that it does not warrant the term *discipline*, and is at best a scholarly profession (and some would dispute even that). For an activity that is institutionalized in teaching and research programs within many universities worldwide this is a serious charge. The second objective of this volume is to explore the alternative proposition, that there is indeed a distinctive field of theoretical knowledge upon which a discipline of landscape architecture is grounded. Such a proposition cannot be proven in a single volume of readings, but it is possible to at least get some sense of the evidence from which a conclusion might be drawn. The selection and ordering of the material is therefore influenced in part by the question of whether it "hangs together" as a coherent body of knowledge.

# INTRODUCTION

SIMON SWAFFIELD

## THEORY IN LANDSCAPE ARCHITECTURE

What is this thing called theory, and what does it do?[1] James Corner[2] has highlighted the contrast between two fundamentally different roles of theory. On the one hand, theory can generalize and codify knowledge, as a basis for practical action. This corresponds to the type of theory described by Garrett Eckbo in *Landscape for Living*, as "the generalization of social experience."[3] Such *instrumental* theory is typically derived from empirical observation. For example, Joan Iverson Nassauer's development of the concept of "cues for care" as a means to "frame" ecological restoration projects in a culturally acceptable way was developed from surveys of the attitudes of Midwestern farmers.[4] Theory can also evolve from practical experience. The staged approach to site planning, codified into a set of principles by Kevin Lynch[5] and John Ormsbee Simonds,[6] is one of the most widely used instrumental theories in landscape architecture. It illustrates the way that such theory can provide a stable and coherent framework for a discipline.

On the other hand, theory can have a more critical role, which resists and challenges taken-for-granted ways of thinking, and puts forward alternatives. Elizabeth Meyer's exploration of landscape architecture as *other* is an example of a *critical* theory.[7] It challenges the modern view of landscape as a largely passive setting (or ground) for architecture, and instead argues for landscape architecture as an autonomous design practice expressing its own language of space and form. A second example of a critical theory is Corner's advocacy of "recovering" landscape, with a consequential recasting of its role from being a passive *product* of culture, to become an active and strategic *agent* of culture.[8] Theoretical work that critiques current knowledge in this way disrupts and destabilizes the discipline, stimulating a search for new forms of knowledge and new ways of working.[9]

Another potential role for theory lies between these two positions. Corner referred to the hermeneutic tradition of interpretation,[10] and *interpretive* theory is well recognized in related disciplines as a form of knowledge that does not attempt to predict and control the world in the same way as instrumental theory, yet neither is it as disruptive as critical theory. Instead, an interpretive theory helps us better *understand* a situation, without necessarily changing it.[11] Much of the knowledge of landscape history expressed in J. B. Jackson's work is interpretive in this sense.

These three roles[12] are not mutually exclusive: empirical research into a taken-for-granted aspect of practice which reveals unexpected knowledge can challenge existing theory and disrupt conventions. Similarly, alternative approaches which arise from critique of mainstream practice can over time themselves become conventions. The "modern" approach to landscape architecture developed during the 1940s and 1950s by Garrett Eckbo, Dan Kiley, and James Rose, among others,[13] arose as a challenge to the conventions of the Beaux-Arts tradition. In due course their perspective itself became the dominant convention, and has been subsequently challenged. This interplay between different roles of theory over time illustrates the fundamentally historical and social nature of theory. It is made by particular people, for specific reasons, in particular places, at particular times.[14]

How then is theory made? It may be derived either inductively or deductively, or more typically through some combination. Inductive theory is built up by generalizing from observation: J. B. Jackson describes this process lucidly in his account of "How to Study Land-scape."[15] In contrast, it is possible to work from first principles, deducing formal hypotheses or propositions which are then tested experimentally. This deductive approach is characteristic of the natural sciences and cognitive social sciences,[16] and has been advocated for landscape architecture by commentators such as Richard Chenoweth.[17] Ironically, much critical theory is also based upon interrogations of principles, rather than by observation, but the "testing" is undertaken by reflection, argument, and design exploration. The validity of such an approach is hotly debated. In practice, as Robert Riley noted,[18] most theory is developed piecemeal through a combination of inductive and deductive activity, moving from one to the other in a series of explorations.

The appropriate level of generalization for theory in landscape architecture is also a matter of some debate. Theory can be expressed at a range of scales. Many of the calls for particular theoretical orientations for the discipline during the 1950s-1980s implicitly or explicitly advocated development of universal or at least widely applicable theoretical models and frameworks. The staged model of design, for example, was intended to be applicable to most if not all design situations. More recently some commentators have argued against this approach. Meyer put it like this: "Landscape theory is specific, not general. Like Feminist criticism, landscape architectural design and theory are based on observation, or that which is known through experience, or the immediate and sensory—that which is known by all the senses, not only visual. Thus landscape architectural theory is situational—it is explicitly historical, contingent, pragmatic and ad hoc. It is not about idealist absolute universals. It finds meaning, form and structure in the site as given."[19]

The extent to which theory is or should be contingent upon circumstance, and in particular the relationship between theory and the social and political setting, is perhaps the most hotly contested aspect of contemporary theory in landscape architecture. It is also closely related to the question of whether theory should be specific to landscape architecture. Riley has been a prominent critic of attempts to develop theory within the discipline. He charged that much of that which claims to be theory in the discipline is in fact *pseudotheory*. One of the main features of such pseudotheory, he claimed, is that it is plagiarized from other disciplines. He also argued for a clearer distinction among theory, models, frameworks, and aphorisms, advocating that the term *theory* should be restricted to knowledge that *explains* some real-world phenomenon. Ideas which link landscape architecture to other disciplines and broader society, he believed, are better described as frameworks.[20]

In contrast, advocates for *critical* theory, such as Meyer and Corner, have emphasized the fundamental linkage between theory and the social and political context in which it is made and used. "Critical theory is a political and strategic phenomenon, not an arcane and autonomous one."[21] Meyer referred to this external linkage in terms of the *mediation* and *reconciliation* of landscape with other cultural ideas. This situated nature of critical theory is related to its role as a point of resistance to dominant social trends. In order to have effect upon society, in this view, theory must be recognized as part of that society. However, recognition of such linkage does not necessarily imply that landscape architectural theory should "borrow" from other disciplines. Like Riley, both Meyer and Corner have advocated the need for a distinctive body of landscape architectural theory.

These differences in approach affect the way the current status of theory in landscape architecture is evaluated. Advocates for a conventional, instrumental type of theory tend to make unfavorable comparisons with scientific disciplines, and argue that landscape architecture should align itself more closely with their methods and procedures. Advocates for a more critical and situated approach to theory typically adopt a historical perspective, highlighting the evolution of the current position (see, for example, Meyer's discussion in Part II), and then offering new directions.

This volume has been prepared on the basis of an inclusive rather than a restrictive view of theory. I see a range of legitimate roles for theory in landscape architecture, and indeed a need for such a range: instrumental, interpretive *and* critical.[22] What is important is that a particular theory should be recognized it for what it is and the knowledge it offers interpreted accordingly. Similarly, there is a need for theory at differing scales of application. We need theoretical understanding that is particular to site, region, and culture, in order that our actions respond sensitively to the richness and variety in the world. But equally, we need to make broader comparisons across regions, countries and cultures if we wish to develop as a discipline with more than local relevance.[23]

I am therefore comfortable with a broad definition of theory. Rather than restricting the term to only those forms of explanatory knowledge that correspond to the formal conventions of science, as Riley proposed, the approach I have adopted is to accept diverse usages, but to qualify the particular meanings (for example by the descriptors instrumental, interpretive, or critical).

Finally, the reader has been prepared based upon the assumption that theory is fundamentally social in character, even when seeking to explain biophysical phenomena. As Meyer and Corner both demonstrate, landscape architecture theory has always expressed broader social and political agendas. This is not to claim that the way we construct theory determines the nature of the world in every respect (as some postmodern theorists appear to imply, and skeptics charge). Rather, the way we represent the world is inevitably shaped by social and political circumstances.[24] Knowledge is always *situated*, as Meyer put it, even when attempting to describe or explain seemingly universal phenomena. Whether and how we choose to utilize such knowledge is a central matter for debate within the discipline.

## The Theoretical Terrain of Landscape Architecture

What is the essential theoretical terrain of landscape architecture? There are three themes which recur explicitly throughout the past fifty years. They are, first, what form should theoretical knowledge in our discipline take; second, what is the process of design in landscape architecture; and third, what are the qualities of space and form, meaning and experience, that the discipline seeks to create?

Three further theoretical themes have emerged in recent years, although they have been implicit throughout. They are the relationship among society, language, and the representation of landscape architectural knowledge; ecological design and the aesthetics of sustainability; and the integration of diverse values through site, place, and region.

Part I contains a selection of extracts which provide a comparison between the essential features of instrumental, interpretive, and critical modes of theory. The two longer extracts also illustrate how different approaches are expressed in the substance of theory: through interpretation of the underlying structure of the North American cultural landscape, and through critique of the picturesque as an aesthetic theory.

Part II explores theories of process. The selection illustrates the way in which the model of a transparent staged process of design developed from the logic of creative problem solv-

Figure 1. Situating knowledge. Central Park, New York as an expression of social ideals, picturesque theory, practical engineering, and horticulture, integrated through design.

ing and became applied both to site planning and ecological design. It shows challenges to different aspects of the process, and several consequential refinements of the model: into a cyclical rather than linear process; incorporating greater client and community participation and recognizing uncertainty and individuality. An alternative view of design process is also presented in which the process of analysis itself becomes a creative act.

Questions of space and form lie at the heart of much theoretical debate in landscape architecture, and provide the focus for Part III. Two contrasting positions on the role of "meaning" in design are evident. On the one hand, the discipline should explore fundamental relationships among culture, technology, and nature through meaningful design. This leads to a strategy of social critique based upon the configuration of landscape as a symbolic system. On the other hand, there is the view that the essence of the discipline lies in creating healthy, functional, and pleasurable places for people and communities, to which significance and meaning will accrue over time. This latter position therefore focuses upon design strategies to enhance sensory experience, use, and enjoyment. The contributions articulate different aspects of this debate. There are also different strategies used to articulate and clarify meaningful form. Earlier writers have tended to adopt relatively static, dualist categories by which to explore questions of meaning: for example, nature and culture, or formal and informal. In recent decades there has been a shift to articulate meaning as part of a more dynamic set of relationships—either conceiving of meaning as part of a dialectic, evolving relationship between two poles, or, more subtly, by conceiving of a field of potential relationships. Both are illustrated in the readings.

The role of language in structuring knowledge has been central to much philosophical debate throughout the later part of the twentieth century. This "linguistic" turn has influenced landscape architecture, and the use of language as a metaphor for both design and landscape has attracted increasing interest. This has led to the reinterpretation of landscape, and related ideas of site, place, region, as if they were a language, text, or narrative. Part IV includes examples of such reinterpretation, which illustrate some of the advantages that arise from a linguistic orientation for theory. These include the complex and multi-layered symbolic nature of language, and its potential to project a coherent structure of meaning over space and time. Questions of authorship, intent, and the relationship of language with power reveal a series of dimensions upon which design critique can draw, and this has opened up a second level of exploration about the way in which landscape representation—through drawings, text, images, and designed landscapes themselves—all express particular social and political relationships and strategies.

Much of landscape architecture's theoretical development has drawn heavily upon other disciplines such as architecture. One important area of differentiation, however, is the central importance of the aesthetic and symbolic configuration of geological, hydrological, and biological forms and processes, and their ecological interrelationships. This has always underpinned questions of space, form, and meaning in landscape architecture, to differing degrees, but in recent decades the aesthetics of ecological design and sustainability has emerged as a primary focus of interest. Part V includes a number of contributions which collectively explore the complex and contested aesthetic relationships between technology and artifact on the one hand and ecology and nature on the other. In recognizing this area as a discrete theoretical theme, I am signaling my own conviction that it constitutes an area in which landscape architecture can make a distinctive disciplinary contribution to wider human knowledge.[25]

The final theme in this reader focuses upon integrating concepts. Although the idea of landscape has historically been a basis for integration of theory and practice, the increasing plurality in meaning of the term *landscape*, and the ever widening scope of landscape architecture, has meant that a number of complementary concepts have been put forward. These include site, place, and region, each of which is explored in different contributions to this final section.

Overall, the six themes by which this reader is organized constitute one possible theoretical map of the discipline. The Conclusion reviews the material covered in the various essays and extracts, interrelating their substantive content, and considering whether they constitute a coherent body of knowledge. I believe that there is a discernible core of theoretical knowledge emerging, particularly when combined with the closely related fields of landscape planning, environmental perception, and land art. I discuss some essential features of this core in the Conclusion.

# PART I

# The Nature of Theory in Landscape Architecture

New ways of thinking about the nature of theory emerge at times when it becomes clear that the prevailing knowledge and methods of landscape architecture are in some way out of step with broader social, cultural, and economic concerns. This has occurred at two important points over the past fifty years: first, in the 1940s, as part of the "modernist" revolution against the prevailing Beaux-Arts tradition, and then again in the late 1980s, as the full implications of poststructuralist thinking came to bear upon the discipline. In the intervening years, the nature of theory received less attention, with greater focus upon its substantive content. Part I includes readings from both these periods of change, and also a classic account of substantive theory.

The section opens with an extract from Garrett Eckbo's *Landscape for Living*. In this, Eckbo first situates landscape architecture within the mainstream of twentieth-century culture and technology. He then argues for the adoption of scientific method as the basis for the theoretical understanding needed by the discipline in its mission to counteract the adverse effects of the post–World War II economic boom. Eckbo characterizes the method in terms of analysis, hypothesis, and experimentation: the constituents of the deductive approach to theory. The next reading is J. B. Jackson's "How to Study Landscape," in which Jackson explains his inductive method, working from the description of particular situations toward generalization of broad principles. The essay is included almost in its entirety, as it embodies an approach to understanding the shape and form of the American landscape upon which the discipline has drawn extensively throughout the latter part of the twentieth century. These two readings encapsulate the dominant approaches to theory upon which the education of landscape architects was based throughout the 1960s and 1970s.

By the 1980s, however, it was clear that despite Eckbo's belief that landscape architecture could and should combine both art and science, in practice it was satisfying the theoretical imperatives of neither. In particular, a new generation of educators drew increasingly upon theoretical developments in the humanities, arts, and social sciences to challenge the conventional stance of the discipline, calling for a much more critical approach.[1] Two short extracts taken from James Corner's extensive two-part essay on the origins of theory set out some basic limitations of the instrumental approach of modern science and argue instead for a more poetic and reflective model of theory. The case for a critical approach is then set out in Elizabeth Meyer's exposition of landscape architectural theory as situated practice. This essay is included both because it is an exemplar of the critical approach and because it is structured around a historical exploration of one of the most enduring and influential aesthetic foundations of the discipline: picturesque theory.

# LANDSCAPE FOR LIVING (1950)

GARRETT ECKBO

Here in the middle of the twentieth century we are left with, not the sterile dichotomy of the official academic theory, but a rich and many-sided octagon of landscape tradition. Here are its parts:

> The formal tradition of Renaissance and Baroque Europe and the Moslem world, with its subcurrent of Greek and Gothic irregularity.
> The informal romantic tradition of China, Japan, and eighteenth-century England.
> The overriding fascination with plants for their own sake, based on the horticultural and botanical advances of the nineteenth and twentieth centuries.
> The conservation movement, with its emphasis on the value and wonder of the indigenous primeval landscape, expressed in our field in the American park movement.
> The urban and regional planning movement, with its compulsion toward reexamination of the relations between buildings and open space, town and country.
> The modern movement in the arts, in architecture, and in landscape design since the mid-1930s.
> The rural tradition, and
> The folk or little garden tradition, two notes of twentieth-century social realism.

If we examine these streams for their relevance to our work in the balance of the century, we will find that they boil back down to another dichotomy, broader, richer, and more fertile than the academic formal:informal dichotomy.

The great problem and the great opportunity of our times is to rebuild, on an infinitely higher plane, the unity and solidarity between man and nature which existed and still exists in primitive communal societies, and which was broken and shattered by the great sweep of history through slavery and feudalism to capitalism. This we can work toward every day on every job and every project, no matter how small or inconsequential it may seem.

On the mention of theory, two questions are apt to arise: one on the need for theory, the other on the nature of the theory needed. We must be able to answer these questions, especially here in practical America, where so much of our environment is built on the sole theory that no theory for its planning is needed—we just go out and build it.

Theory is a generalization of social experience in any particular field, or in all fields. It is at one and the same time a generalization of the past, a vitalizer of the present, and a projection of the future. If it is any one without the others it tends toward sterility, decadence, or frivolity. Only positive exploratory theory can take us beyond the precedents of yesterday. Theory is the vehicle which guarantees the continuous growth and expansion of tradition. Theory and tradition develop together and grow continuously, however unevenly or erratically, through any number of struggles with contradictions. To try to freeze them at any given time in a system of academic rules and proportions is like trying to dam a strong stream with no spillway for overflow control. Sooner or later the stream will find its way over or around the dam, whatever the joints are weakest, and come forth with a burst of vigor equal to the length of time it has been impounded.

Theory, by analyzing the past while working in the present, can project the length and character of the next step into the future. This is the process which has been responsible for all human progress of every sort. Every step forward, technically, culturally, or socially, had to be an idea—a theory—in one or many heads before it could be taken. The whole long chain of development of human tools, from the first flint ax to the most delicate and powerful machinery of today's industry, has come about through this process of analyzing the past in the present toward the future. Theory is theory, whether it is an idea in a clever mechanic's head, or five hundred pages of windy discourse. New shelter and new clothing, steam engine and electricity, Magna Charta and Declaration of Independence and Bill of Rights: all began as theories, as ideas, some of which were called radical. The scientific process of building theory and constantly developing it by analysis, hypothesis, and experiment is basic to our twentieth-century civilization.

Theory in the arts is, of course, the stumbling block for those practical souls who have gone along with us so far. Yet art is only a process of trying to extract the maximum potential human experience out of necessary practical activities. Painting, sculpture, music, architecture, landscape design have all grown from sound, practical, functional roots in the living activities necessary to people. They have grown to cultural heights by the exact process of imaginative building on the past that we have been describing. The architect today can plan a better house than the carpenter, the brickmason, or the general contractor, because, if he is abreast of the possibilities of his profession, he is more aware of the maximum potential for an interior harmony of space, size, and form; for an exterior harmony of open and solid wall; for the most satisfying combinations of materials. Before he can produce this he must, obviously, solve all the practical functional problems in a way which also makes possible a maximum contribution from carpenter, brickmason, and general contractor. Theory—as idea—is not developed for its own sake, even though it precedes practice. It must come from practical necessity, and be based on constant observation and experience.

A good theory of landscape design, then, must be a theory of form as well as of function. It must be artistic as well as practical, in order to produce the maximum for those who will experience work influenced by it. Every work of landscape design, conscious or unconscious, whether it be the utility garden of the southern sharecropper or the Central Composition of Washington, D.C., produces an arrangements of forms, colors, and textures in space which results in some sort of cumulative effect, good or bad, on those who pass through it. We cannot avoid the problem of producing form in the landscape. From the formal western school which went after it with axes and vistas, through the informal eastern school which avoided it with poetry, rationalizations, and subjective grotesqueries, to the horticulturists and the naturalists, who bury it in collections or hide it behind nature—all have produced arrangements of cumulative effect, good or bad, on us who experience them, whether or not we know their literary rationalizations. It should be noted that the good and bad is not necessarily between schools but within schools; all produce good work (pleasing to us) and bad work (unpleasant to us). The goodness or badness, for us, is not necessarily based on the theory of the particular school, but rather on certain questions of the arrangements of spaces, the development of sites, the use of materials, unity and variety, scale and proportion, rhythm and repetition, which we know or can determine are basic to our experiences in our environment.

Our theory, then, must point the way toward good form in the landscape, but it cannot define it rigidly, on an exclusive, selective basis, with dogma and formulae, rules and regulations, precedents and measured drawings. We must base ourselves upon a flexible understanding and assimilation of those basic questions of scale, proportion, unity, variety, rhythm, repetition, which have been the primary guides for good men in all fields in all times and places. We must remember that most landscape problems are so plastic, so little under the control of functional requirements, that any number of solutions is possible. For most, the final best solution is probably as unreachable as the final best solution for a square of canvas on an easel, or a block of stone in the sculptor's yard. Design, like life, has no limits to its development.

It will be said, then, on what shall we base our forms? Where shall we find them? And the answer is, in the world which is around you in space, and behind you in time. If you understand it and love it and enjoy it there is your inspiration. The more you are a part of your world the more inspired you will be, if you find those parts which are streaming steadily forward, rather than the many stagnant backwaters which exist to trap the unwary.

It must be remembered that the great pre-industrial styles of the past were produced by societies of a certain stability, a certain established structure and discipline within which artist and designer found enough security, orientation and direction to produce their best work. The nineteenth and twentieth centuries have been a period of tremendous historical acceleration, of great flux and movement throughout the world, of huge contradictory struggles, of the rise of the common man and the democratic idea. The old relation of the artist to a clientele of the social elite has gradually receded; the new relation of artist to a democratic mass clientele is barely visible over the horizon; in between is the no man's land of commercialism, eclecticism, egocentrism, and escapism in which the artist has been wandering for lo, these many moons. Our theory must be oriented within the social, as well as the technical and aesthetic, potential of the times, if it is to be relevant to the artist as producer and the people as consumers.

Our theory of landscape design for the balance of the twentieth century must be concerned with the realities of the now engrossing problems of the overall outdoor environment of the American people, rather than with abstractions about systems of axes, or poetic subjectivities about nature. We have tremendous problems, of unprecedented social and esthetic potential, ahead of us. As we prepare for them and work on them we can absorb and assimilate the old ideas, build on the strong base of our rich octagon of landscape tradition, and go on to a unified expression of integrated social and natural landscape such as has never been seen before.

# HOW TO STUDY LANDSCAPE (1980)

J. B. JACKSON

It is the accepted European procedure, as I understand it, to start exposing a line of thought by first enunciating a few guiding principles and then providing examples, and this is the method followed by many American professors. But the traditional Anglo-

Saxon procedure is the opposite: it states the facts, provides examples, and only at the end presumes to draw conclusions. This was my approach and I found it satisfactory, if for no other reason than that I had no clear-cut conclusions or generalizations to offer. I had traveled enough in the United States to know the country well, and I had tried to familiarize myself with what can be called its vernacular history; and it was this experience which I undertook to pass on to the students. I confined my introductory remarks to such obvious statements as that a landscape (whether urban or rural) gradually took form when people moved into a place, did what they could to survive and prosper with the resources at hand, and that they soon organized themselves into a group for mutual help and protection and for celebration of one kind or another. I added that landscapes grew and changed and that they had a chronology that was often interesting to explore. This was followed by the display of a few slides illustrating change in certain familiar places.

So, the logical beginning of the course on the history of the American landscape, as I saw it, was a brief account of the arrival of the first settlers in a region—whether Virginia, New England, or North Dakota. The settlers appeared on the scene, explored their surroundings, and then proceeded to make themselves at home. This is also how conventional history books begin. They give a description of the way the new community sets up certain basic institutions; for government, for defense, for communication with the outside world; the way it establishes a school and a church, and builds places to live and work in.

But the student of landscapes has another interest: how space is organized by the community. This means the drawing of a boundary, the efficient dividing up of the land among the several families, the providing of roads and a place of public assembly, and the setting aside of land for communal use. So, while the conventional historian prefers to date the birth of the community as a political entity from that moment when all gather together in a tent or under a tree and pass a number of solemn resolutions, the landscape student likes to call attention to another, equally significant moment—when the first line is scratched in the soil or the first blaze is cut in a tree or the first stone marker is erected. These are the "traces on the Rhodian shore" that Clarence Glacken has described in his wonderful book of that title. The event is no doubt trifling and soon forgotten, but how is a society, even a small pioneer society, to function, how is it to have form and a degree of permanence unless it has its own territory, unless it creates and occupies its own space?

No one has written with greater authority and insight on the subject of space than Professor Yi-Fu Tuan, and his book *Space and Place* continues to be the inspiration and guide of every landscape student. For the significance of space in landscape terms, the allotment of land for private or public use, is that it makes the social order visible. Space, even a small plot of ground, identifies the occupant and gives him status, and, most important of all, it establishes lasting relationships. As the word itself suggests, a boundary is what binds us all together in a group, that which excludes the outsider or stranger. The boundary creates neighbors; it is the symbol of law and order and permanence. The network of boundaries, private as well as public, transforms an amorphous environment into a human landscape, and nothing more clearly shows some of the cherished values of a group than the manner in which they fix those boundaries, the manner in which they organize space. And because these values change in the course of time, the organization of space also undergoes a change. That is one reason why the contemporary landscape is so different from that of even a hundred years ago.

The original layout of spaces is well worth studying, it seems to me, if only because it unconsciously reveals so much about the ideas of the men and women who devised it. If I had to reconstruct my course, or if I were asked what I thought should be emphasized, I think I would say that the significance of boundaries and spatial divisions could hardly be overstressed. Few Americans, I discovered, have any notion of what the national grid system signifies in terms of political philosophy. We either criticize its monotony and its disregard of the lay of the land, or else we assume it was the product of real estate speculators. But as we should know, the grid system is, in fact, one of the most ambitious schemes in history for the orderly creation of landscapes, of small communities. When its scope and purpose are explained, I find that students are quick to respond, and from then on they are alert to other kinds of spatial organization—the careful distribution of land according to the merits of the family in colonial New England, or the laissez-faire procedure followed in the Oklahoma land rush. And what I find most satisfying is that some students even learn to appreciate the grandeur and beauty of the grid.

To talk about the grid means talking about fields and fences and roads and crossroads and schoolhouses, and eventually it means talking about the grid in towns and cities. We have to backtrack and discuss the Philadelphia version of the grid and the Philadelphia way of naming streets versus the southern grid and the southern way of naming streets, and even the Mormon grid—more familiar in the West, of course, than elsewhere. And then there are several kinds of courthouse squares, as Professor Edward T. Price has told us; and while we are on the subject of the spatial organization of the early American town, it is easy to discuss the unique qualities of the American addition or subdivision—which in the old days meant simply the selling of land, the house being built by the purchaser; whereas in Europe, the original landowner also built the houses and thereby created a distinct community or neighborhood. The grid system, at least during its early days, allowed for a wonderful flexibility in the use of space, and even a degree of interchangeability, for all lots, all blocks, all streets were of uniform dimensions and you could build what you liked, *where* you liked. A good illustration of how interchangeability was characteristic of the early, pre-industrial landscape was the popularity until about 1850 of the Greek revival style. It was considered equally appropriate for banks, courthouses, mansions, post offices, college buildings, and churches. Using slides, I showed how versatile the style could be.

It was the pre-industrial town that we discussed, the town which flourished before the factory and the railroad had invaded every part of the landscape, even though there was a water-powered mill in the average town, and often there were steamboats on the river. But a pre-industrial town can be a very complicated element in any landscape, and I long hesitated to discuss the urban scene before discussing the rural scene. There were several reasons, however, why I eventually thought the time had come. First of all, it is one of the peculiarities of the United States, as Richard Wade has pointed out, that in many regions towns came before farms; towns as trading posts, as defense installations, as transfer points in river navigation, were often in existence long before the surrounding forest had been invaded by pioneer farmers. So it was the town that set the pace in the development of the landscape, that established forms and spaces. But another reason for discussing the pre-industrial town was that it still represents for most Americans the most picturesque and appealing aspect of our past. The small town of that period is familiar in our popular art and literature and folklore: the town with its central square or marketplace, with its fairground and local academy or college, its so-called block of offices on the main street, the First Church with its graveyard where the first settlers are buried, and the Greek revival facades along the tree-lined streets leading out to the open country. There is always the danger, in dealing with that remote period, of lapsing into sentimental antiquarianism, a glorification of the simpler ways of the early republic that many young people are very susceptible to. On the other hand, since most students have an urban background, they have an instinctive understanding of how to interpret the town's spaces, and are often expert at discovering its style and its search for order.

My final reason for discussing the town instead of the country was this: the town, particularly the pre-industrial town, offers the best material for studying the house or dwelling.

There is a school of cultural geographers which believes that the dwelling is not only the most important element in the landscape but is the key to understanding all other elements in the landscape: the social order, the economy, the natural resources, the history, and culture. It so happens that the dwelling which these geographers usually have in mind is the European farmhouse or farmstead—a combination under one roof of residence, storage, and work areas. In use and in design and in materials, this farmhouse is closely attuned to the surrounding land, and is, in fact, a product of it. Few American farmhouses, however, resemble the farmhouses of the Old World. Most of them are designed and used as residences, pure and simple, and are essentially like the dwellings in the nearby town, inhabited by lawyers and merchants and clergymen. Indeed, our farmhouses are often copies of these urban counterparts. We ought to be cautious, then, in accepting some of the European theories about the relationship between dwelling and landscape. A house in Juneau, Alaska, is much more likely to resemble a house in Shreveport, Louisiana, than an Eskimo dwelling a few hundred miles away. Perhaps we deplore this circumstance, but it is essential that we learn to live with it; and I can think of no better way for landscape studies to achieve academic respectability than for it to formulate a new and American way of defining house types based not on the nineteenth-century concern for regionalism, use of local materials, local craftsmanship, and local agriculture, but on thoroughly contemporary notions: the dwelling defined in terms of its longevity, of its relationship to work, to the family, to the community, and of its psychological relationship to the natural environment.

What makes an enterprise of this sort easier and at the same time more appropriate is that all students—and indeed all people—have an innate interest in houses. Whether they come from the city or the country, whether they live in a trailer or an apartment or a bungalow or a mansion, students, I have found, immediately respond to any discussion of the dwelling, its construction, its layout, its appearance, its many functions, and its evolution over the centuries. Like every other instructor, I have read many hundreds of term papers. In my case, they discussed some aspect of the contemporary landscape—usually the landscape of the small town or the farm countryside. Those which I found most enjoyable and most perceptive dealt with such modest topics as the front porch or the local Civil War monument, or with barns and roads. I enjoyed them not only for their content—they often revealed obscure historical information—but because they seemed to be based on childhood memories and family traditions. It was from such papers that I learned about the complicated make-up of towns which to the outsider seemed entirely homogeneous: the nicknames for certain sections, certain streets and alleys, the location of all-but-invisible ethnic communities. The papers told of family customs, high school rituals, church festivities; they revealed half-forgotten farming practices and beliefs, and the existence of small gardens where plants unheard of in the region were grown, year after year. All this made for pleasant reading. But there were also papers—not many of them—that recorded everyday sensory experiences of the landscape: the sound of snow shovels after a blizzard, the smell of wet bathing suits, the sensation of walking barefoot on the hot pavement. A woman student from North Dakota wrote of her family driving each fall to the nearest town to see the autumn foliage in the streets and yards; out where she lived there were no trees. We can only be grateful when it comes our way, and encourage students to record such fleeting memories as these, and share them. They often make a whole landscape, a whole season, vivid and unforgettable.

I have already mentioned it in passing and I will say it again for emphasis: this kind of landscape study is essentially preparatory. It deals with the rural or small-town past, with an America which, except in a few isolated regions, has disappeared or changed beyond recognition. Why then, it will be asked, should we bother to study it? Why should we not follow the geographer's precedent, and simply acquaint ourselves with the current scene?

I can think of three good reasons for starting by examining the landscape of the early nineteenth century and before. The studies provide the student with a better view of our vernacular history than do Disneyland and its imitations, or than the student is likely to acquire from tendentious socioeconomic texts. Second, it is an excellent and relatively painless way of learning about the purpose of landscape studies, for it deals with familiar, more or less simple archetypes. And third, we can only start to understand the contemporary landscape by knowing what we have rejected and what we have retained from the past. I doubt if there is any other part of the modern world where the contrast between the traditional landscape and the contemporary landscape is so easy to observe; where the two exist in relative harmony, untroubled by class or race identification.

So there comes a day, usually around midterm, when the students are informed that we are about to embark on the study of a landscape of a very different kind: the landscape which began to emerge around the middle of the nineteenth century and which is now approaching full flower. It is popular to say that we are in a period of transition—and it has been said, with some justification, for the past hundred years. But the phrase represents a kind of evasion, an unwillingness to recognize that in many areas of our culture the final form can be discerned. The notion of a kind of perpetual transition has the effect of making us appraise many things in terms of a familiar past instead of in terms of present-day realities. The widespread belief that ours is a transitional landscape is a case in point: we tend to see it not as it is, with its own unique character, but as a degenerate version of the traditional landscape, and to see its history as a long, drawn-out backsliding, the abandonment of old values, old techniques, old institutions, with nothing developing to take their place.

But a more sensible approach, it seems to me, is to try to discover when some of its characteristics first made their appearance, rather than to dwell on the disappearance of the old. The gradual obsolescence of the traditional multipurpose barn is not so important as the rise of a kind of farming where no barn is needed and all produce is trucked to a local processing plant.

The discussion of the contemporary American landscape should start with the transformation of a basic landscape element: the piece of land or the farm. In the traditional order of things, at least in the United States, the ideal was that the family who owned the land also lived on it and worked it; family status came from the relationship, and in fact many colonial statutes, and even the Homestead Act of 1862, stipulated that a dwelling must be built on the piece of land. But with the sudden availability after independence of immense amounts of federal land for settlement, this concept was gradually abandoned.

In the new territories in the West, land was acquired purely for speculation and its distant owner neither lived on it nor worked on it. Other pieces of federal land were often occupied by squatters who neither bought it or worked it, and still other land was exploited for its timber or its grazing by persons who neither lived on it nor bothered to buy it. This is how a writer on land use in America sums up the situation: after 1812, he says, "we met for the first time on a large scale one of the significant realities to which folk myth has blinded us; independence of the three variables: transfer of land from federal title, actual settlement, and economic development."

As a result of this change, land ceased to indicate the status of the owner or occupant or user. Environmentalists are fond of talking about the need of a bond between man and the land, a biological tie or a mystic relationship. But in the traditional landscape, that bond meant something very specific: it meant that a family was legally and economically and even historically identified with the land it owned and lived on and exploited. The bond was the basis of citizenship. Finally, the house itself symbolized the family attachment, and was, in a sense, the matrix of the landscape.

Thus, when that threefold bond began to lose its power in the course of the nineteenth century, the landscape *had* to change. Land was defined in a new way: as a commodity which could be bought and sold and used in a variety of money-making ways, and the house was redefined in much simpler terms: as a place of residence, to be designed and located as such. Home and place of work were no longer necessarily identical and were even sometimes far apart. Land was put to new and unpredictable uses, or left untouched for future speculation. The fabric of the traditional landscape became loose and threatened to fall apart.

It is when we try to follow this development that we discover the importance of a landscape element which we had previously paid little attention to, and that is the road or highway. It had always been there, of course, but it had been so modest, so limited in its influence that we had taken it for granted. For centuries the country road had merely been a path, a cleared space created by some local ordinance to enable people to come to town to pay taxes, go to church, go to market—a political device, as it were, never given any but the most perfunctory care. But shortly after the Revolution, the building of roads became a matter of national concern, and from then on it began to play a role in the landscape, until (as we all know) it is now the most powerful force for the destruction or creation of landscapes that we have.

There is an enormous amount of writing on roads and railways, and some of it—not all of it, by any means—makes interesting reading. But naturally enough, most of it deals with either the engineering aspect or the traffic which the highway handles, and it is full of superlatives and statistics. When I first decided to discuss the road, I was sure that it could be disposed of in two lectures, illustrated with appropriate slides contrasting old, narrow, rutted roads with the interstate. But I soon found out that from the point of view of the course, the really significant thing about the road was how it affected the landscape; how it started out as a wavering line between fields and houses and hills and then took over more and more land, influenced and changed a wider and wider environment, until the map of the United States seemed nothing but a web of roads and railroads and highways.

And to further complicate matters, I began to see how the road altered not only the way people traveled but how they perceived the world. The first turnpikes, in the early years of the nineteenth century, gave the youth of America its first taste of speed: sulky racing got its start on the turnpikes of New York State, and other turnpikes, by traveling straight across country and bypassing the small villages, revealed the wilderness aspect of the American landscape. The cult of new models and accessories and driving techniques got its start when travelers learned to admire the handsomely painted stage coaches and the shiny harness and the bells on the horses, and when stagecoach drivers competed in style and elegance. The railroad made an even more profound impression: its business methods in those days were the first glimpse most Americans had had of the efficiency of big business, and they were widely imitated. Hard as it is to believe, it was the railroad which taught Americans to be punctual and to watch the clock, and the intricate maneuvering of trains on a single track taught many manufacturers how to organize production and movement.

The automobile, especially in its early days, introduced the notion of exploration. Remote country villages, mountain trails, and the trackless regions of the West were rediscovered by adventurous drivers, and there was talk about the revival of the countryside with country inns and country food.

I suspect that each of these experiences of the road increasingly revealed the abstract joys of relatively effortless fast motion, so that in a sense we were psychologically prepared, even a century ago, for surfing and skiing and kite sailing and even skateboarding.

But the road soon began to change the landscape itself. When the railroad came into town, it destroyed the uniformity of the grid system. Railroad Avenue, with its skid row and its hotels, and with its railside factories and warehouses, introduced an axial development and distorted the original spatial order. The streetcar had much the same effect: it extended the range of commuters and gave them a wider choice of places to live, it decentralized many small businesses, and at transfer points it fostered a cluster of stores and services. And the street itself began to assume a new role: the practice of placing utilities under the street pavement—water, gas, sewerage, light, and eventually telephone lines—gave the street a permanence which it had never previously had, so that it became more important than the property on both sides of it. As in almost every other part of the landscape, the road or street or highway became the armature, the framework of the landscape. The piece of land no longer determined its composition.

What I am saying is an old story. We know, because we see evidence of it every day, that the street or highway is like a magnet that attracts houses, factories, places of business and entertainment to its margins. We are all aware that the important streets and arteries no longer exist to serve the local population, but that they create their own community, their own architecture, their own kind of business, their own rhythm, and their own mobile population. I have found, somewhat to my embarrassment, that students are, generally speaking, far better informed about the highway and its culture than I am, and if there is any risk in discussing the topic, it is the risk of too much enthusiasm, too great a readiness to describe the drive-in, the truck stop, the advertising, and the psychology of the mobile consumer as forms of pop culture, as topics important and attractive in themselves.

That is one reason why I think the emphasis should be put not so much on the road or highway as on the broader landscape created or influenced by the highway. For the highway is merely a symbol of how we learned to organize space and movement; and our zeal to reduce every action, every undertaking to a process of steady, uninterrupted flow of energy and productivity is actually better illustrated in the organization of a factory, a farm, even a university than it is in the incessant activity of the highway. It is in that broader landscape that we can study how the dwelling partakes of the spirit of the highway, and the history of the dwelling over the last 150 years demonstrates the slow emergence of new ideas of community and of mobility. The balloon frame was not the outcome of a gradual evolution of folk building techniques; it was invented by harassed carpenters in boomtown Chicago. It rejected tradition and group collaboration in favor of speed and impermanence. The prefabricated or ready-cut house, developed in the mid-nineteenth century, was popularized by the expansion of railroad lines into the treeless High Plains and made rapid settlement possible. The latest innovation in the dwelling, the trailer, was a response to the need of the motorist for a mobile home. The time has not yet come when we can define the contemporary American home with any finality—in this instance we are indeed in a period of intellectual transition, still thinking of the traditional European dwelling. But the geographers' point is still valid: the house is in many ways a microcosm of the landscape; the landscape explains the house. So let me, in finishing, suggest how the spatial organization of the two landscapes differ—and how, in consequence, the two types of dwelling differ and could be defined.

The old spatial organization, as I mentioned earlier, laid great store on the visible and permanent divisions of space—whether on the land or in the house or city; contemporary space is no less well defined, but the divisions are seen as temporary, and the communication between them is essential; the dwelling favors the open plan.

Spatial divisions often meant permanent social distinctions, and autonomous organizations of work: the farm grew and processed and stored and disposed of its own products; the household was an autonomous society responsible for the education, health, and welfare of its members. We now delegate various stages in a process to another space—or another institution: the processing plant, the packing plant, the wholesale distributor, and so on—and, of course, we delegate domestic responsibilities to the school, the hospital, the various service agencies.

The old spatial organization made much of the need for storage, for provisions for the future, for preserving elements of the past—in barns and attics and warehouses. The modern spatial organization dispenses, whenever possible, with storage space. The supermarket, the factory, the commercial farm depend on trucks either to remove stock or to replenish it. The modern dwelling, without attic or cellar, depends on the mini-storage facility or gives every old item to the local museum or to the Goodwill outlet.

And finally, I would say that the old landscape was conservative and even unimaginative in the use of energy; it saw no further than the visible horizon, and was skeptical as to the existence of sources of energy hidden in the ground or untapped within the individual. As for the modern demand for all kinds of energy in unlimited quantities, the daily paper tells us enough about that. But there are other forms of energy which the past knew nothing about—inexhaustible energy which we are seeking to tap by means of spiritual discipline, self-education, and a new experience of nature. The contemporary dwelling, for all its cultural impoverishment, for all its temporary, mobile, rootless qualities, promises to capture and utilize more and more of this invisible, inexhaustible store of strength. So we can perhaps think of it as the transformer: a structure which does more than depend on the energy provided by the power company, which transforms for each of its inhabitants some of that invisible, spiritual energy we are only now beginning to discover.

# ORIGINS OF THEORY (1990)

## JAMES CORNER

There has been a recent plea by practitioners and academics alike for the creation of a vibrant, all-encompassing body of landscape architectural theory. It is interesting and timely to ask why. What is theory, or what might it be, and why should we need it? What do we expect from theory?

Perhaps, concerned about the relative youth of the profession (certainly not the art itself) or the sparse distribution of work in space and time, we look for theory to provide a foundation—a shared basis and purpose for the practice and performance of the discipline. In this way, theory might be expected to provide a responsible structure with attendant principles and norms from which prescriptions for action may be drawn.

Alternatively, perhaps we look to theory not so much for stability and coherence, as for breakout and rupture. Theory might act as a sort of disruptive catalyst, an inventive prompt, fostering new thought and inquiry within the discipline.

Theory may therefore be sought after, on the one hand, to stabilize and provide a set of codified principles of production or, on the other, to resist the status quo, maintaining heterogeneity and prompting change. In the former case, theory is a stabilizer, while in the latter, it is a disruptive mechanism. This is neither a dichotomy nor a paradox, but remains a poorly understood relation, riddled with misconception and difficulty. To ask what theory is, or might be, and why landscape architecture should need it is to pose questions that escape easy answer. It may be discovered that theory is in fact a much more elusive and enigmatic phenomenon than would first appear.[1]

We might begin our inquiry by asking why bother, why theory? There are those who would argue with conviction that there is no need or time for theory today: "What good is it?" Some might say that we have too much of it already, too much talk, just intellectual games. Others might remind us that landscape architecture is primarily a craft profession, an artisanal practice requiring multiple skills and talents. Such people may tell us of the lifetime commitment necessary to learn and master such skills, in which case theory would just get in the way. This may be true. In much of contemporary discourse, there is considerably divergent rhetoric having very little to do with a profession that is primarily a skill-oriented endeavor, striving toward a greater artfulness and grace in its attendant skills.

However, there is a distinction between craft and motivation, between the skill of making and the purpose that motivates the skill. Craft may often win professional competitions. It can be repeated and, to a degree, taught. Its skills can be deployed without any reference to feelings, history, or ideas. Motivation, however, necessitates the definition of a particular stance toward life—some idea of a culture's relationship toward the world and existential problems. It employs the feeling found in cultural memory and personal experience to general meaning, wonder, and expression. Motivation engenders a heightened sense of purpose. At its greatest, it is an epiphany, a revelation, a new way of seeing the world. Motivation establishes a vital alertness, a sensitive curiosity, and an insatiable sense of marvel. A built landscape may well survive blemishes of craft, but will very rarely survive a creative stillbirth.

This relation between craft and motivation, the how and the why, is the forgotten rule of theory. Originally, art and architecture were understood as a unity between *techne* and *poiesis*.[2] Here, *techne* was the dimension of revelatory knowledge about the world, and *poiesis* was the dimension of creative, symbolic representation. *Techne* made no distinction between the theoretical and the practical. Making was understood as the embodiment of knowledge and ideas; we could say that craft was motivated. This unity fell apart in the seventeenth and eighteenth centuries. *Techne* became a separate body of instrumental or productive knowledge, and *poiesis* became an autonomous creation of subjective and aesthetic reality. This separation coincided with the origin of modern science (technology) and modern aesthetics (art). It also involved an irretrievable alteration of the role of theory in architectural production.

# THEORY IN CRISIS (1991)

## JAMES CORNER

The objectifying logic of technology has emerged as a dominant force in our world during the past two hundred years. It has enabled societies to control the external world in the interests of efficiency and production, while at the same time it has displaced the movement of tradition (because of its progressivist position) and suppressed the poetries of art (because of its ideology of objectivity and optimization), thereby devaluing an already impoverished life-world (at least spiritually). Many humanists have consequently attributed much of society's ills to the alienating effects of technology and capitalism, arguing for the need to transcend the reductionism of techno-economic thinking prior to the realization of a more humane built environment.[1] Indeed it could be argued that the primary problem of survival for the developed cultures of today is less a techno-biological one than it is an aesthetic and moral one.[2]

Landscape architecture has not remained untainted by these developments. As a discipline, it has become increasingly estranged from a sense of traditional and poetic value. In particular, this refers to what might be perceived as the current inability of landscape architecture to simultaneously engage the recurrent and thematic workings of history with the circumstances peculiar to our own time. Traditionally, cultural products (as found historically in literature, painting, music, building, or landscape architecture) represent an infinitely rich array of interpretative gestures and figurative embodiments that have attempted in various ways to critically reconcile the historical with the contemporary, the eternal with the moment, the universal with the specific. Today, however, we find it increasingly difficult to manage this relationship. Many fail to even appreciate the role that landscape architecture plays in the constitution and embodiment of culture, forgetful of the designed landscape's symbolic and revelatory powers, especially with regard to collective memory, cultural orientation, and continuity. It is not unfair to say that contemporary theory and practice have all but lost their metaphysical and mythopoetic dimensions, promoting a landscape architecture of primarily prosaic and technical construction.[3] After all, symbolic and poetic intentions are often rendered naïve in a scientific world, where pragmatic values of efficiency and optimization are often considered more "real."[4]

Theory today is therefore quite different from *theoria*, the original Greek formulation of theory.[5] Whereas *theoria* was mediative and reflective and was derived from the primary realms of human experience and perception, modern theory has largely become an instrument of certainty and control, founded upon autonomous principles of external origin. The predominance of instrumental techniques and rational methods in an anthropocentric world is what has most characterized modern thinking. While the scientific attitude has led to a multitude of accomplishments in modern science, it has also underlain the emergence of a disembodied culture struggling to find access to a lived continuity of being and time. Ours is a landscape of estrangement.

# SITUATING MODERN LANDSCAPE ARCHITECTURE (1992)

ELIZABETH MEYER

How can design theory enrich contemporary landscape architectural practice? In what ways have written treatises, theoretical frameworks (or the collective consciousness),[1] and contiguous physical contexts affected and informed the built works of landscape designers? How do built landscapes embody and embed these ideas, values, and settings within their forms and spaces? These are the questions upon which I designed a course entitled "Theories of Landscape Architecture Design," a lecture course required of first degree graduate students and taken as an elective by advanced graduate students in architecture, urban design, and landscape architecture.

This essay, like the course, hopes to evoke and restore the sense of discovery still possible when studying exemplary built works and treatises. First, I will define theory as a *bridging, mediating,* and *reconciling* practice within the field of landscape architecture and within the time frame known as modern.[2] Then I will focus on one of modernity's primary, yet often misunderstood, figures—the Picturesque—to elucidate these roles for theory. I have chosen to select one theoretical construction, the Picturesque, for analysis and explication rather than describe the course outline. This cross-section of the course exposes a way of thinking, a means of navigating through theory's sometimes murky and frequently turbulent waters.

By framing one aspect of the modern landscape, the essay quickly focuses on the particular instead of the general. This grounding in the particular, this situational stance implicit within the course, and explicit in this paper, underscores a premise of my work— that landscape architectural theory and practice are contingent endeavors; they give form to and illuminate the particulars of a time and place.[3] The framing of the course within the last two centuries engenders in my students a sense of belonging to a tradition—modern landscape architecture history and theory—that is active and alive.[4] These two situations—the physical and cultural boundaries of each built landscape, as well as the temporal or historical boundaries within which a project occurs—form the space for my own theoretical project, the archaeology and reconstruction of modern landscape architecture.

## Bridging, Mediating, Reconciling: Theoretical Analogues

What is the pedagogical value of defining theory through analogy? *Bridging, mediating,* and *reconciling* are verbs that connote a realm of in-betweens. Bridges span. Mediation intercedes.[5] Reconciliation joins. Interpreted as a *bridge*, a *mediation,* or a *reconciliation,* theory occupies a middle ground in between.[6] In between what? Thought and action. Forms of consciousness and built form. The formal and the social realm. A particular project and general principles. General principles and a specific site.

### Why the Picturesque?

One of the most persistent and perplexing of terms that characterize the modern landscape is the "Picturesque." Curiously, this modern landscape—arguably beginning with the Picturesque—was inextricable from the processes of urbanization and modernization. The Picturesque was one of the first theoretical frameworks that embedded the ambiguity a particular society felt toward the progress and loss associated with urbanization and modernization.[7]

Since the scope of the Picturesque encompasses design treatises, political ideologies, world views (or collective consciousness), and conceptual frameworks, it is a versatile tool for exploring how theory can make or clarify connections between the world and design, between culture and form.[8] The evolution, interpretation, and application of the Picturesque from the late eighteenth century through the present day sheds light on the changing meaning of the word as well as on the cultural milieu within which it is interpreted. This picturesque journey should clarify how a course in modern landscape architectural theory might best be understood within the time frame beginning in the mid-eighteenth century[9] and within the context of both cultural/artistic modernity as well as technological modernization.

### Bridging

The tale of the Picturesque begins with four primary sources, which are *bridges* between venerated built works and indigenous woodlands, and the design of future works. These are William Gilpin's *Remarks on Forest Scenery* (1791), Uvedale Price's *An Essay on the Picturesque* (1794), Richard Payne Knight's poem *The Landscape, a Didactic Poem* (1794) and Thomas Whately's *Observations on Modern Gardening* (1770). Through the primary sources, the students absorb the diversity of positions taken by picturesque advocates in the later decades of the eighteenth century.[10]

For instance, Gilpin's guide books—small enough for a connoisseur to carry while walking through the woods—describe and locate British sites for the Picturesque landscape *cognoscenti.*[11] The guide books are a *bridge* (and a screen) between the landscape and the connoisseurs, providing them with a descriptive vocabulary and criteria for appreciating the native landscape. In one passage, Gilpin describes the basic formal characteristics of

Picturesque beauty—form, lightness, and proper balance—before noting how the processes of time and change refine the landscape's character.

> Many of these [picturesque beauties] are derived from the injuries the tree receives, or the diseases to which it is subject. Mr. Lawson, a naturalist of the last age, thus enumerates them. "How many forests and woods," says he, "have we, wherein you shall have, for one lively, thriving tree, four, nay sometimes twenty-four, evil, thriving, rotten and dying trees: what rottenness! what hollowness! what dead arms! withered tops! curtailed trunks! what loads of mosses! drooping boughs, and dying branches, shall you find thee everywhere." Now all these maladies, which our distressed naturalist bemoans with so much feeling, are often capital sources of picturesque beauty, both in the wild scenes of nature, and in artificial landscape.[12]

The elevation of this local scenery to the status of painted pictures suggest that the local is as valuable as the universal (or Italian) and that read landscapes are more precious than *belle nature*.[13] After dedicating Book 1 of *Remarks on Forest Scenery* to the description of trees, Gilpin continues by naming the possible results of combining trees into landscape types—the clump, the park (comprising clumps and interspersed lawns), the wood, the copse, the glen, the open grove, and the forest. As a set of principles or a "scheme of ideas that explain practice," this theory is a *bridge* between observation and making[14]—abstracting general design principles, codes and conventions from the particulars of specific native woodlands.[15]

Price's essay expands Gilpin's distinctions between the Picturesque and the Beautiful (and by association, Kant's distinctions between the Beautiful and the Sublime), and locates the essence of the Picturesque in the physical attributes of the object. This development marks an eighteenth-century tendency to classify and codify by locating Picturesqueness in varied, irregular, asymmetrical, and rough objects or scenes. In contrast, Knight's poem and later essay, *An Analytical Inquiry into the Principles of Taste* (1805), emphasizes the associational and emotive characteristics of the Picturesque over the formal or visual. One knew a Picturesque scene not by its formal attributes, but by the feelings it evoked in the viewer. These two writings provide students with vivid examples of the differences between constructive and contemplative theories, the former engaged with attributes of making and the latter with those of receiving. These primary texts expose the class to the fluidity and complexity of eighteenth-century Picturesque discourse. The Picturesque controversies of the late eighteenth century arose as landscape connoisseurs and designers made claims for differing boundaries for the Picturesque. Comparisons between current popular usage of this term and previous meanings begin to suggest the devolution of the term from a category rich in tactile, temporal, and emotive associations to, by the twentieth century, one solely concerned with the visual.

In addition to theories that *bridge* between empirical observation and general principle, there are treatises that *bridge* the particulars of a certain designer's *oeuvre* (whether written or built) and design practice by others—often in a different country or region. J. C. Loudon's *Suburban Gardener* (1838) or *Villa Gardener* (1850), A. J. Downing's *Treatise on the Theory and Practice of Landscape Architecture as adapted to North America* (1841 and 1865), and H. W. S. Cleveland's *Landscape Architecture as Applied to the Wants of the West* (1873) are examples of treatises that *bridge* the gap between the exemplary built landscapes of Britain and the "wants" of America cities. The *bridging* describes familiar categories such as Beautiful, Picturesque, or Sublime, but emphasizes convenience, fitness, and expression, thus opening up the older categories to invention and interpretation based on the circumstances of the young democracy.

Theoretical texts such as Downing's naturalize a discipline's autonomy and self-referentiality by employing internal languages, building on past precedent, and construing meaning in formal relationships. The codes, principles, and conventions that are described and analyzed in such texts[16] form the basis of a language of design construction and criticism. These "theories from within" are usually aimed at an audience of makers or designers who will build or construct new works upon the foundations of others. Theories from within are significant contributions to the evolution of a specific field of cultural production like landscape architecture because they permit a shared language which facilitates discourse and criticism from within.[17]

## Mediating

An overreliance on theories from within might be the tendency of a designer solely preoccupied with tangible form and corporeal space. This person might be described as having an idealist (versus materialist) perceptive which emphasizes the internal codes and conventions of a designed object or space. The limits of these internal theories emerge if one considers landscape architecture from a Marxist perspective as a cultural product (versus a designed object or space) located within a specific social formation.[18] Cultural products are made both of material products and with human labor, and they are situated in geographically modified social formations. Another place for theory, then, is between a social formation and the act of design, or between the social and the formal. This *mediating* role is active, not passive. It requires "the invention of a set of theoretical terms or codes such that the same terminology can be used to analyze and articulate two or more distinct types of objects or texts, or two different levels of reality." (In other words, built landscapes do not passively reflect their social or physical context any more than an individual's personality is a mere reflection or epiphenomenon of its environment.)

As a *mediating* device, theory can actively reveal the mechanisms that operate to sustain an ideology.[19] As an activity that transforms properties that are themselves both symbols of class status and enablers of power relations, landscape architectural design can reveal the contradictions that underlie a given culture's artistic, political, and economic ideologies. This *mediating* role of theory has implications for both the construction and the contemplation of built works, for the designer and the historian/critic/inhabitant. I will elaborate on this point with three examples: first, with an interpretation of the Picturesque as a *compensation* for the loss of native British countryside to the standardization and modernization of the enclosed agriculture fields; second, with an interpretation of the Picturesque as a *compensation* for European criticisms of America's materialistic values and lack of culture; and finally, as a *displacement* of the continent's only history—its natural or geological history—from the country to the city.[20]

From art historian Mirka Benes's teaching in a prior landscape architectural history course, the students are cognizant of Price and Knight's Foxite Whig affiliations and the transference of their political motives into landscape design. Drawing on that knowledge and readings from Ann Bermingham and Denis Cosgrove, I introduce the concept of *mediation* to the students as it applies to the Picturesque in eighteenth-century Britain. How does the Picturesque contain these motives within its forms? How does the Picturesque *mediate* between the culture and a built landscape?

One might first explain this *mediating* role as a compensatory action. The sort of scenery admired by Gilpin was more than an aesthetic expression of national pride; it was a rapidly disappearing resource because of the standardization of the countryside under enclosure. The local and the particular of the British woodlands were giving way to the universal of both the enclosed agricultural field and the Pastoral improvements of Capability Brown's followers. Inclusion of such Picturesque woodland scenery in one's estate might be interpreted as a compensation for the loss of that regional and local character. The possession of such non-productive property, however, was a luxury that only the wealthy could afford. As such, the Picturesque was as much a projection of social standing as any geometrically configured garden. In fact, one can argue that the Picturesque's pretense of "informality" was less forthright, more deceitful, for its repression of obvious improvements.

This reading of the Picturesque raises immediate questions for students too eager to attribute naturalness (and freedom, liberty, virtue) to any scheme lacking geometrical forms. Such a reading requires a theoretical perspective that pierces the boundary or contour of the garden or landscape under scrutiny and that situates the work in a broader cultural or geographical frame. The Picturesque controversy illuminates how theory can *mediate* the political and formal. What are the implications when the frame changes—a treatise or theory travels from one site to another? Do forms remain constant and meanings vary? Or are the intentions translated into another language? In other words, how is Picturesque theory *mediated* by the particulars of place?

The course traces the Picturesque's travels from eighteenth-century Britain to nineteenth-century France and the United States as a means of illustrating intersections of a theoretical construction with differing environmental and geographical situations. Here, I limit the discussion to the mediation applicable to America.

In the American city, the Picturesque has quite different manifestations and meanings from those in Europe. During an era when the North American continent's vast wilderness was the feature that both differentiated the American from the European psyche and fueled its considerable pride, an urban park replete with Pastoral and Picturesque scenery was a cultural institution capable of inculcating democratic values and embodying national aspirations.

How was the uniqueness of America's landscape given expression in the urban park? Through formal site analyses of the U.S. Capitol Grounds and Prospect Park, I explain the codes Olmsted developed to compose the landscape characters described in Downing, Loudon, and Repton and to suggest ways in which these codes *mediate* between America's collective consciousness about nature, the particulars of the American city, and the generalities of Picturesque theory.

In Prospect Park, the geological structure of the parcel—a transitional landscape which straddles the terminal moraine and outwash plain at the southern extent of the Wisconsin glacier—established three distinct types of landform which Vaux and Olmsted exploited.[21] The flat expanse of the outwash plain to the south was developed into the vast lake; the rolling terrain of the terminal moraine was developed into the Picturesque ravine; and the glaciated till landform to the north was transformed into the Pastoral or Beautiful undulating long meadow, which is defined by real and constructed eskers. An unreal-

Figure 2. Mediating theory: Prospect Park, Brooklyn (John Dixon Hunt).

ized observation tower atop a drumlin would have exposed park visitors to the Sublime of both Manhattan to the northwest and the Atlantic Ocean to the south. Within Prospect Park, geological landforms provide a spatial armature for the arranging, shaping, and sizing of three adjacent landscape types, the Beautiful or Pastoral, the Picturesque, or the Sublime.[22]

Prospect Park's correspondence between geological structure and landscape character or type is contrasted with the correspondence between geometric structure and landscape character at the U.S. Capitol Grounds. Here, the structure of the encompassing city plan designed by L'Enfant—a grid with radiating diagonals—and the plan organization of the existing governmental edifice provide an armature for three landscape characters—the Beautiful, the Picturesque, and the Sublime. The space straddling the central axis and located between the capitol and the Mall was a beautiful, smooth greensward flanked by allées of sycamore lining the extensions of Maryland and Pennsylvania avenues. The northern and southern grounds were densely planted Picturesque plantations of shrubs and trees, through which service drives and walks curved sinuously uphill toward the east forecourt. Within the plantations, two rusticated stone ventilation towers and a hexagonal brick grotto functioned as architectural follies and hygienic services for members of Congress and their constituents. The west terrace offered views across the Beautiful or Pastoral foreground and flanking Picturesque plantations toward the sublime of the (then unrealized) Mall and the country's western expansion implied in that panorama.[23]

Through this interpretation of two Olmsted projects, students see beyond the superficial adjectives such as "Olmstedian" and "informal." This exercise encourages them to work back and forth between texts and built landscapes and their encompassing geographic or underlying geologic structure in order to revive their traditions—to produce new works through interpretation. I hope to instill in them some sense of the artifice and structure inherent in these built works that are too frequently dismissed as amorphous, informal, irregular, anti-urban, and Olmstedian. [24] Furthermore, this part of the course locates theoretical construction within the activity of design. The role of the designer is introduced as that of a theoretically productive agent, one who translates prior theories, principles, and codes and develops new theories, not simply applies precedent. In doing so, the lecture *mediates* between the theory course and the design studio.

*Reconciling*

The last role for a theory of in-betweens I will describe is that of *reconciling*,[25] "making consistent or compatible" or "joining [one piece of work] evenly with another" (*Webster's*). This activity is located between landscape architecture design and socially constructed concepts such as culture, nature, ecology, city, and country. Landscape architectural theory is uniquely positioned to contain, inscribe, embed, and express within its spaces and forms a culture's complex and contradictory attitudes about the natural world. As most models of the natural world and human nature's place within it (or outside it) are based on an intersection of religious and scientific belief structures, built landscapes—understood as expressing a culture's values with nature's materials—can communicate the tension between those intertwined strands of faith and reason, myth and fact.

Theory can be a practice that *reconciles* these values in built form; a practice that explains how forms can mean to those outside the field or discipline. Theory can be a practice that *reconciles* or joins what Carolyn Merchant[26] calls collective consciousness and built form. Societies express their collective consciousness through the forms of "scientific, philosophical and literary texts" and through "rituals, festivals, songs, and myths." A given social formation's forms of consciousness, "through which the world is perceived, understood and interpreted, are socially constructed and subject to change." Landscape architectural theory, constructed by and for practitioners who revel in their roles as spatial translators of cultural values, can be a vital agent in construing new forms of consciousness through the design.

RECONCILING THE RATIONAL AND THE EMOTIVE, THE EMPIRICAL AND THE INTUITIVE

A set of theoretical keywords I employ in the course revolves around the interconnections between the terms "landscape," "Picturesque," and "scientific analysis." How do these terms help illuminate the *reconciliatory* role of modern landscape architecture? Denis Cosgrove's *Social Formation and Symbolic Landscape* and Carolyn Merchant's *Ecological Revolutions* both describe the impact of evolving scientific frameworks on humans' perception of their relationship with the nonhuman natural world. Through the split between "the disembodied analytical mind and a romantic emotional sensibility"[27] accompanying the capitalist ecological revolution, humans became increasingly separated from the non-human world about them. What had previously been an insider's relationship to a vitalist, organic world became an outsider's relationship to a rational, mechanized world. The inhabitant became a connoisseur of visual scenery—the Picturesque landscape—or an observer/measurer of quantifiable landscape variables. This emphasis on the visual and recordable reduced the landscape to two-dimensional surfaces, either the vertical surface of the picture plane or the horizontal surface of the geographer's map. Both facilitated the control of the landscape through abstraction, detachment, and distance. This distancing was complicit with the belief that scientific domination of nature was a prerequisite of progress.

Hence, Picturesque theory's *reconciling* role is a complex one. The idea of the landscape as a scene (versus the site as a place) requires the acceptance of two contradictory conceptual frameworks. The rational and the emotive conspire to distance the viewer (not the inhabitant) from the landscape (not the site) and the specific site from the codified Picturesque. Somehow, these contradictions—held in tension by early theorists of the Picturesque—were to become untenable to late nineteenth- and early twentieth-century designers. Each succeeding treatise or design handbook seemed to extract more and more of the Picturesque's complexity until its meaning was reduced to little more than "a pleasing scene."

Herein lies one aspect of the Picturesque that I find compelling when trying to explain how a theory grounded in the unique character of the British countryside could devolve into a mass-producible, placeless image. The treatises and plan books of the nineteenth century that followed Gilpin's evocative descriptions of native British landscape generalized, abstracted, and reduced his tactile, phenomenal sites to reproducible visual scenery. Even the illustrations reduced the site to landscape by failing to depict topography and by cropping the perspectives into placeless, decorative vignettes.

RECONCILING THE ARTISTIC AND THE ECOLOGICAL: A POST-STRUCTURALIST VIEW

While the Picturesque persists throughout the early twentieth century through sources as disparate as Hubbard and Kimball and Le Corbusier,[28] I would like to shift to the literature of the past thirty years that has served to revise our attitudes about the Picturesque, its place in modern art and architecture, and its reconciliatory role between ecological and artistic endeavors. One of the course's objectives is to reassess the Picturesque's spatial and temporal contributions to modern art and architecture, which have been subjugated by the visual or pictorial in certain historical trajectories. Through writings like Peter Collins's *Changing Ideals in Modern Architecture,* Robert Smithson's "Frederick Law Olmsted and the Dialectical Landscape" and "Sedimentation of the Mind," Yve-Alain Bois's "A Picturesque Stroll Around Clara Clara," and Caroline Constant's "The Barcelona Pavilion as Landscape Garden," the nonvisual aspects of the Picturesque have been recovered.[29] Temporal change, spatial sequence, memory and association, the inability to comprehend in a glance—the experiential, kinetic aspects of the Picturesque have been reclaimed as precursors to both the free-plan and the architectural promenade. Geological layers and cultural memories have been uncovered, thus expanding the Picturesque's grounding in history, time, ruin, and memory. The picture plane of the Picturesque has been thickened to include past and present, natural and cultural history—all understood through movement. As Constant writes in her essay on Mies's pavilion and Bois writes in his discussion of Serra's sculpture, meaning is construed through the interaction of the viewer with, through, and around the work. This active engagement with the piece transforms it from an object into a work. Meaning is produced; it is labored.

If Collins, Constant, and Bois resurrect the bridge between the visual, the spatial, and the temporal inherent in the Picturesque, Smithson's essays are bridges of another sort—between ecological and artistic concerns, between the geological past and the present.[30] His reading of Price's *Three Essays on the Picturesque* (1810) and Burke's *Inquiry into the Origin of Our Ideas of the Sublime and the Beautiful* (1757) recovers the "physical sense of the temporal" Picturesque through an interpretation of Central Park. He recounts Price's Picturesque descriptions of rough slopes overgrown through time, of trees struck by lightning, and of abandoned quarries and gravel pits. He quotes the following passage from Price's *Three Essays on the Picturesque:*

> The side of a smooth green hill, torn by floods, may at first very properly be called deformed; and on the same principle, though not with the same impression, as a gash on an animal. When a rawness of such a gash in the ground is softened, and in part concealed and ornamented by the effects of time, and the progress of vegetation, deformity, by this usual process, is converted to picturesque; and this is the case with quarries, gravel pits, etc., which at first are deformities, and which in their picturesque state, are often considered as such by a levelling improver.[31]

He continues to make connections between early modern landscape architecture and the environmental concerns of his own milieu by defining the implications of locating the Picturesque *between* the Beautiful and the Sublime. "A park can no longer be seen as a 'thing in itself,' but rather a process of ongoing relationships," he writes.[32] Smithson offers a reason for contemporary culture's banal sense of the Picturesque as a visual image. "The reason the potential dialectic inherent in the picturesque broke down was because natural processes were viewed in isolation as so many classifications, detached from physical interconnection, and finally replaced by mental representations of a finished absolute ideal."[33]

Smithson's interpretation, itself a *reconciliation* of the ecological world view of the late 1960s–early 1970s and *mediated* through his own artistic endeavors as an earth artist, recasts our readings of such eighteenth-century texts as Whately, Burke, Price, Knight, and Gilpin. Suddenly, Whately's chapter "On Seasons," in his 1770 *Observations on Modern Gardens,* appears as a rupture in the standard form of garden treatises. Whereas previous architectural treatises concentrated on the constant, universal, and immutable aspects of the garden, this small book revels in the ephemeral, the contingent, and the fleeting—those characteristics of the modern hailed by Baudelaire a century later.[34] Whately's impassioned plea for considering the movement of light and shadow across a garden pavilion, seasonal color changes, and the phenomenal effect of weather in the landscape unequivocally defines the essential conditions and materials of the modern landscape. His respect for the local and the particular assumes a designer's intimate knowledge of a site's processes (unmediated by photographs and maps) in addition to a familiarity with composition, character, and association. In the 1770s, a nascent ecological world view, described by environmental historian Donald Worster[35] as vitalist, infused the theory of modern landscape architecture. This conceptual framework resisted the homogenizing tendency of modernization and the visual biases of modernity by celebrating the differences in every site.

Recovering this resistant stance opens students to the rich legacy of theoretical texts and their associated built landscapes that lie, mostly unread, in our rare book rooms. I believe such a rereading establishes the framework for situating modern landscape architecture's inception within the context of not only the scientific, industrial, and aesthetic revolutions but also the ecological revolution of the late eighteenth century. [36] In this light, landscape architecture can be read as an active but resistant endeavor in the history of modernity and modernization. During a time when a mechanistic world view dominated intellectual discourse and industrial capitalism, one strain of landscape architectural theory and practice held onto the prior vitalist world view that gradually grew into an ecological frame of consciousness later in the nineteenth and twentieth centuries.

This final observation provides a convenient, if arbitrary, moment to terminate this meandering through the Picturesque literature. This one thread of the modern landscape's theoretical tapestry has been unraveled in order to give a concrete example of the ways that a theory course can help students recover the richness of their field's ongoing tradition. Furthermore, by returning to original sources and considering the landscape's own medium and essential characteristics, I hope to disengage landscape architectural theory from its frequent dependence on art and architectural terms and categories. Such distancing is necessary because the marginalization of landscape in the discourses of the modern has blinded many of our practitioners and historians to the multivalent relationships and structures that characterize the modern landscape.

## The Theory Between the Theory and Lectures

As a field of knowledge, a discipline, and a professional activity, modern landscape architecture has been a pragmatic enterprise, reveling in the contingencies of a site. The energies devoted to this enterprise have been translated as nontheoretical, anti-intellectual, or nonexistent by many historians of art and architecture.[37] I would disagree, and argue that a close reading of the reports and treatises written throughout the nineteenth and twentieth centuries supports another interpretation altogether. Our appreciation of modern landscape architectural theory has been hampered not by the work itself but by our reliance on the filters of certain modern art and architectural histories and theories. Landscape as an abstract concept and a real place was marginalized in the discourses of modern art and architecture. Hence our continued reliance on the interpretive lens of those fields which are not concerned with the integration of ecological thinking (or the environmentalist eye)[38] with physical form has limited our understanding of and appreciation for the complexity and form-fullness of the nineteenth-century urban landscape in particular.

In lieu of a rich, descriptive language capable of communicating the ways in which aesthetic theories are both superimposed on and interwoven through specific geographies and viewed through various environmental or ecological eyes, we have been forced to rely on one aspect of the modern landscape: the visual. As such, we have been incapable of resurrecting the spatial, temporal, phenomenal, and material aspects of landscapes of the past.

One objective of this course, then, is archaeological—to uncover the richness of the modern landscape by describing it in its own terms. This endeavor has been facilitated by the theoretical and critical tools developed in the past decade in the fields of cultural history, environmental history, phenomenology, and poststructuralist and feminist theory.[39]

The systems aesthetic that landscape architectural practice developed in the nineteenth century is not easily described or evaluated using the categories of modern art and architecture. The tendency of those discourses to view the relationship between the human and non-human natural world through the lens of binary categories—nature and culture, man and nature, formal and informal, figure and ground—fails to accommodate the in-between quality of the landscape. Theories of the object or thing must give way to theories about the relationships between things. In this respect, landscape architecture prefigures post-structuralism's theoretical critique of the modern project.[40]

As a poststructuralist critic[41] who is researching modern landscape architectural theory and recovering that history from the strictures of art and architectural historiography on the one hand and professional loyalties on the other,[42] I am haunted by the ease with which many modern theories conflate landscape, nature, the irrational, and the irregular with the feminine, while architecture, culture, the rational, and the ordered are aligned with the masculine. What impact do such gender affiliations have on environmental ethics, conceptual frameworks, and theoretical categories? In considering such issues, my role as a feminist theorist is not primarily concerned with recovering the contribution of women producers of landscape architecture; rather, feminist landscape architecture theory can be involved in the "simultaneous deconstruction of the discourses and practices of landscape and architectural history itself."[43]

The course itself is an act of creative destruction and destructive creativity.[44] But I am not as interested in deconstructing the canon for its omission, gaps, and biases as much as I am in mining the archaeological ruin of modern landscape architecture theory and practice in search of the material for a new construction. As a revisionist (as Adrienne Rich defines the term),[45] I hope that "the act of looking back, of seeing with fresh eyes, of entering an old text from a new critical direction" will result in a shift in the future trajectory of landscape architecture theory and practice.

## BRIDGING, MEDIATING, AND RECONCILING: THREE ROLES FOR LANDSCAPE THEORY

Since the cultural products we know as built landscapes, what Michel Foucault called "spaces of nature," are implicated in power structures, landscape architectural theory that *reconciles* quickly becomes entangled in theories of *mediation*.[46] As soon as world views, collective consciousness, and theoretical frameworks are translated into forms of consciousness and cultural products that occupy nature's space, that require human labor and natural and produced material resources, and that signify an owner's or inhabitant's status in a culture, landscape architectural theory oscillates from the symbolic to the ideological realm. I hope it is clear that my analogies do not result in three categories of theory, but rather describe three theoretical projects that all built work can engage in, and that all criticism can bring to bear on built works.

*Bridging, mediating,* and *reconciling*. Theory spans, intercedes, and joins. It removes design from the isolation of the individual ego and from the service of variables, opportunities, and constraints. Theory connects built landscape form to the cares and concerns of humanity. Landscape architectural theory reconciles design form with the particulars of time and place and the aspirations and motivations of humankind. As such, situated theory enables and ennobles practice.

# PART II

# Design Process

Models of the design process are the discipline's *procedural* theory. Just as the overall approach to theory within landscape architecture has evolved over the past half century in response to changing demands and needs, so also have models of design process. Each decade has been characterized by a reconsideration of the way the design activity is understood and taught. For the first two decades (1950–1970), the focus was upon development of a staged model of design, based upon the idea that design is a problem-solving activity. Latterly, there has been greater emphasis upon conceptualization of design as a fine art, with consequential implications for models of process. At the same time, however, staged models have continued to be refined.

The first reading is taken from Hideo Sasaki's (1950) discussion of the need for a structured design process, which prefigured much of the subsequent thinking about a formal process of design during the 1950s and 1960s. As Sasaki's essay makes clear, design was modeled upon systematic research and analysis followed by creative synthesis, and drew directly upon parallel developments in engineering, architecture, industrial design, and project management. This process was elaborated and specifically applied to site planning and design by Kevin Lynch and John Ormsbee Simonds, illustrated by a short extract from the revised version of Kevin Lynch's classic text on site planning. During the 1960s the "environmental revolution"[1] against uncontrolled technical exploitation of the environment stimulated Ian McHarg's reformulation of the staged and systematic design process as "the ecological method." His description of this is included in full.

By the late 1960s, however, alternatives to the classic survey-analysis-design method were being explored. Lawrence Halprin dramatically challenged the presumption that design was a rational, linear process, with a model of *RSVP cycles*, which emphasized instead the creative dimension, cyclical structure, and collaborative nature of landscape design. Other commentators argued for a significant shift of control of the process, toward the community. The extract from Randolph Hester's *Neighborhood Space* includes a number of quotations from planning theorists, illustrating the crossovers between the environmental disciplines that were characteristic of the period.

The main challenge to the staged model, however, arose from a broader theoretical reorientation of the discipline as a whole away from paradigms of science, toward the fine arts. Steven Krog made several incisive commentaries of the rational design process in the early 1980s, and his 1983 essay *Creative Risk Taking* is included in full, as an example of the critique that became widespread during the subsequent decade.

At the same time, though, proponents of a systematic, staged process also adapted and refined their models. A second short extract from Lynch and Hack (1984) highlights the way that each designer adapts the stages of the process to their particular experiences and attitudes, as well as to the needs and characteristics of the project.

The final reading in this section is perhaps the most challenging in the whole collection, in which the French designer and theorist Bernard Lassus describes a design process which encapsulates many of the qualities advocated by Krog. The challenge for the reader of this contribution lies not only in the range of ideas, but also in the style of presentation, which originates in a different language. Nonetheless, Lassus's approach illustrates very well the reconfiguration of design process away from a practical problem-solving tool to an artistic and intellectual exploration, appropriate to the broad cultural and strategic role envisaged by other contemporary commentators.

# DESIGN PROCESS (1950)

## HIDEO SASAKI

It has been customary for landscape schools to teach by the method of projects and solutions. In the course of the normal school year, project-problems dealing with specific situations and falling within specific categories of landscape architecture have been assigned. Customarily, too, these problems have been scheduled haphazardly—perhaps a park, then a subdivision, next a civic center, and so on; or in the advanced years, Landscape Exchange Problems have been assigned as they were scheduled.

Under such a system, coordination of courses (such as construction to design) and the development of design theory in a logical sequence have been difficult if not impossible. Certain schools, therefore, have changed completely to an organized curriculum. The semester work is scheduled to a developmental scheme with all problems related one to another. This method has many obvious advantages.

However, the project-solution or the "case" method of teaching offers some advantages. The change of topics and, where Exchange Problems are used, the stimulation of competition contributes to the general interest and effectiveness of this method of teaching.

Certain facts point out ways and means of using the "case" method of teaching to good advantage. Upon analysis, it is evident that the solution of any given problem is not of primary import; what is of basic significance is the process of thinking which the student undergoes in arriving at a solution. Also, no matter what the given problem, the manifest solution of a particular problem can hardly ever be used to solve another. Conditions change with each new problem, and each solution is unique.

The thing basic to solving all of these problems is the *thinking process*—the critical thought process used in understanding and solving any given problem. Designing is essentially a process of relating all the operational factors into a comprehensive whole, including the factors of cost and effect.

Critical thinking applied to design involves, then: (1) research, to understand all the factors to be considered; (2) analysis, to establish the ideal operational relationship of all the factors; and (3) synthesis, to articulate the complex of relationships into a spatial organization.

Research used in this sense includes more than mere book reading. It involves both the primary and secondary research, and is of three types—verbal, visual, and experimental.

*Verbal research* means reading and discussing. Although recent books on landscape architectural subjects have been scarce, numerous books on art and architecture are available. Also, written materials on social and philosophical matters help in understanding basic problems of environmental planning.

*Visual research* consists of activities of a passive nature—namely, looking at photographs, sketches, and work executed in the field. Some schools are more favorably located for field inspection, but inspiration from the vernacular—grain elevators, high tension lines, cultivated fields, etc.—must not be overlooked.

*Experimental research* is the manipulative activity used to discover new aesthetic possibilities of materials, construction methods, and spatial relationships. A basic understanding of pure design of form, color, and texture, and of space relationships, is a necessity before designs of high quality can be produced. For example, a *collage* problem where amorphous materials (that is, materials having no form in themselves) are taken and arranged in a composition isolates the factor of relationships. This compels the students to think only in terms of relationships and not of objects. In a problem of an abstract space composition, the complex factors of utility are temporarily avoided and pure space relationships are studied. These exercises train the mind and the eye to grasp the fundamental principles of design. And these qualities of proportion, balance, contrast, etc., of pure design are essential in the environment to satisfy the affective nature of human beings.

The second phase of the process of designing is analysis. Given any problem, a systematic analysis of factors involved is necessary before a "design-form" can be articulated. While the experienced and talented designer may be able to perform the analyses quickly and may mentally visualize a synthesis which he can proceed to put directly on paper, the student designer nearly always finds it helpful to make some sort of graphic representation of each phase.

For example, to solve a building problem, the student may approach the problem first by making an abstract "relational" diagram. Such a study considers only the ideal relationships of the various functions involved, such as the kitchen being related to the eating areas, the bath to the bedrooms, etc. Sizes, shapes, location or any other "practical" considerations are temporarily set aside.

The next process may be a "space" or a "sequential" diagram. This analysis attempts to place the various functions in space, i.e., in their order of location in space according to the contributing influences of site, situation, function, etc.

Circulation may be the next consideration. A system which is convenient and operative is worked out in diagrammatic form.

Each problem, of course, will call for a different set of analyses. Moreover, rigid "categorization" is neither necessary nor in itself guarantees a good solution. Factors nearly always have more than one relationship. The process of analysis, therefore, must be multiordinate. It is necessary to make as many analyses as there are types of relationships. Some of the more common types of analyses pertinent to landscape architectural planning are a priori scales according to the relative importance of factors, orientation and exposure studies, indoor-outdoor relationships, etc.

With these basic analyses, the student may now consider the "practical" details of sizes, shapes, materials, construction system, etc. The design-form which finally evolves from this critical thinking process will not likely be arbitrary or preconceived. Rather, it will be a functional expression consistent with structure and materials used, with little concern as to whether it is "modern" or "traditional."

It is this task of synthesis, of articulating all the factors into a design form, which distinguishes a designer from an engineer or a technician. Up to this point, imagination and taste had not entered into the process of designing. The skill of organizing the functional with the touch of aesthetic (proportion, sensitivity, drama, and all the other attributes associated with "beauty") is the particular quality of a designer. It is a moot question whether this quality can be taught. Although the process of research and analysis is molded quite readily by pedagogical efforts, the best that an instructor can hope for is that this genius of synthesis exists in each student in a potentiality great enough so that, with proper guidance and cultivation, it may be harnessed to an acceptable degree.

This process of critical thinking, involving research, analysis, and synthesis, increases fluidity of thinking. Since each problem is approached from an analytical point of view, the synthesis cuts across the archenemies of design, preconceptions and dogmas. Also, since each solution is considered a compromise of the ideal, a multitude of alternatives is offered. The designer, having a thorough understanding of the basic relationships, will have complete control of the problem while he experiments with the various alternatives.

In younger landscape architects' designs today the constructivists' and the expressionists' theories seem to be enjoying a position of dominance. This situation is undoubtedly the result of their fascination with forms and techniques developed by the contemporary arts and architecture movements. However, this need not be the finality of expression in landscape design.

As indicated, the expression of each problem will differ; and the expression developed in landscape architecture need not be imitative of its sister arts. Landscape expressions will resemble architectural expressions in so far as its problems are similar, but the valid and varied expressions of contemporary landscape architecture will evolve from the basic ingredients of its materials, methods, and functions.

Numerous examples of experimental projects which have led to new forms in environmental planning may be found, such as contour plowing, freeway traffic routes, Radburn and the greenbelt towns, etc. New concepts applied frankly to solving problems of functions create new forms.

A basic approach to design, then, plus problems of a more investigative and experimental nature are necessary in the educational institutions. Schools should teach students more than mere techniques of earning their bread and butter. The questioning and exploration of new ideas should be encouraged in educational institutions, since limitations are largely theoretical and consequences accountable only to semester grades. It is only then that the students will be provided with tools to forge new knowledge to meet existing and new situations and to contribute toward social progress in their professional life.

# THE ART OF SITE PLANNING (1984)

## KEVIN LYNCH AND GARY HACK

To summarize, there are eight stages in the typical site planning cycle in which the designer is properly involved. (But often, alas, the designer has little to do with the first and the last.) Beyond this cycle of events, of course, other actors are engaged in other actions: the consideration and approval of plans, for example, or the securing of financing. Nevertheless, the stages of site planning proper are

　　1. defining the problem;
　　2. programming and the analysis of site and user;
　　3. schematic design and the preliminary cost estimate;
　　4. developed design and detailed costing;
　　5. contract documents;

6. bidding and contracting;

7. construction; and

8. occupation and management.

Reciting these stages makes them sound logical and linear, but the recital is only conventional; the real process is looping and cyclical. Knowledge of a later phase influences conduct of an earlier one, and early decisions are later reworked. Site design is a process of learning in which a coherent system of form, client, program, and site gradually emerges. Even after decisions are made and building begins—even after the site is occupied—the feedback from experience continues to modify the plan. . . . The designer thinks that her organization will have an absolute, permanent influence on all later occupants. In reality, this is only partly so, since whatever she does will soon undergo some modification. Every site has a long history that bears on its present. Every site will have a long future, over which the designer exerts only partial control. The new site form is one episode in a continuous interplay of space and people. Sooner or later, it will be succeeded by another cycle of adaptation.

Some critics assert that our physical settings determine the quality of our lives. That view collapses under careful scrutiny, and then it is a natural reaction to say that the spatial environment has no critical bearing on human satisfaction. Each extreme view rests on the fallacies of the other. Organism and environment interact, and environment is both social and physical. You cannot predict the happiness of anyone from the landscape he lives in (although you might predict his unhappiness), but neither can you predict what he will do or feel without knowing his landscape and others he has experienced. People and their habitat coexist.[1] As humans multiply and their technology comes to dominate the earth, the conscious organization of the land becomes more important to the quality of life. Pollution impairs the living system, and some of our technical feats threaten all life. Careless disturbance of the landscape harms us; skilled siting enhances us. Well-organized, productive living space is a resource for humanity, just as are energy, air, and water.

Site planning, then, is the organization of the external physical environment to accommodate human behavior. It deals with the qualities and locations of structures, land, activities, and living things. It creates a pattern of those elements in space and time, which will be subject to continuous future management and change. The technical output—the grading plans, utility layouts, survey locations, planting plans, sketches, diagrams, and specifications—are simply a conventional way of specifying this complex organization.

# AN ECOLOGICAL METHOD (1967)

IAN MCHARG

In many cases a qualified statement is, if not the most propitious, at least the most prudent. In this case it would only be gratuitous. I believe that ecology provides the single indispensable basis for landscape architecture and regional planning. I would state in addition that it has now, and will increasingly have, a profound relevance for both city planning and architecture.

Where the landscape architect commands ecology he is the only bridge between the natural sciences and the planning and design professions, the proprietor of the most perceptive view of the natural world which science or art has provided. This can be at once his unique attribute, his passport to relevance and productive social utility. With the acquisition of this competence the sad image of ornamental horticulture, handmaiden to architecture after the fact, the caprice and arbitrariness of "clever" designs can be dismissed forever. In short, ecology offers emancipation to landscape architecture.

This is not the place for a scholarly article on ecology. We are interested in it selfishly, as those who can and must apply it. Our concern is for a method which has the power to reveal nature as process, containing intrinsic form.

Ecology is generally described as the study of the interactions of organisms and environment which includes other organisms. The particular interests of landscape architecture are focused only upon a part of this great, synoptic concern. This might better be defined as the study of physical and biological processes, as dynamic and interacting, responsive to laws, having limiting factors and exhibiting certain opportunities and constraints, employed in planning and design for human use. At this juncture two possibilities present themselves. The first is to attempt to present a general theory of ecology and the planning processes. This is a venture which I long to undertake, but this is not the time nor place to attempt it. The other alternative is to present a method which has been tested empirically at many scales from a continent, a major region, a river basin, physiographic regions, subregional areas, and a metropolitan region town to a single city.[1] In every case, I submit, it has been triumphantly revelatory.

First, it is necessary to submit a proposition to this effect: that the place, the plants, animals, and men upon it are only comprehensible in terms of physical and biological evolution. Written on the place and upon its inhabitants lies mute all physical, biological, and cultural history awaiting to be understood by those who can read it. It is thus necessary to begin at the beginning if we are to understand the place, the man, or his co-tenants of this phenomenal universe. This is the prerequisite for intelligent intervention and adaptation. So let us begin at the beginning. We start with historical geology. The place, any place, can only be understood through its physical evolution. What history of mountain building and ancient seas, uplifting, folding, sinking, erosion, and glaciation have passed here and left their marks? These explain its present form. Yet the effects of climate and later of plants and animals have interacted upon geological processes and these too lie mute in the record of the rocks. Both climate and geology can be invoked to interpret physiography, the current configuration of the place. Arctic differs from tropics, desert from delta, the Himalayas from the Gangetic Plain. The Appalachian Plateau differs from the Ridge and Valley Province and all of these from the Piedmont and the Coastal Plain. If one now knows historical geology, climate, and physiography then the water regimen becomes comprehensible—the pattern of rivers and aquifers, their physical properties and relative abundance, oscillation between flood and drought. Rivers are young or old, they vary by orders; their pattern and distribution, as for aquifers, is directly consequential upon geology, climate, and physiography.

Knowing the foregoing and the prior history of plant evolution, we can now comprehend the nature and pattern of soils. As plants are highly selective to environmental factors, by identifying physiographic, climatic zones and soils we can perceive order and predictability in the distribution of constituent plant communities. Indeed, the plant communities are more perceptive to environmental variables than we can be with available data, and we can thus infer environmental factors from the presence of plants. Animals are fundamentally plant-related so that given the preceding information, with the addition of the stage of succession of the plant communities and their age, it is possible both to understand and to predict the species, abundance or scarcity of wild animal populations. If there are no acorns there will be no squirrels; an old forest will have few deer; an early succession can support many. Resources also exist where they do for good and sufficient reasons—coal, iron, limestone, productive soils, water in relative abundance, transportation routes, fall lines, and the termini of water transport. And so the land use map becomes comprehensible when viewed through this perspective.

The information so acquired is a gross ecological inventory and contains the data bank for all further investigations. The next task is the interpretation of these data to analyze existing and propose future human land use and management. The first objective is the inventory of unique or scarce phenomena, the technique for which Philip Lewis[2] is renowned. In this all sites of unique scenic, geological, ecological, or historical importance are located. Enlarging this category we can interpret the geological data to locate economic minerals. Geology, climate, and physiography will locate dependable water resources. Physiography will reveal slope and exposure which, with soil and water, can be used to locate areas suitable for agriculture by types; the foregoing, with the addition of plant communities, will reveal intrinsic suitabilities for both forestry and recreation. The entire body of data can be examined to reveal sites for urbanization, industry, transportation routes, indeed any human land-using activity. This interpretive sequence would produce a body of analytical material but the end product for a region would include a map of unique sites, the location of economic minerals, the location of water resources, a slope and exposure map, a map of agricultural suitabilities by types, a similar map for forestry, one each for recreation and urbanization.

These maps of intrinsic suitability would indicate highest and best uses for the entire study area. But this is not enough. These are single uses ascribed to discrete areas. In the forest there are likely to be dominant or co-dominant trees and other subordinate species. We must seek to prescribe all coexistent, compatible uses which may occupy each area. To this end it is necessary to develop a matrix in which all possible land uses are shown on each coordinate. Each is then examined against all others to determine the degree of compatibility or incompatibility. As an example, a single area of forest may be managed for forestry, either hardwood or pulp; it may be utilized for water management objectives; it may fulfill an erosion control function; it can be managed for wildlife and hunting, recreation, and for villages and hamlets. Here we have not land use in the normal sense but *communities* of land uses. The end product would be a map of present and prospective land uses, in communities of compatibilities, with dominants, co-dominants and subordinates derived from an understanding of nature as a process responsive to laws, having limiting factors, constituting a value system, and exhibiting opportunities and constraints to human use.

Now this is not a plan. It does not contain any information of demand. This last is the province of the regional scientist, the econometrician, the economic planner. The work is thus divided between the natural scientist, regional planner-landscape architect who interprets the land and its resources, and the economics-based planner who determines demand, locational preferences, investment and fiscal policies. If demand information is available, then the formulation of a plan is possible, and the demand components can be allocated for urban growth, for the nature and form of the metropolis, for the pattern of regional growth.

So what has our method revealed? First, it allows us to understand nature as process insofar as the natural sciences permit. Second, it reveals causality. The place is because. Next it permits us to interpret natural processes as resources, to prescribe and even to predict for prospective land uses, not singly but in compatible communities. Finally, given information on demand and investment, we are enabled to produce a plan for a continent or a few hundred acres based upon natural process. That is not a small accomplishment.

You might well agree that this is a valuable and perhaps even indispensable method for regional planning but is it as valuable for landscape architecture? I say that any project, save a small garden or the raddled heart of a city where nature has long gone, which is undertaken without a full comprehension and employment of natural process as form-giver is suspect at best and capriciously irrelevant at worst. I submit that the ecological method is the sine qua non for all landscape architecture.

Yet, I hear you say, those who doubt, that the method may be extremely valuable for regional rural problems, but can it enter the city and reveal a comparable utility? Yes, indeed it can but in crossing this threshold the method changes. When used to examine metropolitan growth the data remains the same but the interpretation is focused upon the overwhelming demand for urban land uses and it is oriented to the prohibitions and permissiveness exhibited by natural process to urbanization on the one hand and the presence of locational and resource factors which one would select for satisfactory urban environments on the other. But the litany remains the same: historical geology, climate, physiography, the water regimen, soils, plants, animals, and land use. This is the source from which the interpretation is made although the grain becomes finer.

Yet you say, the method has not entered the city proper; you feel that it is still a device for protecting natural process against the blind despoliation of ignorance and Philistinism. But the method can enter the city and we can proceed with our now familiar body of information to examine the city in an ecological way. We have explained that the place was "because" and to explain "because," all of physical and biological evolution as well. To do this we make a distinction between the "given" and "made" forms. The former is a natural landscape identity, the latter is the accumulation of the adaptations to the given form which constitute the present city. Rio is different from New Orleans, Kansas City from Lima, Amsterdam from San Francisco, because. By employing the ecological method we can discern the reason for the location of the city, comprehend its natural form, discern those elements of identity which are critical and expressive, both those of physiography and vegetation, and develop a program for the preservation and enhancement of that identity. The method is equally applicable when one confronts the made form. The successive stages of urbanization are examined as adaptations to the environment, some of which are successful, some not. Some enter the inventory of resources and contribute to the *genius loci*. As for the given form, this method allows us to perceive the elements of identity in the scale of values. One can then prepare a comprehensive landscape plan for a city and feed the elements of identity, natural process, and the palette for formal expression into the comprehensive planning process.

You still demur. The method has not yet entered into the putrid parts of the city. It needs rivers and palisades, hill and valleys, woodlands and parkland. When will it confront slums and overcrowding, congestion and pollution, anarchy and ugliness? Indeed the method can enter into the very heart of the city and by so doing may save us from the melancholy criteria of economic determinism which have proven so disappointing to the orthodoxy of city planning or the alternative of unbridled "design" which haunts architecture. But here again we must be selective as we return to the source in ecology. We will find little that is applicable in energy system ecology, analysis of food pyramids, relations defined in terms of predator-prey, competition, or those other analytical devices so efficacious for plant and animal ecology. But we can well turn to an ecological model which contains multifaceted criteria for measuring ecosystems and we can select health as an encompassing criterion. The model is my own and as such it is suspect for I am not an ecologist, but each of the parts is the product of a distinguished ecologist.[3] Let us hope that the assembly of the constituents does not diminish their veracity, for they have compelling value.

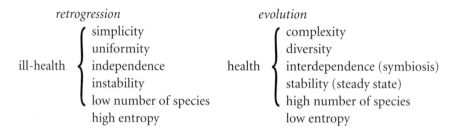

The most obvious example is life and death. Life is the evolution of a single egg into the complexity of the organism. Death is the retrogression of a complex organism into a few simple elements. If this model is true, it allows us to examine a city, neighborhood, community institution, family, city plan, architectural or landscape design in these terms. This model suggests that any system moving toward simplicity, uniformity, instability with a low number of species and high entropy is retrogressing; any system moving in that direction is moving toward ill health.

Conversely, complexity, diversity, stability (steady state), with a high number of species and low entropy are indicators of health and systems moving in this direction are evolving. As a simple application let us map, in tones on transparencies, statistics of all physical disease, all mental disease, and all social disease. If we also map income, age of population, density, ethnicity, and quality of the physical environment we have on the one hand discerned the environment of health, the environment of pathology and we have accumulated the data which allow interpretation of the social and physical environmental components of health and pathology. Moreover, we have the other criteria of the model which permit examination from different directions. If this model is true and the method good, it may be the greatest contribution of the ecological method to diagnosis and prescription for the city.

But, you say, all this may be very fine but landscape architects are finally designers—when will you speak to ecology and design? I will. Lou Kahn, the most perceptive of men, foresaw the ecological method even through these intractable, inert materials which he infuses with life when he spoke of "existence will," the will to be. The place is because. It is and is in the process of becoming. This we must be able to read, and ecology provides the language. By being, the place or the creature has form. Form and process are indivisible aspects of a single phenomenon. The ecological method allows one to understand form as an explicit point in evolutionary process. Again, Lou Kahn has made clear to us the distinction between form and design. Cup is form and begins from the cupped hand. Design is the creation of the cup, transmuted by the artist, but never denying its formal origins. As a profession, landscape architecture has exploited a pliant earth, tractable and docile plants to make much that is arbitrary, capricious, and inconsequential. We could not see the cupped hand as giving form to the cup, the earth and its processes as giving form to our works. The ecological method is then also the perception of form, an insight to the given form, implication for the made form which is to say design, and this, for landscape architects, may be its greatest gift.

# THE RSVP CYCLES (1969)

## LAWRENCE HALPRIN

This book [*RSVP Cycles*] started as an exploration of "scores" and the interrelationships between scoring in the various fields of art. Scores are *symbolizations of processes* which extend over time. The most familiar kind of "score" is a musical one, but I have extended this meaning to include "scores" in all fields of human endeavor. Even a grocery list or a calendar, for example, is a score. I have been interested in the idea of scoring—not any one particular system of scoring, but scoring generally—for many years. This interest grew, quite clearly, from two different sources: first, because I am professionally an environmental designer and planner involved in the broad landscape where human beings and nature interface; and, second, because of my close relationship to dance and theatre due largely to my wife, the dancer and choreographer Ann Halprin, who is Director of the Dancers' Workshop in San Francisco.

Both sources—the new theatre-dance and the environment as Ann and I have been practicing them—are nonstatic, very closely related in that they are process-oriented, rather than simply result-oriented. Both derive their strengths and fundaments from a deep involvement in activity. In both fields, the process is like an iceberg—nine-tenths invisible but nonetheless vital to achievement. Both deal with subtleties and nuance, intuition, and fantasy, and go to the root-source of human needs and desires—atavistic ones at that. In both, values, though there, are not *really* demonstrable. At all events, I have been searching for years (and still am) for means to describe and evoke processes on other than a simply random basis. I thought that this would have meaning not only for my field of the environmental arts and dance-theatre, but also for all the *other* arts where the elements of time and activity over time (particularly of numbers of people) would have meaning and usefulness.

I saw scores as a way of describing all such processes in all the arts, of making process visible and thereby designing with process through scores. I saw scores also as a way of communicating these processes over time and space to other people in other places at other moments and as a vehicle to allow many people to enter into the act of creation together, *allowing* for participation, feedback, and communications.

I hope that scores will lead into new ways of designing and planning large-scale environments of regions and large communities whose essential nature is complexity and whose purpose is diversity. I hope that the idea of scores will make it possible to work in these regional communities as a method for energizing processes and people and the natural environment in a constantly evolving and mutually involving procedure over time. I hope to see scores used as catalytic agents for creativity leading to a constructive use of change.

The book itself [*RSVP Cycles*] has been a score. It was not preconceived, and has developed its own shape while a work in progress. I started out with many scores for ephemera that I have done for dance or for environmental events over the years. I explored primitive scores, mystical scores, scores for happenings, based on my wife's work, and my friends', who, too, have been pushing the boundaries of their arts. Inevitably much of my own personal experience comes out of the "scores for environment" which is my professional interest as well as the field in which I have had my most personal experiences. Thus, the second half of the book explores street scores, ecological scoring, city scores, and finally community scores.

As I worked on the score for the book, however, one fact kept on emerging to plague me—it demanded consideration, and this became increasingly clear as I worked in communiscores. The scheme was not complete. As I worked on "scores" *only*, there were elements that kept cropping up in the creative process which were not being covered by the scoring procedure, especially as the projects became more and more complex. I found that scores are nonjudgmental—this is one of their primary characteristics. Yet, in many instances some outside witnessing must be reached, some selectivity must be exercised. But scores do not do that, they don't perform that function.

As I continued to develop the characteristics of scores, I found that often before actual scoring starts the scorer has a great deal of preliminary work to do in collecting resource material, inventory items to use in his scores. I found too that a clear differentiation has to be made between the score, which is usually graphic and precedes the fact, and the performance, which is the resultant of the score. Much of my own professional life has been involved in this apparent dichotomy: between the score and the performance, which are not the same but have an intricate relationship to each other. Finally, I found that scoring has to allow for feedback, for analysis before, during, and after a score is created in order for the score to develop and allow for change—to grow. All of these important functions were not, I found, taken care of in scores themselves.

In the long run, I found that what I had really been working toward, what I really wanted to explore, was nothing less than the creative process—what energizes it—how it functions—and how its universal aspects can have implications for all our fields. Scores alone were not doing this. I was not interested exclusively in what the score-performance relation was—how the particular event, the building, or piece of music, or piece of legislation, was beautiful, but how the process of arriving at it came about. I found that I had to understand the context in which it all had happened and to see if, by understanding what had been required to make it happen, I could apply the principle across many fields, in a multidimensional way, to a life process. Perhaps most importantly, I found that by themselves scores could not deal with the humanistic aspects of life situations including individual passions, wills, and values. And it seemed necessary to round out the scheme so that human communications—including values and decisions as well as performance—could be accounted for in the process.

When that became clear, I found that the procedures I needed to get all these inputs into some context had four parts and they were all interrelated. Each part had its own internal significance, but got really cracking only when it related to the others. They have similarities to Jung's cycle which he called the compass of the psyche.[1]

**R**    *Resources* which are what you have to work with. These include human and physical resources *and* their motivation and aims.

**S**    *Scores* which describe the process leading to the performance.

**V**    *Valuaction* which analyzes the results of action and possible selectivity and decisions. The term "valuaction" is one coined to suggest the action-oriented as well as the decision-oriented aspects of V in the cycle.

**P**    *Performance* which is the resultant of scores and is the "style" of the process.

Together I feel that these describe all the procedures inherent in the creative process. They must feed back all along the way, each to the other, and thus make communication possible. In a process-oriented society they must *all* be visible continuously, in order to work so as to avoid secrecy and the manipulation of people.

Together they form what I have called the RSVP cycles.

The diagram above describes the multidimensional and moving interconnectedness between all the elements of the cycle. It can as correctly read, P, R, S, V or any other combination. It is important to emphasize this point. The cycle operates in *any* direction and by overlapping. The cycle can start at any point and move in any direction. The sequence is completely variable depending on the situation, the scorer, and the intent. By chance, when I finally put the headings together, they spelled out RSVP, which is a communications idea meaning "respond."

This is, obviously, an essential ingredient of the cycle. As I and others have worked with this cycle it has become increasingly clear that the cycle must work at two levels. The first of these is the personal, private level of the self, which I use with a lower case "s" according to the Gestalt psychology. This cycle is an inner one, appropriately, and refers to one's own personal Gestalt: the people who are close to you, your personal environment, attitudes, interests, even hangups; one's motivational inner world as distinct from one's outer-oriented world. This self RSVP cycle appears graphically at the center of the community or group RSVP cycle which is in effect composed of all the individual self-cycles engaged in the activity of scoring.

The private, self-oriented inner cycle and the community, group-oriented outer cycle together make up the RSVP cycles necessary to encompass all human creative processes. Thus, this book deals with the two RSVP cycles. The inner cycle as the separate self and the outer cycle as the collective self: individual and community.

The book then, as it finally emerged, describes the effects of the various parts of the RSVP cycles on the process of scoring and on what has emerged from the scores. Particularly in the environmental section the entire RSVP cycles are in use all the way through, since in the planning of environments every facet of the total cycle has importance. In other activities, the whole cycle is not desired or required. When that is the case it has been so

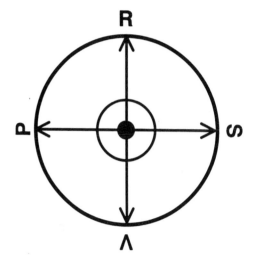

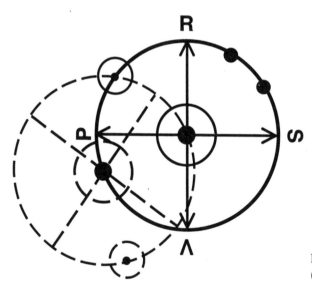

Figure 3. The RSVP Cycles
(after Lawrence Halprin).

indicated. I believe, however, that it is important for anyone working with the cycle to understand where he is concentrating and which parts are operating. If, for instance, you jump immediately to Performance (P), you are improvising. There are times when improvisation, for example, or spontaneous responses are vital to the release of creative energies which might remain locked up otherwise. But these energies can often fruitfully feed back into the rest of the cycle or remain isolated for their own sake.

The same is true of other portions of the cycle, which does not have to be in complete operation at all times in order to have validity. A personal word to my friends in the various art fields. I know how resistant artists are to the notion of "systematizing" the processes by which art evolves. There is a feeling that to enclose gossamer is to destroy it. These RSVP cycles and the point of "scoring" are not meant to categorize or organize, but to free the creative process by making the process *visible*. I have found, in my own work, that my hangups come when there is some buried obstacle that I don't understand and can't flush out. When I can "see" obstacles or get in touch with what's blocking me, I can deal with them. I hope the RSVP cycle can do that; it already has for me and others with whom I have discussed it.

Nothing in the RSVP has attempted to define talent or ability or the final making of a decision which, of course, remains at the very core of personal creation. The magic of magic remains.

For me, professionally, the significance of the RSVP cycles lies in the fact that as an ecological designer I have always been interested in pluralism and the generative force of many contributions to solutions. I view the earth and its life processes as a model for the creative process, where not one but many forces interact with each other with results emergent—not imposed. I see the earth as a vast and intricately interrelated ecosystem. In this system all of the parts have value, and they are all moving toward balance.

The essential characteristic of community in the ecological sense is that all of the parts are functioning within their own habitat, that no one element outweighs the other, that each contributes to the whole. Thus, the total ecological community has the characteristics of an organism which lives and grows and reproduces itself in an ongoing process.

Human communities, too, have many of the same characteristics, to which we have given the name "tout ensemble," that is, the sum is itself valuable and has more qualities than simply one additive of its ingredients. Such a "tout ensemble," recently threatened by a freeway in New Orleans, has been saved by the decision not to allow that one factor to undermine the balance of the whole community. The balance of climax communities in natural or human communities is tenuous and easily destroyed—it is not static—it exists as long as no one force outweighs the others. This I believe to be true of all human affairs and a model for all the life processes in which we need to integrate ourselves.

One of the gravest dangers that we experience is the danger of becoming *goal-oriented*. It is a tendency that crops up on every hand and in every field of endeavor. It is a trap which goes like this: things are going poorly (in the realm of politics or religion or building a city or the world community or a personal relationship or whatever). As thinking people we must try to solve this problem that faces us. Let us set ourselves a "goal" upon which we can all agree (most goals after all are quite clearly moralistically based and incontrovertibly "good ideas"). Having set ourselves this goal we can then proceed posthaste to achieve it by the *most direct method possible*. Everyone can put his shoulder to the wheel, and systems engineering, technology, and our leader (or whatever) will get us to the agreed goal.

It doesn't work! The results of this oversimplified approach, now coming into general vogue, are all around us in the chaos of our cities and the confusion of our politics (or other politics—fascism and communism are clear statements of this approach). It generates tension in personal relationships by burying the real problems; it avoids the central issue of education, which is why today's young people are dropping out; it is destroying the resources and physical beauty of our planet; and it avoids the basic issue.

There are evidences of this kind of thinking in the attempt to make a science out of community design, as if by assigning it the term "science" then the goal of perfection can be reached. Human community planning cannot ever be a science anymore than politics can rightly be called political science. Science implies codification of knowledge and a drive toward perfectibility none of which are possible or even desirable in human affairs. When ekisticians, for example, say that the "search for the ideal is our greatest obligation" they are making the same basic error that all goal-oriented thinking does—a confusion between motivation and process. We can be scientific and precise about gathering data and inventorying resources, but in the multivariable and open scoring process necessary for human lifestyles and attitudes, creativity, inquantifiable attitudes, and openness will always be required. There is a vast difference between being idealistic, which is life-oriented and process-oriented, and utopian, which implies a finite and formal goal. In that sense scores are nonutopian.

We don't really want to be involved in goal-making or goal-solving. Fritz Perls says, "Scores face the possible where goals face the impossible."[2] What we want, what we desperately need, is a feeling of close and creative involvement in processes. It is the *doing* that we all enjoy and which is meaningful to us. That is what is needed in education, in the ghetto, and in the young and the downtrodden who feel that they are excluded from the process of decision-making in our communities; certainly it is needed in personal relations. It is ongoingness, the process that will build and develop great cities and regions and a world community on this planet Earth. By involvement in process we all interact, our input is significant, visible, meaningful, useful, and no one point of view can hold us in thralldom. Scores are not goal-oriented; they are hope-oriented.

This is why "scores," which describe process, seem to me so significant. It is through them that we can involve ourselves creatively in "doing," from which, in fact, structure emerges—the form of anything is latent in the process. The *score* is the mechanism which allows us *all* to become involved, to make our presence felt. Scores are process-oriented, not thing-oriented. In dance and theatre this works through open scoring, which establishes "lines of action" to which each person contributes and from which a final performance then emerges. In personal relations scoring allows a constant interaction devoid of the moralisms and shoulds and shouldn'ts which inhibit growth and deep contacts and involvements. In the planning of communities a score visible to all the people allows each one of us to respond, to find our own input, to influence *before* the performance is fixed, *before* decisions are made. Scoring makes the process *visible*. For that reason scores seem to me the key link in the entire RSVP cycles—though only one link, still at the core of the whole procedure.

The RSVP cycles is a balanced scheme in which all the parts are mutually related and constantly interacting. It functions best when all parts are operating. Its purpose is to make procedures and processes visible, to allow for constant communication and ultimately to insure the diversity and pluralism necessary for change and growth.

# COMMUNITY DESIGN (1974)

## RANDOLPH HESTER, JR.

[We need] new policies to make the design profession more responsible for the social suitability of the neighborhood environments they create. Particularly, we need policies (1) to clarify to whom the designer is responsible, the owner or the user of neighborhood space, (2) to guarantee the input of users' *values* into the neighborhood design process, (3) to eliminate professional ethics as a justification for the high cost and questionable results of neighborhood space design, (4) to provide for socially suitable neighborhood environments in both old and new communities, and (5) to guarantee increased user involvement throughout the neighborhood design process.

### POLICY 1

The designer should be responsible to the users in creating socially suitable neighborhood spaces. This is what Norman Newton called for when he said that the only intelligent measure of a successful design is its impact on the users,[1] and what Herbert Gans advocated when he asked for user-oriented planning. This is the policy that advocate planners implemented in the late 1960s, and the issue that Jan C. Rowan raised in a *Progressive Architecture* editorial: "Architects are, of course, masters at rationalizing and idealizing whatever they happen to be doing. But such verbal acrobatics, good only for ego placation of the designers involved, obscure the more basic issues. The issue at stake is an important one: who should the architect serve—the owner or the public?"[2]

Further articulating this point of view, Rowan advanced the idea that what is good for the architect and the private client is not necessarily good for the public. Similarly, what is good for the private client is not necessarily good for the residents of a neighborhood. To provide socially suitable neighborhood space, it is evident that there must be a new operational policy that makes the designer responsible to the *user*.

### POLICY 2

The designer should incorporate the users' values into the neighborhood design process instead of relying exclusively on his own values. Often the user's values are different from the designer's. Hugh C. Davis has described this problem as being particularly acute in the planning and design of neighborhood space. When answering the question, "Who is neighborhood open space for?" designers generally say "for all the people." But Davis notes that many open spaces are not for all the people. They are for the affluent white middle class who know how to use and respect them:

> They are not for anyone with "different" ideas as to what constitutes relaxation and enjoyment in the out-of-doors. If you have money, if you have middle or upper class values, you are welcome. If you don't, go some place else. And this often means don't go anywhere. For those who do not appreciate and respect nature, as the middle-class are trained to do, we have only supplied second-class places with second-class maintenance and facilities.[3]

Samuel Z. Klausner described the conflict between designers' and users' values in this manner: "Typically, individuals project the recreational culture of their own social circle, or social class, on the larger society. Members of each class or circle either believe that others share their recreational interests or that it would be good for them if they did. The absurdity is now apparent."[4]

After considering this value conflict between users and designers in greater detail, Davis suggested that "open space might best be identified in terms of use rather than by the amount or kind of vegetation or degree of so-called naturalness"[5] that have traditionally been the designer's major concerns. Such an attitude would begin to counteract the designer's value bias by identifying the uses in terms of the user's behavior. This would not exclude the designer's bias from the design process. The designer's opinion is desirable but represents only one of several points of view that need to be considered in the design process. John Friedmann described how the designer-user value conflict can be resolved through transactive planning. In this planning process, the values of both the designer and user are openly discussed in "face-to-face, person-centered relations within small groups." Friedmann indicates how drastic a change in the planning process this approach would represent by comparing it to the process that Taylor established a century ago, which is still widely practiced:

> Our inherited notions of planning are dead. The planning with which most of us are familiar today was invented nearly one hundred years ago by the originator of scientific management. Under the kind of planning Taylorism inspired, the individual person was treated as an instrument for the attainment of an extrinsic goal. He was reduced to complete passivity: his behavior was to be engineered to conform with the plan. The transactive planning of the future, on the other hand, is deeply rooted in face-to-face, person-centered relations within small groups. If Taylor's discipline was the ratio of resources to final product, the discipline of transactive planning is the radical openness required by dialogue.[6]

In such a process all the participants realize that planning "is too important to be left entirely to experts."[7] The designer shoulders the responsibility of incorporating into the design of neighborhood space not only his own values but also the values of the users.

## POLICY 3

The designer should not use professional ethics as a justification for the high cost and questionable results of neighborhood space design. The public neighborhood environment suffers from a lack of design attention, and planners give several "ethical" excuses for this lack of quality. For projects that will adversely affect a neighborhood, planners often say, "if I don't do it, some other planner will who is less qualified to do a good job." Often there seems to be a convenient confusion of ethics and economics. The designer says to himself, "if this project is economically beneficial personally, it is ethical, but if it is not economically beneficial, the project is unethical." This confusion of economics and ethics has been used by designers to justify designing apartment buildings on the last remaining open spaces in neighborhoods, strip commercial districts in residential sections, and highways through local communities. In many other cases the professional designer has substituted his own financial success for the public's safety and welfare. This is "economic justification" to the profession and "malpractice" to the public. That professional design services are too costly for most neighborhood groups to hire designers to advocate their point of view has exacerbated the problem. The public neighborhood environment has received not only second-rate consideration but also direct abuses at the hands of designers. The end product has been neighborhood environments that do not meet the needs of the residents.

POLICY 4

The designer should be concerned about the social suitability of both old and new neighborhood environments. Planners and designers have had noticeable success in providing suitable neighborhood space in new communities. For example, by leaving undeveloped linear systems along drainage ways, planners have shown that outdoor neighborhood space can be created at the same time that development is kept away from sensitive flood-prone areas. Such space allows a more natural pattern of water runoff and prevents costly soil erosion and flooding. This provision for neighborhood open space came about through such innovations as clustering,[8] New Towns Development, Planned Unit Development, and open-space zoning,[9] which allow higher-density development in those areas best suited for development and no development in the ill-suited areas. Therefore, a neighborhood environment is provided without taxpayer cost. Actually, the environment provided is a potential environment in the sense that it is left totally undeveloped until the residents move in and decide what uses they want—tennis courts or basketball courts, bike paths or sitting areas, nature walks or hanging areas. Flexibility is clearly the key to social suitability in the case of new neighborhood development.

But the success in new neighborhoods has been overshadowed by the failure to provide socially suitable neighborhood space in older central-city communities. In the early 1960s Garrett Eckbo asked when designers would begin work with the long-neglected ordinary and typical landscapes of the central city.[10] And Theodore Osmundson, speaking as president of the American Society of Landscape Architects in 1969, frankly admitted the designers' failure in the older central-city neighborhoods:

> To put it bluntly, the landscape architecture profession is not used to working in the central city. The landscape architect generally works in the suburbs and beyond for a client whom he knows and with whom he can easily relate. Most landscape architects are white, and of middle income. Consequently, they're not familiar with—and have trouble understanding—the needs and life style of urban citizens who are not white and have a lower income.
>
> Landscape architecture, like many other segments of American life, is poorly equipped psychologically to contribute the technical service it has available to the solving of the urban design problem. However, it's the only profession we have, and we must find ways to make it work.[11]

The American Institute of Architects National Policy Task Force sought to make the design professions work by encouraging the rebuilding of cities at the neighborhood scale. They concluded that a national growth policy should concentrate on improving the present and future conditions of the existing urban neighborhoods: "We believe the first priority should go toward improving the condition of the older core cities, more especially the condition of those trapped in poverty and the squalor of declining neighborhoods."[12]

Here, the design professions have identified their responsibility to both old and new neighborhoods in creating environments that are socially suitable. The AIA policy makes it clear that the design and rebuilding of older neighborhoods can only succeed socially when undertaken in partnership with health care, employment, education, and other human services.

POLICY 5

The designer should foster user involvement throughout the neighborhood design process. A black student recently described the greatest urban ill as being feudalism.[13] He referred to anonymous decision making on the part of the elite, including the design professionals, whom he called "fat cat, establishment-oriented reactionaries"[14] for their part in urban renewal and the accompanying neighborhood disruption and Negro removal. Charles A. Reich called this part of the American crisis. He contends that "we no longer understand the system under which we live, hence the structure has become obsolete and we have become powerless; in turn, the system has been permitted to assume unchallenged power to dominate our lives, and now rumbles along, unguided and therefore indifferent to human ends."[15] Applying this to the design of the neighborhood environment, neighborhood residents and designers are dominated and stifled by unsuitable environments but do not know what to do. The student called this design *against* people and suggested that decisions about neighborhood change should be made *with* people. Design is undergoing a change in this regard from design *against* or *for* people to design *with* or *by* people. In this simplistic paradigm, design *against* people has been cast as design by the elite, with a substantial lack of concern for the user's needs. In addition to the urban renewal example offered by the student, it is characterized by inner-city freeways and public-housing projects that disrupt neighborhoods and displace families with little regard for their special life patterns. Design *for* people likewise has been cast as design by the elite: subdivisions, new towns, corporate sites, and large city and regional plans are generally examples offered. Some design *for* people has been successful in providing socially suitable neighborhood space, as discussed previously, particularly in the provision of potential environments that users could later design to meet their own needs.[16] In designing *with* people, on the other hand, decisions are made jointly by the users, designers, and others; adversary, advocacy, collaborative, and transactive planning are examples of this type of design. In design *by* people, the users exclusively make the decisions. The goal is not to bring the designer closer to the people, as in transactional planning, but to educate the users to do without the designer.[17] The built environment is the result of the collective decisions of those people who will occupy that environment. Grass-roots design,[18] guerrilla architecture,[19] self-help design,[20] and plural planning[21] characterize design *by* people. In each of these, the users rely on their own knowledge of their needs and their own skills in building rather simple environments. They may use manuals that designers have prepared as tools in the building process. Few of these efforts have succeeded on a large scale.

Although these descriptions of design *against, for, with,* and *by* people are oversimplified, there seems to be a movement in design toward neighborhood design "*with* peo-

| | Against People | For People | With People | By People |
|---|---|---|---|---|
| Decision made By | Elite | Elite | Jointly | Users |
| Users Involvement | None | None | Major | Exclusively |
| Characterised By | Urban Renewal, Inner City Highways, Public Housing. | Subdivisions, Large Cities or Regional Plans, New Towns. | Collaborative, Adversary, Advocacy and Transactive Planning. | Plural Planning, Guerrilla Architecture, Self-Help Design, Grassroots Planning. |
| Example | Pruit Igoe Inner Belt in Cambridge, Massachusetts. | Jacob Riis Plaza, Columbia, Maryland. | Putnam Gardens, Tot Lot. | Self-Help Housing, Squatter Housing, Neighbourhood Commons. |

Figure 4. Design Against➔For➔With➔By People: approaches to community design (after Randolph Hester).

ple." The designer's responsibility is to facilitate design *with* people by fostering user involvement throughout the neighborhood design process. . . .

A Methodology

The preceding policies suggest that an overhaul is needed in the methodology applied to the design of neighborhood space. A holistic, process-oriented methodology is needed. Such a methodology, the community development process, applied widely by the Agricultural Extension Service, the Peace Corps, and various antipoverty groups, has existed for years and can serve as a model. It operates on the basis of guidelines that are applicable to the design of neighborhood space:

1. The process begins at the grass-roots level under the users' direction, and it requires continued resident support to succeed.
2. The designer serves as an environmental problem solver by offering and facilitating the evaluation of alternative choices.
3. Different points of view may be advocated by various user groups.

4. There is an emphasis on face-to-face, collaborative, group decision making.

5. Goal setting and problem definition are emphasized before a design program is written.

6. A suitable program is secured before implementation begins.

7. The designer can advocate a no-design alternative.

8. The designer's commitment to the residents is long term.

9. The creative, form-giving process remains within the purview of the designer.

Consider these community development guidelines one at a time. First, that users direct the process implies that participation in the neighborhood change process is just as important to the users as the product itself. J. B. Jackson concluded that participation was important in his critique of the overemphasis by nineteenth-century designers on aesthetics rather than activity in neighborhood spaces: "The city dweller is still exhausted, to be sure, by city existence, and he still relishes a glimpse of rural scenery. But weariness is no longer his chief complaint, and participation rather than passive contemplation is what he is asking."[22]

Whereas the users of the last century wanted designers to include participatory activities in neighborhood spaces, today users are demanding that they be involved in the entire process of designing neighborhood spaces. Meaningful participation is necessary for neighborhood design to be socially suitable, because only through involvement will users overcome their lack of understanding of how the decision-making process operates to change their neighborhood. And only by overcoming this lack of understanding can users overcome their sense of powerlessness and regain the control of neighborhood change. When the users have this power and responsibility to direct change at the grass-roots level, design can then adequately serve the user client and produce socially suitable neighborhood space.

The designer's role in this process is to offer various alternatives and to aid the residents in evaluating the costs and benefits of each. Herbert Gans has clarified the role:

> The planner does not determine goals; this is the job of the community and its elected representatives. Even so, the planner should try to help those representatives in the process of goal determination by analyzing their present activities to show them what implicit goals they are pursuing—and by making studies of the behavior patterns and attitudes of the citizenry that would provide data on the goals of various sectors of the community's population.
>
> In his goal-determining function the planner is thus a technician-aid to the elected decision maker.[23]

But the planner functions as more than a technician; it is his responsibility to present different ways of defining a problem. Is the problem slum clearance? Or is the problem the elimination of the social, psychological and economic problems of slum dwellers?[24] Or is the problem housing? What is the cost of each? What do the residents want? The designer offers insights into problem definition by offering choices and assisting the users as they evaluate the choices. He becomes a designer *with* people in this process.

After the designer presents the alternatives, different points of view may be advocated by various user groups. The designer can then present different "solutions" based on the different perspectives of the user groups. These "solutions" are then openly examined and debated by the neighborhood residents. Such a process is based on the premise that no single public good exists. Since wealthy special interests often determine the public good, this process simply allows less powerful minority interests to be represented in the decision-making discussions. Paul Davidoff described the process as follows:

> The recommendation that city planners represent and plead the plans of many interest groups is founded upon the need to establish an effective urban democracy, one in which citizens may be able to play an active role in the process of deciding public policy. Appropriate policy in a democracy is determined through a process of political debate. The right course of action is always a matter of choice, never fact. In a bureaucratic age, great care must be taken that choices remain in the area of public view and participation.[25]

Only by presenting the various viewpoints can the unique needs of local, diverse interests be incorporated into the community development process and reflected in the design of socially suitable neighborhood space.

Throughout this process there is an emphasis on face-to-face, collaborative group decision making. During the advocate debates, personal exchanges occur. David R. Godschalk describes this process as the "systematic combination of innovation diffusion and citizen involvement in a cooperative public planning process."[26] It springs from the belief that two heads are better than one for designing suitable neighborhood environments. John Friedmann has described the process more eloquently than anyone in *Retracking America: A Theory of Transactive Planning*. He suggests that in the face-to-face encounter the planners contribute "concepts, theories, analysis, processed knowledge, new perspectives, and systematic search procedures" and the users contribute intimate knowledge of the context, details of behavior, insights into neighborhood idiosyncrasies, "realistic alternatives, norms, priorities, feasibility judgments, and operational details."[27] The result is more complete information, better understanding of the problem, and a better design for a neighborhood environment aided by the process of collaborative group decision making.

The community development process emphasizes goal setting and problem definition before writing a program for the activities in a space. In this way, positive values, ideals, and goals are incorporated into a picture of what can be. Within that context, a problem that will prevent the accomplishment of what can be is identified. This lessens the likelihood of solving either the wrong problem or a symptom of the real problem. As an example, the need for a freeway through a neighborhood may be considered the problem, but upon study the problem may be identified as being the need for jobs closer to home. Once this problem is identified, the neighborhood might then seek appropriate industry and the designer might plan for an industrial site rather than a freeway. The Fletcher School Playground offers a more sobering example. The designers assumed that a recreation facility for teenagers would reduce their disruptive behavior in the neighborhood. Without questioning the real problem, the adults and the designer proceeded to design areas for basketball, hanging out, and street and ice hockey. But, in fact, the teenagers needed jobs to help support their families, not recreation to absorb their frustration. The result was a design catastrophe: a playground that was irrelevant because it solved the wrong problem. It could have been averted by focusing on community goals and by more carefully defining the problem prior to plunging headlong into a predetermined solution.

It is equally important that a socially suitable design program be firmly established before implementation begins. Even after the problem has been adequately defined, the specific considerations for user needs are incorporated into the program, needs including setting, "people," psychological comfort, symbolic ownership, physical comfort, safety, policy on use, relatedness, and cost. By using established techniques, . . . the designer should be able to gain insight into the most critical user needs. The inclusion of such idiosyncratic user needs in the design program makes a design socially suitable.

In some cases the designer may advocate a no-design alternative. After having studied the problem, the designer may feel that the solution lies outside the domain of physical change, possibly requiring a policy or procedure change. In this case the designer can refer the users to the appropriate policy-making body, just as a general practitioner refers a patient with a fracture to an orthopedic surgeon. Some designers feel that the responsibility does not end with the referral. One professional designer, speaking about the need for a city government change rather than the need for a new park, remarked: "Maybe we're abdicating our responsibility as professionals by not advocating these needed changes and fighting to change administrative regulations. . . . It's not the community's responsibility to solve the problems. It's really the parks department's responsibility, but somebody's got to politicize the issue and confront the parks department."[28]

In other situations, after having assessed the impact of a physical change, the designer may advocate a no-design alternative, which resembles the negative environmental impact statement at the neighborhood scale. In the same way that highway engineers have been forced to consider the no-design alternative, neighborhood designers should consider the no-design alternative when that is compatible with user needs.

In fulfilling his responsibility to the users in the community development process, the designer's commitment to provide socially suitable neighborhood spaces is long term. Through a change in the structure of fee payment, designers should be retained for long periods of time to prevent the short-term approach of many designers. Long-term commitment fosters greater social suitability in the design of neighborhood spaces by allowing the designer to respond to change on a daily and incremental basis, and by forcing him to continuously evaluate projects and to receive continuous feedback from the users.

In spite of increased attention to user needs and user involvement in the community development process, the creative, form-giving methodology remains within the purview of the designer. Public concern that designers take unwarranted artistic liberties in designing neighborhood open space[29] and that the residents' sense of aesthetics should be most important is matched by a fear among some design professionals that a methodology like the community development process, involving conceptual framework of user needs and user-needs techniques, will stymie the designer's creative process. Such a fear is no more valid than the fear that accurate soils information stifles the creative process of the national park planner. The methodology simply exposes more relevant information and opens the process to closer scrutiny and critical evaluation. The creative act remains the same. The analogy of designer as magician or designer as black box remains the same. At some point in the process, the designer must take the available information and creatively give form to a solution in the process partly out of his conscious control.[30] In the community development process there may be less pretense to magical acts, but the creative act remains in the domain of the designer.

# SITE DESIGN (1984)

## KEVIN LYNCH AND GARY HACK

Design is the search for forms that satisfy a program. It deals with particular solutions, while the program is concerned with general characteristics and desired outcomes. Design begins in the programming, and programs are modified as design progresses.

By common account, design is a mystery, a flash of revelation. The genius who receives this flash learns to receive it by following the example of other people of genius. After the revelation, there are details to be developed and the labor of carrying out the revealed solution. This afterwork is separate from design, however, whether one thinks of it as a grubby nuisance or as facing up to realistic issues.

This common account is correct on one point: there *is* a mystery in design, as there is in all human thought. Otherwise, the account is mistaken. Design is not restricted to genius, or separate from practicality, or a sudden revelation. Fine places develop out of an intimate understanding of form possibility, which has been gained by constantly reframing the problem, by repeatedly searching for solutions. Revelations go by the inch and the foot, rarely by the mile. Particular methods, learned by experience, help the designer to make this journey of discovery.

A site design deals with three elements: the pattern of activity, the pattern of circulation, and the pattern of sensible form that supports them. The first, symbolized in the activity diagram, is the arrangement of the behavior settings, their character, linkage, density and grain, following the requirements of the program. The second is the layout of the movement channels and their relations to the activity locations. The third centers on the human experience of place: what we see, hear, smell, and feel, and what that means to us. The designer is concerned with what it is like to act in a place, to move through it, and to experience it. These are the subject matter of her first sketches, and remain dominant themes throughout the work. Each element implies the other, and so she faces a multitude of interlocking possibilities. She must make a set of simultaneous decisions which seem at first too numerous to grasp, which all depend on each other, like linked dancers in a ring.

Design is a process of envisioning and weighing possibilities, mindful of past experience. "What if I thought of the site this way?" the designer asks, bringing to mind one of a number of possible solutions. A wooded slope is as a "cascade," with houses "spilling" down it. Solutions frequently begin with metaphors, and the logic of the metaphor guides its elaboration. The practicalities of servicing, cost, or foundation stability then come to mind as tests of the idea. Each initial solution will fail to achieve the outcome sought. Failure points to another way of thinking about the problem. The problem is reframed,[1] and a new cycle of invention and testing follows. Thus design is a dialectic of framing and making. Leaping from metaphor to metaphor, attending to this aspect and then to that, neither dismayed by dissonance nor seduced too early by some momentary consonance, the mind begins to understand the significance of decisions in all their important dimensions. The designer imagines total systems—precise at the critical points, loose and unresolved where decisions have less significance.

To do this, designers need to construct a "virtual world," a model of what they know about site and program, which allows possibilities to be tested quickly. Diagrams and physical models are of service, but these virtual worlds are mental pictures. A site seems "fragmented," which shapes what one sees and calls to mind the virtues of unifying devices. Through past experience, designers accumulate a repertoire of analogous situations. Before each new situation, one asks what others it is like and most unlike. Likeness and unlikeness are understandings that help to imagine and test possible solutions. This virtual world will almost always extend beyond the original site boundaries, since a site depends on its context. The designer is suspicious of limits and yet cannot deal with the universe. Therefore he decides: Where shall my focus be? What shall be its context? How shall they connect? This is often a larger universe than the one first given, and thus some tension arises. The design need not harmonize with its context, should that be undesirable or ephemeral, but it must take it into account.

Designers develop a preference for a particular way of structuring their process of design and hold strong attitudes about appropriate procedure. Some prefer to make decisions along the way, moving deliberately from one step to the next, while others engage in a free-flowing inquiry in which nothing is frozen until all aspects seem right. These personal styles help shield them from the anxieties of the open search. But since the design process should fit the problem as well as the designer, a personal style is also a limitation of possibilities, a latent distortion of the problem. Ideally, designers should be eclectics. Where this is not psychologically possible, they should at least be aware of other ways of doing business and have a sense of the type of problem to which their own manner of working is best fitted. All design methods are laden with values; none are objective. Each emphasizes some environmental qualities over others and favors particular ways of judging.

# CREATIVE RISK TAKING (1983)

## STEVEN KROG

Why are there so few manmade landscapes which persuade us to launch a purposeful excursion or cause us unexpectedly to change an itinerary? Why are there so few fascinating, new landscapes that we *must* see? And why do many of those which *are* provocative so often come from the pens of building architects—Ambasz, Rob and Leon Krier, and SITE, to mention a few? Or from the so-called Earth Artists who manipulate large-scale earth forms?

I would suggest that the prevailing lack of interest in, or commitment to, artful "works of genius" predestines many well-intended efforts at landscape design to be shallow or feckless—not worth a detour.

Why this languidness, this disinterest? First, while the thoughtful, but puzzled stare has become a ubiquitous expression on the face of architects, landscape architects remain complacent and undaunted behind a Maginot Line ideology of functional geometry generated by design process. Insecurity and its attendant winds of controversy (which blew even before Tom Wolfe) are productive, heuristic springboards. They are the source of architecture's vitality and a guarantee of its evolution. Landscape architecture is the lesser for its "security."

Secondly, landscape architecture is suffering an interregnum of significant consequence.

In a different context, but toward a not so different end, D. H. Lawrence wrote, "... men cannot live without masters. There is always a master. And men live in glad obedience to the master they believe in, or they live in fictional opposition to the master they wish to undermine."

Present-day landscape architects lack both.

To learn how landscape architecture is made today, one must study the machinations of its nearly deified design process. Certainly there is no denying the essentiality of methodical analysis of program, site, and their fit. After all, the landscape is a much-varied entity, difficult to understand and manipulate.

When in doubt, we stoke the fire under design process, hoping it will produce one more alternative, one more flash of insight. But while, breeder reactor-like, the design process often manufactures more information than it consumes, it has sadly never produced one gram of insight.

This is not the fault of the process. It never promised us solutions to our problems—just a means toward their logical scrutiny. In our haste, confusion, or indolence, we overlook the fact that the process collapses just when we approach the fearsome gap between the functional diagram and design development. Up to this point, the process is well illustrated. But then it provides only a blank space or a vague innuendo. Halprin acknowledges this dilemma in his *RSVP Cycles*, but went on to say, "Scores tell what and why, but they leave the 'how' up to the individual." So now he tells us: No Trade Secrets! Well, I suspect that none will ever be forthcoming. We admittedly are talking about the moment of artistic creation. And if John Dewey was correct in his assessment of art as a nondiscursive symbol,[1] words must prove inadequate.

So, this prescribed retreat to process must be seen as an expedient, yet hopelessly self-deceptive strategy. We delude ourselves in believing that by energetically invoking the process, we will definitely arrive at a creative design solution. We can only dissolve this obeisance by facing the great risk—by recognizing that creation/invention is an emotion-, intuition-, intellect-, and energy-intensive task. We must learn to tolerate two experiences that the design process is explicitly intended to circumvent: substantial personal terror and uncertainty—even good designers usually do no know exactly where they are going when they are creating/inventing.

Blasphemy? Not at all. Consider the fictional attempt by would-be novelist Daniel Martin. John Fowles writes:

> He suddenly saw the proposed novel as a pipe dream, one more yearning for the impossible. The terror of the task: that making of a world, alone, unguided, now mocked, like some distant mountain peak. He could never do it. Never mind that what he felt was felt by all novelists, all artists, at the beginning of a creation—*that indeed not feeling the terror was the worst possible augury for the enterprise.* (Author's emphasis)[2]

I am not saying that landscape architects do not experience terror. But most of us feel frustration with the process, not fear of the task. "The process has brought me this far," we think. "Why won't it bear me across that final design chasm?"

I do not assert that there is a causal relationship between terror, doubt, and creative excellence. Rather, I do suggest that despite written programs, site analyses, elaborate design concepts, and processional massaging or incubation, most landscape architects still do not know where their designs are headed even while using the process. And because they perceive this as an *apparent obstacle,* they avoid design innovation. The methodical process of deduction can satisfy site planning's functionalist requirements. But landscape architecture is a more demanding mistress. Designers must accept personal terror as inherent to an act of discovery. This is the landscape architecture of experience, not objects.

In the epilogue to his 1961 *Landscape Architecture,* John Simonds briefly discussed his revelatory comprehension of the prepotence of experience over plan, or designed shapes, spaces, and forms: "The living, pulsing, vital experience, if conceived as a diagram of harmonious relationships, will develop its own expressive form."[3] The profession's ready deference to a regimental design process is the result of Simonds's and others' uneasiness with this emancipatory discovery and the sincere yet unsuccessful effort to make that discovery serviceable.

We should not be surprised by these halting attempts; their potential consequence is far greater than the introduction of some mere style. They entail the wholesale modification of the way we *think about* the purpose of landscape architecture ("what" we do) and the means of accomplishing it ("how" it's done). Succinctly, in the words of writer Donald Barthelme, "[Art] is a process of dealing with not-knowing; a forcing of what and how."

If we abandon the design process as the fountainhead of inspiration, but keep it as an information gatherer, it can be cathartic—and frightening. The best analogy I know is that of artist Robert Irwin's description of his experience in shutting down his studio after he decided that paintings and sculpture were a false means toward his artistic intent.

So what is a "new way" of thinking? I submit that successful landscape architectural art will involve the simple recognition, or the subtle creating and transformation, of a place's "presence" (to use Irwin's term); along with, or perhaps through, the minimizing (Frank Stella would claim "elimination") of metaphor.[4]

To begin this new approach we must divest ourselves of the notion that we engage in creating art only as rampaging self-expressionists with little or no interest in communication, or that when we practice the art of landscape architecture we are incapable of addressing functional concerns. It was with these distinctions that Norman Newton was grappling when, in response to my "Is It Art?" essay, he looked down his nose at labeling landscape architecture a fine art and wrote, "In the fine arts—as in painting or sculpture, for examples—the creator of a work is engaged primarily in solving his own problems—doing what he feels he must get out of his system or explode. The landscape architect, on the other hand, is trying primarily to solve other people's problems."[5] My own differentiation between site planning and landscape architecture notwithstanding, I believe Newton's to be one of the principal misconceptions about the making of art. I believe that for most artists today the situation is almost exactly the opposite of that suggested by Newton; that making art is a quest, a looking for something that artists don't have, can't find, or wish existed. Says Fowles's Daniel Martin, "You create out of what you lack, not out of what you have."[6]

The realization of this point is central. What is sought after by the artist cannot be an object, it must be an experience. Richard Williams got it all wrong when, in response to "Is It Art?" he wrote, "one infers that Mr. Krog associates art with beauty."[7] The search for "beauty" presupposes that the artist's purpose is the production of an *object* which is to be consciously approached *as* a work of art; and that, if the object lacks "beauty" it is therefore poor art. Objects need not be beautiful to qualify as works of art. Few would defend as beautiful Edvard Munch's painting *The Shriek,* but few would dismiss it as artless.

Turning aside from this diversionary question, "Is it beautiful?" we are free to accept artist James Turrell's imperative that "the media of art are perception."[8] Small wonder that Robert Smithson, Carl Andre, Christo, Michael Heizer, Dennis Oppenheim, and other artists turned to the landscape as their forum and/or medium. The landscape teems with factors which heighten one's perceptual awareness and one's artistic experience precisely because it overflows with latent present, is subject to relatively few metaphorical associations, and is largely lacking in museum pretension.

However, because of the landscape architect's bent for practicality (i.e., the client's needs), the application of these windfall advantages presents a problem. If we agree that the subject of art is aesthetic perception itself, and if we wish to claim for landscape architecture a seat among the other fine arts, then we ultimately must confront the messy dilemma of whether the profession's works are to be a service to society or a commentary on society.[9]

Most designers would define their professional role with one of these two terms. Most landscape architects and/or site planners could be expected to choose "service" over "commentary." The recognition of one's own orientation is crucial, since it establishes and regulates the actual physical forms and, therefore, impact of the resulting landscapes, available to the artist/designer.

Over the past two decades, many leading characters have taken note of the findings in the field of semiotics and tried to apply them to the design of buildings, so they can serve more successfully as the cultural symbols their designers claim them to be. If the public is to "read" a building as a house, school, church, or whatever, the design should include those signs the public are most likely to interpret as indicating house, school, or church.

So here we finally arrive at the critical fork in the landscape architect's road—whether to try to design a cultural symbol by molding signal-laden forms and materials, and thereby provide a valuable service to society, or to mold those or other forms and materials so that they are assigned new meanings evoking rich, fundamental thoughts and images, and thereby comment constructively upon society's ideas and visions. Both are mighty endeavors, both are potentially artful, and both employ the insights of semiotics. Because it necessarily relies upon known, communicative signs, I would define designing cultural symbols as an inventive task; whereas assigning new meanings is creative.

In spite of herculean efforts by semioticians, however, architecture and the physical environment steadfastly prove *not* to be a language. There does not yet exist a comprehensive, recognizable system of object-meaning relationships which would allow designers merely to choose from a vocabulary of forms and be sure they are successfully communicating.

Neither do I suggest that one orientation is "better" for society. Nonetheless, it is apparent that the "creative" aim to heighten perceptual awareness often stands in opposition to the "inventive" task of designing cultural symbols by instilling metaphorical traits in a new project through the skillful use of culturally accepted meanings. That is, to design what is recognized as "a church," the designer must give it characteristics which make it appear "like" the culturally accepted equivalent of a church. The same can be said for a park, a parking lot, or a street mall. Anyone working to change the workaday environment must succeed in managing these familiar symbols. You cannot design a communicable—and therefore truly habitable—environment without this skill. And one is surely not condemned to repeat available and familiar forms. As Widdowson has observed, "The existence of a common verbal language does not stifle creative verbal expression, it guarantees an audience and enhances communicability."[10]

But if Irwin is correct in his belief[11] that we move through the world with a high expectation-fit ratio (that is, we block out supposedly noncritical information, or see only what we want to see or think we see), then the metaphorical characteristics of places and things will further homogenize our experiences. The more the metaphorical content is increased—the more something is made to be "like" what we expect it to be—the less likely it is that it will be truly seen or experienced. Therefore, while "inventions" are more likely to successfully communicate certain types of information, they are less likely to heighten awareness; and conversely, while what I have termed "creation" is more likely to heighten awareness, it is less likely to be easily understood.

When I insist on preeminence for "creation," I am responding to the apparent need for forums which help us explore the truth of what it means to be socially conditioned being in a physical/nonphysical world. From Descartes to Einstein it has been established that what we think we experience is seldom the accurate representation of reality—no matter what we may believe. The artist's purpose must not be to explore the frontier and then return to document his/her discoveries for a sedentary and complacent audience, but rather to create a laboratory for the audience to investigate the physical and psychological boundaries of its own perception. No life-changing revelation or astounding news need result—a momentary knitting of brow or widening of eyes is sufficient, provided the work of art has made some contribution to one's perception of the world. I do not suggest this as the ultimate orientation of art or landscape architecture. Art is a product of the society which creates it and is therefore ever-subject to change. Our over-programmed society simply demands art *of* experience.

Can or should landscape architecture enter this arena? I believe it has no choice if it is to contribute to a better understanding of our humanness. Whether or not it is done as landscape architecture, the sculpting of exterior space is now, and will continue to be, a principal scene for this investigation.

How do we proceed? The current reliance upon a design process provides an obvious starting point. Composed of ephemeral, temporal, and spatial qualities, the landscape is difficult to describe, evaluate, or interpret. Yet landscape architecture cannot afford to overlook or neglect the very necessary, though admittedly unsettling, confrontation with these interactive, nonmappable, nonquantifiable, and difficult-to-predict components.

Along with stewardship must come respect for our interaction and participation with the land. Nowhere is there evidence to suggest that our simple, artificial constructs are sufficient for examining and, subsequently, manipulating the landscape. It is therefore unconscionable, to me, that we justify our self-indulgent preparation of two-dimensional drawings by manufacturing the myth that alluring graphic plans practically guarantee desirable landscapes. Despite lip service to the contrary, the "plan" has become the object (both noun and verb) of landscape architecture. Are we jealous of the architects' building elevations? We admonish our students and ourselves not to design solely in plan, but no effective alternate mechanism for designing is proposed.

Perhaps the Minimalists' reductivism of the 1960s provides some clues. These artists discarded complex imagery and its metaphorical content to permit access to purer emotions and experience. Landscape architecture could engender similar results. Complexity of meaning, perhaps; complexity of forms, only from the masterful.

The enhancement of presence and subduing of metaphor may not require works of genius, but Mary Gordon's charge to writers should also ring true for landscape architects involved in the act of artistic creation:

"The important thing is that they must express *reality*; they must express their *genius*, not *themselves*. . . . For pitted against reality . . . the self is puny; it is of no interest."[12]

The implications for landscape architecture are many. For me, the "reality" of the landscape involves exploration of the limits of experience, of what a "place" can do to me or for me. I am interested in landscape architecture as a three-dimensional discussion of the interaction of persons and the environment but only when "news of the world" is the topic. I want landscape architects to create settings where I can discover special, unknown aspects of my own perception and understanding. This can only be accomplished through the evaluation, interpretation, and transformation of selected experience. Landscape architects' continuing tendency toward geometric exercises in molding, compressing, and diluting familiar things to make them fit immediate projects is inadequate.

To accommodate contemporary needs, wholly new combinations or assigned meanings may be necessary. And herein lies the rub, because bestowing new meanings will startle and confuse the audience until it learns the new vocabulary. (Three-quarters of a century after its introduction, Cubism continues to perplex.) Our options are not many, though. As Barthelme explains,

"Art is not difficult because it wishes to be difficult, rather because it wishes to be art. . . . [The artist] discovers that in being simple, honest, straightforward, nothing much happens."[13]

An example is that of architect Peter Eisenman. While developing singular residential projects based on an interpretation of linguist Noam Chomsky's theories of grammar and syntax, Eisenman assigned new meanings to walls, doors, windows, floors, stairs, etc. For this he endured considerable abuse. Today, even Eisenman admits to the limits of the experiment. But note, at no time were we asked to believe that he was creating a new prototype for Levittown. What is important is that we now have one interpretation of how the organization of language and of architecture might correlate. I believe we must consider this to be valuable even though it has not changed the face of architecture. How is art to progress if someone isn't prepared to take a risk, to put a finger in the flame?

To the inevitable charge of "inaccessibility," artist Ben Shahn responds:

"It is not the degree of communicability that constitutes the value of art to the public . . . however difficult its language, [great art] will serve ultimately to dignify that society in which it exists. By the same argument, a work that is tawdry and calculating is not made more worthy by being easily understood."[14]

Still, so-called esoterica is not the sole approach to artistic experience, nor are cultural symbols and perceptual awareness totally distinct events. Surely such achievements as Le Corbusier's Notre Dame du Haut at Ronchamp, Gaudi's Güell Park, and Picasso's *Guernica*, illustrate how new cultural symbols can result from forms given new meanings. This is attainable when the new meanings are *required* by issues dealing with elemental truths concerning existence. The works may not always be simple and clear, but they are usually filled with wonder and possibility. Without exception they are devoid of gimmicks or tricks.

Why isn't landscape architecture nearer the artistic mainstream? One reason is that landscape architects rely too heavily upon their own built projects for most of the clues about design. We need to do more research and to engage in more experimentation. Consider those cartoonish thumbnail drawings which serve as a testing ground for architect Michael Graves and others who do them. They permit description and dissection. They encourage evaluation and interpretation. They allow (limited) experimentation—without building. Of course they, and models also, are imperfect tools. But they may be the best architecture has.

Landscape architecture, too, needs to develop a more productive relationship with graphics and models without deluding itself about the authenticity of these representations. And landscape architecture must resurrect its interest in its own rich history, not for answers, but rather as a secure and informative benchmark.

Even our workplaces hamper us. It is hardly surprising that landscape architects' commonly chaotic or bustling offices and university design studios seldom nurture works of genius. Barragan is right when he recalls that "art is made by the alone, for the alone." Creation is an intimate act.

But despite the most perseverant efforts, there will be no life in your art if you have no experience to draw upon. To my mind, the only way to produce experience-supportive landscapes, is to have an experience-supported reservoir of understanding. I think we should visit places not just to see them and record them with our snapshots, but rather to *feel* them. Let the seeing be documentary, but the feeling enlightening. Our designs will be the better for it.[15]

# THE OBLIGATION OF INVENTION (1998)

## BERNARD LASSUS

The dissociation that has now become widely established between landscape and concrete space hides another one, between appearance and concrete space, and that for two reasons: one relative to their respective scales, the other to the omission of the evocative power of appearance.

Now that daily life has been overwhelmed by this process of dissociation, would it not be time to try to illuminate the relationships between landscape, appearance and concrete space, for those who are interested in landscape through development?

### VISUAL APPEARANCE AND TACTILE DISCOVERY

If, while walking in 1961[1] along the quays of the port in Stockholm, I suddenly saw before me the silhouette, which had remained until then invisible, of an imposing warship, it was undoubtedly because, in the background beyond the ship was the landscape of the port. The background had helped the thin layer of paint (akin to a paratrooper's battle dress) covering the ship to play the role of camouflage. That is, to destroy, through mimesis, the appearance of the boat and to create instead an ensemble in which the vegetable element [trees, etc.] dominated that of the port all the way to the horizon. Such a silhouette could only be perceived in that port, because it appeared suddenly in the same line as if it was a piece of that landscape, and revealed its scale at the same time. In the open sea it would not be the same.

To that first shock was added a second, the fact of seeing, over against a mass of several thousand tons of metal, a thin layer of paint. Then a third, necessitating that I retrace my steps in order to assist it, because of the change of distance and point of view. . . . I recorded the experience with three indissociable photographs: two showing the landscape in which, although omnipresent, the ship was not visible, the last one revealing abruptly the shape of the ship alongside the quay. In the case of that ship, irrespective of the camouflage colors relating to the vegetable world in lights and shades, it is the scale of the fractionalization as well as the dominant colors that induced the obliteration of the limits of the "ship" outline. Thus there was a scale of common reading between the internal fractions of the camouflaged ship and the port as far as its horizon. The fractions as isolated appearances were vaguely reminiscent of numerous objects built or planted, but they were also an ensemble of numerous specific shapes, although with indeterminate meanings. Hence the gargantuan shock of the ship entity appearing suddenly, in its own scale, out of the landscape of the port. If the port had been covered with snow and the ship painted white, there probably would have been also the elimination of the proper limits of the ship, but that effect would have been fragile, resting only on the common denominator of the white. The slightest shadow produced would have revealed its presence.[2]

In that movement of retracing my steps, standing back, then coming forward again toward the ship, began the discovery of concrete space, a movement that incites us to go and check with our finger whether, in entering a landscape, some object guessed from a fragment of its appearance, corresponds truly to our expectation.

From a wider look, the landscape is thus a reading that crystallizes the fractions of appearances. Halfway, one can wonder about the nature of these fractions, of that toward which one is making one's way: that maroon stain has the appearance of being the roof of a house, but can be the appearance of a truck's canvas cover or the autumn foliage of a chestnut tree. Close up, it is just a simple wall in the sun, with the distance of the wall of a few moments ago in its appearance, which is superimposed in my memory on the fraction of the previous landscape.

The elaboration of the appearance can thus be oriented in its relation to the object, as well as in its relation to the possible landscapes, by a play of fractions between appearances.[3] That notion of an ensemble of fractions of appearances forming a landscape is a drawer full of imaginary landscapes, whose concreteness is not verified. Nor, obviously, are its visual appearances in situ.

I explored that inversion of camouflage in the project put on at the Lainé warehouse in Bordeaux in 1979–1980 (the Entrepôt Lainé, now the Bordeaux Museum of Contemporary Art), where I combined a huge camouflage canvas with, placed before it, a desk, at which by pushing buttons it was possible to select a sound: seagull cries, wind in the pines, etc. Thus by summoning up his own memory, the experimenter with the mechanism could transform the camouflage canvas into a succession of imaginary landscapes, chosen according to an ensemble of landscape possibilities suggested by the sounds.

Now I go back to my approach in order to confront the visual appearance with what will be apprehended in tactile terms, that difference between visual appearance and tactile discovery of the concrete that results in a "going toward."

I move forward in the direction of the current, evaluating at each step the spot on which to place my next step.

At certain moments diverse choices are posed. Here I prefer a more linear progress, chopped by vertical ruptures, or there, a more horizontal, though extremely sinuous, course. Compared to those of a walk through town, these movements have length and depth at the same time. With each step, in varying proportions, and/or interchanged.

The question is rarely posed as clearly, since the nature of that on which I walk is not given, but is there to discover. Reflections, dark depths of water . . . luminous bottoms . . . at what depth will I strike the bottom? Will it support my weight? Hence the preference conceded to what appears the hardest: rock. And, will this rock be slippery in spite of my striated rubber soles?[4]

Why that insistence on tactility, if it is not because we know that new landscapes will no longer be offered to our sight, extracted via the discovery of oceans, as were those of Cook?

Nowadays television is giving us access to many things; therefore as landscapers we really have to make contact, to be interested in things, to encounter them in order to create them out of the dominance of the visual. The finitude of the world leads us to go beyond the nostalgia of discovery in order to approach the effective invention of things, of materials, of their sounds and their new appearances.

That new concrete space will thus be available for new landscapes. Alternately, one could also start, for the elaboration of parts of that concrete space, from specific landscape hypotheses.

The revelation of the necessity to give shape to the concrete world has led me lately to consider a distinction between tactile scale and visual scale, that is, between a scale where it is possible to confront the visual information with physical presence, and another where the phenomena are only visual.

The tactile scale is linked to everyday life by a direct encounter with things; let us take, for example, perception in an urban milieu. The tactile scale is the one in which we move, in which it is required to locate ourselves with precision: to park our car, locate the stairs, and open our door. This tactile scale is the zone within which the confrontation of imprecise information, transmitted by the eye, must correspond to images registered in our memory, in order to allow ourselves to move easily. The space may not be faked, but at least it may be animated, with the proviso that what is there remains subject to everyday requirements of judgment on distances.[5]

Above and beyond the tactile scale is the visual scale, a zone in which phenomena, even if they provide us with various sensations, are only visual.

When one goes in search of landscape's objects, diverse things offer themselves for verification. Simultaneously those things, by evoking others and participating in them, can be inserted in other ensembles. These may not be obvious at the beginning, and may be reminiscent of strata of entities not necessarily present in totality on the places of exploration. Nevertheless, each creates a certain extension of perception, more or less well-defined.

Those landscape objects, regrouped in different categories, belong to proper and different scales corresponding to entities that are spatially abstract, that cannot be grasped by a broad look, as can a landscape. In certain conditions, however, they can evoke imaginary landscapes, as the home-landscapers have discovered for themselves on the scale of their tiny gardens.[6]

## THE LANDSCAPE ENTITY

While studying a project for the third phase of the Parc du Roi Baudouin in Brussels in 1984, I was able to see that the surface of the park was composed of fractions of very different elements: one of the oldest woods on the outskirts of Brussels, an old reed bed, places considered as the image of the typical landscape of Brabant (meadows, hedges of poplars, and cows), the whole lot on a slope. Instead of constituting the park as a new object on that slope, the aim of my proposal was to dilute its limits so that the fractions of the elements would be strengthened in their differences. My proposal allowed the surface to be the public fraction of a public-private space: the *landscape entity* of the slope of the valley of the Mollenbeek, the local river.

In that way I avoided adding a supplementary object to what had already been superimposed in that place. This is because in addition to the fractions of tangible elements previously mentioned, there were also fractions of other elements, imaginary this time. For example, the old mills and the archaeological remains of the Roman occupation—those elements being themselves fractions, or rather, remains of different superimposed moments of that site.

My proposal was therefore not to add another fraction (or object), not to destroy one of the previous remains, but, on the contrary, to reveal their successive and simultaneous presences in a chosen expanse (the landscape entity).[7] I did this by linking its characteristics to a morphological fraction: one of the portions of one of the slopes of the Mollenbeek valley.

Other places: other entities, rarely linked with the surface planned for the intervention. At the beginning of the study of the recreation area of the new town of Marne-la-Vallée,[8] the general hypothesis was that the image of a recreation area can correspond, before any notion of activity, to the notion of a place called "natural." While walking across the park of the château at Champs-sur-Marne, I realized that in the middle of that garden *à la française,* surrounded by numerous trees, a continuous sound of cars was clearly audible. Therefore I proceeded with a series of sound surveys on the whole area that revealed the passage of numerous airplanes, the intensity of the noise of the highway, and a thermal power plant, situated on the east of the site. Subsequently, I questioned the people who frequently visited this place (fishermen, people who had discovered this spot through the years and who came on Sundays for a walk). Those people did not hear either the cars or the planes! It was probably out of the question for them anyway to be able to hear those noises. Having been lucky enough to discover that "wild" place, to be attentive to that sound nuisance would in effect have destroyed their discovery and forced them to see the deteriorated banks, the car wrecks, the greasy bits of paper . . . .

Let us imagine that this place would really become a recreation center advertised by leaflets and signposts at the entrance: would they not hear, then, the sounds of planes while eating their picnics on the grass?

In the center of the "wildest" zone of the site, located not far from the Meunier chocolate factory, beneath the breeze a delicious smell of chocolate spread through the undergrowth.

It would not have been judicious to isolate the fraction of the site called "wild" or that rather extensive area (of the order of 350 hectares) from those smells and noises. Rather I was tempted to exalt its presence. Facing the power plant, a high ramp crowned by a crenellated tower, partially collapsed, would have produced a critical response stigmatizing the noises and, just as at Jericho, the power plant, with its noises, would have succeeded in destroying the tower.

Further, in the wood, in the center of the wildest zone of the site, a panel would announce: "Courtesy of the west wind, chocolate mousse."

## Minimal Intervention

The fact that a place exists before one proposes to do something to it has repercussions on the nature of the intervention and poses, in a radical way, the question of knowing whether or not one has to intervene. On September 14, 1981, Senator Ludovico Corrao had consulted Lucius Burckhardt and myself, at a conference in Gibellina-Nuova, in Sicily, in order to try to determine how to preserve the ruins of the old town in the mountain a few kilometers away, which had been entirely destroyed at the time of the 1968 earthquake.[9] To try to evaluate the possibility of a physical intervention, we proposed the concept of *minimal intervention,* and to introduce that concept I chose to mention my work on the tulip.

Belonging to the family *Liliaceae,* the tulip has a caducous perianth shaped like a bell and divided in six. It blooms alone at the top of its erect stalk. Let us say it is red. But is there anything else? To try to enlarge on what I know about it, with a pair of scissors, I take a sheet of white card and cut out a narrow strip whose width is less than the internal diameter of the flower. This allows me to insert it right to the bottom of the bell while still retaining a part of the card outside. I hold the strip delicately, in such a way that it neither brushes against the walls or the petals, nor touches the bottom of the bell. This action allows me to ascertain that the white surface plunged deepest into the floral volume has become rose, a rose which, as it approaches the upper part of the flower, becomes lighter in color. "Un air rosé."

That reflection of light inside the tulip reveals to me, in a flash, that the rose hue is only the sign, the mark, and that it is the totality of the volume into which I have plunged that strip of card that is rose. The reason is very simple: the light reflecting on the petaloid divisions from one to the other, in a play of multiple reflections, each time coloring with a little more red, has formed a volume of colored light.

Then I just as delicately withdraw the card from the tulip. If the flower appears to be the same, it is not and no longer will ever be.

Is not also the landscape a deepened, tangible knowledge of what the concrete can offer, a certain apprehension of what is and was there? It is therefore not necessary that a physical transformation occur for there to be a landscape intervention. From that point of view, the minimal intervention is to bring other tangible dimensions to what is already there.

But must the cardboard be left in the tulip? And if it has to be, on what conditions? Those questions appear to me all the more interesting because in the tulip of France itself they propose to develop a national highway network.

## The Indivisible Places

To intervene in a place, to find a form for the passage of a highway, for example, has nothing to do with the fact of passing through there or not. To create a highway, however beautiful it may be, in a place where it should not pass, does not solve the problem of passage. This is because it is the passage itself which is the most important factor, and makes the place into something else by cutting it in two. In other words, there is a value of identity particular to certain places, which makes them for a moment indivisible.

Thus the decision to pass or not to pass through a place, which is of a symbolic order, must not be confused with the fact of finding an artistic solution for that passage. The artistic solution can, after all, be a success or not, but is dependent on the other, symbolic problem.

An example: the difficulties raised by the passage of a highway near the Puy de la Nugère, at one of the extremities of the chain of puys, or extinct volcanoes in central France. I gave advice at that time not to venture into that landscape entity. That entity, by its geological nature, must be considered totally unique, on the national and even the European scale. Besides, it corresponds approximately to a national park, the park of the volcanoes.

Another example: one would no longer dig a tunnel beneath Mont Blanc, as we did a few years ago for a number of reasons at the time held to be convincing, because today one no longer seeks to oppose the human mastery of the technical to the natural power of Mont Blanc. Our actual mastery is rightly not to dig and not to breach that natural power. For that more subtle mastery, the taking into account of new values emerging from a place is part of the decision to make.

## NATURE AND DISPLACEMENT

The passage of a highway thus supposes a thorough specific knowledge of places. But what are these places? If one refers to the maps of the sites affected by the proposed highway at the Ministère de l'Equipement, one establishes that they are just as much places where man has introduced no construction, as places which man has more or less modified, either as visitor or as producer of significant non-natural elements: villages, monuments, bridges, etc.

Now, if one puts on the same level what on the one hand would be in the category of the natural, or is wished to be, and what on the other hand is undoubtedly the result of human presence, we create a tension. Let us implicitly suppose we give a similar landscape value to a village or a cascade, for example. Now from the point of view of the possibility of making a passage for the highway, the value of nature is not identical.

In addition, to distinguish the natural from the artificial is not as simple as one could first think, because the choice of a place as natural is already in fact a human intervention. Furthermore, close to apparently natural cascades, there might have been an earlier clearing of certain views, plantations of trees, etc.

In that new scale the natural would be what has been less modified. However, such a definition would not take into account the effects of the *displacement,* which can tip mixed places into the category of the natural, by the simple fact of adding obviously artificial objects.

> If you introduce a new element into your visual field, it will be inserted either between the natural and the artificial, or it will become the most natural element, or the most artificial: whence displacement of one or several earlier elements. More or less natural, more or less artificial, it is an identification that leads to a classification.[10]

When we are faced with the question of addition to a site, it is the value of nature of that site which is displaced, or more precisely, impelled toward the most natural. To pass around or through—these are interventions that have to be considered in relation to setting categories of appreciation of places by referential or dominant factors; in the circumstances here, classifying places from more to less natural, insofar as the factor "nature" takes more and more weight.

Thus, in that way, before the effective passage in a site, the plan of a highway can, in the visual field of the affected residents, make them perceive that site as still more natural; hence a still stronger attitude of rejection of the highway. The project thus helps, despite itself, to constitute locally a visual field that appears more natural. The effective passage of the highway poses then either as a force opposed to the natural power, or, beyond the passage in the visual field, as a destroyer of the infinitely vast entity of nature, of which the visual field is only a fraction. In both cases, to pass is to scar. The identification of the residents with the entity of abstract nature evoked in that way, an identification that is sometimes confined to anthropomorphism, will make the passage be experienced like the destruction of a loved one.

That explains why the concept of landscape entity, here as in nature, cannot be approached only as a visual problem, since it is situated at symbolic levels. It also explains the importance played by maps in the actual debates on the passage of the highway. The map indeed represents, with its diverse irregular spots of a certain color, the surfaces and forms of the entity of nature associated with that color. That designation by a colored surface with precise limits is a choice. By that choice, the value of nature is revealed. Over and above this, does not the delimitation join what is shown by the ring of Rouault's paintings or the halo of the saint, by giving it the character of the infinite? Thus it is that one cannot clip off the marshes at Poitiers at their *margins*.

## LITERALITY

Literality, which is not (like minimal intervention) a renewed reading, but the action of leaving places in their state, in total respect of their possibilities, must be challenged. First let us distinguish between concrete literality and mythical literality.

The first would consist in conserving nature in its biological processes.

The second would signify to protect the acquired because how does one know if what one wants to do is better than what one destroys in the name of the new.

Now even if it is not a similar notion of time that underlies those two positions, do they not both suppose a common idea, the idea of reversibility? On one side, the feeling that one can go back to a prehuman, natural state; on the other, the imaginary attempt to reconstitute human history, to make again, nostalgically, the journey that seemed to have succeeded so well.

In the end, these two literalities are both mythical.

## THE INVENTIVE ANALYSIS

The current grand debate on conservation and rehabilitation is linked to the difference between fixity and the process of evolution. In the particular cases of the Garden of Returns and the project for the Tuileries, it appears to me that it was necessary to make possible an interpretation of landscape that would not deny the natural given, or the patrimonial given, or the social given. It would also make clear the necessity of the conception, provided that one include the importance of *inventive analysis*, both in order to make an account of the physical and historical places and to identify the process of physical evolution and practices in those places. And, through those diverse times, to discern what would be most appropriate to the specific relation between a place and practices of that place, the place reflecting the practice, and vice versa.

That question was raised in the course of consultation for the restoration of the garden in the Tuileries. Should we privilege Le Nôtre to the detriment of Mollet or de Dupeyrac, the nineteenth-century garden or the site as it was before the Revolution, or, on the contrary, opt for the present? I did not want to choose by elimination because each of these strata had a reason to be present on the spot. Therefore I preferred to perpetuate through fractions the interventions of the different landscapers who had followed in turn in that garden. In other words, it was about, at the time, respecting their contributions and remaking them in another form—what they had themselves made in other times and what I have called *interlacing.*[11]

> One reinvents while pursuing a contemporary creation (*at the scale of the whole site, and not only by a simple formal localised adjunction*) the logic of the articulation between successive compositions of the site in the course of its development. . . . The progressive development of the garden does not result from successive adjunctions of new parts, but from a succession of rewritings on the same space and from reinterpretations, by the society which uses it, of the sense of the garden at each moment of its history. . . . It is thus that multiplicity of the site that had to be made poetically tangible and to be followed in the present.[12]

## The Inflection of the Landscape Process

The term "process" itself designates the ensemble of the interactive movements of the place. It indicates how it is necessary not to stop the place, not to fix it. One could almost say that it is required to catch the place "on the move."

Consequently the role of intervention, which for diverse reasons has revealed itself to be wished for, will take form in that movement and in the game of various processes. It can also tend to reanimate the movement of certain fixed factors and eventually to add others, all of that joining in the process of what is already in place. I call that type of intervention of a landscape project the "inflection of the landscape process." I intend that way to escape the usual term of composition, installation, which implies a reversible and therefore reconstructible temporality. It claims that the landscape process, usually called the project, is situated, that is, participates in the various movements of the concrete. Facing interventions which would be inserted in a successiveness, an agglomeration of objects, would it not be better to choose the reinvention of elements or fractions? The treatment of each new fraction is therefore conceived by revealing and taking into account the totality of the chosen moment/moments that are given. . . .

In a new optics, each fraction is not only an object situated horizontally in relation with others in the same temporality, but a fraction of its own time. Beyond the displacement of a given, one finds oneself no longer before a juxtaposition of objects that are able or not to gather in a landscape, but before a simultaneity of different moments, of vertical fractions each having its own necessary space, so that it results in an ensemble of associated structures mutually given significance by their temporal differences. That is what I proposed for the park at Duisburg-Nord.

This last project distinguishes itself from the one at Brussels, in that in Brussels I only posed "colors" that were naturally present, when what seems important to me now, is to create "spectra," that is, ensembles of "colors" valorized in their individuality, reconstructed and reinvented in their autonomy by cuts, by faults. This renewal in a "spectral" whole, endowed with its own scale, is therefore not a literal juxtaposition of "colors," too concerned with the "natural given" that it mystifies.[13] For each intervention it is necessary to understand each time if we have to reinvent the "spectrum" and the "colors" that correspond to it. In that "spectrum" the "color" is reinvented in a triple relationship: to itself, to its neighbors, and to the "spectrum" where it is located and which it makes possible.

Therefore, the problem of landscape is not to bring in one or several new elements, by thinking in terms of coherence, integration, insertion, but finally to put in place a new "spectrum" in a system of structures. The common denominator is, indeed, from the moment, the structure, since we can have structures with different dominant factors. Let us take the example of the superimposition of several jigsaw puzzles whose motifs, the sizes and shapes of the pieces, would not be identical. Each puzzle would furthermore be incomplete: here and there slits between pieces would correspond from puzzle to puzzle and create narrow breaks, some deeper than others, suggesting regroupings, both horizontal and vertical.

At the present time, when the finished appears ineluctable, any contribution appears as inevitably destructive and the real extent of that destruction is never known. Nevertheless, one has to choose, hence the necessity to envisage an inflected conception fitting into a history, a given multiple, undulating, unpredictable, resuming or opening other potentialities, especially those so important to daily life and the economy which cannot be dissociated from it.

I shall take Rochefort as an example, for there, in connection with the project of the Garden of Returns, a politics of horticultural production takes place progressively with the development of that garden. That production, centered on the begonia, has a profound connection with Rochefort because it is there that the species was named, in other words, invented. That birthplace had thus to be selected for its production, and that production in turn gains from the relation of the symbol that is the notion of "return." Besides, that connection has incited the European authorities to help start that production. The existence of the garden and its use as a place of daily activities are still other expressions of that symbol.

It is inventive analysis that has made possible those various propositions, because the sensory choice of the landscape entity gathers in it numerous factors nourished by the processes of the place itself, processes that find themselves inflected in return. Thus the military arsenal of Rochefort has now become a botanical arsenal. By that progress, the preservation/improvement of our patrimony has allowed a process of production to emerge.

Beyond the symbolic landscape, we have nevertheless to cross the road each day, to take paths by walking on slow or fast grounds to get to work, to hurry or to wander around in passages of light or shade, of sun or foliage, later on to walk in the garden, to breathe its smells, to listen to its murmurs. That, we do by *successions of ambiances*,[14] a concept it is difficult not to evoke as soon as we understand that where a landscape appears, we are already in place.

# PART III

# Form, Meaning, and Experience

The multiple interrelationships among form, meaning, and experience in landscape have been a focus of theoretical debate in landscape architecture since its inception. A range of perspectives and design strategies has been explored and advocated. The majority of readings in this section reflect the dominant view in the discipline that its role is to create meaningful landscapes. That is to say, the designer orders landscape in a way that expresses particular ideas or concepts that will be meaningful to those who experience it. Typically the "ordering" is through reconfiguration of the form of landscape, although the influence of land artists has also led to a strategy of minimal intervention, in which meaning is created through "reframing" the way we experience a particular setting. A number of readings below set out different strategies by which to achieve "meaningful" landscapes. However, there has also been a consistent alternative critique, which questions the possibility of "creating" meaning, and instead focuses upon strategies to enable meaning to accumulate through use.

In the strategies to "create" meaning, landscape is typically used as a basic frame of reference, to articulate the interrelationship between nature and culture. However, this has been dealt with in subtly different ways. Most fundamentally, there has been a shift over time from a focus upon how landscape might express some aspect of a dualistic relationship between nature and culture, toward the conceptualization of landscape existing within a field of relationships, involving both nature and culture, but that also allows a wider range of possibilities. As with the changing understanding of theory and of design process, discussed in Parts I and II, this shift in landscape architectural thinking reflects broader intellectual trends in society. However, the shift is not simply from "modern" to "postmodern," or from "structuralist" to "poststructuralist,"[1] nor is there a steady change over time. Rather, the following readings map out a series of explorations into ways of reconfiguring our understanding of landscape that draw in different ways upon this wider intellectual debate. Two particular lines of inquiry—into the symbolic dimensions of landscape design, and the aesthetics of ecological design—are continued in Parts IV and V.

The first five short readings each argue in different ways that meaningful landscape design should express a distillation of the essential qualities of human experience. They all explore the enduring questions expressed by J. O. Simonds in the epilogue to his classic text on site planning. "[The] consuming search for the central theme of all great [site] planning was like that of the old lama in his search for truth," he wrote, "Always we felt its presence in some degree, but always somehow the essence seemed to escape us. What were these planners trying to do? What was the aim of their planning? What was their planning approach?" Later in the epilogue, Simonds recounts the revelation that was to inspire subsequent generations of landscape architects: "What must count then is not primarily the plan approach, the designed shapes, spaces and forms. What counts is the experience!"[2]

In the first reading, Laurie Olin argues that the primary inspiration for meaningful experience in landscape has always been Nature, and draws upon historical precedent of French and English landscape traditions to illustrate his case. The next three readings focus upon human artifacts as the source of meaningful form in landscape. Geoffrey and Susan Jellicoe (1987) express a vision of the search for a "single great idea" of landscape as the meaningful middle distance, mediating between the individual and infinity. Their references to the urban fabric of a medieval town, the American regional grid, and the painting of Jackson Pollock as sources for a humanistic landscape prefigure contemporary ideals of landscape as meaningful infrastructure. Infrastructure is also prefigured in Nan Fairbrother's (1970) advocacy of the aesthetic and experiential possibilities of the functional "new industrial" landscape, seeking meaning from the way landscape has itself become artifact.

Patrick Condon (1988) also focuses upon human artifice as a source of experience, drawing upon familiar architectural metaphors to compare different types of spatial experience in landscape and arguing for a shift from a modernist idea of space defined by the placement of objects to a more phenomenological approach based upon enclosure.

In the last of the shorter extracts, Peter Walker reasserts the vitality of the classical tradition in the search for essential experience in landscape design, exploring the role of minimalism (1997) as a relief from the "increasingly bewildering, spiritually impoverished, overstuffed and undermaintained garden Earth." Like Olin, Walker expresses his belief in the continuing significance of classical historical sites as exemplars of the convergence of form, meaning, and experience.

Despite differences in scale and focus, each of these preceding writers advocated a search for meaningful experience in landscape through the clarity of the designer/artist's vision of nature and humanity. In contrast, there has been a line of critique which questions the desirability or even possibility of designing meaningful landscapes. Marc Treib's (1998) essay "Must Landscapes Mean?" starts by offering a summary classification of more recent trends in the search for meaningful design in landscape architecture. However, Treib is highly circumspect about accepting contemporary claims to create "meaning" in design. He argues that contemporary plurality of culture and society makes it difficult if not impossible for a singular meaning to be created. Instead, meaning can only accrue "like a patina" through use over time. Nonetheless, a designer can encourage the use from which meanings will emerge, and he argues that designers should therefore focus upon providing pleasurable experience.

The next reading pushes the argument further. Edward Relph has consistently offered a critical perspective upon modern landscape with his explorations of place and placelessness. In the extract included here, he sets out an agenda for place reclamation based not upon the grand vision of the artist/designer, which he sees as vulnerable to manipulation by "the instant environment machine" of contemporary capitalism, but upon working "from the inside out." That is to say, meaningful landscapes, or places, can only arise "through the involvement and commitment of the people who live and work in them."

A belief that meaning accrues to landscape through the accumulation of everyday experience represents a shift of focus away from dualistic categories such as nature and culture, and instead conceives meaning in terms of a more complex set of layered relationships. In the final three readings in this section, meaning in landscape is explored as part of a "field" of relationships. Robert Thayer, Catherine Howett, and Peter Jacobs have all articulated subtly different tripartite conceptual fields within which landscape meaning can be understood and elaborated. First, an extract from Thayer's *Gray World Green Heart* (1994) proposes two complementary frameworks, one identifying how technology acquires perceptual, functional, and symbolic meaning in landscape, and a second which argues that all contemporary landscapes exhibit tension between topophilia (love of place), technophilia (love of technology), and technophobia (fear of technology). He argues that the way people assign meaning to landscape will depend upon their response to these attitudes. Howett offers a broad-ranging overview of recent landscape thinking, arguing that it draws together three types of knowledge: ecology, semiotics, and environmental psychology, and that these provide the basis for the creation of meaningful landscapes focused upon the concept of dwelling.

The final extract, from Jacobs's *De/In/Re[form]ing Landscape* (1991), reconsiders the relationship among nature, culture, and technology, and looks to sustainability as a goal by which meaning will become invested in landscape. Drawing upon a seminal article by Rosalind Krauss,[3] which mapped out the place of modern sculpture in relationship to architecture and landscape, Jacobs proposed a similar "expanded field" of landscape architecture, interrelated with society, environment, and artifact. From this conceptual base he then argued for a threefold structure for landscape design, comprising social equity, ecological integrity, and a sense of belonging. The designer faces the challenge of not only locating his or her work within this expanded field, but of configuring landscape in a way which expresses the multiple influences upon it.

Common to all the readings in this section is a belief that humans have become alienated by modern technology and culture, and that the fundamental role of landscape architecture is to distill what it is to be human and to seek a greater sense of belonging in the world. While the conceptual strategies that are proposed differ, all express an ideal of redemption, or recovery of a sense of purpose. Landscape architectural theory of form, meaning, and experience, as expressed here, is thus both *critical* of current cultural practice, and *normative*, in its belief that there is a "better" way. It continues the underlying pastoral sentiment that launched the profession. However, as the last readings in the section illustrate, and the next sections elaborate further, there is a current crisis of representation. That is, when broader changes in culture cause familiar categories upon which our design vocabulary is based to dissolve (such as nature and culture, ecology, and technology, individual and society), where do we turn for the source of meaningful forms?

# FORM, MEANING, AND EXPRESSION (1988)

LAURIE OLIN

## LANDSCAPE FORM

Everything that exists has form. The words "formal" and "informal" as used in everyday speech are meaningless and an obstacle to a discussion about design, which by definition always contains formal properties of some sort. Where do forms come from? Forms come from forms first. Forms do not come from words. They cannot. Words can describe physical forms, but they do not (or did not) originate them; nor can they perform operations upon them. One must be familiar with a repertoire of forms before one can use them or manipulate them. This includes the forms found in nature and the forms of art, our art and that of others—other media, other cultures, and other periods. In nature are all the forms. In our imagination is their discernment and abstraction.

Art, and landscape architecture as a subfield of art, proceeds by using a known body of forms, a vocabulary of shapes, and by applying ideas concerning their use and manipulation. Landscape architecture, like other fields, evolves as it finds new ways to perform operations upon a particular corpus of forms—reusing, reassembling, distorting, taking apart, transforming, and carrying forward an older set of forms—often quite limited in range, but constantly making new things with new meanings. Occasionally a few new forms will be let in or discovered, but more generally new material consists of the re-presentation or recombination of material that has been forgotten or has been deemed banal or out-of-bounds for some reason.

Once again, where does this repertoire of forms come from? As I have remarked elsewhere in a discussion about places and memory, the only thing that we can ever know for certain about the world is that which exists now or has existed in the past. To make something new we must start with what is or has been and change it in some way to make it fresh in some way. To merely repeat or rebuild that which has existed is not creative and does not advance the field, eventually devaluing that which is repeated. How to make old things new, how to see something common and banal in a new and fresh way is the central problem in Art.

Arthur Danto, in the essay "Works of Art as Mere Real Things," goes so far as to say that the central activity of art is to transform ordinary (or extraordinary) real things into things that are art, i.e., no longer ordinary or mere real things.[1] Examples range from representations of landscapes (say in Claude or Innes) to Marcel Duchamp's declaring a urinal or bottle rack to be art works. The planting of trees in rows, whether good or bad, new or old, is an act of transformation and can under particular circumstances be art of a very high order.

Two of the greatest landscape designers that ever lived are André Le Nôtre and Lancelot Brown. Neither of these artistic giants invented the elements that comprise the parts of their greatest compositions. In the case of Brown, the meadows, clumps, and belts of trees, lakes, dams, classical pavilions, even the positioning strategies, all existed in the landscape gardens of his contemporaries and immediate predecessors. Nevertheless, he produced unique, startlingly fresh, and profoundly influential designs which still possess energy and authority. The elements he used can be found in the works of Kent, Bridgeman, and Wise and the villas of Rome, especially the vignas of the Villas Madama and Eiulia, but it was his particular assemblage that blended these elements into cohesive and tightly structured (albeit large-scale) compositions that were not episodic or disjointed, but plastic and "whole." The source of cultural authority for these pastoral compositions was literature (from classical verse to the Georgian poets) and graphic art (from Roman frescoes to Claude and Dutch landscape school especially Ruisdael, Hobbemaa, and Cuyp). Also, there was a predisposition on the part of his audience to understand and appreciate his constructions, both as sensual environs and as emblematic representations of agrarian social views.

For Le Nôtre, one could say the same thing. Every shape and form he used exists in seventeenth-century pattern books and in the sixteenth-century Italian and French gardens which he knew as a child and young adult. What then is so special and creative about his work? Like Andrea Palladio in his work at Il Redentore or the Villa Rotunda at Capra, he is working in a tradition, using standard elements, yet the results are more than a skillful or interesting repetition, more than traditional. He was highly original. His invention is one of recombination and transformation, frequently accomplished through a jump in scale with the simplest of elements and unexpected juxtapositions. Take Chantilly as an example: every shape—oval, square, circle, rectangle, ramp, parterre, and cascade—can be found in any of a dozen Roman gardens of the sixteenth and seventeenth centuries. Part of the transformation was to take elements originally conceived as furnishings for terraces or small garden rooms adjacent to houses (admittedly villas and *pallazzi*) and to change their scale, enlarging and frequently stretching them, and then to use these new figures to organize and unify entire estates or large tracts of land, reversing the relationship until the building was essentially a furnishing or embellishment of the landscape composition. This is true even when, as was usually the case, the building was the seed about which the enormous garden had grown. If Vaux-le-Vicomte and Versailles are two of his central and most fundamental creations, Sceaux and Chantilly are possibly his most original. This is largely because of the amount of transformation from prototype and the relegation of the chateaux in each case to a peripheral or tangential relationship to the composition, especially in its relationship to the most important water elements which exist as if for themselves with the parks subservient and organized about them. Here the shape, spirit, and meaning of these axial bodies of water and verdure are transformed from those that preceded them in France and Italy, in his own work as well as that of others. The source of their energy and authority is similar to that of Brown's work: foreign precedent and aesthetic paternity (especially Roman literature, archaeology, and Renaissance masterworks) plus contemporary science, particularly optics. How does one go about doing such things? How did he know to do this? It is hard to say. It is obvious that he had to abstract, perhaps I should even say extract, the forms, the types of basin, terrace, and bosque from the works he was exposed to, from his practical and immediate experience, and from representations in views, prints, and plans. Then, too, there was probably a certain felicitous amount of change and direction given by the society, his clients, their budgets, programs, and desires, as well as the capabilities and constraints imposed by the site, the climate, and technology.

If one returns to my opening thesis that the strength of landscape architecture derives from the fulsome sensual properties of the medium, its expression of the relationship of

Figure 5. Blenheim Park (John Dixon Hunt).
Figure 6. Chantilly (John Dixon Hunt).

society to nature, and the centrality of nature as the ur-metaphor of art, it is not difficult to understand why the works of Brown and Le Nôtre are among the very greatest in the field. Despite their differences in geometric form and organization, both men worked with the same limited palette which reduced the elements of their designs to the most basic— earth, trees, turf, stone, water—and arranged them at a scale that dwarfed the individual and created an ambience which, if not resembling any natural scene, by its very extent, diversity, and texture possessed the attributes of one. It is difficult to exaggerate the impact of their work upon one's sensibilities when on the spot, moving through their compositions. Artificial as they may be, ecologically simplified as they are, the effect is that of being in a landscape larger than oneself and beyond the immediate comprehension or control of oneself, of many of the feelings one has in a "natural" landscape—of light and space, of amplitude and generosity. Although two generations apart, both men produced work that responded to a particular moment in the economy and social structure of their society, that could not be sustained beyond their own life and career, and that was impossible to imitate or extend. Both refer to agriculture—whether that of pastoral herds or forest plantations, irrigation, and drainage schemes—the larger organization of the cosmos, and whether it is knowable or not. Both were masters of the simple detail and the subtle, complex, large design, thereby rendering their work truly analogous to the natural landscape. Redundancy and profligacy does not appear to have been a concern or issue, another natural analogue. Neither ever designed or built a composition that visually or formally imitated nature; both abstracted their forms from nature, farming, and art. The lakes at Blenheim and Stowe, at Vaux-le-Vicomte and Versailles all were, in part, responses to an abundance of rainfall, surface water, and poorly drained soils. Each one expanded or drowned the work of a predecessor with an uncanny sense of organic logic. Until one has actually seen these works, on foot and with one's own eyes, one cannot appreciate their character, achievement, or worth. Students who only know this work from slides or plans in books have no idea what they are like. In this way they also resemble natural environments of great scale, beauty, and cohesion.

# THE LANDSCAPE OF MAN (1987)

## GEOFFREY AND SUSAN JELLICOE

The philosophy of landscape design began as belief in myth, merged into humanism based on the establishment of fact, and is now grappling with the realization that facts are no more than assumptions. Humanism is passing into another, unknown, phase. It is possible for instance, that the present disruption of the environment can be traced beyond the manifest reasons to one basic cause: the subconscious disorientation now in man's mind concerning time and space and his relation to both.

Artists in the nineteenth century had already sensed not only that all things were in flux (as had the Greeks), but that time and space were not two entities, but one. Now that it has been scientifically proved, the concept is so overwhelming and the break with history so abrupt, that this may be the main reason why today, significantly, time plays little part in the arts. It is the present that matters. The imagination, for example, no longer cares to bridge the gap, peculiar to landscape, between the seedling and the tree: landscape must be instant. Architecture is created for a short life and the discord between old and new is without historical precedent. Such absence of a sense of time is contrary to all previous philosophy, metaphysical or humanistic. It is as though action supersedes contemplation. In extreme contrast, Egypt, ancient India and pre-Columbian America were almost wholly preoccupied with abstract time. China considered buildings to be self-reproducing, like plants; but the new landscapes were to be everlasting. Western civilization has consistently balanced time with space; the Italian philosopher-architect Alberti and the English astronomer-architect Wren held equally that all architecture should be built for eternity.

While man's sense of time has diminished, his sense of space seems to have expanded beyond control. He has a command of it, both in microcosm and macrocosm, that would have amazed the ancients; but in filling it he is tending to become personally dissociated from it; it is too big and he is too small. During the last few hundred years, the mathematical laws of the universe, extracted from outer space by scientists and engineers, have slowly come to dominate the biological laws of the biosphere. Second only to the particular significance of nuclear power lies that of pure mathematics. Civilized life for the human race, as emphasized by J. Bronowski in *The Ascent of Man* (Chapter 12: "Generation upon Generation"), is dependent upon a diversification planned with incredible ingenuity by nature. But mathematics is based on repetition; repetition implies mass production; and this inevitably could lead to the static, efficient and deadly civilization of the bee. Pressure to stamp out individuality is everywhere and is most manifest in state housing or hive; it is not wonder that, under such conditions, the subconscious human instinct for self-expression finds vent in violence and illogical vandalism.

Now that we know and can assess the forces battering our planet, can they first be resisted by the defensive mechanism of instinct and then controlled and put to work by the intellect? Balanced and self-renewing ecosystems had already been evolved by past civilizations (notably the eastern), but their scope was limited and their evolution by trial and error slow and laborious. The possibility now before man is the creation, with the services of computer, of an ecosystem that is immediate, comprehensive and based on unlimited recurring energies known to exist in the universe. This can achieve on current theoretical knowledge, but it is not enough. Can we also, as did the simpler past civilizations, turn scientific data into abstract thought and art, thus to sustain and identify ourselves as humans and not as animals in this extraordinary continuum?

The concept of a middle distance, or link between smallness-bigness and immediacy-infinity, is peculiar to the human species. It is primarily concerned with *idea*: that there is a largeness beyond human comprehension and that this can be approached by an intermediary or stepping-stone. All religions are intermediaries, and so is art. In landscape design, the first projection of individual personality has been the complex of home, garden and forest tree; this is the stable foreground from which spring the eternally changing middle distances. In history, the middle distance was almost always metaphysical and abstract, such as the ascending progression of man-sphinx-pyramid-eternity. Although the scene has changed from the metaphysical to the material, the same progression in scale can be experienced today through the enigmatic sculptures and monster structures of Atlanta. As the manmade world grows increasingly superhuman, so the concept of a meaningful middle distance must be extended and deepened.

What abstract form will this middle distance take? Man's new relation to environment is revolutionary and the landscape designer, unlike the artist, is conditioned by many factors that debar immediate experiment. We must therefore turn to the artists for a vision of the future, gaining confidence in the knowledge that the abstract art that lurks behind all art lives a life of its own, independent of time and space. The interpretation of art into landscape is personal to every designer, but a combined study of the aerial view of Urbino, the aerial survey of the Philadelphia region, and the painting by Jackson Pollock may suggest the grandeur of a fresh humanistic landscape that will have grown out of history and now lies within our grasp.

For the first time in history, the shape of the world that is unfolding expresses collective materialism rather than prescribed religion. In the advanced countries, the individual is evolving his own personal beliefs within his own home. The greatest threat to his existence may not be commercialism, or war, or pollution, or noise, or consumption of capital resources, or even the threat of extinction from without, but rather the blindness that follows sheer lack of appreciation and the consequent destruction of those values in history that together are symbolic of a single great idea.


# NEW LIVES, NEW LANDSCAPES (1970)

NAN FAIRBROTHER

Our only hope is exactly that—to *imagine* what we know and to plan creatively for the future. Industrial man must live in an environment organized for industrial uses, and this he must consciously create. "The real want is want of a plan," as William Robinson said of nineteenth-century London, for just as blind preservation of the past will not work, neither will blind trust in a future where new land-uses work out their own salvation without benefit of planning. The new landscapes for our new lives must now be consciously achieved by positive and clear-sighted adaptation of the habitat to our new industrial condition.

The old farming landscape evolved. Through generations of our farming ancestors the rural countryside developed by a long process of trial and error to suit the slowly developing business of agriculture. Our field-pattern is a centuries-long creation, our lanes are older than the cottages which border them, our villages were here in Domesday Book, and long generations of workers developed the traditional ways of plowing and hedging and planting trees—all the farming operations which created and maintained the old countryside. And this landscape which is the product of centuries of controlled evolution developed its present beauties slowly. Crude and primitive farming merely exploits the habitat, causing erosion and dust bowls: it is mature agricultural landscapes which are beautiful, and if our crude and primitive industrial land-uses are ugly, so equally our mature industrial landscapes could develop their own beauties.

It is possible in fact that given enough time good industrial landscape would also evolve of itself to suit our new land-uses. But there is no longer enough time. Swiftly changing conditions are part of our impatient new world, and have not only swept away old traditions but leave no chance for new ones to develop. Before any new method is perfected it is replaced by a newer and that by the newest. The proverb is now reversed, and though the mills of God may grind small they also grind exceeding slow, and we no longer wait for the grinding. Our landscapes no longer evolve but are crudely manufactured by destruction of the old.

New ways therefore no longer produce their own aesthetic solution—it is a new and depressing truth of the industrial age which is only too evident everywhere. And the conscious control which must now replace unconscious evolution to achieve good design must do so in the whole of our environment from small-scale to large—cups and chairs and rooms and houses and streets and towns. And also landscape. This realization began with the small and has gradually climbed the scale as far as towns. "A city is not a tree," said W. H. Auden, and no one now imagines that left to grow like a tree an industrial city will achieve spontaneous beauty—or if they do there are plenty of examples all over the world to disabuse them. It is in fact the disastrous results of uncontrolled industrial growth which have convinced a reluctant public that control is essential.

What we have not yet accepted, however, is that the design process must now also include landscape; that the days of spontaneous rightness are over here as everywhere else in our environment, and that to achieve good landscapes for our new ways of living we must deliberately design new settings to suit our new land-uses. And the past cannot help us. There are no traditions for industrial landscape, nor for mechanized farming, nor pylons in the countryside, nor urban housing in rural areas, nor mass motorized leisure, nor for any of our other new land-uses.

The choice then is not between old and new but between good landscape and bad. But it *is* choice, and even though it is said that the old must go (as it always has been), the true tragedy is not that the old must go but that the new should be bad.

Nor need the old beauties go with the old pattern, for though we cannot preserve them in the old landscapes we can re-create them in new ones. We want our leafy lanes and bosky hedge-bottoms, the country flowers and birds and casual wild places; above all we want the trees whose loss is reducing much of our countryside to large-scale allotments. We also want much more besides; cities which are a pleasure to live in and roads to travel on, properly planned areas to play in and attractive places to work in. We want in fact new landscapes for our new lives, and if they are to be valid and therefore viable they must be created in terms not of the past but of our new industrial condition.

# CUBIST SPACE, VOLUMETRIC SPACE (1988)

PATRICK CONDON

This discussion focuses on two distinct designed space types: modernist space, first made explicitly manifest through the time/space explorations of Cubist painters and thus characterized as *Cubist space,* and its antithesis, *volumetric space.* Cubist space, to simplify drastically, is made by placing solids in space; volumetric space is made by enclosing space with solids. Examples of Cubist spaces would include the Waterfront Park in Boston, Nicollet Mall in Minneapolis, Greenacre Park in New York City, Harlequin Plaza in Denver, and "housing projects" all over the world. Examples of volumetric space would include the Piazza San Marco in Venice, Prospect Park in Brooklyn, Paley Park in New York City, the Piazza del Campo in Sienna, and the European space type known as the medieval city.

Volumetric space in the landscape can be as large as the "outdoor" room experienced when adrift at sea—that is, the room formed by the apparent celestial sphere resting on the horizon.[1] Conversely a volumetric space can be as small as a closet. Volumetric space is therefore distinct from enclosure. Enclosure is a relationship between volumetric space and human scale. When adrift at sea one experiences the least enclosure possible on this planet; when sequestered in a closet one experiences the greatest possible enclosure short of the grave.

The example of the Piazza San Marco in Venice will serve to illustrate the important characteristics of volumetric space. The Piazza San Marco is a large bounded space with few fixed elements inside. What gives it distinction is the character and proportion of the "floor," "walls," and "ceiling" of the space. The two rooms of the space, the Piazza and Piazzetta, share a continuous and level floor. Except for the Basilica façade, the walls of the space are continuous planes or, in essence, simple rectangles. Again with the exception of the Basilica, the equal height and continuous cornice line of the other buildings defines the perceived ceiling, thereby bringing the blue sky down to cap the space explicitly at a more intimate scale than is usually experienced. The much studied proportional relations between floor and wall[2] provide unity. The delicate filigree and solid-void contrast of the carved masonry walls provide all the richness and variety one could wish for; by imagining the space with windowless concrete walls but otherwise unaltered, it becomes evident how critical this aspect is.

As in many other volumetric spaces (the Piazza San Pietro and the Piazza Navona to name but two), the detached object is used in ways that contribute to, rather than contradict the boundaries of the space. At the Piazza San Marco, the freestanding object of the Campanile hinges the Piazzetta to the Piazza. The freestanding columns at the south end of the piazzetta define the south "wall" of the space; the columns act as "mullions" and make a hue "bay window" that opens onto a "balcony" overlooking the sea. When arriving in this volumetric space from the many narrow access ways, there is an unmistakable sense that one has "arrived," in both the literal and metaphorical sense of the word. To construct a simile, having arrived at Piazza San Marco is much like the fantasy image of having "arrived" at the heart of regal society after moving through the protected layers of palatial entry, up the grand stair, and down the gilded vaulted hallway terminated by great double doors that are swept open by twin doormen to reveal, in the brilliance of ten thousand candles and the ebullience of five hundred seductive voices, the immense ballroom of one's

Figure 7. Piazzetta San Marco, Venice: volumetric space (Kevin Connery).

Figure 8. Waterfront Park, Boston: cubist space (Patrick Condon).

destination. At San Marco, one wants nothing else but to linger there forever. The nature of the containment is such that no worthy egress, not even the portal of the Basilica, can tempt a person; only the "balcony" overlooking the Laguna Veneta at the far end of the Piazzetta offers sufficient enticement to draw one forward, affording a suitable space for a brief flirtation before returning to the ball.

I have chosen to compare the Piazza San Marco with Waterfront Park in Boston because both relate to their urban contexts similarly, and to water virtually identically; as space types, however, they are opposed. At the Piazza San Marco the two "rooms" of space are explicitly defined. At Waterfront Park, however, explicit enclosure is lacking; it is traded away for highly complex spatial fields activated by sculptural forms. Here the walking surface is not a level plane but it is quite animated and changes grade frequently with stairs and ramps; these changes of level make the base highly complex, a relief sculpture that prevents the participant from perceiving it as a floor. "Walls" are intentionally indistinct; existing contextural walls of waterfront structures and elevated highway are neither acknowledged nor completely obscured, but are mitigated or counterpointed by intervening freestanding elements. Design unity derives not from the proportion of the "room" but from a complicated asymmetrical balance between the park's sculptural objects; the most noticeable of these is the overscale arbor. Within this strategy, where unity is so difficult to achieve, one might expect variety to take care of itself; in large measure it does, but for insurance a relatively rich plant palette is deployed in a number of different but thematically unified ways. The themes are asymmetrical balance, sculptural dynamism, natural growth patterns, and painterly concern with color.

Likewise, structural elements are individually sculpted as distinct independent objects that are expressive of a concern for purity of form and materials. Whereas at the Piazza San Marco the objects were used in ways that supported clearly defined "rooms," here, at Waterfront Park, it is fair to say that there are no "rooms" to define. Rather the numerous objects in the space must, by the relationship one to the next, establish the quality of spatial experience. In this way the objects of the space (some of which, like the arbor, are large enough to enter, but are still fundamentally sculptural objects) are similar to the rocks intuitively arranged in a Zen garden. To invoke Gertrude Stein, at Waterfront Park "there is no there there." This does not suggest a weakness in the design itself, but rather points out the logical impossibility of creating sense of arrival without specific space definition. The "there" quality of knowing precisely when you are "in" has been sacrificed to gain a dynamic quality of experience, whereby the moving participant experiences an environmental field that dramatically changes with each step. As a consequence, each person in the park will be experiencing quite a different set of visual stimuli at any single moment. This interest in motion, spatial dynamism, and singularity of perception so evident at Waterfront Park can be seen as the hallmarks of modernist aesthetics, arguable best and certainly first popularized in Cubist painting. In this light, the term "Cubist space" has been chosen as the most adequate shorthand descriptor for the space of Waterfront Park and many other modern landscape designs.

The choice between the two types of space is not just a matter of the designer's preference; it is far more fundamental. Recent explorations in landscape design theory have productively questioned modern era foundations for landscape design ethics,[3] process,[4] and meaning.[5] Work that suggests the implications of such shifting theoretical foundations for actual space-shaping in landscape design is vitally needed, since the way in which space is presumed to exist is linked to the ethical, procedural, and semiological issues mentioned above; these issues are, in turn, linked to the political, scientific, and philosophical notions that underlie culture. Given the dramatic erosion of formerly secure precepts in all of these realms it is logical to expect a revised space aesthetic to emerge. The central hypothesis of this paper is that volumetric space is a supportable candidate for this revised space aesthetic, based on arguments grounded in environmental holism,[6] a comprehensive paradigm that includes political, scientific, and philosophical components.

# MINIMALIST LANDSCAPE (1997)

## PETER WALKER

### MINIMALISM IN THE LANDSCAPE

Distinct from the specificity of its art world argument relating to a certain group of artists as a certain moment in the 1960s, minimalism in the landscape seems to me to represent a revival of the analytic interests of the early modernists that parallel in many respects the spirit of classicism. It is the formal reinvention and the quest for primary purity and human meaning that dignify its spiritual strength: an interest in mystery and nonreferential content are thereby linked to the quest of classical thought.

As with the term and idea of classicism, minimalism has entered our fast-paced society and been further defined and redefined by varying artistic and cultural disciplines. In this greater context, minimalism continues to imply an approach that rejects any attempt to intellectually, technically, or industrially overcome the forces of nature. It suggests a conceptual order and the reality of changing natural systems with geometry, narrative, rhythm, gesture, and other devices that can imbue space with a sense of unique place that lives in memory.

Despite the broader scope of my use of the term *minimalism,* a reference to the quintessential minimalist artist in illuminating. Donald Judd insisted that minimalism is first and foremost an expression of the objective, a focus on the object in itself, rather than its surrounding context or interpretation. Minimalism is not referential or representative, though some viewers will inevitably make their own historical or iconic projections. In correlation, though minimalist landscape exists in the larger context of the environment, and though it may employ strategies of interruption or interaction one can see beyond the designed "objects" to the larger landscape, the focus is still on the designed landscape itself, its own energy and space. Scale, both in context and internally experienced, remains primarily important. And as with minimal art, minimalist landscape is not necessarily or essentially reductivist, although these works often do have minimum components and a directness that implies simplicity.

With these parameters, minimalism in landscape architecture opens a line of inquiry that can illuminate and guide us through some of the difficult transitions of our time: the simplification or loss of craft, transitions from traditional natural materials to synthetics, and extensions of human scale to the large scale, in both space and time, of our mechanically aided modern life. And minimalism in this context suggests an artistically successful approach to dealing with two of the most critical environmental problems we currently face: mounting waste and dwindling resources.

An inquiry into minimalism in the landscape now seems to be especially timely. Recent developments in landscape architecture, architecture, and urban design during what has been termed our postmodern era have questioned the legitimacy of modernist design, with some favoring a return to classicism. Much of the recent work and thought in this area has focused on formal and decorative issues on the one hand and sociological and functional issues on the other. Minimalism, one of the manifestations of the last moment of high modernism in the visual arts, has itself, of course many compelling affinities with classicism. Rather than focusing on design and functional issues as mutually exclusive, minimalism leads to examination of the abstract and the essential, qualities of both classicist and modernist design.

It is interesting to recall that when the youthful Le Corbusier journeyed through the Middle Eastern and Mediterranean lands before World War I in 1911, he was drawn to Turkish mosques, Byzantine monasteries, and Bulgarian houses, because of certain qualities, particularly silence, light and simple, austere form. On the Acropolis of Athens, however, he was overwhelmed and awed by the Parthenon, the "undeniable master," which he later interpreted as a distillation of form, and unexcelled product of standardization. A moment had been reached, he concluded, when nothing more could be taken away. It was a moment of perfection, a defining of the classic. It so happens that I felt a similar response to one particular Le Nôtre garden when I visited it in the 1970s. Chantilly, a great garden of stone, water, space, and light, also represents a superb example of form reduced to its essential perfection. Chantilly seemed to me then and seems to me still to share in its essence an understanding and intent that is both classic and minimal.

These thoughts are a progress report of my personal journey as a landscape architect who came of age at the height of modernism in American environmental design. They are informed by the gardens, landscapes, designs, artists, and insights that have helped to shape my perceptions and to chart my particular course of inquiry to this point. They offer one personal approach to the making of environments that seems to be especially needed at this time in human history: environments that are serene and uncluttered, yet still expressive and meaningful. More than ever, we need to incorporate in our built environment places for gathering and congregation, *along with* spaces for discovery, repose, and privacy in our increasingly bewildering, spiritually impoverished, overstuffed, and undermaintained garden Earth.

# MUST LANDSCAPES MEAN? (1995)

MARC TREIB

I

During the last decade, the amount of writing purporting to deal with meaning in landscape design has grown impressively.[1] Landscape architects now write of their attempts to imbue designs with significance by referring to such conditions as existing natural forms or to the historic aspects of the site. Cultural geographers, calling upon a collective body of study that extends back well over half a century, interpret ordinary landscapes by first looking at the world around them; in their eyes, meaning congeals in setting, dwelling, and use—and not alone from the designer's intention.[2] Historians of gardens and landscape architecture tell us of those makers of places past who tried earnestly to create landscapes in which meaning would be apparent and understood. At times relying on iconography and inscription, the creators of these gardens and parts sought to convey to the visitor a message as well as a sensuous impression. Within the garden confines, the visitor would take pause, and perhaps ponder the meaning of existence or at least his or her part of it. Since the visitor, owner, and maker tended to share class and culture, intelligible communication was feasible.

These are only a few examples of the interests that have surfaced in the last decade and that have appeared in numerous publications. Principal among them, *The Meanings of Gardens,* edited by Mark Francis and Randolph Hester, Jr., in 1989 collected a series of essays that ranged in topic from religion to pop culture, from sex to pets, and geographically from Israel to Norway.[3] In the book, authors drawn from diverse disciplines questioned the significance of the landscapes we create; there were no generic conclusions, although the essays were somewhat neatly arranged under the headings of idea, place, and action. In a 1988 essay titled "From Sacred Grove to Disney World: The Search for Garden Meaning," Robert Riley also tracked the search for meaning—and its loss over time—and concluded: "Gardens have been a locus of meaning in many cultures, but not in modern America."[4]

What are we to make of all these renewed attempts to discern meaning in landscapes? Is it really possible to build into landscape architecture a semantic dimension that communicates the maker's intention to the inhabitant? If so, how? In addition, *should* we try to reveal meaning in environments, and if so, why? Where does the audience enter the process? Admittedly, this is notoriously treacherous territory, and every author begins— and often ends—by hedging his or her bets. Laurie Olin stressed the "daunting" task of defining meaning and suggested that there were two broad categories in which the term was positioned. The first he termed "natural" or "evolutionary": "Generally these related to aspects of the landscape as a setting for society and have been developed as a reflection or expression of hopes and fears for survival and perpetuation."[5] More simply stated, significance accrues through use and custom. Olin's second category, and the arena in which most designers operate, concerned synthetic or invented meanings, and it is these to which he devotes most of his essay and criticism.[6] My own effort will probably be no different from that of almost all previous writers in that I will discuss the question of significance without precisely defining it.[7] To some degree this lacuna is problematic, in other ways it may not be so troublesome.[8] I would like to think that we can discuss the meaning of meaning in landscape without a definition applicable to all landscape circumstances. Or at least I will operate under that premise. We can at least establish a broad theater in which meaning is taken simply as an integral aspect of human lives, beyond any basic attachment to the land through familiarity. Meaning thus comprises ethics, values, history, affect, all of them taken singly or as a group.

We could first try to establish *why* the pursuit of meaning has resurfaced at the close of the twentieth century. One reason might be the rejection of history, and all the baggage it carried, by those formulating a modern(ist) American landscape design in the late 1930s. Unlike their European colleagues, who continually confronted history in the world around them, American designers often started with a relatively clean slate. James Rose and Garrett Eckbo, among other writers, aggressively challenged the value of history as a lexicon of styles or typologies to be unquestioningly applied to contemporary problems and projects. Like their architectural contemporaries, they looked forward to solving problems of open space and form, and not backward to any book of given solutions. The received body of historical landscape architecture was taken as meaningless because its significance belonged to other places and other times.[9]

Rose, probably borrowing from the Canadian-Englishman Christopher Tunnard, argued for what he termed a "structural" use of plants: vegetation selected for a given climatic zone, but configured to create spaces to be used from within rather than to be viewed from without.[10] A continuing theme in Eckbo's writings well into the 1950s was the condemnation of the axis, which had "run out of gas in the seventeenth century."[11] Like Rose, Eckbo envisioned an enriched landscape configured for use, rather than one restricted to a linear spatial structure based on formal principles.

There was little or no discussion of meaning in these writings, as there was—quite remarkably—no argument for any specific vocabulary. Significance derived from forms and spaces appropriate to their use and times; meaning was a by-product, or so the text implied. Although the zigzag was a popular feature in the gardens of Eckbo and Thomas Church, and the biomorphism of Jean Arp and Isamu Noguchi informed much postwar California garden design, no published texts connected these idioms with either modern art or the modern era—or argued for their significance.[12] In fact, very little was written specifically about syntax—that is, the relationship between the elements—much less about semantic production.

Landscape writings of the period paralleled—almost always with a bit of a time lag—discourse on modern architecture. Sigfried Gideon, the central theorist for what came to be termed the International Style, rationalized the new architectural vocabulary by setting it against spatially vital architectures past.[13] The modernist art critic Clement Greenberg saw painting first and foremost as marks upon a canvas and found its culmination in nonobjective works; Gideon saw in modernist building the culmination of architecture as space.[14] In so doing, he actually recast history to accord with a twentieth-century vantage point. In anthropological terms, he was etic rather than emic, that is, looking at the subject from beyond its cultural limits rather than on its own terms. While a vast repertoire of Western architecture had accumulated over time, to Gideon its quest had ultimately been spatial rather than stylistic, and as such it reached a fruition in the modern era. Because he found space more central to architecture than either iconography or human affect, Gideon was more focused on architectonics (that is, an architectural syntax) than on semantics. Or perhaps he saw as synonymous significance and the means of spatial production. Eckbo's *Landscape for Living* of 1950 provided the modernist argument with its text and laid out the concerns and parameters for modern landscape architecture.[15] More fully developed in breadth and depth than earlier writings by either Tunnard or Rose, Eckbo's work reinforced the need for reflecting time and place and human presence in landscape architecture: but there was no discussion of what it meant.

In many ways, the next major ideological and highly polemical tract was Ian McHarg's *Design with Nature,* published in 1966. Focused on the evolving study of natural ecology and rooted in landscape management, McHarg cited the natural world as the only viable source of landscape design. His text provided landscape architects with sufficient moral grounds for almost completely avoiding decisions of design—if design be taken as the conscious shaping of landscape rather than its stewardship. No talk of meaning here, only of natural processes and a moral imperative.[16] Olin, among others, has pointed out that design decision normally derive from a greater complexity of factors than those of ecology alone, among them social and cultural issues including aesthetics, and he cautions: "This chilling, close-minded stance of moral certitude is hostile to the vast body of work produced through history, castigating it as 'formal' and as representing the dominance of humans over nature."[17] McHarg mixed science with evangelism—a sort of eco-fundamentalism as it is sarcastically known by some parties—taking no prisoners and allowing no quarter.

The McHargian view was focused to the point of being exclusive, confusing two rather different arenas of landscape intervention modulation as if they were one.[18] To manage a region without thorough "scientific" investigation and analysis would be fatuous, if not dangerous. Viable design begins with study and analysis. But the planning process rarely requires the active form making that is central to landscape architecture. Reams of analysis and overlays will establish the parameters for making a garden for a suburban backyard, but they will hardly provide the design. McHarg's method insinuated that if the process were correct, the form would be good, almost as if an aesthetic automatically resulted from objective study. Presumably, meaning would accompany the resulting landscape. The 1960s and the 1970s were dominated by attempts to rationalize the practices of architecture and landscape architecture, giving favor to social utility rather than the pursuit of form or meaning. By the end of the decade, however, the limits to this way of thinking, coupled with an emerging desire by younger landscape architects to again become visible, began to generate a reaction to the anti-aesthetic and antisemantic climates of the preceding decade.

Admittedly, this is a cursory explanation of a professional condition that derived from a complex series of interrelated factors. Landscape architecture is, after all, part of a cultural, technical, and social milieu and as such is informed by a multitude of factors and considerations. But . . .

## II

During the 1980s, declarations of meanings began to accompany the published photos and drawings of landscape designs. At conferences, landscape architects would describe their intentions, their sources, and what the designs meant. Some authors merely claimed they were touching base once again with the vernacular matrix in which High Style design was embedded. Martha Schwartz, for example, reexamined the materials of the ordinary landscape and the typologies of the small, private garden and the shopping center. George Hargreaves spoke of a perceptually complex space at Harlequin Plaza in Inglewood, Colorado, from 1984, although he shied away from making direct claims about its meaning(s). The emerging generation of designers displayed a new interest in making form; and many of them claimed that these new forms would be meaningful. In reviewing landscape architecture from almost two decades, I have found it helpful to classify five roughly framed approaches to landscape design and, by extension, to significance, used by the makers or their critics: the Neoarchaic, the Genius of the Place, the Zeitgeist, the Vernacular Landscape, and the Didactic.

A sort of primitivism constituted one attempt to retrieve that which had been lost at some unspecified point along the way to modernity. Borrowing from approaches that ranged from the body works of Ana Mendieta to the stone markings of Richard Long to the theories of entropy proffered by Robert Smithson, landscape architects began to reconfigure the land in a manner we could term *Neoarchaic*. Whether the landscape architects referred directly to neolithic sources, or only to the sculptors who had drawn upon them is impossible to determine. Perhaps they tapped both resources. But in neighborhood playgrounds and in suburban office parks, one began to encounter hills coiled with spiral paths, cuts in the earth aligned with the rising or setting sun (or the solstice), circles of broken stone and clusters of scared groves. Granite steles evoking the stone circles of ancient Scandinavia—or was that England's Salisbury Plain or Easter Island?—appeared in backyards and plazas. Myriad versions of Jai Singh's eighteenth-century astronomical observatories at Delhi and Jaipur popped up like mushrooms, including one reinterpretation in a fine garden by the master Isamu Noguchi.[19] One can almost hear designers saying, sotto voce: "If they meant something in the past (of course, we have to like them as forms . . .), then they will mean something again to us today." Gary Dwyer's proposal to link the two sides of the San Andreas Fault in California with crisscrossed topographic band-aids curiously developed from the Ogham writing of the Celts is extreme to be sure—and a bit difficult to support with rational argument—but it was not at all that bizarre in the context of contemporary projects.[20] As Catherine Howett once aptly phrased it: "By the early 1980s, every landscape architect student project had been equinoxed to death."[21]

If archaicism was one school of semantic creation, the worship of the *Genius of the Place* marked a second. Alexander Pope had enjoined Lord Burlington to consult the spirit of the place as a means of rooting landscape design in a particular locale. A garden was not a universal concept to be applied uninflected upon all sites. Instead, the garden revealed the particularities of its place as well as the profundity of the garden's idea. Long driven underground by the onslaught of urbanity, suburbanity, and modern technology, the genius was a bit hesitant to reemerge into the twentieth-century sunlight and, as a result, came out squinting. A renewed cult figure, the genius—or what was left of him or her—could be consulted in many places in only a desultory way, since "the place" had been so disturbed over the centuries by industrial development. While writers such as Christian Norberg-Schultz based their discussion of the genius and place in the phenomenology of Maurice Merleau-Ponty, and others decried the rise of placelessness, designers often adopted a more superficial approach to connect human inhabitants to their landscape setting.[22]

History became an image to be dusted off and applied to any current proposal as a means to validate it. In a glance over the shoulder of history, the tiny urban park was planted with prairie grass to show what vegetation had once thrived there. Like the caged animal in the zoo, however, an urban prairie is hardly a prairie at all; it is an urban garden planted with unmown grass and little else. Since the frame for reading—that is to say its context— has been so drastically altered, the subject of view is not easily understood as a reference to the past by contemporary citizens. The grass has been reduced from an inherent and meaningful component of early settlement to a design, or at best museological, element; a plastic or metal plaque normally provides its meaning to the residents with credits to the designer, the sponsoring body (usually a benevolent foundation for Green America), and of course the mayor in office at the time. Still, passersby wonder quietly to themselves: "When are they going to cut that lawn? I'm sure there are rats and Lord knows what else living in it. And they should water it; it looks dead."[23]

The presence of the genius is a bit more obvious in the undisturbed land, but there is precious little of that around these days; the genius is hardly unaffected by changes in atmosphere and climate. Still, the genius provides major support for landscape design and its rationalization today. Technically, studies of vegetation, hydrology, soil conditions, and the like are indeed the basis of design. But do these suggest a significant form for the design? If there is a stand of oaks, do you plant more oaks? Or should the stand be complemented by another species that even to the untrained eye appears to be foreign to the site?[24] So much of landscape architecture in the past has been created to *overcome* what the genius of the place offered the "unimproved" land—for example, by bringing water to the desert or by constructing conditioned enclosures to grow oranges in colder climates—that it is obvious that the genius's ambiguous advice can be taken rather freely. In instances such as the Patio of the Oranges in Seville, the human contrivance of irrigation was elevated to an art form, creating a garden of exceptional pleasure, refinement, and calm. Needless to say, this was not an approach to xeriscape using native plants; admittedly, it was collective and religious, rather than an anonymous, private, vernacular garden. But this courtyard, like other pieces of greenery and water in arid climates, nevertheless illustrates that, while one should consult Genius and Company, one need not accept the advice in precisely the manner it was given. Like any consultation, the information must be evaluated and some decisions need to be made, including those of form.

Buried within this approach to shaping the landscape is the belief that reflecting a preexisting condition creates a design more meaningful to the inhabitants. But I'm not sure. Many of them were not even on the planet at the time the land was pristine. I recently heard a project presentation that noted that as the principal concept for a natural preserve the designers and clients had recently restored the historical ecology and its pattern. That they had also created a pond where none had existed—assumedly as much for the visitors as for the birds that were to be lured to this reserve—was passed over without question. It is difficult to fault the good intentions of restoring disturbed wetlands. But why does the original pattern need to be "restored," when in fact the reserve serves as much for human recreation as it does for open space preservation? Is it because the "natural" pattern, masquerading as nature, is less open to question by client and visitor alike? Or could it be that the designers somewhat defensively do not believe that the natural pattern can be improved upon and brought into greater accord with the new uses and the drift of the times? Or is it a conscious or unconscious harking back to received picturesque values? Does the genius really grant significance or just point out the easiest path to follow, what in the zoological world is called a "target of opportunity"?

Approach number three borrows from related disciplines, which suggests a belief in the Zeitgeist (that is, "the spirit of the times") as a determining force for any aspect of contemporary culture. If artists, and the battery of cultural critics who support and explain their work, have produced a body of work deemed illustrative of the spirit of our times, then landscapes designed with contemporary art-like elements must share that significance. Such an approach intersects at times with the Neoarchaic, particularly in recent years when a new regard for prehistory has informed at least one major strain of art making.[25]

The boulders that constitute Peter Walker's Tanner Fountain at Harvard from 1984 bear a striking resemblance to those Carl Andre had neatly arranged in his Stone Field Sculpture in Hartford, Connecticut, some seven years earlier. Andre, in spite of his ultraminimalist proclivities, had actually consulted the genius in creating the work, choosing a range of stone types from the surrounding area as the basic material of the installation. (Because the rocks had been removed from their native context, however, this fact required a written or verbal explanation.) Walker's stones are all more or less the same size and species, and their circular configuration—like certain elements of his IBM Solana, Texas, campus—cites rather directly the work of sculptor Richard Long. Certainly an aesthetic transformation has resulted; neither the fountain nor courtyard design is plagiarized. But much of their novelty and appeal, at least at the time of their initiation, derive from their seeming correlation with art forms of the times. From sculpture, the designer receives both the instigation of ideas and, to some degree, of validation. Landscape architecture becomes in the process a part of the ethos of the era, and its own identity as an art is confirmed.

Perhaps the most prominent recent example of the Zeitgeist approach is the 1988 Parc de la Villette in Paris, won in competition by Bernard Tschumi. Bounded on one edge by the Périphérique (ring road), described by architectural historian Norma Evenson as the concrete moat that surrounds Paris,[26] the site was offered little by the Genius Loci, and a Didactic (see below) approach would have demanded a strong evocation of the site's history or even the reinstitution of the slaughtering that once existed on the site.[27] Instead, Tschumi used ideas of cinematic sequences and poststructural theories concerning the fragmentation of postmodern culture as sources for the park's design. The "outmoded" concept of park was supposedly dissolved by this new idea, instead producing a design that effaced the boundary between city and park and eliminated the hard line between built and green zones.

The drawings used to explain the competition design were brilliantly conceived and included an exploded axonometric view that masterfully conveyed the design concept of point, line, and surface—a visual equivalent of a sound bite. Unfortunately, parks are rarely seen from the air, and even less frequently as exploded entities. In fact, as a totality, the noncomposition recalls too closely the bland and amorphous open spaces of Paris's *grand ensembles* (housing projects) of the 1950s and 1960s. La Villette's red follies, while intriguing as investigations of architectural form, do little to energize the park's sensual appeal beyond the visual. Ultimately there is precious little of genuine, that is to say *experiential*, interest as landscape architecture on the site. Basically, the landscape comprises some lawn and some trees.[28] The ideas used to conceive the park are rich and evocative; the experience on site is limited and spatially uninteresting, however. At what point does concept end and experience begin? Is an intriguing concept sufficient to create meaning in the minds of the beholders? What of the beholder not privy to the designer's convoluted explanation? The Parc de la Villette illustrates the problems that plague borrowing parallel ideas or forms from other disciplines, and the distortion that often accompanies translation. In this particular Parisian example, what has been written about the project is far more intriguing than what one encounters on site.[29] The success or failure of such landscape designs does not ultimately derive from their intellectual origins, but whether they "work" on their own merits as places and landscapes without recourse to jargon and verbal explanations. One might also ask in the end: What is the nature of the pleasure they provide?

Like architects such as Robert Venturi and Frank Gehry, landscape architects such as Martha Schwartz also look at the *Vernacular Landscape.* This is a hip glance at the Genius of the Place, of course, but the genius is culturalized and the selections suave. The vernacular is a rich source of materials and forms; after all, it constitutes the "real" world in which we dwell. But just as the meanings of historical landscapes are affected by reframing, the Vernacular Landscape is inevitably transformed when borrowed by design professionals. And when vernacular elements reappear in High Style projects, they have semantically virtually nothing in common with their sources. They have been reframed. The vernacular environment is treated by designers as a quarry for raw materials to be reconfigured and thus transfigured. The unselfconsciousness, the appropriate sense of the makeshift and the accepted transience of vernacular building are usually lost along the way.[30] A glass gazing ball optically enlarges the confines of a small backyard garden, while serving as a sign of neighborly propriety. When it is extracted from the backyard, repeated at length, and arranged in a grid, however, only the basic reflective properties remain unaffected. Similarly, a concrete frog accompanying a cement deer and perhaps a gnome are tender companions in an intimate setting. Multiplied by the hundreds and painted gold, they are no longer the common vernacular element they once were, but fodder for High Style designers. This is not to say they possess no merit of their own, they do; but the meaning is no longer vernacular. Like fine wine, significance does not travel very well, and wine *is* different from grape juice.

The fifth approach to "constructed meaning" goes down the *Didactic* path. This is the one I have found most appealing, and one that has formed the only more or less stable leg of anything our office has tried to design. In fact, it was the observation by a friend while examining a current project that made me realize that much of what we do is a somewhat desperate search for meaning in landscape.[31] The Didactic approach dictates that forms should tell us, in fact instruct us, about the natural workings or history of the place. This is related—as all the approaches are to some degree—to the Genius Loci school, but the Didactic is usually more overt in its intentions. Not only should we consult the genius about its basis, but our resultant project should render an exegesis on what the genius told us.

Curiously, we often try to restore what has been previously destroyed. Perhaps a stream long culverted and buried is restored to its "original" state (of course, it really isn't—everything has changed around it). One of the rules formulated by Joel Garreau in *Edge City* is that one names a place for the features that have been destroyed to make room for the new development.[32] Shady Hills Estates commemorates the trees that were cut to build the houses, and the natural undulations that were flattened to make construction less challenging; and incidentally, the houses are hardly estates. But like the photo caption, the name of the development directs our reading of the place and asks us to complete that which is missing in the picture. A design didactically conceived, like the photo caption, is both informative—possibly normative—and certainly directive. The "factual" base is intended to validate the designer's work.

A Didactic landscape is supposedly an aesthetic textbook on natural, or in some cases urban, processes. Alexandre Chemetoff's sunken bamboo garden at La Villette purposefully allowed the elements of urban infrastructure to remain, reminding the visitor that this small, green respite was actually but a fragment of an urban agglomeration that to exist required massive amounts of servicing. Water mains, sewer pipes, and electrical ducts crisscross the site; the retain walls are constructed of precast concrete elements commonly used to support the walls of adjacent sites during excavation for new construction. The landscape architect did not leave these elements of infrastructure untouched, however; the scheme itself developed in relation as a give-and-take between the didactic exposure of services and its aesthetic complement in wispy green and gold foliage. Sculptors—who almost by definition are allowed to consider the aesthetic parameter in isolation—have also created places structured on the Didactic dimension. At the National Oceanographic and Atmospheric Administration in Seattle, Washington, for example, Douglas Hollis's Sound Garden (1983) captured the wind to activate an environmental organ; the vanes aligning the field of erect pipes into the gusts added a visual signal of wind direction. Here, the presence of the wind was thus given both aural and visual expression.

In these two instances, the work of landscape art addressed either natural or urban process with an assumption—which I have since come to suspect—that designs revealing these processes are both more viable and more meaningful. I don't think the answer is quite that simple. Didactic thinking provides a good point of departure for the work, but the success of the place ultimately hinges on the skill and care with which the design is made and on what it offers the visitor. Didacticism per se is not enough. (In these two instances, however, the final success of the resulting works did not depend on its Didactic aspects alone.)

And then there is the *Theme Garden*. It is curious to me how many people deride the world's Disneylands and other theme parks, and then propose Theme Gardens. A theme, in this context, constitutes a perceptually apparent idea used to fashion the garden's form. Roses, Mother Goose, the color yellow, or even electric light could all be used as themes, and I imagine that all of them have been used as such somewhere at some time. One could argue that the gamut of themes deriving from horticultural or environmental ideas or cultural borrowings are inherently more genuine than the contrived imagery of a theme park created in plaster or plastic, but they are themes nonetheless.[33]

A theme, it must be admitted, is not necessarily an argument for significance, but there is an underlying assertion of validity that accompanies any obvious concept. Even today, the landscape professional can accept a Chinese garden, for example that by Fletcher Steele at Naumkeag, or the copper tents at Frederik Magnus Piper's eighteenth-century Haga Park in Stockholm. Perhaps we use the word "charming" rather than "beautiful" to qualify them. If well done, in fact, the effect of the pavilion or cultural borrowing is far greater than its semantic theme. It can be pleasant, calming, restful, stimulating in its own right; that is, it can affect us. Which tells us something about the experiential dimensions of the garden.

The white garden at Sissinghurst is a well-known example of color used as a subject, but the themed approach is widespread in time and place. The recently opened Parc André Citroën in Paris includes "black" and "white" gardens, although in both gardens green seems to be the predominant color that meets the eye. One could argue that the restriction to a single color suggests a poverty of horticultural invention or an overly zealous pursuit of minimalism. It can also, of course, create a garden of stunning beauty, employing incredible horticultural acrobatics and subtle chromatic mixtures even with a single color range.

Gilles Clément, the landscape architect for a considerable section of the park, has also applied his idea of a "garden in movement" to one of its riverside zones. Here, a score of wild flowers and grasses has been planted with little regard as to where or to which will survive. Paths through these meadows will be determined by human movement rather than by formal design; the paths will fix the traces of occupation and use. This Darwinian approach to park design, which joins the Didactic and the Theme with instructive aesthetic consequences, addresses both the social issues brought to the fore in the 1960s and aspects of urban ecology. While these parts of the park will evolve in terms of horticultural species—and over time run the risk of looking like a vacant lot—they suggest the human presence only through a relatively few wooden seating platforms raised slightly above the ground. The idea of replicating evolution to establish an appropriate urban landscape is engaging, although the form may not be attractive at all times. But do such replications mean anything to anyone today?[34]

## III

Is it really possible to imbue a place with meaning from the outset? It would seem that history tells us yes, if the users possess sufficient experience in common. For one, significance is culturally circumscribed and, ultimately, personally determined.[35] If we examine a Chinese poem executed in ink on silk, as nonreaders of the Chinese language we are denied access to the poem's linguistic dimension. Should we be uninitiated into Chinese calligraphy, and the propriety and taste conveyed by the chosen style, the marks will have even less meaning to us. We can appreciate the work solely on its formal dimension, of course, as fluid black marks on a white ground. It is obvious, however, that possessing linguistic abilities in Chinese would enrich both our understanding and our pleasure: the two-dimensional writing on the page would acquire multiple semantic dimensions.

The same is true of gardens. The uninitiated may or may not appreciate a dry Zen garden for its formal properties alone, for the pattern of its raked sand and the composition of its rocks, but the meanings of the garden will remain communicated imperfectly at best. The absence of many of the elements that say "garden" to members of foreign cultures denies access to meaning as the mores deny access to physical entry.[36]

The Zen garden provides a valuable case study for considering the construction of meaning. Japan's centuries of cultural homogeneity fostered an attitude toward simplicity as the compression of complexity (rather than its reduction or elimination, as it has been in the West). One could say, with perhaps only a little exaggeration, that until recently a Japanese of a certain class-educational level could understand the intentions behind the making of the garden. He or she could appreciate the framing of the space, the nongeometric order within the enclosure, the quality of the rocks and their arrangement, the shaping of shrubs, the almost complete absence of brilliantly flowering species. Unless a person is initiated into Zen doctrine, however, the meaning as the embodiment of religious belief, and as possibly intended by the gardenist, would remain beyond comprehension. And since Zen reflects continually back on the self for understanding and ultimately enlightenment, there is an implicit denial of meaning within the garden itself. Instead, the garden stimulates individual contemplation; it can be seen as a vehicle for understanding the self rather than the place. The meaning of the garden is nonmeaning. In Zen belief, the place bears no meaning per se, but can perhaps evoke a call for meaning within the individual.

Allusions to worlds beyond the garden in place and time have appeared with some regularity in the polite traditions of landscape design in both East and West.[37] Replicas or recollections of Roman temples often appeared in the English landscape garden. At Katsura Rikyu in Kyoto, a small spit of water-worn stones was intended to cast the visitor's musings toward the peninsula of Ama-no-hashidate, long regarded as one of Japan's most outstanding shoreline landscapes. The shorn bamboo-covered slope at Koraku-en in today's Tokyo, on the other hand, specifically invoked the Mountain of the Chinese Immortals. Unlike the abstract Zen landscapes that were intended to summon a multitude of (ultimately personal) interpretations and associations, the aristocratic villa gardens often established intimations of legend and land. Meaning accrued from allusions to real or mythic geography outside the immediate landscape.

John Dixon Hunt has cogently argued that the world of the English landscape garden, like many garden traditions before it, was a coherent system of signs devised to be legible to both maker and visitor.[38] Here the signs were made tangible: a temple based on a Roman predecessor, a vale with mythological reference, an architectonic emblem of Englishness. References could be manifest in a landscape feature, a structure, or even a written inscription to reduce ambiguity. Although falling under the common heading of signification, they actually concern two structures of meaning, differentiated in time. The first regarded the production of meaning used at the time of the garden's creation and its effect(iveness) on the visitor. The second concerned the greater orbit of meaning that is part of the garden as institution and semiotic constellation. "Gardens, too, mean rather than are," claims this garden historian. "Their various signs are constituted of all the elements that compose them—elements of technical human intervention like terraces or the shape of flowerbeds, elements of nature like water and trees—but they are nonetheless signs, to be read by outsiders in time and space for what they tell of a certain society.[39] Hunt also states, at first seemingly in contradiction with what he has written earlier in the essay, that even the most specific of references (probably textual ones) become time worn and lose their significance: "Castle Howard and Rousham provide excellent examples of garden experience we have totally lost. We no longer see a representation of English landscape; we just see it."[40]

Any symbolic system demands education and the comprehension of both the medium and the message. One might understand, for example, that Diana was the goddess of the chase and even know of her association with the moon, but still might have absolutely no idea why her likeness stands in the garden. Were we unaware of Louis XIV's self-association with the sun, would we not believe Versailles to be a glorious homage to cloudy France's sunshine lost or to Apollo himself? We have lost the ability to read the original intensions, but we can still decipher the original garden elements on our own contemporary terms. That these two worlds of meaning mutate over time suggests that meaning is indeed dynamic and ever-changing.[41] It also suggests that the meaning with which the designer believes he or she is investing the garden may have only minimal impact in the beginning, and even less in years to come. On the other hand, the designer does have power over the artifact and its immediate effect on the sense—and its potential to mean.

Communications theory tells us that the two parties in conversation mush share a common semantic channel or there will be no communication; no meaning. Can the garden operate as such a channel, and does the designer possess the power to create a significant landscape, especially given the multitude of communication channels in today's pluralistic world? When a society is relatively homogenized, the task is far easier because the designer shares the values and belief system of the people. Folk cultures produce places that are almost immediately communicative, and communicative over long periods. Because their connections between form and intention are understood within the culture and evolve only slowly over time, it is possible for the makers, the people, and the meaning of place to remain in contact.[42]

The Woodland Cemetery outside Stockholm, designed between 1915 and 1940 by Gunnar Asplund and Sigurd Lewerentz, tapped into the religious and value systems of the Swedish Lutheran congregants. This landscape of remembrance has remained both meaningful to its parishioners and appreciated by them from the time of its realization. The triumph of the cemetery lies not only in its magnificent joining of architecture and landscape, and the modulated juncture of re-formed land with the existing pine forest, but also in its ability to conjure a sense of sanctity without relying on overt Christian iconography. Perhaps the power of this funeral landscape ultimately derives from an almost animistic feeling of pre-Christianity that addresses the forest, the land, and the heavens as a primeval setting. Perhaps the design also tapped into something basic to Swedish religion and culture. It might still be possible to create a landscape equally attuned to its time and place today, when Swedish society is far more diverse. But is would be far more difficult to devise the forms and symbols that would resonate within the contemporary Swedish population in quite the same way.[43] Not that it was ever easy; but it was easier earlier in the century. The communication channels are no longer so few, nor are the elements of the Swedish landscape so simple.

To summarize:

> Can a (landscape) designer help make a significant place? Yes.
> Can a (landscape) designer design significance into the place at the time of its realization? No, or let's say, no longer.

When the society was homogeneous and shared a common system of belief, when the symbolic system was endemic, when the makers of places operated unselfconsciously fully within the culture, it was possible.[44] But even then, meaning was enriched through habit and the passage of time. Given the fragmentation of contemporary American society, and especially with its current emphasis on difference, the concord necessary for instant meaning is, to say the least, deficient.

Since a commissioning body might include meaningfulness as part of its brief, why commission a (landscape) designer?

Of course, there are the pragmatic aspects of design that can best be addressed by those with an education, technical knowledge, and experience. One also hopes that the landscape architect possesses equal skill in understanding people and culture, as well as horticulture and form. Creating significant landscapes remains a quest of the profession, as well it should. But calling attention to Celtic inscriptions, solar alignments, the spirit of the place, the Zeitgeist, the vernacular landscape, or even a didactic lesson in the derivation of form does not create meaning. Providing symbols is not the same as creating meaningful places, although it may be one point along the path. To my mind significance lies with the beholder and not alone in the place. Meaning accrues over time; like respect, it is earned, not granted. While the designer yearns to establish a landscape that will acquire significance, it is not possible to use pat symbols alone as a means to transmute syntax into semantics, that is, tectonics into meaning.[45]

Familiarity and affect are not quite the same as significance, although they can serve as vehicles for its creation. To recall the site of one's first camping trip, or the park where the football championship was won, or even the flowers of one's family home ground establish associations among place, act, and form that cohere in landscape meaning. If these places were designed by landscape architects, all well and good. Meaning condenses at the intersection of people and place, and not alone in the form the designer's idea takes.

The design itself constitutes a filter that creates the difference between what the designer intends and what the visitor experiences. This is the difference between the intended perception and the perceived intention. Differences in culture, in education, in life experience, in our experience of nature will all modify our perception of the work of landscape architecture. While this transaction between people and place is never completely symmetrical, I do believe that we can circumscribe the range of possible reactions to a designed place. We cannot make that place mean, but we can, I hope, instigate reactions to the place that will fall within the desired confines of happiness, gloom, joy, contemplation, or delight. This range of possible reactions, while tempered by cultural norms and personal experience, is still physiologically dependent on the human body. The limits of thermal comfort, the olfactory faculty, the capability to perceive chroma and natural process, and our basic size are characteristics shared by virtually every human inhabitant of the planet. Could we not start with these physical senses rather than with the encultured mind? Could we not make the place pleasurable?

## IV

In historical garden literature, a considerable amount of text describes the pleasure of the garden, that is, its comfort, its delight, its sense of well-being. The pleasures of the imperial palace garden backdrop the rather limited action and plot development in the twelfth-century *Tale of Genji*. Pleasure and its appreciation were so much a part of gardens in the past that we can well wonder why landscape architects today seek significance rather than pleasure. Could it be that pleasure is trite, hedonistic, and ephemeral, while meaning is deep and long-lasting? Or perhaps pleasure seems to be too solitary an enterprise, while meaning is taken as collective embodiment of values? Or is it that meaning is the dimension that distinguishes landscape architecture from mere "gardening"?

Roland Barthes argued that to read is to seek the pleasure of the text. He tells us that, to provide pleasure, "The text must prove to me *that it desires me*" (italics in the original).[46] Knowledge, a magnificent use of language, plot, linguistic constructions all contribute to the ultimate goal: the pleasure of reading. Is it not possible to believe that pleasure is one of the necessary entry points to significance (certainly, horror would be another as the sublime school once believed, but our quotidian world seems to provide enough of that)?

It seems curious to me that, in most professional design publications, the aspect of pleasure is almost completely missing from the discourse, while it thrives in popular gardening magazines and in seed catalogs. This is not to say that pursuit of pleasure is not a part of professional work; one assumes that park design, for example, is to a large degree predicated upon the contented use of its grounds. But a discussion of pleasure is rarely a part of trade and academic writing. Professional publications often talk of the site, the client,

the plant materials, perhaps the particular ecological system or cleverness on the designer's part in solving a particularly thorny drainage problem. More recently, some discussion of the alignment of the garden's axis to the summer solstice or its relation to some geomantic construction might also come into play. The lay publications, in contrast, discuss the delight of the garden and that making one is so easy—like summer cooking recipes—you can do it in, or to, your own backyard. Color and fragrance and delight are givens; and it is the perfect place for a barbecue. Magazines such as *Sunset* have expanded the world of the house and the garden to the world of lifestyle.

Today might be a good time to once more examine the garden in relation to the senses, while putting conscious mental rationalizations on the back burner—to create a mixed metaphor. Although the world's peoples vary greatly in terms of linguistic and cultural matrices, we do share roughly similar human senses, although admittedly these can be honed or dimmed by culture. Is there not a link between the senses and significance, or is meaning necessarily restricted to the rational faculties. Barthes would argue that there is a connection. "What is significance?" he writes; "it is meaning, *insofar as it is sensually produced*" (italics in the original).[47]

When an interlocutor once accused Charles Eames of designing furniture only for himself, the designer openly admitted that he did. But he did not design for what was idiosyncratic to himself alone, but for a self indicative of the greater population of chair users. Why not try to reinject the same sense of pleasing the individual or self into the landscape design? I do not talk here of Gaia and other forms of touchy-feely expression that constitute yet another form of Neoarchaicism—since telephone lines have superseded ley lines—but of trying to understand at what level our experience can be shared by others. Not as an abstract symbolic system referring back to Celtic times, but places—and ideas—that acknowledge our time, our sensitivities, and our people. This takes more than a pseudosignificant landscape loaded with the designer's explanatory voice-over, or captions built into the landscape itself. It would seem that a designer could create a landscape of pleasure that in itself would become significant. "Art should not simply speak to the mind *through* the senses," wrote Goethe, "it must also satisfy the senses themselves."[48]

There are various arguments for a concern for pleasure in garden design.[49] For one—at running the risk of sounding too Californian—pleasure can be a valuable pursuit in itself, as valid as the pursuit of meaning. Even Vitruvius constructed his triad of desirable architectural qualities on commodity, firmness, and delight.[50] In the past, sensory pleasures have served to condition meaning. Consider the expression of taste in the selection and arrangement of cut flowers in Japan or the ecstasy of religious experience that underwrote so much Counter-Reformation art and architecture. Sensory experience *moved* the viewer, causing him or her to reflect upon religious meaning as well as one's position in the universe—powerful stuff indeed. Third, despite the influence of culture, individual physiological characteristics, and even transitory psychological states, pleasure is still more predictable than meaning. As in the past, and despite the collapse of collective social norms, pleasure may provide a more defined path toward meaning than the erudite approaches to landscape design discussed earlier in this essay.

Significance, I believe, is not a designer's construct that benignly accompanies the completion of construction. It is not the product of the maker, but is, instead, created by the receivers. Like a patina, significance is acquired only with time. And like a patina, it emerges only if the conditions are right.

# PLACE RECLAMATION (1993)

EDWARD RELPH

## THE INSTANT ENVIRONMENT MACHINE

"The perfection of Art in an American's eyes," wrote James Fergusson in 1862, "would be attained by the invention of a self-acting machine which should produce plans of cities and designs for Gothic churches or Classic municipal buildings at so much per foot super, and so save all further trouble and thought."[1] It took most of the century to achieve Fergusson's invention, and the effort was as much European as American. But the twentieth century has created just such a self-acting machine, which can level places and mix histories in any way desired. Capable now of making or destroying environments of almost any type or scale, from sensory deprivation chambers to entire cities, modern builders have at their disposal an "instant environment machine."

This machine is big but subtle. It is, in Lewis Mumford's term, a mega-machine and comprised of the interacting components of ideologies, economic linkages, institutions and corporations, methodologies for planning and design, huge organizations and communications systems, and a veritable panoply of technologies. It is fueled by money and lubricated by the personal gratifications that come with increasing levels of comfort and leisure. It is steered by an unswerving conviction in growth and progress. Places, landscapes, buildings, and cities seem largely incidental to its purpose; new or old, distinctive or ordinary, they are treated like other economic resources. They are commodities to be exploited, managed, preserved, or otherwise manipulated in whatever ways promote the self-maintenance and profitability of the machine. . . .

## STYLES OF PLACE RECLAMATION

From the perspective of the instant environment machine, places are not significantly important. Yet a concern with place and sense of place has become an important theme in several different professions and academic disciplines since the early 1970s. Place has also become a frequent focus in popular culture, as is apparent from articles in magazines like *Esquire* and *Harper's*. This emergent concern can be understood in at least three ways.

From one perspective, the interest in place is a desperate rearguard action first mounted as the full force of modernism became apparent in the late 1960s and early 1970s. In this case, the interest in place is a form of romanticism and nostalgia—a reaction against the decay of personal and group identity. Its effects include the designation of historically significant buildings and districts, presumably on the principle that in the face of onslaught one saves what one can. While all these efforts are valuable, they look backward and come to terms with the environment machine only in a limited way. This approach to place museumizes the best fragments of *genius loci*. The results are often pleasant, informative and exquisitely restored, but they do nothing to challenge the placeless processes of modern development methods.

In a second, more compliant sense, the recent concern with place has been an attempt to improve the products of the environment machine by making pleasant, arresting spaces, like the Barnyard, instead of the dreary angular ones that were often built in the 1950s and 1960s. The principle here appears to be that if we have to live with a monstrous machine, we might as well decorate it to look attractive. One might question whether this approach constitutes place making at all, or whether it is some form of subtle co-option by the agencies of the environment machine. Such "placey" environments can be the product of intensive technical and behavioral research used to manipulate a supposed sense of place, and in such cases the chief purpose seems to be to persuade a docile population to spend money and not to worry about environmental dilution.

A third, more radical concern with place has attempted to come to an understanding of its existential importance and has been critical of the instant environment machine. The aim has been to reclaim the specificity and originality of places by thinking carefully about their nature and the ways in which it might be possible to make new types of places without simply copying outdated approaches. Perhaps this radical concern has been based partly in the conviction that a heightened sense of place is an essential aspect of any attempt to redress the enormous injustices and dangers to survival that threaten us all. This approach attempts to break free from ideology and technical abstraction and to contact people, things, and landscapes directly. This approach has led to a growing awareness that places do matter to people, and that they need to be reclaimed as integral parts of human environments.

## PLACE RECLAMATION AND PLACE MAKING

Place reclamation is not a simple task. The environment machine, with the full weight of development corporations and government agencies behind it, has acquired a powerful momentum so that it is not easy even to deflect, let alone stop or reverse. A direct confrontation is likely to be futile. And more sophisticated design techniques make about as much sense as prescribing better quality wines as a cure for alcoholism. Kevin Lynch,[2] Christopher Alexander,[3] and others have recognized these difficulties in dealing with modern environments, and they have found it necessary to make proposals for place making and environmental design that owe very little to conventional approaches. Within most of these proposals lies a straightforward idea that is central to all issues of place and place making—one that offers the possibility for the emergence of *genius loci* and that challenges the environment machine without necessarily being co-opted by it. This idea is simply that *places have to be made largely through the involvement and commitment of the people who live and work in them; places have to be made from the inside out. . . .*

## CONCLUSION

*Genius loci* cannot be designed to order. It has to evolve, to be allowed to happen, to grow and change from the direct efforts of those who live and work in places and care about them. Here, the technical methods employed in corporatization and the electronic media are of no value. No matter how sophisticated technical knowledge may be, the understanding of others' lives and problems will always be partial. Just as outsiders cannot feel their pain, so they cannot experience their sense of place. I believe, therefore, that it is impossible to make complete places in which other people can live. And, in a world dominated by international economic processes and global telecommunications, there can be no return to an environment of integrated and distinctive places.

Nevertheless there is an important role for architects, landscape architects, planners, and social scientists to play in reclaiming and making places. Their task is, first, to develop a sensitivity to the attributes of places and then to find ways of initiating and directing locally committed developments. These ways must simultaneously acknowledge the global character of almost everything in modern life. In short, the task is to find some means of balancing local considerations with broader social and ecological concerns. How this is done will surely vary enormously from situation to situation, but it always has to be based on the recognition that places are the contexts of human life and in some manner are themselves alive, for they grow, change, and decline with the individuals and groups who maintain or ignore them. Trying to design or reclaim places is, therefore, rather like trying to make or modify life itself. In this effort, it is wisest to adopt the gentle and patient manner of an environmental midwife, while rejecting utterly the machine-driven arrogance of some environmental equivalent to a genetic engineer. By such gentle means places might flourish again, but also the world might become less threatened.

# THREE DIMENSIONS OF MEANING (1994)

## ROBERT THAYER

### THREE DIMENSIONS

It is possible to construct a three-dimensional framework for examining the meanings of landscape—particularly that which has been influenced by technology and utilitarian necessity—and its impact on human affect or emotional response. We respond to landscapes as forms and patterns of light and dark distinguishable from background; as the result of their context for human functions and actions; and as symbols of particular social or personal value. Let us assume a three-dimensional model where each dimension can be displayed as perpendicular to the other two dimensions. The first row will be called the *perceptual* dimension, where technological manifestations in the landscape are categorized according to their degree of *perceivability* and *conspicuousness* in the landscape as differentiated from the so-called "natural" background. The second dimension consists of the major, familiar *functional* associates or groups of technologies the typical American might recognize in the landscape. Finally, the third dimension organizes technologies in terms of their *symbolic* implications with respect to the land.

A simple experience in the author's life may help to illustrate the three basic meaning dimensions of any technological landscape feature. While on a backpack trip twenty years ago across a section of the Continental Divide in the Colorado Rockies, my friend and I paused for a breather part way up the trail. About one mile away we could see the saddle of land between two peaks—a pass across the divide which would take us down to our lakeside destination for that evening. There in the distance, but in plain site [*sic*], were several patches of a very shiny material against the rocky background. We immediately entered into a debate, my friend insisting that these surfaces were of natural origins—perhaps a patch of ice or snow, and I asserting they were manmade. The debate spawned a bet for a bottle of wine. Traveling another two hundred yards, we both concluded that I had won the bet. Although we were not yet near enough to make out many details, the shiny patches were definitely metallic in origin and did not seem to be arranged in a pattern we recognized as part of the normal mountain context. (At this point, we had experienced the *perceptual* level of this technological landscape intrusion.) Only when we had approached within several hundred feet of the metallic surfaces did we recognize them as the wreckage of a light airplane (we had then experienced the *functional* level). Upon arriving at the scene, we were relieved to discover that the wreckage was at least several weeks old, and the pilot and any similarly unlucky passengers or their bodies had long since been evacuated. We lingered at the wreckage site for some time, excited but saddened, pondering the unfortunate accident. Picking up the pilot's headphones, my companion examined them, put them on his head, and after a serious and introspective pause, speculated about the possibility of living humans communicating with the dead. Hence my companion and I had successively experienced three basic significant levels of human intrusion on the landscape. Attracted initially to a visual stimulus set off from its context, we first perceived the stimulus as "technological" and human-made without knowing its function. Later, we recognized the function, and finally, made some symbolic connections.

My purpose in developing this framework is to suggest that each dimension contributes, both individually and perhaps synergistically, to a participant's *affective response* to a particular utilitarian or technological landscape, and that by examining each dimension separately and more closely, we can learn much about how we react to the technologically influenced landscapes that form the context of our daily American existence. In the case of our encounter with the airplane wreckage in the Rockies, my companion and I had approached in a linear fashion, and our experience of each dimension was therefore sequential. Had we stumbled upon the wreckage suddenly, however, we might have experienced all levels simultaneously. Whether the experience of complex levels of landscape meaning is linear (i.e., information processing) or simultaneous (e.g., Gestalt) and whether the perceptual, functional, and symbolic levels act independently one of another or in an interactive, interdependent manner is unclear. However, I am convinced that humans evaluate the three meaning dimensions according to inner "positive—-negative" scales or operative procedures. In short, each meaning dimension or significance level contributes something to overall affective or emotional response, be it negative or positive. Our response to utilitarian, technologically influenced landscape is partly dependent on characteristics of each dimension, and each dimension can be broken down into more discrete categories which further influence affective response. . . .

## Topophilia, Technophilia, and Technophobia

Most landscapes, examined at any scale, embody elements of all three social attitudes of topophilia, technophilia, and technophobia. At the Marine World/Africa USA theme park in Vallejo, California, stylized versions of natural animal habitats coexist with water-skiing demonstration lagoons. Here topophilia is represented in the landscape plantings and animal displays, technophilia in the lighting effects and waterski boats, and technophobia in the concealment of the irrigation system, water pumps and filters, and air conditioning units, and the visual screening of the parking lots. Characterizing the proportional mixture of these three attitudes or forces for any landscape can be facilitated by the use of a triangle, with topophilia at the top, technophilia at the lower left corner, and technopho-

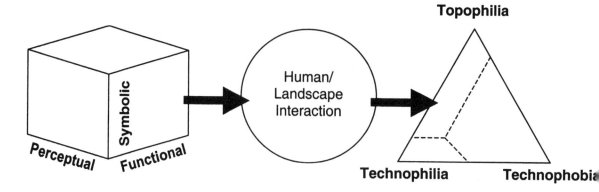

### "Meaning" Dimensions of Technological Landscapes

Through repeated experience with many landscapes, participant mentally constructs a cognitive framework of subjective meanings based on perceptual, functional, and symbolic dimensions.

### Emotions/Attitudes toward a Specific Landscape

Participant responds to a specific landscape as if it were an "objective" stimulus, placing it in a relative "field" of various proportions of topophilia, technophilia, and technophobia.

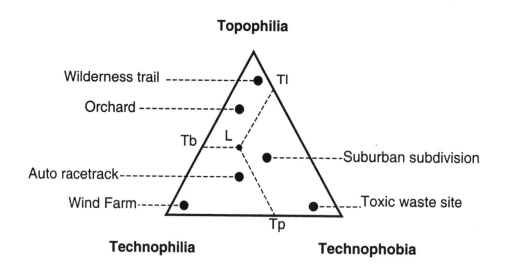

For any landscape L, L(Tp) = % Topophilia,

L(Tl) = % Technophilia, and L(Tb) = % Technophobia

Figure 9. Topophilia, Technophilia, Technophobia: three attitudes toward technology and landscape (after Robert Thayer).

Figure 10. Wind farm, Altamont Pass, California: making technology visible (Robert Thayer).

bia at the lower right corner. Any landscape in question can be "located" on a triangle based upon the proportion of each of the three generalized attitudes embodied in the landscape.

This model is hypothetical and not meant to be mathematically precise, for in any given landscape, the symbolic meaning is often arguable and the causative forces hard to determine. However, the triangular framework allows some comparisons between landscapes and facilitates the "framing" of the main body of landscape meaning by extreme examples near the corners of the triangle. For instance, a toxic waste repository can be considered an almost entirely technophobic landscape, while a wilderness trail is nearly completely topophilic. An automobile drag strip exemplifies a near-complete technophilic landscape. A housing subdivision is a blend of all three. Subdivisions are frequently given topophilic names of the natural or pastoral features in the landscape (e.g., "Quail Ridge," "Green Meadows," "Arlington Farms") they have replaced. Although subdivisions are structured for easy automobile access, automotive themes are visually downplayed, and technological features like TV aerials, utility meters, and power lines are often screened, disguised, or buried.

A wind energy power plant, on the other hand, is a highly technophilic landscape. Telephoto views of modern wind turbines have been used in marketing as positive symbols of quiet power to sell automobiles (British Honda Motor Company) and Christian music compact discs (Petra). However, some people find modern wind farms to be an objectionable visual (i.e., technophobic) assault on romantic pastoral conditions.

A fruit orchard such as any found in the Central Valley of California represents a similar combination of topophilia and technophilia. Its material manifestations (i.e., trees) are less threatening to many people than the mechanical appearance of modern wind turbines. However, orchards are nearly as mechanized as wind farms; the strict geometric grid patterns of the fruiting trees is an unmistakable sign of human manipulation, and planting, irrigating, spraying, and harvesting of orchards are increasingly done using machines and chemicals. In spite of this, most people would attribute a sense of "natural" order, harmony, bounty, and beauty in an orchard landscape that combines both topophilia and technophilia.

There are, no doubt, other variables on other dimensions which could have been included in this framework. A major point, however, is that *some proportion of the three attitudes or social forces of topophilia, technophilia, and technophobia are embodied in simultaneous, tensile relationship to one another in nearly every landscape.*

## SYSTEMS, SIGNS, AND SENSIBILITIES (1987)

### CATHERINE HOWETT

A critique of certain fundamental preconceptions of the picturesque canon will be implied in the observations that follow, which point toward potential sources in three separate disciplines from which we might garner ideas and insights—into ourselves, our lives, the world we make and the world that nature presents to us—needed for a new and more appropriate landscape aesthetic. These three critical and theoretical currents, each of which is already at the center of research, experiment, and argument within the profession, are: (1) the new ecology, which over the last two decades has fundamentally recast our vision of the natural world and the human community's place within its systems; (2) semiotics, which in proposing analogies between language and architecture has forced a fresh understanding of the expressive meanings of built form and the devices of architectural communication—sign systems as critical to the designer of landscapes as natural systems; and finally, (3) environmental psychology, including as well the work of such geographers as Yi-Fu Tuan who speculate on the nature of place experience and the profound conscious and preconscious bonds that make us respond in specific ways to various environments.

Curiously, the very notion of aesthetic values has become suspect in the view of many within each of these three domains. For the ecologist, aesthetic concerns are frequently identified with high-art traditions that are perceived as having been ruthlessly insensitive to the effects of certain kinds of development upon vulnerable natural systems. Architectural theorists have deplored the elitist cast of judgments based on uncritically accepted, inherited aesthetic values—hence the studied embrace, in recent years, of vernacular buildings and landscapes and "pop art" iconography. Environmental psychologists, too, see aesthetic evaluations as too often favoring somewhat arbitrary visual criteria at the expense of other, less obvious but ultimately more important, experiential ones. This shared suspicion works against the possibility of developing mutually satisfactory aesthetic norms that might reflect a cross-fertilization of values important to all three of these constituencies.

This should not discourage us, however. Landscape architecture is by its very nature interdisciplinary, combining science and art, as we are fond of saying. It is up to us to forge an intellectual synthesis that can act as the foundation for an aesthetic canon capable of generating new forms, new landscape styles. Olmsted's strength, as we have seen, had as much to do with his energetic involvement in the intellectual, political, and social discourse of his day as it did with his literary and artistic genius. Albert Fein has suggested, in fact, that Olmsted's work is best understood as the expression of a social and institutional ideal that was the highest achievement of nineteenth-century America, as central to its cultural identity as was the Acropolis to Athens or the cathedral to medieval France.[1] Our profession's historic isolation, since Olmsted, from the central philosophical, ideological, literary, and artistic debates of our own time must finally be overcome if a new generation of landscape architects is to be capable of imagining and creating the landscape forms that would similarly express the highest values and aspirations of American culture on the eve of the third millennium.

Until that dialogue has been engaged, however, it is absurd to ask what, exactly, these new landscape forms will look like, or how they will operate. Who can precisely describe the physical form of tomorrow's art? These forms will emerge from the play of mind and spirit, from risk-taking experiment and painstaking work. Our task right now is to lay the groundwork, seeking to discover what characteristics such a new art ought to have.

Surely these new forms must reflect the awakening of our generation to ecological consciousness, and the growing popular understanding of the degree to which the natural world is, in Aldo Leopold's words, "interlocked in one humming community of co-operations and competitions, one biota."[2] Suppose we acknowledge this ecological awareness as the ground of values to which we want our society to be dedicated—a kind of "post-humanist" environmental consciousness defined by Del Janik as one that "values all living things and the inorganic environment on which they depend, recognizing that all life and the conditions that sustain life are interrelated. It asserts that man can be, if he abandons his anthropometric assumptions, a contributor to, rather than the destroyer of, the pattern of nature."[3] The implications of this revaluation within the discipline of landscape architecture should be far-reaching. Baird Callicott, in an essay on what he termed the "land aesthetic" implicit in Leopold's writing, expressed regret that artists (he was speaking of painters) are not able, because of their medium, to awaken the public to a more holistic appreciation of the natural world; because it is not represented and interpreted through art, that more evolutionary-ecological aesthetic of nature remains unappreciated by the average person.[4] It is the art of landscape architecture, obviously, that ought to take up this challenge. Ian McHarg's now classic *Design with Nature* (1969) revolutionized the way that we approach urban and regional planning, proposing a methodology marked by greater responsiveness to the environmental contexts in which human activity acts as a dynamic shaping force for good or ill. But we are still worlds away from achieving the widespread and consistent application and interpretation of ecological principles in the designed landscape that Callicott hints at. We have for the most part been guilty of turning our backs on this ethically compelling opportunity, and our addiction to the picturesque aesthetic is principally to blame.

Nan Fairbrother called this dominant model the "park-and-garden style" and tried to explain to the readers of *New Lives, New Landscapes,* how vegetation in a designed landscape differs from the way plants grow naturally. Speaking of the English countryside, she pointed out that:

> In natural growth the layers of the vegetation intermingle, with tall herbs growing through low shrubs and shrubs merging with trees, with no definition and with no gaps between them[.]

Simply therefore to separate vegetation into grass, shrubs and trees immediately creates an unnatural effect[.] It is also unnatural if we omit a layer, as with trees in grass[;] or if we change the order of the layers, as by growing trees and shrubs with grass between them[.] Whatever the actual plants these common modifications of natural growth produce a garden effect.[5]

She went on to recommend a more natural style of planting in "country areas"—one that took natural competition into account, depended on indigenous plant communities, and reflected the way plants grow in nature:

The growth of 20 square yards . . . of natural woodland, for instance, might start as 200 seedlings, which as they grow and the weak are progressively crowded out are reduced in the end to a single tree—the fittest of 200. When we on the other hand want a tree on such an area we transplant a single part-grown specimen to grow exposed in unnatural isolation—no question of choice by competition, nor survival of the fittest plant for the situation, nor of the close shelter natural to young trees.[6]

Fairbrother's recommendations for more natural planting composition in rural areas offer a model that emphasizes process over time and authentic patterns of growth as an alternative to an artificial appearance of closure, of static and idealized perfection.

There is no reason why this more ecologically based approach should not be used in urban areas as well. And indeed there have been encouraging signs, within the last few years, of a growing interest in planting design and vegetation management approaches that take their inspiration from natural associations and processes. Starting in 1982, the British journal *Landscape Design* published a series of essays under the title "New Directions: Ecological Approaches"[7] that surveyed recent examples of alternative, "natural" landscapes, including significant numbers of fairly large-scale projects in Sweden and the Netherlands. One author, O. D. Manning, ventured a definition of ecological design as "an approach which seeks to substitute for the restricted, artificial and expensive creations of conventional design, a looser and apparently more natural landscape, marked by species-diversity, structural complexity and freedom of growth, and achieved above all by the use of indigenous vegetation sensitively managed in order to exploit natural growth processes (especially successional) and the natural potential of the site."[8] Darrel Morrison's early work in replicating and restoring Midwestern prairie landscapes represents the most significant American expression of this new enthusiasm, and has helped to popularize in this country the idea of using native plant communities in what would normally be considered "ornamental" planting situations. Morrison's example represents the best possible thrust for this effort, because he begins by justifying the planting on ecological grounds, a lesson first patiently imparted to clients and then absorbed slowly, by observation over time, by the general public.[9]

Too often, however, advocates of this new direction defend it by invoking values borrowed from more orthodox stylistic traditions, and become preoccupied with management devices meant to overcome what one hostile critic has described as "the monotony so often seen in these ecological landscapes."[10] But when such natural plantings periodically—perhaps seasonally—take on an appearance that challenges conventional notions of the beautiful or scenic, this transformation ought not to be seen as a disadvantage for which their picturesque beauty at other phases of growth offers compensation. From the point of view of the argument being developed in this essay, the time has come to see this characteristic as a positive asset of such plantings, because it makes more present to our awareness the desiccation, death, and decay that are part of a natural cycle. Perhaps the best illustration of an actual landscape that has prophetically rejected picturesque values in favor of an emblematic ecological integrity is the work of an artist, Alan Sonfist, and is part of his *Time Landscape* series, begun in 1965. Sonfist took an 8,000 square-foot plot of ground in the heart of densely developed urban blocks in downtown New York City and sought to reintroduce the makeup of the original woodland of lower Manhattan Island. Lucy Lippard described the project in this way:

> It is an image of wild pre-Colonial land in the midst of a colonized and exploited human site. I live near it, and can vouch that it's not one of those unreal projects that has forgotten death. In winter the *Time Landscape* is a tangle of brush, its beauty ravaged and hidden. In spring you watch it awakening, and in summer it's green and lush—though in some ways less interesting, more conventionally parklike.[11]

For another work in the series, in the South Bronx, Sonfist did a similar kind of planting and then painted a realistic mural on a building wall adjacent to the site that showed how the place would look after twenty years, when the trees had matured.

It may seem at first as if the advocacy of more ecologically based landscape design will demand the sacrifice of cherished and legitimate values, the simple pleasure taken in creating or experiencing compositions that please the eye. But what is being called for is an expansion, not a diminishment, of sensibility. We must come to see that we are trapped not just in a tyranny of the visual imposed by an inherited picturesque aesthetic, but that even the range of possibilities for visual stimulation and pleasure has been needlessly narrowed. And we have deprived our other senses and, indeed, our own minds and souls, of a potentially richer and more profound delight. Baird Callicott has made the point that just as we can develop the capacity to enjoy dissonance in music or "the clash of color and distortion of eidetic form in painting," we can come to appreciate qualities in a landscape that initially confound our preconceptions of what is pleasing.[12]

A cognitive element must come into play, however; it is our understanding of what is at work that will enhance our pleasure in the denser, more complex images that an ecologically grounded aesthetic will promote. To foster this deepened understanding, those of us who live in cites might begin by reading Anne Whiston Spirn's comprehensive study *The Granite Garden: Urban Nature and Human Design* (1984), a work that vividly conveys the awesome scale of our habitual indifference to critical ecological processes in the design of urban environments. Nurturing positive aesthetic responses to more natural kinds of planting may suggest a wholesome reorientation of our awareness, but much more far-reaching and radical departures from familiar solutions are demanded by the holistic vision that ecological science reveals to us. The domain of aesthetics must come to be seen as coextensive with the ecosphere,[13] rather than narrowed to its traditional applications in art criticism, so that aesthetic values may no longer be isolated from ecological ones. Thus every work of landscape architecture, whatever its scale, ought first of all to be responsive to the whole range of interactive systems—soils and geology, climate and hydrology, vegetation and wildlife, and the human community—that come into play on a given site and will be affected by its design. In the measure that the forms of the designed landscape artfully express and celebrate that responsiveness, their beauty will be discovered.

The important consideration of the way in which our perceptual faculties must be expanded and our understanding deepened by increased knowledge of ecological processes is related to the next area in which we hope to find the seed-ideas of a new landscape aesthetic—the realm of signs and symbols, semiotics. Within the limits of this essay I can only hope to suggest the critical relevancy of this field of philosophical, linguistic, and literary analysis to the formation of a new aesthetic for landscape architecture. *Signs, Symbols, and Architecture,* edited by Charles Jencks, Geoffrey Broadbent, and Richard Bunt (1980), is a valuable study of some of the ways in which theory and principles borrowed from semiotics can be applied to the world of built form. Basically, scholars and critics pursuing this mode of analysis argue that architecture can communicate visual and conceptual messages according to the way a vocabulary of meaningful formal signs is ordered, much as a spoken or written language makes sense to us because it follows rules of syntax and grammar in the arrangement of words whose meaning we know. Semiotics provides a structural and analytic framework for a reality that is familiar to all of us, once intellectual and affective responses that are automatic and preconscious are called to our attention. For example, when Marx suggests that part of the attraction that suburban life exercises for many of us may have to do with an unconscious nostalgia for a simpler way of life identified with rural America and opposed to our ideas about city life, he is implying that the suburban landscape communicates to us, that its winding roads and tree-dappled lawns say "country," say "retreat from the city," and say it deliberately. If a developer were to put up a steel and glass tower in the middle of a suburban neighborhood, it would "read" all wrong to us, and we would object to its presence in that context. Similarly, Sonfist's *Time Landscape* intends to communicate a message; the artist has told us that he wants to make the city-dwellers who see his wooded landscape aware of a past environment that time has erased but history has not. It is part of their own history, suddenly made real and present to them in the work.

A better understanding of the sign-systems available to us will contribute to a revitalized, freshened imagery in the landscapes we design. We do not, after all, want to express a more uncompromising commitment to the clear demonstration of ecological processes in even the most routine landscapes we design, by making every one of them into a fragment of wild nature. I see no reason, however, not to propose that at this juncture in our history every landscape we design ought to be in some measure an *icon* of the natural world as we have come to understand it—an ecological sign, or cluster of signs. Jencks uses the term "univalent" to describe the architecture "created around one (or a few) simplified values,"[14] the expressive possibilities of which have been severely reduced and impoverished. When landscape architects rely upon conventional compositional devices and use forms and materials in predictable ways to achieve nothing more than a pleasant or tasteful scenic effect, we are perpetuating a univalent, hackneyed design tradition. We earned the scorn of Robert Smithson, who castigated contemporary landscapes that summon up "memory traces of tranquil gardens as 'ideal nature'—jejune Edens that suggest an ideal of banal 'quality'—[as they] persist in popular magazines like *House Beautiful* and *Better Homes and Gardens*. A kind of watered down Victorianism. . . ."[15] I might add that the cure for the rut we are in is not to begin decorating our landscapes with icons borrowed from a postmodernist architectural vocabulary; a proliferation of latter-day "eyecatchers" and follies will mire us more deeply in picturesque values, not liberate us from them. The real solution will demand profound changes and much more difficult work, both intellectual and imaginative.

We will need to create landscape forms that express a multivalent symbolism of the sort that Joseph Grange has recently described:

> When a designer looks at an environment, three principles must be foremost in his mind. First, things are *meanings*, not material objects. Second, these meanings are nodal points of expression that open out into a field of relationships. Third, the goal of environmental design is to knot together these concentrations of meaning so that the participant-dweller can experience the radical unity that binds up these different qualities.[16]

Grange recognizes, moreover, the centrality of our society's attitude toward human death to this potential matrix of meaning. At the present time, he says, we are surrounded by a landscape "littered with the bloated corpses of desire. Everywhere one looks, the objects of failed desire obstruct our view: Shopping malls, parked cars, discarded furniture, and obsolete appliances—to name but a few elements of our *de trop* culture."[17] He believes, following Ernest Becker, that a rejection of the idea of death is deeply ingrained in our culture[18] and separates us from nature, whose lesson is one of limited and incomplete parts, belonging to a process that evolves over time—a "luminous" wholeness.

It is true that in the desacralized, secular world in which we live, the ancient stories of the race and its ritual and dance no longer serve to illuminate our place within the cosmic order, giving meaning to daylight and darkness, seedtime and harvest, and the struggles of heroes, saints, and ordinary men and women. The landscapes we design and manage are most often meant to obliterate any real or symbolic suggestion of disorder, decay, or death, any hint of risk, vulnerability, or of mysteries beyond our understanding. In the nineteenth century, the rural cemetery emerged as a landscape form that frequently gave eloquent expression to that society's preoccupation with the mystery and pain of human mortality. In our own day, the debate over the Vietnam Veterans Memorial in Washington, D.C., affords a rare and splendid example of a work so full of visual and experiential meaning that it created a storm of controversy. The truth that we sense in this work is not factual, not quantifiable, not translatable into language, least of all the triumphalist slogans to which a nation's experience of war is often reduced. The power of this elegantly simple wall incised in the earth, bearing the individual names of so many thousands of the fallen, has to do with the complexity of its message, the ambiguity of its form, virtues in the designed environment to which Amos Rapoport and Robert Kantor have called to our attention:

> The problem with much contemporary architecture and urban design is that it has been simplified and cleaned up to such an extent that all it has to say is revealed at a glance. A range of meanings and possibilities has been eliminated. This loss leads to a loss of interest—there is nothing to divert or to hold one as a result of lowered rates of perceptual inputs. We may visualize a range of perceptual input from sensory deprivation (monotony) to sensory saturation (chaos). In the case of the former, there is not enough to observe, to select, to organize; there is an excess of order. In the latter, there is too much to observe, there is no relation between the elements, so that one is overwhelmed by multiplicity.
>
> In between, there is an optimal perceptual rate (an "ideal") which enables one to explore, to unfold gradually, to see, to give meaning to the environment. One needs to roam back and forth—either physically or with one's eye and mind—not taking it all in at a glance. If there

is no ambiguity, the eye is attracted only once and interest is lost. If all is designed and settled, there is no opportunity to bring one's own values to the forms . . .[19]

This is another formulation of Jenck's "multivalency"—or, for that matter, Robert Venturi's "complexity and contradiction."[20] Maya Ying Lin's design for the Vietnam Memorial possessed these qualities in sufficient measure to arouse critics of the work, who finally succeeded in their demand to have a second memorial erected nearby on the same site, a predictably univalent figural sculpture of three GIs by Frederick Hart.

Another work of contemporary landscape architecture that probed richer layers of meaning by seizing upon antipicturesque visual metaphors was Richard Haag's Gas Works Park in Seattle, Washington, begun in 1972. Here, too, the designer called down upon himself the wrath of politicians, journalists, and other members of the community who were outraged by his intention to retain as the central feature of a new urban park the hulking ruins of an early twentieth-century industrial complex that occupied the site. Haag's plan forced people to consider not just the degree of positive visual and spatial interest possessed by this relic of an outdated technology, but what its meanings might be for the community it had served for fifty years. For one thing, the lakefront site had been severely polluted by the plant's operations, so that inevitably the labyrinth of rusting pipes, towers, and other remaining structures must have seemed haunted by the shadow of harm done to earth, air, and water. The aim of the design was to redeem this history by recycling the site as a playful place, a *sign* of wholesome life and health salvaged, literally, from an industrial wasteland.[21] Once implemented, the project enjoyed a spectacular critical success, winning numerous awards, including the 1981 President's Award of Excellence in Land and Water Reclamation and Conservation of the American Society of Landscape Architects. Ironically, the park had to be closed to the public for a period of time, three years later, when it was discovered that poisonous materials remaining in the soil posed a threat to human health. The potency of Gas Works Park as a symbolic landscape for our own time has not been diminished by this tragic turn of events; more than ever, the park speaks to us now of the fragility of the natural systems upon which our life depends. It serves as a *memento mori* for the city of Seattle; would that every American city had the same message inscribed in its skyline.

To speak of the ways in which landscapes can communicate values shared by our culture, meanings whose discovery is part of our aesthetic response to the places we inhabit or encounter, brings us quite naturally to the third subject area that can help us to frame a new landscape aesthetic, the world of environmental psychology. Scholars in may disciplines, but especially philosophy, psychology, and cultural geography, have in recent years contributed to a growing body of literature analyzing the nature of human place experience. The subject area ranges over a spectrum from the rigorous methodologies of scientific inquiry, measurement, and evaluation at one extreme, to highly subjective and intuitive speculation about affective responses to place on the other. All of it is concerned with helping us ultimately to understand better the dynamics of the myriad different kinds of relationships we humans can have with the environments we shape and that are shaped by us, included the natural world. It has been more than ten years now since the geographer Yi-Fu Tuan published a ground-breaking study in which he tried to bring together strands of inquiry and insight from many disciplines in order to provide an overview of the factors that contribute to what he called "topophilia," "the affective bond between people and place or setting."[22] Tuan explored the compelling evidence for the essential role that culture plays in determining how we read and respond to environment; distinct cultures provide, as we know, the conceptual structures that imbue environments with meanings and values particular to a given group. He described as well a class of responses that all human beings seem to share by their very nature, such as our tendency to organize phenomena in binary pairs or to invent rational justifications for nonrational drives and aspirations; these physical and psychological characteristics of the human community also determine the character of the environments we favor. In a telling passage, Tuan explored the difference between the occasional native response to environment, unmediated by culturally imposed criteria, and the more distant, intellectualized experience that is especially common in advanced societies. A child, he observed, cares less for a composed picturesque view at the seashore than for the particular things and physical sensations he or she encounters there. "Visual appreciation, discerning and reflective," Tuan concluded, "creates aesthetic distance."[23]

Within recent years a growing number of philosophers, psychologists, and designers have begun to challenge more forcefully the almost exclusive identification of aesthetic perception with visual (or, to a lesser degree, aural) norms and modes of experience. They want to overcome the conventional assumption of a contemplative distance that separates us in some way from the environments to which we respond aesthetically. Martin Heidegger's phenomenology, with its frontal assault upon Cartesian arguments positing a world of things—the "other"—arrayed outside a thinking self, has appealed strongly to those who see a need for reshaping the philosophical premises underlying our culture's approach both to nature and to the built world. Heidegger's essay "Building/Dwelling/Thinking"[24] has achieved the status of a cult classic in schools of architecture and environmental design, and statements such as the one that follows, as Neil Evernden has shown, have made his thinking provocative for many ecologists and environmentalists as well: "Mortals dwell in that they save the earth. . . . Saving does not only snatch something from a danger. To save really means to set something free into its own essence. To save the earth is more than to exploit it or even wear it out. Saving the earth does not master the earth and does not subjugate it, which is merely one step from boundless spoilation."[25]

Evernden tellingly juxtaposes this passage with another from an essay by Joseph Grange, outlining a new "foundational ecology":

> In our human being we want nearness to that which distances itself from us. . . . Yet that neighbor, the earth, and even our body, gives itself without cost and without price, freely of itself to us—if we but respect it and let it be what it is. Ecology is therefore learning anew *to-be-at-home* in the region of our concern. This means that human homecoming is a matter of learning how to dwell intimately with that which resists our attempts to control, shape, manipulate and exploit it.[26]

Arnold Berleant, in turn, argues for a "participatory" model of experience as the basis for a new aesthetics; such a model "enables us to grasp the environment as a setting of dynamic forces, a field of forces that engages both perceiver and perceived in a dynamic unity":

> In such a phenomenological field the environment cannot be objectified; rather it is a totality continuous with the participant. An environment can be designed to work in this mode or

it can be structured to oppose it. It can be shaped to encourage participation or to inhibit, intimidate or oppress the person. When design becomes humane it not only fits the shape, movement and uses of the body; it also works with the conscious organism in an arc of expansion, development, and fulfillment. This is a goal which a consciously articulated aesthetic can help accomplish, and the challenge of such an aesthetic can be a powerful force in the effort to transform the world we inhabit into a place for human dwelling.[27]

The best of Lawrence Halprin's work in landscape architecture bears witness to his awareness of environment as just such a "totality continuous with the participant." Halprin acknowledges the important influence that choreography has had on his designing, affirming process over product, open-ended interactive dynamics over goal-setting and the predetermined channeling of behavior. His landscapes might be described with another of Berleant's terms, as "invitational," inviting the fullest kind of physical and psychological involvement of the participant. He has substituted the idea of "scoring" for more traditional "planning" to emphasize a more spontaneous and creative, as well as a more self-effacing and communitarian design process. Ecology, moreover, is a perfect model for the kind of design activity he wants to pursue, because in Halprin's own words, "the science of ecology is a *science of process,* and . . . in ecology what is significant is not so much the understanding of what exists at any given moment in time, but that the existence is ephemeral and in constant motion, constant change."[28]

Halprin's sense of his own creative process as metaphorically analogous to ecological process is a good example of the kind of sympathetic connections—a mutuality of interest, approach, and even, in some instances, of vocabulary—that seem to link the three subject-areas under discussion. Upon analysis, we can see in these three contemporary sciences an interrelated triad of descriptive concern that has in it the seeds of a new cosmology.

# DE/RE/IN[FORM]ING LANDSCAPE (1991)

PETER JACOBS

*RE(FORM)ING LANDSCAPE*

In a marvelous and inventive critique of recent sculpture, Rosalind Krauss suggests that Rodin's *Gates of Hell* and his statute of *Balzac* mark the transition from site-specific monuments to that of nomadic markers, siteless without a sense of place and largely self-referential. Brancusi's *Endless Column* becomes both base and sculpture, transportable to any "where." By the mid-1960s, sculpture was what was not-architecture on the one hand, and not-landscape on the other. It was, as Krauss explains, a combination of exclusions. The fact that

sculpture had become a kind of ontological absence, the combination of exclusions, the sum of neither/nor, does not mean that the terms themselves from which it was built—the not-landscape and the not-architecture—did not have a certain interest. This is because these terms express a strict opposition between the built and the not-built, the cultural and the natural, between which the production of sculptural art appeared to be suspended.[1]

With these sentences Krauss sets out an expended field of binary opposites, a positivist schema that embraces the subjective and the indeterminant.

The ideas of the essay entitled "Sculpture in the Expanded Field"[2] become clear when the set of binaries, architecture-not architecture and landscape-not landscape, is displayed as "a quaternary field which both mirrors the original opposition and, at the same time, opens it" using the analysis formats developed in mathematics (the Klein group) or in structuralism (the Piaget group). In the expanded field, sculpture is no longer the privileged middle term between two things it isn't, but rather only one term on the periphery of a field occupied by marked sites, site-construction, and axiomatic structures. Marked sites ranged from Smithson's *Spiral Jetty* to Christo's *Running Fence*. By contrast, the axiomatic structures that fall between architecture and not-architecture have been created by Robert Irwin, Bruce Newman, Richard Serra, and Sol Lewitt in their indoor work.

For us, perhaps the most interesting axis, that of site-construction, suspended between landscape and architecture has been occupied, among others, by Robert Smithson, Robert Morris, Michael Heizer, Walter de Maria, and Mary Miss. It is precisely this point (site-construction) that might well be occupied by landscape architecture.

What would happen were we to apply the same expanded field analysis to landscape? While I have defined landscape as a concept in which sculpture mediates our idea of nature and of culture,[3] landscape is neither nature nor culture, but rather is "suspended" between the two. The quaternary field occupied by culture-not culture and nature-not nature gives rise to a rich periphery of concepts that includes landscape displayed to the north of society, and environment displayed to the west of artifact.

The purpose, in fact the necessity, of perceiving the landscape in the context of environment, artifact, and society is threefold:

- To reintegrate the idea of landscape into fields from which it has been temporarily excluded,
- To rearticulate the values that animate the landscape, and thus
- To participate in the task of re-forming the shape of landscape.

And the position of landscape on the axis, between nature and culture, points to the dialectical strength and vulnerability of the milieu. Because of the cumulative effects of the cultural distancing from landscape in the twentieth century, there has been a corresponding move toward the pole of nature in the idea and practice of landscape architecture.

Peter Walker expresses the opinion that our preoccupation with the environmental crisis may well have arrested the development of landscape form over the past twenty years. He may be correct, yet I would argue that it was and continues to be a "pause that refreshes." The concept of sustainable landscapes, inconceivable at the height of the unbridled growth ethic in the 1960s and 1970s, adds a dimension of understanding to our sense of the landscape that only a very few had glimpsed and even fewer were prepared to support.

To feed and shelter the growing communities of the world and to continue to sup-

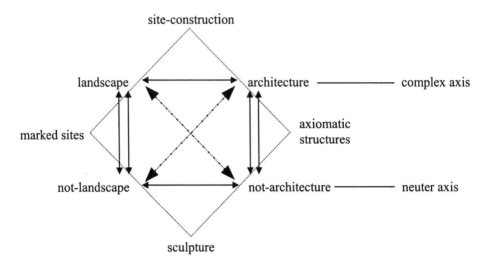

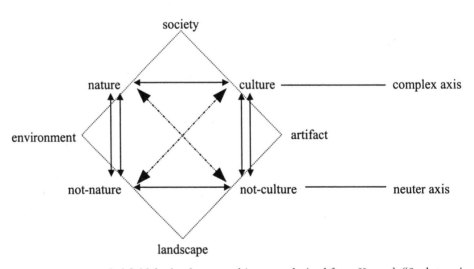

Figure 11. An expanded field for landscape architecture, derived from Krauss's "Sculpture in the Expanded Field" (after Rosalind Krauss and Peter Jacobs) (see also Figure 19).

port economic growth, more land has been cleared for cultivation in the past 100 years than in all the previous centuries of human existence combined. Part of this process contributes to the 6 million hectares of land that are degraded to desertlike conditions every year and to a new desert the size of Saudi Arabia every three decades. More than 11 million hectares of tropical forests are destroyed annually. Over thirty years, this amounts to an area about the size of the Indian subcontinent. As a direct consequence of this destruction (between 10,000 and 100,000 species), an enormous number of species are becoming extinct each year.

The "Brundtland" report[4] proposes continued growth as the path toward an equitable and sustainable tomorrow. It is unlikely, however, that we can grow our way out of our problems; we will have to solve many of them through informed design and through changes in our behavior and perceived needs. Robert Thayer[5] goes so far as to suggest that the concept of sustainable landscapes represents a "counterculture" with respect to design-driven "cosmetic" notions of aesthetic quality.

The shape of the landscape has always been informed by our literature and philosophy, and it is not unreasonable that science fiction be used as the medium of information. In Frank Herbert's *Dune* landscape, the essence of humanness is coping—acknowledging and adjusting to circumstances created by the natural environment, as opposed to adapting the environment to the needs of oneself or one's species, that is, the imposing of order. Humanness distinguishes human beings from other animals not by their ability to control the natural environment, but by their ability to control themselves—their bodies, their minds, their emotions.[6]

Yet an instrumental value system has dominated our perception of the environment, and our modern landscape forms are expressive of this vision. The extent to which we are prepared to embrace the intrinsic worth of environment may provide us with a new mix of "witness" landscapes against which we might compare and admire our continuing efforts to shape the sacred and profane landscapes of today and tomorrow. Christopher Stone[7] argues for a pluralistic approach to our values and our ethics with respect to each other and to other sentient beings, pressing further that the scope and complexity of our relationship is such that any one ideology, any one ethic, any one form is unlikely to satisfy all "shapes of content." So too is it unlikely that a unique and singular landscape form will emerge in response to these relationships.

The "artifact" is to the object as society is to the subject. To most, an artifact is what we hold in our hand or what we propel to the moon. To others, the landscape itself is an artifact, worked and reworked through human intervention until it too is assimilated into our productive processes and subject to the "sciences of the artificial," as described by Herbert Simon[8] thirty years ago.

Yet some have struggled to give formal expression to the symbolic and poetic components of landscape. Stonypath, the garden of Ian Hamilton Finlay, is a composition of objects set in a garden setting where the relationship of the forms of landscape and poetry are explored and celebrated. The form of the poem has been extended by Finlay from lines on a printed page to objects in a natural environment, and the relationship between poetic structures and the picturesque landscape.[9] Bernard Lassus has focused much of his work on creating new tales and myths in the garden and in the landscape.

In a recent critique of the avant-garde landscape architectural designs for the Harlequin Plaza in Denver and Las Colinas plaza near Dallas, Laurie Olin[10] suggests that they transgressed what is culturally acceptable regarding the choice of materials, form, and composition and that they embraced design devices or strategies that lead away from the central source of its power: nature. Olin suggests that "in nature are all the forms, in our imagination is their discernment and abstraction" and that new material consists of the re-presentation and recombination of material that has been deemed banal or out of bounds for some reason.[11] Olin's article on form, meaning, and expression in landscape architecture argues passionately and persuasively that the strength of the field of landscape architecture lies in its ability to express the relationship of society to nature.

Have we come full circle? I think not; we can never return to the unitary focus implied by the beautiful (or the sublime), or for that matter the avant-garde. Jacques Derrida's deconstruction of texts[12] challenges the autonomous order of avant-garde art. By juxtaposing the image and the text and by insisting that the viewer-reader be engaged in the "decoding of the social constraints that are often concealed behind the talk of aesthetic autonomy of form," he questions the very basis of the avant-garde discourse as well as that of much of Modernism. Both Derrida and Michel Foucault[13] offer new opportunities to juxtapose our ideas of nature and culture, and thus to re-form our concept of landscape.

Landscape is part of an expanded field. Landscape is both of nature and culture, it is the expression of who we are at any one of a number of periods of time and at any one of a number of places and events. Landscape, too, incorporates the collective memory of nature and of culture: landscape design seeks to give this concept form.

The quality of design that has produced the built landscapes that we inhabit today reflects our traditional values, many that we still cherish. Some of our current designs are experimental, others are patterned after design solutions that have been tested previously and found to be appropriate to both the cultural and physical context in which they were developed. Others have yet to be imagined.

What are the icons that will inform our landscape designs in the future, and to what extent can we be criticized for eschewing the "modern" and the "avant-garde"? How indeed can we develop meaningful form that speaks of diverse traditions, of collective memories, and of shared visions? I would maintain that landscape design has struggled to assert a profound sense of place, of climate, biology, and culture in the face of an overwhelming drive toward landscape homogenization, internationalism, and functionalism that we have not totally escaped.

We must now be more forthcoming with respect to our ideas and our ideals. We can articulate criteria against which we offer to evaluate progress in the management and design of the emerging landscapes of the twenty-first century. I have suggested previously that these might focus on maintaining the integrity of the biosphere, its habitats and inhabitants, on celebrating the specificity and identity of place and thus the sense of belonging, and on increasing the adaptability of our institutions in support of more equitable and sustainable development.[14]

Landscape design will have to contribute to the need to build landscapes that are equitable—equitable in the way the living resources of the landscape are used and distributed, equitable in terms of those whose environments are at risk and those who benefit from landscape development, equitable in providing opportunities for those generations that will follow our own.

Landscape design must also seek to express the sense of integrity that is present within living communities that are biologically and culturally adapted to the landscapes in which they dwell. If landscape research and management strategies provide the knowledge and strategic framework for a committed understanding of landscape processes and for ways in which these processes can be conserved and harvested sustainably, then our landscape designs must express these relationships with clarity and conviction.

Finally, we must account for our individual and collective need to develop a sense of belonging to and within the landscape. A sense of equity and of integrity, of course, contributes to our sense of belonging and even our sense of cherishing the landscape that is our own. Yet our design expressions must reach beyond these criteria to explore our collective past and the history of the landscape, to seek to imagine our future and the ways that we might achieve a fitting sense of dwelling within that future.

The search for landscape form imbued with a sense of equity, of integrity, and of belonging; the strategies that we evolve to manage such landscapes; and the knowledge base necessary to inform our judgments and value systems constitute the challenge we face in shaping the landscapes of the expanded field bounded by our artifacts, our society, and the environment.

# PART IV

# Society, Language, and the Representation of Landscape

Many of the questions of form and meaning in landscape architecture hinge upon how to *represent* different relationships involving nature, culture, and technology. Representation is a form of communication, and, as noted in the Introduction, the metaphor of language has become increasingly influential in a range of disciplines. It now informs landscape architectural theory in a number of ways, and in the past decade there have been a number of attempts to express landscape architectural knowledge and practice as a form of language. The first reading in this section is from Ann Whiston Spirn's *Language of Landscape*, which sets out the claim that "Landscape has all the features of language," justified with a rich selection of examples. The legitimacy of such a broad claim has been debated and challenged, but there is no question that specific metaphors such as text and narrative have proven to be fertile ground for theoretical critique of landscape. In the following shorter extract, James Corner (1991) links landscape as text with landscape as site, and in "Reading and Writing the Site" (1992) John Dixon Hunt further develops the proposition that gardens and landscapes are "readable," arguing that the interpretation of their symbolic content deserves as much emphasis as does analysis of their formal properties. Matthew Potteiger and Jamie Purinton extend the argument in *Landscape Narratives* (1998), proposing three realms within which landscape can be interpreted as narrative: as story, context/intertext, and discourse. Using the Crosby Arboretum as an example, they illustrate how these linguistic concepts can usefully inform landscape architecture.

James Corner (1992) turned the linguistic critique back upon landscape architectural practice. In "Representation and Landscape: Drawing and Making in the Landscape Medium," he explored how the way landscape is represented—as plan, sketch, and so on—influences and structures its form and meaning. This essay is included almost in its entirety. The subsequent short extract from Denis Cosgrove's *Social Formation and Symbolic Landscape* (1984) then raises a central issue of all forms of representation, which is the question of *whose* language is being used, and for what *ends*? Part IV closes with Elizabeth Meyer's argument for greater attention to the development of a theoretical base for landscape architecture that utilizes language and categories specific to the discipline, as opposed to borrowing from others. An extract from "The Expanded Field of Landscape Architecture" (1997) shows how linguistic techniques can be used to critique contemporary practice and open up alternative ways of knowing about landscape. The extract also introduces a feminist perspective, exploring Cosgrove's argument that any language of landscape inevitably serves particular interests, and excludes others.

# THE LANGUAGE OF LANDSCAPE (1998)

ANN WHISTON SPIRN

## LANDSCAPE IS LANGUAGE

The language of landscape is our native language. Landscape was the original dwelling; humans evolved among plants and animals, under the sky, upon the earth, near water. Everyone carries that legacy in body and mind. Humans touched, saw, heard, smelled, tasted, lived in, and shaped landscapes before the species had words to describe what it did. Landscapes were the first human texts, read before the invention of other signs and symbols. Clouds, wind, and sun were clues to weather, ripples and eddies signs of rocks and life under water, caves and ledges promise of shelter, leaves guides to food; birdcalls warnings of predators. Early writing resembled landscape; other languages—verbal, mathematical, graphic—derive from the language of landscape.[1]

The language of landscape can be spoken, written, read, and imagined. Speaking and reading landscape are by-products of living—of moving, mating, eating—and strategies of survival—creating refuge, providing prospect, growing food. To read and write landscape is to learn and teach: to know the world, to express ideas and to influence others. Landscape, as language, makes thought tangible and imagination possible. Through it humans share experience with future generations, just as ancestors inscribed their values and beliefs in the landscapes they left as a legacy, "a treasure deposited by the practice of speech," a rich lode of literature: natural and cultural histories, landscapes of purpose, poetry, power, and prayer.[2]

Landscape has all the features of language. It contains the equivalent of words and parts of speech—patterns of shape, structure, material, formation, and function. All landscapes are combinations of these. Like the meanings of words, the meanings of landscape elements (water, for example) are only potential until context shapes them. Rules of grammar govern and guide how landscapes are formed, some specific to places and their local dialects, others universal. Landscape is pragmatic, poetic, rhetorical, polemical. Landscape is scene of life, cultivated construction, carrier of meaning. It is language.

Verbal language reflects landscape. Up and down, in and out—the most basic metaphors of verbal language—stem from experience of landscape, like bodily movement through landscape.[3] Verbs, nouns, adverbs, adjectives, and their contexts—parts of speech and the structure of verbal language—mirror landscape processes, products, and their modifiers, material, formal, and spatial. Just as a river combines water, flowing, and eroded banks, sentences combine actions and actors, objects and modifiers. The context of a word or sentence, like that of hill or valley, defines it. Verbal texts and landscapes are nested: word within sentence within paragraph within chapter, leaf within branch within tree within forest. Words reflect observation and experience; dialects are rich in terms specific to landscape of place, like "estuary English," described so vividly by John Stilgoe.[4] Shakespeare, Mark Twain, T. S. Eliot, Anthony Hecht, and Adrienne Rich, like verbal poets of every literature, mine landscape for structure, rhythm, and fresh metaphors of human experience; so do poets of landscape itself, "Capability" Brown, Frederick Law Olmsted, Frank Lloyd Wright, Lawrence Halprin, Martha Schwartz.[5]

Landscape is the material home, the language of landscape is a habitat of mind. Heidegger called language the house of being, but the language of landscape truly is the *house of being*; we dwell within it. To dwell—to make and care for a place—is self-expression. Heidegger traced that verb in High German and Old English; in both, the root for "to dwell" means "to build." In German, the roots for building and dwelling and "I am" are the same. I am because I dwell; I dwell because I build. *Bauen*—building, dwelling, and being—means "to build," "to construct," but also to "cherish and protect, to preserve and care for, specifically to till the soil, to cultivate the mind."[6]

Landscape associates people and place. Danish *landskab*, German *landschaft*, Dutch *landschap*, and Old English *landscipe* combine two roots. "Land" means both a place and the people living there. *Skabe* and *schaffen* mean "to shape;" suffixes *-skab* and *-schaft* as in the English "-ship," also mean association, partnership.[7] Though no longer used in ordinary speech, the Dutch *schappen* conveys a magisterial sense of shaping, as in the biblical Creation. Still strong in Scandinavian and German languages, these original meanings have all but disappeared from English. *Webster's Dictionary* defines *landscape* as static, "a picture representing a section of natural, inland scenery, as of prairie, woodland, mountains . . . an expanse of natural scenery seen by the eye in one view"; the *Oxford English Dictionary* traces the word to a Dutch painting term *(landskip)*.[8] But landscape is not a mere visible surface, static composition, or passive backdrop to human theater; therefore dictionaries must be revised, and the older meanings revived. The words *environment* and *place*, commonly used to replace *landscape* in twentieth-century English, are inadequate substitutes, for they refer to locale or surroundings and omit people. In midcentury, the declining use of *landscape* was in part a reaction to the Nazis' adoption of "blood and soil," a linking of native landscape and racial identity. *Environment* and *place* seem more neutral, but they are abstract, disembodied, sacrificing meaning, concealing tensions and conflicts, ignoring the assumptions *landscape* reveals. *Landscape* connotes a sense of purposefully shaped, the sensual and aesthetic, the embeddedness in culture. The language of landscape recovers the dynamic connection between place and those who dwell there.

Landscape is loud with dialogues, with story lines that connect a place and its dwellers. The shape and structure of a tree record an evolutionary dialogue between species and environment: eucalpt leaves that run their edge to bright sun, deciduous leaves that fall off during seasonal heat or cold. And they record dialogues between a tree and its habitat. Tree rings thick and thin tell the water and food of each growing season of the tree's life. Size, shape, and structure—low-branched or high, densely branched or spare—reflect dialogues between a tree and a group of trees in open field or dense forest. Each species has a characteristic form from which individuals deviate, as true of human body shape—muscled or fat, short or tall—as of trees. A coherence of human vernacular landscapes emerges from dialogues between builders and place, fine-tuned over time. They tell of a congruence between snowfall and roof pitch, between seasonal sun angles and roof overhang, wind direction and alignment of hedgerows, cultivation practices and dimensions of fields, family structure and patterns of settlement. Dialogues make up the context of individual, group, and place. The context of life is a woven fabric of dialogues, enduring and ephemeral.

Humans are not the sole authors of landscape. Volcanoes spew lava, remaking land; rain falls, carving valleys. Mountains, gardens, and cities are shaped by volcanoes and rain, plants and animals, human hands and minds. Trees shade ground and shed leaves, produce a more hospitable place for life with similar needs. Beavers cut trees and dam streams to make ponds: a dwelling place. People mold landscape with hands, tools, and machines, through law, public policy, and actions undertaken hundreds, even thousands, of miles away. All living things share the same space, all make landscape, and all landscapes, wild or domesticated, have coauthors, all are phenomena of nature and culture. Others share the language, but only humans (as far as we yet know) reflect, worship, make art, and design landscapes like the gardens of the Villa d'Este that "set the formal structures" within a natural context "where the tension lectures us on our mortal state."[9] . . .

Metaphors grounded in landscape guide how humans think and act. George Lakoff and Mark Johnson demonstrate what Emerson observed: that humans understand and experience one kind of thing in terms of another, projecting bodies and minds onto the surrounding world: trees and clouds seen as bounded, a river seen as having a mouth, a mountain as having a foot, front, back, and side.[10] One might just as easily see things as continuous and undifferentiated; viewing them as separate is more a function of individual consciousness than an inherent quality of landscape. Many metaphors are grounded in fundamental relationships with landscape—moving, making, eating, wasting. The most common refer to space and direction: in and out, up and down. In American culture, high and in are good, down and out are bad; central is important, marginal is not. Landscape imagery conveys feelings and ideas: emotions churning like a stormy sea, rivers of time, clouds where gods live, sacred mountains, Father Sky impregnating Mother Earth with rain as the seed, Zeus and Thor hurling thunderbolts in anger, Siva flashing lightening from his Third Eye, a flare of cosmic intelligence, the god of Jews and Christians dispatching plagues of locusts and disease to punish the wicked. Personification, the attribution of human feelings like intention, anger, love to natural forms and phenomena, is the foundation of myth and religion.

Landscapes are the world itself and may also be metaphors of the world. A tree can be both a tree and The Tree, a path both a path and The Path. A tree in the Garden of Eden represents the Tree of Life, the Tree of Knowledge. It becomes the archetype of Tree. When a path represents the Path of Enlightenment of Buddhism or the Stations of the Cross of Christianity it is no longer a mere path, but The Path. The yellow brick road in *The Wizard of Oz* is both path and Path. The similar is the stuff of metaphor, simile, and personification; contrasts are the stuff of paradox and oxymoron. Landscape actors, objects, and modifiers may enhance meaning without rhetoric: rivers reflect and run, but they do not pun.

Built landscapes may be rhetorical. Landscape features, like hill and street, may be emphasized or embellished for effect, slope steepened to make climb difficult, street broadened and lined with trees to impress the viewer. Gardens of allusion reflect oral and written literature: Shakespeare gardens allude to the bard's plays and poetry, their herbs and blooms references to his works; eighteenth-century English gardens, with their buildings in classical style and pastoral landscape refer to classical literature. When Mussolini built a monument in 1938 to those who died in a battle of the First World War in Redipuglia, near Italy's northwestern boundary, he used the language of rhetoric. More than one hundred thousand soldiers are buried there in twenty-two terraces of tombs, arranged from bottom to top in alphabetical order, sixty thousand buried at the top of the hill in a common grave surmounted by three crosses, like Calvary. Words engraved in the pavement tell how these soldiers died for the glory of Italy, immortal in memory. Facing the hill of tombs is the grave of their general, as if addressing his entombed soldiers. Their inscriptions answer, "*Presente.*" "I am here."

The language of landscape can be spoken and read even though never codified, without recourse to rules. People follow paths and make them, plant gardens, are awed by the scale of mountains and cathedrals; great designers use landscape fluently, all without dictionaries or grammars. Thomas Jefferson linked landscape and learning at the University of Virginia, where he designed and sited the original buildings. Sigurd Lewerentz and Gunnar Asplund comforted the bereaved in the Hill of Remembrance and Woodland Chapel at Forest Cemetery in Stockholm. Glenn Murcutt associated people, sun, wind, and water in a house at Bingie on the coast of Australia. Even those who exploit landscape cynically may do so masterfully, as Mussolini did when, at Redipuglia, he fostered feelings of heroic nationalism to promote fascism, or as Disney has exploited it, for profit, at Disneyland and Disney World.

Landscapes are a vast library of literature. The myths of Japan's Fuji and Australia's Uluru, the folksy tales of trolls and pink flamingos on American lawns, the classical works of earth, water, and wind at Yosemite and the Grand Canyon, the high art of the Alhambra and Manhattan's Central Park, and countless other places, ordinary and extraordinary, record the language of landscape. The library ranges from wild and vernacular landscape, tales shaped by everyday phenomena, to classic landscapes of artful expression, like the relationship of ordinary spoken language to great works of literature. Worship, memory, play, movement, meeting, exchange, power, production, home, and community are pervasive landscape genre. To be fully felt and known landscape literature must be experienced in situ; words, drawings, paintings, or photographs cannot replace the experience of the place itself, though they may enhance and intensify it.

Landscape literature is a resource to be treasured. Several decades ago, archeologists in Israel discovered ancient water-gathering systems in the Negev Desert that employed simple channels, check dams, and broad depressions. These techniques, lost for many centuries, have inspired the landscape architect Shlomo Aronson and others to reshape whole landscapes to gather water; they planted groves and grassy meadows in the desert, all sustained by dewfall and rain. The water engineer Ken Wright is working with archeologists to study the water systems of the Incas in Peru, not just to understand, but to use their knowledge. I have studied dozens of community gardens in Philadelphia as landscape expressions. The literature of landscape contains a vast repertoire of similar examples, adaptations to a wide range of circumstances, not just in the diversity of genes and behavior, but in ideas and cultures. Some are cherished and cared for, others are being rediscovered, but entire volumes of landscape literature are being lost and forgotten, whole libraries destroyed.

## LANDSCAPE HAS CONSEQUENCES

The language of landscape is a powerful tool. A person literate in landscape sees significance where an illiterate person notes nothing. Past and future fires, floods, landslides, welcome or warning are visible to those who can read them in tree and slope, boundary and gate. Knowing how to tell what one wants to express—pragmatics—makes landscape authors more adept; making landscapes appeal to emotion and reason depends on understanding rhetoric. To know landscape poetics is to see, smell, taste, hear, and feel landscape as a symphony of complex harmonies. Natural processes establish the base rhythm that is expressed in the initial form of the land, to which culture, in turn, responds with new and changing themes that weave an intricate pattern, punctuated here and there by high points of nature and art. Landscape symphonies evolve continually in time, in predictable and unpredictable ways, responding to process and to human purpose, and, in landscape symphonies, all dwellers are composers and players.

The language of landscape humans have always known but now use piecemeal, with much forgotten. People still read paths and create them, identify boundaries and define territory, delight in a flowering tree comparing it to a lover, but most people read landscape shallowly or narrowly and tell it stupidly or inadequately. Oblivious to dialogue and story line, they misread or miss meaning entirely, blind to connections among intimately related phenomena, oblivious to poetry, then fail to act or act wrongly. Absent, false, or partial readings lead to inarticulate expression: landscape silence, gibberish, incoherent rambling, dysfunctional, fragmented dialogues, broken story lines. The consequences are comical, dumb, dire, tragic. Those who admired the yellowwood's excessive, early flowering on the campus in Philadelphia were blind to what the bud scars told, failed to read the flowers' poignant message, were unable to imagine the tree's connection to soil, plaza, and contractor. When I tried to convince the dean, himself an architect, to find another site for the contractors' trailer and tools, he refused, unconvinced or not caring that the yellowwood would die as a consequence. Those who first built houses over the buried creek in West Philadelphia and those who rebuilt in the same place were illiterate in the language of landscape and so could not read the creek's presence. I tried and failed, at first, to convince planners at the City Planning Commission and engineers at the Philadelphia Water Department that the buried creek was a resource to be exploited and a force to be reckoned with. The yellowwood is dead, but it is not too late to restore Mill Creek—the water, the people, the place.

Ironically, the professionals who specialize, reading certain parts of landscape more deeply than other parts and shaping them more powerfully, often fail to understand landscape as a continuous whole. Once those who transformed landscapes were generalists: naturalist, humanist, artist, engineer, even priest, all combined. Now pieces of landscape are shaped by those whose narrowness of knowledge, experience, values, and concerns leads them to read and tell only fragments of the story. To an ecologist, landscape is habitat, but not construction or metaphor. To a lawyer, landscape may be property to regulate, to a developer, a commodity to exploit, to an architect, a site to build on, to a planner, a zone for recreation or residence or commerce or transportation or "nature preservation." As in the story of the blind men who each touch a different part of the elephant—trunk or tusk or tail alone— then arrive at a false description of the whole animal, so each discipline and each interest group reads and tells landscape through its own tunnel vision of perception, value, tool, and action. And as each shouts its own fragment, landscapes of cities, suburbs, and regions are severed, become impoverished, dysfunctional. It is even fashionable now to design buildings, gardens, and cities deliberately as dislocated and unconnected fragments to emphasize the erosion of common ground, a misanthropic view of cultural differences.

Loss of fluency in the language of landscape, in turn, impoverishes verbal language. Words like *bore* and *guzzle* refer to features and processes many no longer perceive—and which can injure or even kill. To know the meaning (and location) of bore and guzzle is to be safe, to survive: a bore is the "noisy rush of the tides against the current in a narrow channel"; a guzzle, the low place in the dunes where water drains and the sea comes crashing through in a "century storm."[11] To know bore is to avoid it at high tide; to know guzzle is to decide not to build and settle there. Such nuances, preserved in specialized, professional language, are now lost to common verbal language. Aboriginal peoples become more "civilized" and less attuned to landscape; young Papua-New Guineans, for example, no longer learn to sing with waterfalls and birds. A loss of language and loss of knowledge limits the celebration of landscape as a partnership between people, place, and other life and further reduces the capacity to understand and imagine possible human relationships with nonhuman nature.

We shape landscape and language; they shape us. To know landscape is to read in Boston's Fens and Riverway artful reconstructions of places laid waste by human occupation. Not to know is to fail to discern what merely grew and what was planted, and thus, for example, to mistake the Fens and Riverway as "preserved" wetland and floodplain forest; they were, rather, the product of human purpose mindful of natural processes of regeneration. Failure to recognize the Fens and Riverway as being *designed* and *built*, not happenstance, blinds us to the possibility of designing and building similar transformations elsewhere.

Landscape metaphors modify perceptions, prompt ideas and actions, molding landscape, in turn. To see wilderness as chaos provokes fear and prompts flight, perhaps even the urge to destroy; to believe it sacred fosters appeal, reverence, and the desire to cherish. To know nature as a set of ideas not a place, and landscape as the expression of actions and ideas in place not as an abstraction or as mere scenery promotes an understanding of landscape as a continuum of meaning.[12] Not to know, and to confuse landscape and nature, is to equate landscape with mountain, meadow, farm, and country road, but not highway or town. Yet a designed urban park is no less a landscape than a planted cornfield, the island of Manhattan no less a landscape than its Central Park. Notions of landscape as countryside, but not city, falsely fragment intimate connections and produce such ironies as inner-city schoolchildren bused out of town to study old-field meadows, ignoring the same plants growing on vacant lots next door.[13] To see landscape as mere scenery gives precedence to appearance at the expense of habitability and risks trivializing landscape as decoration—landscaping—concealing the significance of sense other than sight and of parts hidden from view, the deep context underlying the surface. To call some landscapes natural and others artificial or cultural misses the truth that landscapes are never wholly one or the other.

# THE HERMENEUTIC LANDSCAPE (1991)

JAMES CORNER

The landscape is itself a text that is open to interpretation and transformation. It is also a highly situated phenomenon in terms of space, time, and tradition and exists as both the ground and geography of our heritage and change.

Landscape is distinguished from wilderness in that it is land which has been modified by humans. But it is more than this. Landscape is not only a physical phenomenon, but is also a cultural schema, a conceptual filter through which our relationships to wilderness and nature can be understood.

It is the well-formed world of occupied places as opposed to the world outside of that—the unplaced place. In other words, prior to language, "landscape" is a phenomenon beyond immediate comprehension; it is not until we choose a prospect and map what we see, marking some aspects, ignoring others, that the landscape acquires meaning.[1] Such interventions include paintings, poems, myths, and literature, in addition to buildings and other interventions upon the land. These works are the encodings that set and enframe human situations. They are the posts that map out a "landscape."

As time passes, this marked landscape weathers, ever subject to the contingencies of nature. Other points of view are chosen as circumstances change and new ways of marking are overlaid upon the old, producing collagic and weathered overlays. Residua in this topographic palimpsest provide loci for the remembrance, renewal, and transfiguration of a culture's relationship to the land. Such are the familiar and unexpected places of authentic dwelling.

As a human-made projection, landscape is both text and site, partly clarifying the world and our place within it. The textual landscape is thus a hermeneutic medium. Landscape architecture might therefore be thought of as the practice of e-scaping and rescaping our relationship to nature and the "other" through the construction of built worlds. In the desire to reflect both on our modern context and on our inheritance, landscape architecture might practice a hermeneutical plotting of the landscape—a plotting that is as much political and strategic as it is relational and physical. The landscape architect as plotter is simultaneously critic, geographer, communicator, and maker, digging to uncover mute and latest possibilities in the lived landscape. With every "projection" there might follow a rebirth: the artifact of culture and the enigma of nature rendered fuller with every pass.[2] To plot, to map, to dig, to set: Are these not the fundamental traditions of landscape architecture?

# READING AND WRITING THE SITE (1992)

JOHN DIXON HUNT

By way of orientation, . . . it is worth announcing, somewhat schematically, four themes. . . . The first, and the lengthiest, concerns how we process the so-called natural or physical world for our consumption. The second briefly addresses gardens as an art of milieu—how gardens, where humans exercise control over space and nature, become the most eloquent expressions of complex cultural ideas. The third invokes the notion of cultural translation—whereby one particular period receives and shapes for its own specific purposes ideas and forms inherited from predecessors elsewhere. The fourth derives from and builds upon the previous three: it explains the claim . . . that gardens and landscapes are "readable."

I

The Roman writer Cicero termed what we would call the cultural landscape a second nature *(alteram naturam)*.[1] This was a landscape of bridges, roads, harbors, fields—in short, all of the elements which men and women introduce into the physical world to make it more habitable, to make it serve their purposes. Cicero's phrase "a second nature" of course implies a first; though he does not specify this, we may take it that he implies a primal nature, an unmediated world before humans invaded, altered, and augmented it, a world without any roads, ports, paths, terraced vineyards, etc. Today we might call it the wilderness.

In sixteenth-century Italy, when gardens began to flourish and be elaborated as never before, this art was likened to a third nature by various commentators; one of them, Jacopo Bonfadio, wrote of gardens as being "nature incorporated with art . . . [and made] the creator and conatural of art, and from both is made a third nature [*una terza natura*]."[2] The implication of this third nature, as indeed of Cicero's second, was its augmentation of an existing state of affairs. Gardens went beyond the cultural landscape, and therefore those humanists, drawing upon Cicero, invented new terminology. Gardens were worlds where the pursuits of pleasure probably outweighed the need for utility and accordingly where the utmost resources of human intelligence and technological skill were invoked to fabricate an environment where nature and art collaborated.

The point to emphasize here is the fashion in which first nature has constantly been processed for human consumption, either into second or into second and then third natures, or sometimes directly into third nature. Consumption may involve a search for habitation, agricultural needs, transportation, religious beliefs (whereby sacred places are marked by temples and shrines), and eventually leisure and aesthetic pleasure. To whatever end, though, human reworking of the first nature renders the physical world more amenable, useful, tolerable, pleasant, beautiful (the specific emphasis will clearly depend upon the historical moment, and many—not just ecological enthusiasts—would today of course add ravaged or ruined).

But consumption has also taken less obvious or less palpable forms. One of these [is] the picturesque. . . . Much has been written about picturesque taste, both at the time of its greatest popularity and subsequently by modern commentators,[3] but what is never explicitly emphasized is that it was and continues to be a mode of processing the physical world for our consumption or for our greater comfort. The primal world of physical nature— Cicero's implied first nature—can be raw, hostile, discomforting, dangerous: just because few readers of this book may have themselves experienced this first nature in that form does not deny its existence. Whenever humans have encountered it, they tend to tame it, utilize it, and otherwise process it.

This processing can be intellectual as well as physical. A frequent response to the terrifying and threatening spaces of mountains, sea, or desert has been to annex them mentally to what is termed the "sublime," at which point we start talking of the grandeur of the mountains, and so on; while still allowed its primal forcefulness, first nature has now been subsumed and managed culturally (and arguably has ceased to be a pure form of first nature, slipping into a version of the second).

Yet another intellectual intervention into first nature which makes sense and proportion out of empty waste is narrated in Wallace Stevens's poem "Anecdote of the Jar," a parable somewhat in vogue with landscape architects at present. The poet tells how he

> placed a jar in Tennessee
> And round it was, upon a hill.
> It made the slovenly wilderness
> Surround that hill.

The wilderness rose up to it,
And sprawled around, no longer wild[4]

The art work—vase or jar—transforms how we regard the first nature in which it is positioned, through without physically altering the hillside (the jar is ecologically sound, so to speak). Gardens, too, may be thought of as jars, set down in otherwise artless landscapes; part of their appeal is that they reorganize our thinking, especially about the natural materials from which they are crafted. Unlike Stevens's jar, though, a garden is itself a consequence of fresh perceptions of second and first nature.

By the end of the eighteenth century the picturesque had become another example of how humans came to accommodate potentially unprepossessing scenery. The physical world could be seen more pleasantly, occupied and visited more safely, if it were thought of as a painting. So it was filtered through sensibilities honed on a study of graphic representations of the world (not necessarily the natural world—). . . . William Gilpin, the great popularizer of this picturesque mode, helped his readers to travel and look at the various parts of Great Britain as if its various topographies were safely pictorialized; the world "out there" in Wales, Scotland, the Lake District, even in the Home Counties and the south coast, was turned into "landscapes" or "scenery."[5] Both of which terms, by alluding respectively to paintings and theatrical sets, announced the safe and sanitized nature of the picturesque vision. . . .

That garden art had become intimately allied with the picturesque vogue by the end of the eighteenth century should recall us to the essential fact that gardens, too, have always been ways of mediating the physical world. . . . Gardens are, if not ways of actually coming to terms with the first and second natures, at least retrospective ways of registering how we have come to terms with them. By being sophisticated products of our relationship with the world beyond their walls, gardens represent, as do landscape paintings, an art of milieu.[6]

## II

Our second point may now be made more quickly. Human beings have processed nature in different ways and for different motives. One such mode is the garden. Each phase of garden art is culturally specific, determined by a whole congeries of ideas and events few of which are explicitly horticultural or architectural: they may be political, social, economic, religious. But because, as the Renaissance humanists implied by the invention of a third nature, gardens go one stage further than the cultural landscape of second nature in representing the extent and significance of control over their environment, gardens may arguably offer a more refined, more acute, and more intricate expression of human experience. This expression will be both conscious and unconscious, just as the subsequent analysis of it will confront both the obvious and the unexpected (there is, however, no automatic correlation between what was taken for granted then and what is seen as obvious about it now).

This is not the place to enquire into exactly what range of human experience gardens have at various times managed to express.[7] But what is today termed landscape architecture has always realized a particular society's, even a particular person's, attitudes toward space and nature. This deliberately constructed milieu invokes selected forms and materials to express, often in a concentrated fashion and certainly in a special way, some human response to and recognition of an environment; this environment will be physical, topographical, but it will also include less tangible, spiritual values. Landscape paintings have also attempted the same expression of experience, though in their case the space is necessarily two-dimensional and therefore illusionary; it is also "easier," in that it requires no physical intervention on the ground as gardens do. To bestow such and such a shape upon a parcel of land is to declare explicitly or implicitly some of the landowner's and designer's more fundamental ideas about their environment.

### III

The cultural declarations of landscape architecture . . . are perhaps most visible . . . whenever a society attempts to borrow and shape to its own purposes ideas from or about previous cultures, [for example] in the English eighteenth century; . . . [and] in French impressionism's reformulations of garden imagery or twentieth-century landscape architecture's dialogue with its past. In this process of cultural translation it is the translator's own preoccupations that come to the fore and determine the outcome, which can be better appreciated by comparing it with its original.

In England during the eighteenth century, as is well known, there was much backward contemplation of ancient Rome: classical writers were invoked as contemporary models, and where (as with architecture and certainly landscape architecture) perhaps insufficient antique examples existed, the classical legacy could always be accessed via, say, the works and writings of Italian Renaissance practitioners. But the cult of Palladio in England, for example, makes a further point: his Renaissance buildings were extrapolated for his contemporaries from a careful study of classical remains which were then made anew by him in a fresh context. The English emulation of Palladio in its turn added a further translation: from classical remains into Renaissance buildings, then from those directly or via Palladio's writing in *I Quattro Libri* (1570) into northern ones of the seventeenth and eighteenth centuries.

But a country like England has its own indigenous architectural forms, let alone its own distinct landscapes where (it could be argued) neoclassical buildings did not necessarily sit too happily. Coexisting with the neoclassical taste had always been a fascination with the native Gothic traditions (in literature as well as in architecture) and gradually during the eighteenth century this taste increased. So when writers or architects translated the classical languages of their models, they were obliged at least to address the question of how Vitruvius, Palladio, Horace, or Pliny would function in England and in English. Alexander Pope was actually urged by a friend in the 1720s to "make Homer speak good English," and when he turned his attention to Horace in the 1730s he was even more concerned to register what was capable of translation and what, for various cultural reasons, resisted it.

Exactly the same attitudes to translation seem to have been applied in garden design during the first half of the eighteenth century. The absence of classical precedents forced Englishmen back upon yet further strategies of translation: if they sought to relocate themselves in the villa and garden traditions of Pliny, Horace, and Martial, then they had to translate old verbal accounts into new visual forms.

All this cultural processing of the past for the present and of ancient Rome for modern England could be and was explained by a scheme known as the progress of the arts.[8]

What had been the glory of Greece and Rome had (so the narrative went) been lost sight of during the "dark" ages, been recovered and reconstituted by the Italian Renaissance, and from that point of time and place had progressed northward to its final flowering in—according to your nationality—France, the Low Countries, or Great Britain. But at least in the last of these territories the progress of the art of landscaping began to be celebrated as an accommodation of those classical traditions to a new and different culture. Hence, just as Homer and Horace were required to speak modern English in Pope's translations, so landscapes like Castle Howard felt obliged to honor their indigenous languages of architecture and topography.

One extra example will be useful. When William Kent was called in to redesign Rousham, General Dormer's garden in Oxfordshire, in the late 1730s, he drew attention by various visual hints to that beautiful garden's place in the progress of its art from Rome to England. Allusions to the new garden's Italian models—to the ruined Temple of Fortune at ancient Praeneste or to a sculptural group in the grounds of the Renaissance Villa d'Este—were offered along with indications of the cultural changes that the act of translation had wrought upon the classical originals. Further, throughout the relatively small garden Kent emphasized both the old and the new, classical and Gothick,[9] often side by side; by these juxtapositions our attention is drawn to the new English location of classical ideas and forms.

All this was apt for a family with strong English pedigree: a Dormer had married the aunt of Sir Philip Sidney; the family had been royalist in the Civil Wars, held court appointments in the seventeenth and eighteenth centuries; and yet in the eighteenth century they were attentive to classical culture, especially through architecture and sculpture.[10] Perhaps the most economical and witty fashion in which this cultural translation is underlined occurs on top of the screens with which Kent linked the seventeenth-century house, remodeled to look Tudor-Gothick, to its new wings. Giving the "old" central block wings was in the classical-Palladian mode; yet gothicizing them with ogive niches and "battlements" was British, "medieval." So the linking walls have crested parapets or castellations in the shape of the stone balls which decorate similar screen links on the front of Palladio's San Giorgio Maggiore in Venice.[11] Thus we are advised that what we see is a translation from an old into a "new" language with a consequent elision of the two.

## IV

We have just surveyed what might be called the writing of a site, the inscription of meaning—sometimes with actual words, but just as often by a dumb visual language—onto some segment of terrain. If such a description of the cultural making of gardens is allowed, then it follows that what has been written may also be read, at least if we take the trouble to learn the language. The visual forms that we see at Rousham have a meaning, a content, that is also available to us. In the terms that most of Kent's contemporaries would have understood, his architecture and landscape architecture were "speaking pictures."[12]

It may be objected that a garden like Rousham, or its not too distant neighbor Stowe in Buckinghamshire, is exceptional in the conscious deliberation with which its owners and designers encoded meanings in it. It is indeed true that it was all meant to be readable. Rousham and Stowe have in this respect at least to be situated toward the end of a tradition that found architecture as meaningful, for example, as heraldry.[13]

But it is [my] underlying argument that as historians and theorists of landscape architecture we are also able to "read" garden "texts" which did not lay claim to that specific kind of readability. All human creations, especially—it is here argued—gardens, declare their creators; it is the business of cultural historians to extrapolate ideas, beliefs, and other modes of *mentalité* from them. Reading gardens, in other words, does not consist wholly in taking notice of their inscriptions. Many do not have any such verbal devices, and they present themselves substantially if not totally through formal, visual means.

Yet forms have significance and content, even if that content itself signals a refusal of meaning. No gesture is unreadable. If this neglects formal analysis in favor of what forms may contain, that is because the importance of the latter approach needs to be reasserted.

# LANDSCAPE NARRATIVES (1998)

## MATTHEW POTTEIGER AND JAMIE PURINTON

To link the practices of making landscapes to narrative practices requires an expanded notion of text, of the role of readers in producing meaning, as well as recognition of landscape as a spatial narrative shaped by ongoing processes and multiple authors. Design practice derived from understanding these conditions forms "open narratives," as opposed to the current trend for highly scripted and controlled narratives.

Narratives intersect with sites, accumulate as layers of history, organise sequences and inhere in the very materials and processes of the landscape. In various ways, stories "take place." The term "landscape narrative" designates the interplay and mutual relationship between story and place. More than just a backdrop, places become eventful changing sites that engender stories. And we come to know places because we know their stories.

Narrative is an increasingly common intention in contemporary landscape design. However, landscape narratives are typically conceived in terms of literal storytelling, being highly scripted and controlled with explicit references to histories, biographies, local emblems or other codified or textual forms. While this does begin to communicate a local sense of place and extend the repertoire of landscape expression, it is a limited conception of the significance and potential of both narrative and landscape.

Narrative need not be conceived as an explicit storyline grafted *onto* a site as if it were once a blank slate. Narratives are already implicit in landscapes, inscribed by natural processes and cultural practices.[1] They can reside in very ordinary forms, routine activities and institutional structures. However, beyond the frame of the garden or the parking lot of the theme park, these implicit narratives may be difficult to read if one is looking for conventional stories with clear beginnings, middles and ends. There are also different protocols for reading the landscape as a visual and spatial narrative. Viewers enter at different points, are free to pause, take in the whole image, inspect its parts or review. This changes the traditional relationship between author, text and reader where the author exerts control over the *telling*. Instead, the spatial narrative is more about *showing*, relinquishing control to the viewer/reader who must put together sequences, fill in the gaps and decipher meaning.[2] And since most landscapes are shaped by environmental and cultural practices, they may not have a single author or narrator. Instead they develop from multiple and often competing groups.

Rather than a limitation, these conditions on the spatial narrative offer distinct opportunities for what we refer to as "open narratives." These narratives are open to interpretation, multiple authorship, competing discourses and change, making landscape such a vital phenomenon. Out of the interdisciplinary and evolving field of contemporary narrative theory, we can identify certain critical moves that re-conceive narrative and landscape in ways that can engender these new practices. First, landscape and narrative can be redescribed as cultural systems of signification, as language. Second, landscape and narrative are also linked by an expanded notion of *text* and the network of *intertextual* associations. Further, landscape narratives are not directly homologous to language, but meanings and interpretations are both enabled and constrained within social discourses.

Proceeding from these conceptions, we can describe the diversity of landscape narrative forms and practices as they are produced within three related realms:

- The story realm
- The contextual/intertextual realm
- The discourse realm

The story realm is the world of the story itself. The emphasis is on the author/designer's intentions to create meaning within the structures of story (event, plot, character, etc). However, it is important to see how stories relate to contexts and other texts. The emphasis in the contextual/intertextual realm is on the role of readers, community or memory in the making of landscape narratives. The third realm of discourse requires attention to whose story is told and to what ideologies or world views are implicit in the telling. In this paper, the three realms and their relationships will be illustrated by one contemporary example, the Pincote Interpretive Center of the Crosby Arboretum in Picayune, Mississippi. The Arboretum tells a story with strategies as sophisticated as those in any renaissance garden. However, in this "regional garden" the narrative of ecological change becomes an open narrative engaged in reconstructing contemporary discourse on nature and culture.

## The Story Realm

Gardens, whether renaissance or regional, are distinct storytelling realms. The term "story realm" designates the world created within a narrative—its content, or the *story*, as well as the means used to shape that world, or the *narration* (telling). In this narrative space we look at how the units of story, event, sequence, place, character, agency, point of view, and so on, all work as a system of signification to conjure and sustain a coherent and believable story. Our purpose is to conceptualize narrative as an analyzable system whose basic structural components are shared by narratives of all sorts, from literary texts to film, paintings, and landscape.[3]

A story develops through the placement, combination and substitution of events and the other structural elements of character, agency, and place. To substitute one event or place for another, to leave a gap or to change in some way the order of the sequence, changes the meaning of the story. In this manner the structure of a story is homologous to the structure of language and the two axes of signification: combination and substitution (syntagmatic and paradigmatic). Thus, the construction of meaning in both language and landscape is spatial.

Axis of Substitution
|
woods
|
garden
|
bean stalk
|
fear

That very night in Max's room a forest grew and grew and grew, until . . . Axis of Combination—placement—sequence—movement—

Structuring sequences also structure time, and narrative has been referred to as a language of time.[4] A story creates a virtual space in time: what happened yesterday, last year or in hundreds of years of ecological process. Access to and knowledge of this realm is through some form of narration. Narration time and story time are integral but different. The time represented in a narrative may be one week, a moment or a millennium; but the actual time to tell, hear or read these stories may be just five minutes. Likewise, in landscape the sense of time can be accelerated (installing mature vegetation), frozen (preserving), and modulated in many ways. Nature is often perceived as a "slow event" that can be retold, organized into epochs and summarized. In the Crosby Arboretum thousands of years of ecological succession can be experienced in an afternoon's walk. The time it takes to walk the trails is the *time of narration*, whereas the *story time* is the time of the actual geological and ecological processes.

In landscape narratives the temporal language becomes spatialized, "plotted." We can analyze not just how stories take place, but the placement of events and the way in which they create patterns of lines, circles, branching patterns, and other forms of plot. These spatial forms of stories vary in complexity, reflecting differences in determinism, choice, contingency, and chance. Instead of linear structures, authors such as Italo Calvino or Jorge Luis Borges create an experience of time that is simultaneous, embedded, and multiple, resembling a labyrinth or the complexities of ecology, rather than a single storyline.

RETELLING THE ECOLOGY OF MISSISSIPPI'S PINEY WOODS

The sixty-four-acre Pinecote Interpretive Center of the Crosby Arboretum reverses the plot of cultural narratives of progress by restoring the semblance of an original natural order to a site that had been logged, farmed, and abandoned. Healing, then, is one of the metaphors which structures the plot of the site. This story, however, began by reading the existing ecological narrative and "letting the site reveal itself."[5] Ed Blake lived on the site for four years and learned how to read plant signatures, such as how big blue andropogon

Figure 12. Crosby Arboretum, South Mississippi (Ed Blake and Mississippi State University).

indicates drier ground. He also made a grid which cut through the vegetation as a device for revealing how these subtle changes occur along a "moisture gradient."

The design then retells the region's ecology by reestablishing the structural combinations of plants in relation to processes. Bringing water to the site sets it all in motion. A pond was invented "as if" a beaver had dammed a meandering stream in a possible ecological world. This wetland zone forms part of a mosaic of interlocking ecotones. Each of the zones is managed so as to reflect different stages of ecological succession. In the savanna habitat, for instance, fire is used to suppress the growth of certain species while encouraging others. In other zones the process of succession toward diversity is "nudged" or accelerated, by planting native species that had disappeared from the site over the last one hundred years. By these means, the zones become metaphors of different times, some reflecting the recent past, some telling of first contact with this nature as the landscape "represents the dominant pinewoods which the early European settlers encountered."[6]

The series of "journeys" that structure narrative sequence weave through the zones, juxtapose edge with edge, move back and forth through different stages of succession or follow a transect along the moisture gradient in order to develop themes, break down the complexity, and build it back up again into an understanding of the whole. Rather than explaining in words, these design devices structure ways of reading signatures and signs in the landscape, replicating the ways ecologists read the landscape. Meanwhile, the site is in the process of becoming a complex, braided and evolving narrative of ecological time.[7]

*Closure and Control of Meaning*

The pleasure and power of stories lies in their ability to create coherent and believable worlds. This is achieved by the play of narrativity—the units of story: frame, events, characters, plot, space, authority, etc. A story is contingent upon a reader who participates and believes in the possible world created in the story. We can enter the various spaces and times of stories—myth, natural history, magic realism, etc.—only to the extent that we let their conventions determine what we look for and do in them.

## THE CONTEXTUAL/INTERTEXTUAL REALM

Despite the illusion of closure, stories are necessarily interrelated with aspects outside their control. They contain references and traces of other stories by many different authors, and they are interpreted by readers from multiple points of view in different contexts.

The terms *contextual* and *intertextual* designate a realm of narrative where meanings cross boundaries between the story and sites outside the story. Instead of closure, the contextual/intertextual realm opens a story to multiple readings, references, associations, and constellations of stories. The control of meaning shifts from the intentions of the author to the role of the readers within particular cultural contexts.

*From Context to Intertext*

Contextualism is a familiar ideology in landscape design. But the context of this nature is actually integral to the structuring of meaning inside the story. It is similar to the realistic novels of the nineteenth century in which the story is a "natural" outgrowth of the circumstances and milieu of the time and place. As causes are linked to environment, the novels reflected the prevailing ideology of environmental influence and determinism of the nineteenth century.

The Crosby Arboretum, as a "regional garden," is a sophisticated blending of the story realm and the world it is immersed in. The stepped edges of Fay Jones' Pinecote pavilion, for instance, imitate the effect of filtered light through the tree canopy. Fragments or miniaturized representations of the larger context are incorporated into the space of the story. Story space and contextual space are contiguous, linked in a sequence or influenced by the same processes.

"*. . . [E]very text is constructed as a mosaic of quotations, every text is absorption and transformation of another text.*"[8] Despite the ability of stories to carefully position their meanings in relation to a context, stories are necessarily related to aspects outside their control. The devices used in a story to bring closure—metaphor, metonymy, etc.—also have the potential to open other associations, references and codes beyond the intentions of the author. Metaphors have "entailments" or extra connotations that come inadvertently with their usage. In addition, multiple authorship of landscape narratives increases the plurality and complexity of meaning. The Crosby Arboretum is shaped by the collective work of the designer, consultants, a board of directors (both local and national, and from different professions), the Crosby family, marketing, and an implied public audience.

More fundamentally, the difficulty in controlling meaning inside a story arises, as post-structuralists argue, from the very nature of language itself. Meaning as structured through language is relational—produced by differences between one thing and another—which results in a constant deferral or slippage of meaning without a final, "transcendental signifier" (such as "nature"). Not only is there a potentially limitless network of meaning beyond the work, but within the work itself there are gaps, silences and an array of meanings which can disassemble the sense of unity of the work.

A story then is intertextual in two senses:

- in the layering of texts and references to other texts within the work itself that are considered relevant to its meaning.
- in the dissemination of meaning from the work across a network of other texts, contexts, genres and forms (written, oral, visual, social behavior, landscape).

The pattern of water which features at the Crosby Arboretum is a collage of the straight lines of existing drainage ditches that become the source for the new curvilinear pond. Its ecological narratives are based on ecological texts, as well as Japanese and English design traditions. In addition, the narrative of restoration is connected to a global network of other restoration projects. But in Mississippi, restoration also parallels a narrative of the emergence of "The New South," to regain national economic and cultural significance with its own regional distinctiveness.

### Reading the Landscape as an Intertextual Practice

In the article "[Re]reading the Landscape," geographers James and Nancy Duncan agree that meaning is unstable, but they criticize the notions that the interaction of texts is autonomous, and that meanings can be freely construed by any individual reader. Instead, the Duncans assert that while meaning *is* unstable and plural, it is not infinite, because texts also interact with social contexts which work to enable and constrain the range of interpretations.[9]

The intertextual realm of dispersed and unstable meaning can then be grounded in specific social contexts where meaning is not only dispersed but also gathered. In fact, part of the strength of narratives lies in how extensively they become imbricated or woven into the fabric of a community. The term "interpretive communities" designates the context of social practices in which narratives are interpreted and produced. This concept maintains the plurality and fluidity of meaning, but identifies limits to the endless play of signification.

### THE REALM OF DISCOURSE

Landscape narratives are also a discursive realm for negotiating and structuring values, beliefs and ideologies. A discourse is more than the moral of the story: it is a "social framework of intelligibility" which influences all practices of signification, including narrative and landscape. Discourses are found and produced within social institutions such as law, medicine, economics, art, biology, the family, the office, the nation, and so on. Duncan emphasizes that discourses are not rigid, deterministic frames, but fields where ideas are "communicated, negotiated or challenged."[10]

Attention to discourse focuses on the uses of stories, the purposes to which they are put, and the institutions and the world views they create and sustain. Since narratives help to establish systems of belief and authority they reproduce relationships of power in a society. Often dominant groups tell their story in the landscape, controlling interpretations as well as preventing others from making history.[11]

### Naturalizing/Denaturalizing Discourse

The discursive space of landscape narratives is difficult to apprehend, because it is effectively embedded in the ordinary, the commonplace, and the very means of telling a story. Below this horizon of critical awareness, ideologies become "naturalized." As Eagleton states: "It is one of the functions of ideology to 'naturalize' social reality, to make it seem as innocent and unchangeable as Nature itself."[12] In a sense, instead of the landscape functioning as a locus of memory, it is also a site of "cultural amnesia." The landscape is replete with "dead metaphors"—sites where original conjunction of meaning is taken-for-natural.

### The Discourses of Ecological Design at Crosby Arboretum

In both the interpretation and design of the Arboretum the discourse of ecology is primary. Carol Franklin, a principal in Andropogon who were the landscape design consultants for the project, eschews conventional, formalist design as arbitrary, capricious, and inconsequential.[13] Instead, all the interventions—the extensive "native" plantings, controlled burning of the savanna, and accelerated processes of vegetation succession—are authorized within an ecological discourse. The most dramatic intervention, the creation of the pond, was cast not as arbitrary, but something that could have occurred ecologically or historically. The water level of the pond is regulated by a small dam which simulates the water fluctuation created by the beaver dam.[14] Ecology also serves a discourse of scientific management which judges decisions according to "energy inputs" (mowing grass is inefficient) and functional relationships. But, unlike engineering, ecological design has an aesthetic ideology as well.[15]

It is the narrative of environmental crisis, however, which creates the imperative for ecological design. Carol Franklin tells this story and its implications: "We don't have time to debate about styles, about fashions. They are irrelevant to the survival of the diversity of life on our planet. . . . Passion should come first in putting systems back together, reconnecting us spiritually and functionally to the earth."[16] As this quote indicates, the ecological narrative of the site is also an allegory, a means for telling other morally charged stories of restoration: the emergence of a new south and continuity of enlightened paternalistic control of the land.

The discursive issues raised by the Crosby Arboretum characterize a more pervasive issue for the designer engaged in making places. On the one hand, narratives structure the values people live by; on the other, the strength of narratives lie in their fictions. As Hayden White argues, this situation is unavoidable, since tropes and narratives constitute the way we understand and explain the world.[17] It is an ironic but also critical position.

## REALMS AND PRACTICES

The three realms provide a framework for understanding the narrative qualities and production of places. Across these realms, landscape narratives are shaped by a variety of practices: framing, naming, sequencing, revealing/concealing, erasing, gathering, opening, and so on. These are fundamental practices of narrative as well as cultural practices that reach beyond those of professional design to include the vernacular, the rituals of daily life, journeys or memory. *Gathering*, for instance, is fundamental to narrative in that stories gather and configure time, event, and place. Likewise, places serve as a means of gathering collective experience and memory.

*Opening*

The practices of opening perhaps hold the greatest potential for new forms landscape narratives *derived from* rather than *opposed to* the multiple, indeterminate, intertextual, and discursive aspects of landscape. The idea of open landscape narratives is particularly important in the context of a growing trend to create closed narratives, such as theme parks, theme restaurants and gated communities. Controlled and scripted by certain authorities, the places formed from closed narratives can silence or displace diverse voices, erase layers of history and complexity, and draw distinct boundaries between themselves and the living, changing places they simulate.

In the story realm, opening is a way of resisting the semblance of closure or single authorship and storyline. Rather than explicit referencing or controlling sequences, the open narrative encourages the creation of multiple stories, or complex sequences, which offer choices, chance events, or recombinations. In this manner, the Crosby Arboretum uses the indeterminacy of ecology to engender an evolving, incomplete narrative. In addition, simply leaving space open and unprogrammed without specific emblematic references, can allow others to appropriate and add their stories to a place. The Vietnam Veterans' Memorial in Washington, D.C., is notable in this regard for its rhetorical silence, which evokes a multitude of responses from others.

By encouraging and incorporating multiple stories by leaving gaps, disjunctions, ambiguities and indeterminacies as intentional aspects of the work (in other words, without resolving the stories into a smooth coherence), open narratives become intertextual creations. Opening also shifts the production of meaning from the author to the reader, so that the vitality of the work is created by the active engagement of many readers. In a sense, a work is always opened by a reader who brings new life to a text.

Multiple or alternative readings also have the potential for opening the discursive space of landscape narratives. Opening is a strategy for denaturalizing ideologies that appear to be inherent or closed to interpretation. Irony, as in Martha Schwartz's project *Splice Garden*, is an effective means of unmasking and denaturalizing hegemonic discourse. What appears convincing and natural can also be challenged by multiple stories, alternative readings or counternarratives. The project *De-Code/Re-Code Atlanta* by Conway and Schulte[18] reveals the discourse inscribed in the written regulations and government processes that determine the form of public space. Their project denaturalized (de-coded) the often unseen codes by rewriting them (re-coding). They treated "language as infrastructure." Because landscape narratives so effectively materialize beliefs to make them seem natural, strategies of opening this discursive realm are some of the most critical acts of design practice.

Opening the discursive space of landscape narratives changes the relationship between designer, story, readers/community and landscape. Landscape narratives need not be controlled and plotted stories. Instead, designers can open the discourses constituted by narratives that inhere in very ordinary landscapes. Instead of emphasizing closure and unity, opening involves the ongoing processes of narrative production. In effect it engages the practices of how people make places and stories a constitutive part of their own experience, interpretation, and memory.

# REPRESENTATION AND LANDSCAPE (1992)

JAMES CORNER

A central characteristic of the often ambiguous term "landscape" is that it is first a schema, a representation, a way of seeing the external world, and, based on one's point of view, such schemata vary significantly. Geographers and painters see the land in different ways, as do developers and environmentalists.[1] If asked to draw the landscape, each party would no doubt produce a wholesome variety of graphic models and representations, reflecting their own peculiar mode of (re)cognition. Drawings might range from a cartographer's map, to an ecologist's transect, to an artist's perspective rendering. A poet might prefer words and tropes to visual images when describing a landscape. Collectively, each of these texts would "draw out" of an existing landscape a particular description, or analytique, as seen through a specific conceptual lens, and would subsequently alter or transform the meaning of that landscape. Landscapes are thus the inevitable result of cultural interpretation and the accumulation of representational sediments over time; they are thereby made distinct from "wildernesses" as they are constructed, or layered.[2]

From a landscape architectural point of view, a major aspect of landscape is that it is not only a phenomenon of analysis, but is more significantly something to be *made*, or designed. The landscape architect is very much interested in physically manipulating the land to reflect and express human ideas about Nature and dwelling therein. After all, landscape architecture is not simply an ameliorative or restorative practice, but is more precisely a figurative and representational art, providing culture with a sense of existential orientation through the construction of a built symbolic environment. Like any text, landscape architecture is conceptual, schematizing Nature and humankind's place within it, but at the same time it differs from other landscape representations in that it operates through and within the medium of landscape itself. In other words, the actual lived landscape is the medium of both construal and construction; the representation is not only encoded in various related textual media, such as literature or painting, but is more significantly embodied in the constructed landscape. As such, landscape architectural drawing—a textual medium which is secondary to the actual landscape—can never be simply and alone a case of reflection and analysis; it is more fundamentally an eidetic and *generative* activity, one where the drawing acts as a producing agent or ideational catalyst.[3]

The relationship of drawing to the production of the built landscapes remains, however, obscure. Indeed, this obscurity is made all the more difficult to understand when one stops to reflect on just *why* drawings have become so extensive and prevalent in the making of landscapes: do not drawings seem particularly abstract phenomena when compared with the phenomena of landscape? This peculiarity is made all the more apparent when one compares drawing in landscape architectural production with other modes of artistic endeavor, such as painting or sculpture. It is not insignificant that many painters and sculptors often admit to not knowing where they are going with their work when they first begin. Instead, the work "unfolds" as the artist is personally engaged with the medium and the possibilities that emerge from the work. Invariably, the fine artist's most focused attention is on the making, the touching and holding of the same worked artifact that will become the final piece.[4] During the time of engagement there occurs a spontaneity of feeling and expression arising both from a reactive response to the medium and from an imaginative source deep within. Here, the body and the imaginal are joined, inextricably involved with one another in a concentrated and creative, yet unselfconscious, unity. The making is itself a dialogue, a perceptive conversation between the medium and the imagination that cannot be intellectualized or thought of external to experience.[5] The ancient Greeks knew this; an important connotation of *poiesis,* meaning to create or to make, is that only through the sentient perception of tactile and creative activity—the actual *work* of making—can discovery and revelation occur, the longed-for "moment" of disclosure. As Heidegger has recognized, the hidden "truth" of things, their essence or *aletheia,* is something brought forth through human agency.[6]

The difficulty in landscape architecture, however, is that the actual work of building and construction is usually done by people other that the landscape architect. The instrumentality of modern construction procedures leaves little room for emotive or tactile involvement. Unlike the painter, the musician, the sculptor, or the traditional gardener, the landscape architect rarely has the opportunity to significantly touch and mould the landscape medium as it plays out in response to intervention. Although landscapists ultimately make places out of plants, earth, water, stone and light, they are caught at a peculiar distance from these same elements, working instead with a completely different medium, an intermediary and translatory medium that we call drawing. Creative access to the actual landscape is therefore remote and indirect, masked by a two-dimensional screen.

This problem of distance and indirectness is further complicated by the apparent disparity or incongruity between drawing and landscape. While the preliminary sketch bears an obvious and similar relationship to the work of painting and sculpture, a drawing, any drawing, is radically dissimilar from the medium that constitutes the lived landscape. The disparity between the phenomenon of drawing and that of the landscape means that there is often a discrepancy between what is represented and what gets built. It is significant—but not necessarily disadvantageous—that the nature and embodied meanings of drawings and landscapes belong to different worlds, as do their modes of experience.

Drawing in landscape architectural design is also different from the art of the landscape painter. In a brilliant essay called "Translations from Drawing to Building," Robin Evans has described how architectural design drawing differs from other pictorial artist in that it is not done *after* the subject, but *prior* to it, that is, prior to building and construction.[7] Landscape architectural drawing is not so much an outcome of reflection on a preexisting reality, as it is *productive* of a reality that will later emerge. The built landscape must be determined in advance, and will exist after the drawing, not before it.

Therefore, as a preface to the argument that follows, it is possible to state that the difficulties of drawing, with respect to landscape architectural production, lie primarily in three characteristics: (1) the designer's indirect and detached, or remote, access to the landscape medium; (2) the incongruity of drawing with respect to its subject—its abstractness with respect to actual landscape experience; and (3) the anterior, prevenient function of the drawing—its generative role. Paradoxically it is these same three characteristics that make such drawing enigmatic in both a negative and positive sense. On the one hand, the drawing can be an impotent imposter, an impossible analog, dangerously reductive and misused; whereas, on the other hand, drawing holds the possibility of forming a field of revelation, prompting one to figure previously unforeseen landscapes of a richer and more meaningful dimension. . . .

## The Medium of Landscape

The landscape is primarily a medium that is irreducibly rich in sensual and phenomenological terms. Traditionally, the landscape has provided a great experiential quarry from which a variety of ideas and metaphors have inspired artistic and cultural attitudes toward Nature since antiquity. As a medium of symbolic representation, the landscape and its constitutive elements—stones, plants, water, earth, and sky—when artfully composed—have provided humans with some of the most sacred and powerful places of embodied meaning. Nothing, and certainly not a picture, can replace or equal the direct and bodily experience of such places. In particular, there are three phenomena unique to the medium of landscape and the experience of the same that evade reproduction in other art forms and pose the greatest difficulty for landscape architectural drawing. These may be tentatively called landscape spatiality, landscape temporality, and landscape materiality.

## Spatiality in Landscape

Unlike paintings or novels, there is very little opportunity to wander or turn away from the experience of landscape. Spatially, it is all-enveloping and surrounds us, flooded with light and atmosphere. Irreducible, the landscape controls our experience extensively; it permeates our memories and consciousness, and enframes our daily lives.

Not only does the landscape surround us, but it does so in a limitless way. Its scale is big. Scale refers to both size and measurement, but more directly it denotes the relative size of something, the relative extent or degree. When people normally speak of landscape scale, they are referring to its bigness, its enormity relative to themselves. The limitless immensity of the landscape is felt to be spacious, sweeping, vast, enveloping and engaging of the subject. Scale engages not because it is an object—something external—but rather because it is a phenomenon that penetrates our imaginary consciousness. Bachelard has written of this experience, distinguishing the "immediate immensity" of the world, the apparent limitlessness of the great forests and oceans, from the "inner immensity" of the human imagination, the inner space of the self, infinite and luminous. Bachelard has speculated that the vast world of external Nature invokes a primal response within the subject, calming the soul and distilling a paradoxical though comforting sense of "intimate immensity" with the world. A dream-space of infinite magnitude opens wherein vast thought and imaginative extension are reciprocally engaged with the spatial corporeality of landscape.[8] Landscape scale not only envelops the body but also the imagination and the spirit.

This all-enveloping nature of landscape space, its overriding bigness and sheer sense of scale, and its inevitable correspondence with the poetic imagination are peculiar to the landscape medium. The full plenitude of landscape spatial experience cannot be represented without alteration or reduction: it can neither be drawn, for it is not in essence pictorial, nor can it be quantified, without gross simplification, for it is not all-measurable.

Furthermore, landscape space is a highly situated phenomenon, literally bound into geographical places and topographies. The spatial interrelationships of cultural and natural patterns that constitute a particular landscape mean that places are interwoven as a densely contextual and cumulative weave. Every place is unique and special, nested within a particular *topos*, or "topography." For the ancient Greeks, *topos* referred to a tangible place that immediately brought to mind a variety of associations. Places, like things, conjure up a wealth of images and ideas; we place topics and rhetorical arguments as much as we do topography and space. We always find ourselves inextricably caught up with and bound into places. Our knowledge and experience of space is therefore more ontological, or "lived," than it is mathematical or Cartesian. Heidegger recognized the situatedness of space when he wrote:

> Space is in essence that for which room has been made, that which is let into its bounds. That for which room is made is always granted and hence is joined, that is, gathered, by virtue of a location. . . . *Accordingly, spaces receive their being from locations and not from "space."*[9]

Locations "gather" and interconnect phenomena; they "admit and install" relationships to become "places." "Space is not the setting (real or logical) in which things are arranged, but the means whereby the position of things become possible," wrote Merleau-Ponty, describing how space is the "universal power" that enables things to be connected, and is fully dependent on the subject's ability to experience and move through it.[10] As such, each of us "spaces" the world around us. Through spacing we orient ourselves and construct our geographical being.[11]

Spacing also implies a conceptual ability to "think across" space. As Heidegger has shown, thinking can "persist through" distance and time to any thing or place.[12] When one moves through landscape space, that person is going "somewhere," he/she has a destination, and, in a phenomenological sense, part of the individual is already there, occupying, thinking, pervading.

The subject in the landscape is therefore a fully enveloped and integral part of spatial and phenomenological relations. The experience of landscape space is never simply and alone an aesthetic one but is more deeply experienced as a lived-upon topological field, a highly situated network of relationships and associations that is perhaps best represented as a geographical map of collagic dimensions. The topological experience of landscape obviously challenges the spatial instrumentality of Cartesian geometry and algebraic measurement that is so prevalent in the most contemporary representations of space. The Cartesian coordinates that constitute purely technical projection drawing neither originate nor end in earthy space—they are not situated in place but float in an abstract frame of analytic-mathematic relations.

## TEMPORALITY IN LANDSCAPE

Meaning, as embodied in landscape, is also experienced temporally. There is a duration of experience, a serialistic and unfolding flow of befores and afters. Just as a landscape cannot spatially be reduced to a single point of view, it cannot be frozen as a single moment in time. The geography of a place becomes known to us through an accumulation of fragments, detours and incidents that sediment meaning, "adding up" over time. Where, when, and how one experiences a landscape precipitates any meaning that is derived from it.

Moreover, as Merleau-Ponty has identified, there are no events without someone to which they happen. He has written: "Time is not a real process, not an actual succession that I am content to record. It arises from *my* relation to things. . . . Let us not say that time is a 'datum of consciousness;' let us be more precise and say that consciousness deploys or constitutes time."[13]

The disclosure of meaning in a given landscape can only occur when the subject is present, moving through it, open to sensation and experience. This phenomenological observation not only means that one's comprehension of landscape is bound to a particular cultural view. Such are the periods that constitute history. We today "see" Versailles differently from the seventeenth-century courtiers and festival-goers, for example.

Temporality in landscape experience is further complicated by the movement of the body itself, a phenomenon we call kinethesis. When moving across landscape space there is not only a dynamic flow of perceptions derived from external sources, but there is also the muscular and nervous movement of the body itself through space and time.[14] One may run, stroll, dance or ramble across, down or along a landscape, changing relational meanings through the pace and nature of bodily movement. This is further complicated by the fact that moving bodies in the landscape are often in a distracted state, the individual paying little, if any, concentrated attention to their immediate environment. We rarely pay such conscious and sensorial devotion to landscape space as we do in a painting or an object. Rather, as Walter Benjamin has recognized, the meaning derived from landscape and architectural space is received "by a collectivity in a state of distraction," slowly appreciating its symbolic environment through "habitual appropriation," or through every day use and activity.[15] The experience of landscape *takes time*, and results from an accumulation of often distracted events and everyday encounters.

A third aspect of temporality in landscape distinguishes it from buildings and other spatial artforms: landscape is a living biome that is subject to flux and change by natural processes operating over time. The dynamic action of erosion, deposition and the effects of growth and weather continually transform the structure and pattern of the shifting landscape. The same landscape may be experienced in radically different ways when it is in flood, engulfed in fog, covered with snow, or burning with fire, meaning that the qualities of space, light, texture, and ambience are ever subject to change. Not only does this dynamism challenge the art and intentionality of landscape architectural meaning (because of the impermanence of a medium caught in flux), but it also makes it difficult, if not impossible, to represent and experience it externally, as through a drawing for example.

## Substance and Materiality in Landscape

The landscape is further complicated because it is a concrete and substantial medium, composed of elemental matter. Matter is the raw, brutish stuff from which things are made. It is what constitutes material properties, making them perceptible to our senses. Materiality is the *quality* of being material and is best understood through the tactile and bodily perception of things, senses distinct from any form of secondary or objective deduction.

The tactile not only includes surface phenomena, such as roughness and smoothness, stickiness and silkiness, but also substantial phenomena such as density and viscosity, elasticity and plasticity, hardness and rigidity. Materials in the landscape radiate a host of sensory stimuli that are deeply registered by the sentient body: the aroma of material; the feeling of humidity or dampness; the intensity of light, dark, heat and cold. Different woods burn in different ways. They give off varying flame patterns—some crackle, some hiss, their embers may glow, sparkle, or smoke. As living trees, the same woods are known to us in significantly different ways. In the pine stand the wind whispers and whistles; in the gnarled oak forest it broods and wallows; in the aspen grove it rustles. Things and places become known to us because of what they impart to our senses through the very organization of their sensible aspects. The significance of anything encircles and permeates tangible matter.

Today's fascination with the visual image, the pictorial, makes it all the more important to recall how the greater part of landscape experience belongs to the sensorium of the tactile, the poetries of material and touch. A bogland for example can be quite monotonous or uninteresting visually, but it can be appreciated completely different way through bodily and tactile experience—the muttering squelch and lisp of water underfoot; the springy return of the spongy ground; the dampness of cold, gray, windless air; the peaceful *softness* of it all. Obviously, drawing is as limited here as it is in the realms of space and time. While a drawing can perhaps signify qualities, it cannot reproduce or represent the actual qualitative experience of materials which constitute the tactile landscape.

Thus, the phenomenological qualities of landscape space, time and material present unsurmountable difficulties for drawing and representation. First, the flatness and framing of the graphic presentation fails to capture the all-enveloping quality and sheer scale of landscape space. What is presented is a picture, a flat frontality approached from a distance as an object. Second, the drawing is autonomous, equally at home in a gallery or book. It is not situated as are places and locations, and remains unaltered when estranged from the complexity of life-situations. Third, the drawing is static and immediate, meaning that it is quickly decoded as the eye scans the image from a totalizing and singular point of view. Landscape experience, meanwhile, is received in moments, glances, and accidental detours, kinesthetically unfolding through rambling and habitual encounters over time. Fourth, a drawing is made of its own materials—it has its own substance, and is therefore unable to reproduce and actualize the sensuous and tactile experience of the corporeal landscape, even though a drawing may oftentimes possess the power to make humans more cognizant of a landscape's attributes. Fifth, and perhaps most significantly, the drawing is experienced optically, with rapt and full attention being paid to the image, whereas landscape is so much more, experienced as much if not more through the body than the eye. The subject in the landscape is a fully enveloped and integral part of spatial, temporal, and material relations, and nothing can reproduce the meaning that comes from this lived experience, no matter how accurate or skilful is the representation in other mediums.[16]

## THE MEDIUM OF DRAWING: PROJECTION, NOTATION, AND REPRESENTATION

The phenomenology of landscape experience eludes drawing to such a point that one might feel the need to end the discussion at this point, perhaps doubting or at best wondering how drawings can relate to landscape at all. Yet useful and imaginative relationships have evolved over the centuries (no matter how partial or indirect these may at first seem). Landscape and architectural drawing can be discussed as three quite distinct and separate types. We shall call them projection, notation, and representation.

*Projection*

Projection has to do with *direct analogies* between drawing and construction, and includes the plan, the elevation, the section, the axonometric, and, in a lesser way, the perspective. In *Natural History,* Pliny the Elder offered one myth of the origin of drawing when he told of the story of Diboutades tracing the shadow of her departing lover on the wall.[17] Robin Evans has beautifully compared David Allan's painting of Pliny's tale, entitled *The Origin of Painting,* of 1773, with the architect Frederick Schinkel's painting of the same title, done in 1830.[18] In both, light rays project the shadow of a figure onto the flat wall and constitute a traced outline which may be called a "projection." A shape is projected through space to be captured on a flat picture plane. Evans has described how, in Allan's depiction, the projected drawing was the outcome of a single-point light source casting the shadow of the seated lover onto a refined interior wall, whereas in Schinkel's painting, a man better known as an architect than a painter, the drawing was the result of solar illumination (and therefore the result of parallel projection), casting the shadow of a figure onto an uncut stone. For the architect, therefore, the projection drawing serves as a precedent to artifice, acting as a template of transfer from figure to cut-stone, or more precisely, from *idea* to built artifice.

The projection drawing is thus directly analogous to construction. One constructs a drawing as one does a building. Both are "projects." A drawing that surveys and measures an existing landscape is a literal projection of that topography onto the picture-plane. On the other hand a drawing that proposes a new and as yet unrealized landscape acts as the mediator between the designer's vision, or ideational project, and the actual construction of that project on the site. The survey drawing is projected from the ground, whereas the construction drawing is projected onto the ground. Both types of drawing are demonstrative as they reveal otherwise hidden aspects of the building or landscape. A plan, or a map for example, makes visible an aerial topography that is otherwise inaccessible.

For Vitruvius, the parts of a construction were arranged according to the "ideas of disposition," which were constituted in three ways: *ichnographia,* the plan; *orthographia,* the elevation; and *scaenographia,* the sectional profile.[19] These drawings embodied in themselves the "ideas" necessary for architectural translation and construction. Thus, the plan drawing literally demonstrates the layout and organization on the ground, akin to the marking and pegging out of a foundation: the elevation drawing demonstrates the raising and construction of a vertical face, akin to scaffolding; the section or profile-cut demonstrates the details and relations between parts; and the sectional linear perspective allows for the optical correction of proportion and scale.[20] The Vitruvian "ideas" were less graphic conventions than conceptual strategies analogous to the reality of execution. Another projection, which is more peculiar to landscape and gardens, is the planometric, probably first devised by the ancient Egyptians and developed during medieval times. Here, the vertical elements of a building or garden are "laid down," as in elevation over the plan. This "double" projection embodies both the map-like topography of landscape terrain, as seen from above, and the frontal, or elevational, composition as seen by the standing subject, and it demonstrates to the gardener the layout and distribution of the various plant forms as well as the relationships between the parts. Unlike buildings, which are raised volumetrically as floors,

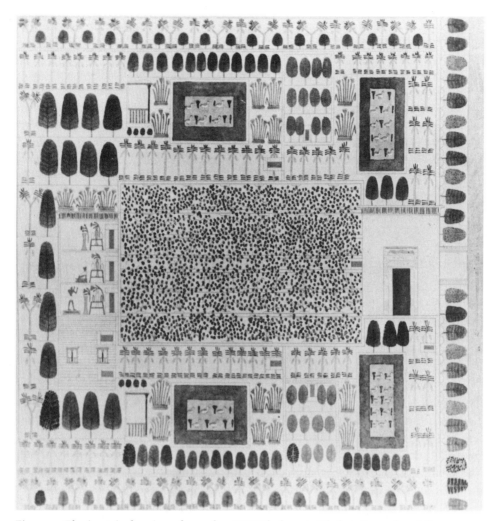

Figure 13. Planimetric drawing of a garden. XVIIIth dynasty Thebes. Reproduced from Geoffrey and Susan Jellicoe, *The Landscape of Man* (New York: Thames and Hudson, 1987), fig. 164 (photograph by Susan Jellicoe).

walls and roofs, the construction of a landscape is much akin to the workings of the planometric, emphasizing both the ground plane and the frontal identities simultaneously.

Danielle Barbaro, commenting on Vitruvius's Treatise in 1569, believed the projection geometries of plan, section and elevation to be superior to perspective, making a clear distinction between "ideas" and "expression on the paper."[21] Projective drawings are neither a picture nor a neutral set of information, rather they embody in themselves architectural ideas through co-similar and complementary projections which are ontologically conceived as being analogous to the symbolic intentions of the built work itself. This practical relationship has largely been forgotten today, displaced by a more instrumental and descriptive use of projective geometry. Alberto Perez-Gomez has described how, during most of the seventeenth century, architects could still distinguish between ontological drawing and illusionary drawing, i.e., between "practical" drawing and artificial perspective. Describing the degeneration of eidetic projective drawing into the functional and systematic methodology developed at the Ecole Polytechnique in Paris, Perez-Gomez has written: "The original architectural 'ideas' were transformed into universal projections that could then, and only then, be perceived as reductions of buildings, creating the illusion of drawing as a neutral tool that communicates unambiguous information like scientific prose."[22]

In other words, the power of demonstrative drawing lies in the fact that it is *open* to interpretation, both prior to and after the built construct. Such drawing is an integral part of the whole artistic "project," making visible what is hidden and prompting one to understand something at a higher level. One attribute of William Kent's *oeuvre* of drawings, for example, or of Bernard Tschumi's portfolio for the Parc de la Villette, is that the images significantly affect the way one sees and understands the landscape to which they refer. Never is drawing merely a mute and instrumental document. However the purely procedural techniques of modern-day projection drawings tend to alienate both designer and builder from a synesthetic and hermeneutical mode of making and knowing. From the eighteenth-century pattern books of Batty Langley, replete with a menu of geometrical templates for garden layout and design, to the current-day wide acceptance of "graphic standards" and glossaries of forms and "types," projective drawing has degenerated into a prescriptive recipe for relatively harmless, but thoughtless and trivial production. The contemporary belief that drawings are either objective communicative devises (instrumental construction drawings) or illustrations (facile presentation drawings) significantly misunderstands the traditional symbolic and ontological basis of projection.[23]

*Notation*

Some systems of standard projection belong to a family of drawing called notation. Notation systems seek to *identify* the parts of a schema, enabling them to be reproduced, enacted or performed. They include itinerary schedules, piano scores and dance notations. Measured plans, sections, elevations, and written specifications are also notational, as their main purpose is to specify the essential properties of a particular work in order for it to be translated with minimum ambiguity. In *Languages of Art*, Nelson Goodman has written that notation schemes must employ a symbol system that is "syntactically differentiated within unambiguous and finite parameters."[24] Notations are therefore strictly denotative constructs rather than connotative ones. Edward Tufte has remarked that "Design strategies for recording dance movements encompass many . . . display techniques: small multiples, close text-figure integration, parallel sequences, details and panorama, a polyphony of layering and separation, data compression into content-focused dimensions, and avoidance of redundancy."[25] The unambiguous nature of the notation is an attempt to avoid connotative or subjective misinterpretation—even though the playing of a musical score, for example—is still open to interpretation by the musician. Obviously, the quest for strictly denotative objectivity remains a fundamental principle for notational work, but, at the same time, we cannot forget that interpretative semiosis remains an inevitable part of notational reading, even though the tolerance of variation may be small.

Notation systems in landscape architectural design are not only useful for their communicative and translatory status, but also because they enable one to consider the simultaneity of different layers of experience, including movement and time. Rudolf Laban, for example, developed a system of dance notation called *Labanolation*, which precisely choreographs the movement of the body through time and space, enabling dancers to enact a

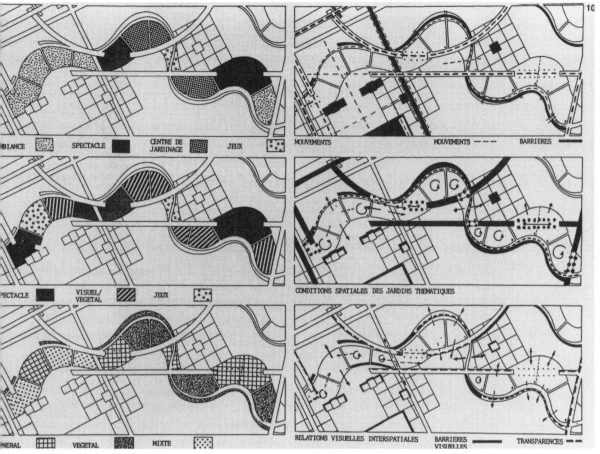

Figure 14. Cinematic path notations, Parc de la Villette, Bernard Tschumi, 1988. Reproduced by permission of Princeton Architectural Press.

particular performance.[26] It successfully challenges the view that complex motion is too difficult a subject-matter for notational articulation through a layered deployment of abstract symbols and encodings. The landscape architect Lawrence Halprin has also devised notational scores to design and coordinate fountain displays as well as to consider the disposition and experience of elements along a particular route or sequence. Halprin also developed a method of "scoring" that enabled group participation in decision making and planning. The complicated, but highly active, score itself becomes a performed piece as the creative process is graphically played out.[27] Apart from Halprin, however, notational developments specific to landscape architecture have been few and far between, and yet the analogous qualities of landscape to narrative, dance, theater, or film, suggest that notations would be a promising area of research. One might begin by studying the theatrical scores developed by Moholy-Nagy or the film storyboards of Sergei Eisenstein, who effectively separated the various layers of cinematic experience in order to coordinate the movements of the camera with the playing of the soundtrack, the dimming and brightening of light, and the timing of editing and cutting. Eisenstein called the intersection of the various layers "correspondences," explaining how the full meaning embodied in the film would be a result of their simultaneous correspondence—an overlay known as *montage*.[28] Bernard Tschumi adopted a similar strategy, layering spatial, temporal, and material phenomena into a notational sequence for a "cinematic path" at the Parc de la Villette. The notation successfully plays down visual aspects of the experience while highlighting programmatic and spatial ones.

Such notations afford a coded matrix upon which to design narratives of time and space, enabling one to orchestrate the simultaneity of spatial, temporal and tactile experience. However, these syntactically complicated graphics remain limited because of the need for specialist reading to decode the complex score and understand it as experience. How many of us can actually hear the music where we read a piano score, or experience a movie sequence from looking at a storyboard? On the other hand, notations cannot, nor should they necessarily try to, portray or depict experience; their function is simply to identify the parts which constitute it.

*Representation*

Unlike projection and notation, representational drawings aim to *represent* a given landscape or building, seeking to elicit the same experiential effects but in a different medium—to give the same effects again.[29] Pictorial perspective is therefore a representation in this sense as it depicts the depth and spatiality of a scene at eye-level from a certain vantage point. An accurate perspective structure, with carefully observed and applied chiaroscuro, texture and color, will closely resemble and imitate a particular scene, as if drawn on a pane of glass positioned between the viewing subject and the landscape. Constable, for example, strove to capture in his painting the "truth" of a scene, recording the landscape before his eyes with an almost scientific precision and discipline. With equal if not more emphasis on chiaroscuro than perspective, Constable's "naturalistic" school of painting sought to make a canvas as perfect an imitation as possible, accurately recording a retinal, almost photographic, impression. Constable's genius lay in his ability to surpass formulaic and technical approaches to painting, such as the "Claude-glass" (a polished copper mirror which made a scene appear more as it might in a canvas by Claude), and in his skill at transcending the rigidity of methodical schemata and technique, especially with regard to the innate attributes of oil paint on canvas. The lively one-to-one correspondence between scene and picture, unimpeded by the cultural codes of vision, was the aspiration and success of Constable's "art of truth."[30]

However, the realism of direct imitation poses problems for landscape architectural design. Let us not forget how landscape architectural drawings *precede* the subject-matter, unlike Constable's which were derived from a pre-existing subject. Therefore, to draw a "scene" which is yet to be built is to reverse the direction of artistic production. Whereas a painter's picture is a representation of a scene as *perceived*, a landscape architectural picture is a representation of a scene *imagined*, and, in turn, the built landscape becomes a representation of that picture. Rosalind Krauss, in her essay "The Originality of the Avant-Garde," has explained how the Picturesque paintings of Rosa, Lorrain, and Gilpin were conceived as pictorial "copies" of nature, formulaic and therefore reproducible, which actually preceded how the "original," the landscape, was subsequently seen and understood. Gilpin, for example, wrote extensively about how to look at a landscape scene and observe the "effects" of foreground, distance, perspective and "roughness." In describing this, Krauss has written, "the priorness and repetition of pictures (were) necessary to the singularity of the Picturesque," and the understanding and meaning derived from a particular landscape was "made possible only by a prior example"—a picture.[31] Krauss is describing how pictures can affect the reception and understanding of a landscape, the basis of the Picturesque, but pictures can also work to affect the production and management of landscapes. Andrew Wyeth's paintings, for example, have helped the aristocracy of Chester and Delaware Counties, Pennsylvania, form a regional landscape aesthetic which they (indirectly) employ to control the design and management of their estates.[32] Furthermore, pictures can also be used to literally transform a landscape physically. The *Red Books* of Humphry Repton, for example, show the beautification of a series of rural landscapes through the use of "before and after" paintings of specific scenes. The logic of the picture plane determines the landscape composition, subtracting and adding earth, water, and vegetation to an existing "inferior" view. Both the existing and proposed views are compared or overlaid so that one might understand the precise nature of the transformation. Of course, many eighteenth-century landscapes were laid out as an arrangement and disposition of scenes. One might stroll through such a landscape catching glimpses and then fully composed views of scenes evocative of contemporary paintings. The moving bodies of the visitors themselves often provide the action necessary to complement the scene, now backdrop.[33] The problem, however, with scenographic approaches to landscape architectural design is that they demand that the subject's primary mode of attention be visual and participatory. Vision is, of course, only one part of landscape experience; rarely is one's full attention devoted to the aesthetics of sight. Landscape perception is more fully the result of an accumulation of incident, impression and detour, more like a rambling and unpredictable sequence of events than a contrived picture-show. Reduced to a scene, the pictorial landscape is often conceived in a manner remote from both the laws of its own constituency (the effects of time and ecological flows of energy for example) and from the experiencing subject (aspects of distraction and the tactile for example). The danger of pictorial representation lies in the designer making "pictures" as opposed to "landscapes," scenes and visual compositions based upon the illusionary logic of the picture plane, rather than upon the sensual arrangement of landscape form, replete with a fullness of spatial, temporal and material qualities.[34]

However, there are other types of representation which are perhaps better able to articulate a greater sense of experience than the singularity of perspectival pictures. These representations deploy graphic signs and symbols which are rich with *connotative* value, unlike the strictly denotative symbol system used in notational drawing. Expression in representation works because of the way in which semantically rich symbols (marks, gestures, shapes, colors) can be related to metaphoric labels, figures that disclose an infinite network of associated meanings due to what Goodman has called their "semantic density."[35] The experience of inference and association in art is called *synthesia*, which means the splashing over of impressions from one sense mode to another. For example, Kandinsky illustrated how shape and color, purely visual phenomena, could be juxtaposed so as "to weep," or "to shout" or to "kill each other." We speak of "loud colors," "bright sounds," or "cold light."[36] It is the signifying capacity of a semantically rich representation which speaks to us, as in Duchamp's powerful *Genre Allegory (George Washington)*, wherein the iodine-soaked bandages pinned to a canvas with military stars ironically recall a rather disordered American flag and also silhouette the distinctive facial profile of Washington.

While such highly suggestive works are clearly visual, they are not images. That is, they

Figure 15. *Genre Allegory (George Washington)*, Marcel Duchamp, 1943. Cardboard, iodine, gauze, nails, gilt-metal stars, 53.2 x 40.5 cm (Musée Nationale d'Art Moderne, Paris). © Marcel Duchamp, 1943/ADAGP. Licensed by VISCOPY, Sydney, 2002.

do not directly resemble the optical image of things, the *image*, or the retinal specter, but rather they point to the *idea* which underlies things. In other words, the *cause* of a particular effect is shown. We may call this the archetypal essence of things: that which remains ever open to new interpretations. Drawing of this sort is therefore re-presentational; that is, it does not simply represent a world already in existence, a quantity we already know, but rather it tries to re-present the world in ways previously unforeseen, thereby making the old appear new and the banal appear fresh. The fact that drawing in landscape architectural design precedes a built reality means that it might also have first to transform a society's vision about landscape, perhaps playing less on the picture and more on the phenomenological enigmas inherent in the landscape itself. To understand representation as (de)sign—as portent or harbinger—one must first learn to forget the scenic surface of the image and think behind it, beneath it, around it.[37]

## THE MISUSE OF DRAWING

Projections, notations, and representations are all, though in differing ways, indirect, abstract, incongruous, and anterior in relation to the landscape medium. These qualities have led to two major misconceptions about the value and action of drawing in contemporary design.[38] The first misuse occurs when emphasis is placed on the drawing itself, as if the drawing is the artistic and prized artifact. In this camp, the seductive qualities of drawing promote a detached and personal preoccupation with it, whereupon the drawing is over-privileged as an artform unto itself. It is commonplace today to see autonomous and self-referential drawings as bearers of effect and the focus of attention. Such works are eminently consumable, affording a visual feast for those with the appetite, while remaining ineffectual with regard to the actual production and experience of landscape. The wide availability of images and their mass dissemination has prompted John Whiteman to write:

> First, in critical magazines, architecture becomes its own market, both producing and consuming its own images. Second, the ideology and impulses which then surround architectural drawing no longer aim toward the production of architectural experience, but instead lead to images that can only be picturesque in their hidden drive to be available for distribution.[39]

The second misuse of drawing is a reaction against the former. This party is suspicious of any meaning a drawing may hold beyond that of the strictly instrumental. Consequently, the potential richness of drawing is suppressed through a reductive and overly technical practice. Here, the emphasis is on the mute language of objective, denotative systems (plans, sections, isometrics). An outcome of the eighteenth century, this scientific view of drawing is widely practiced today owing to the emphasis on rational methodology in the design professions and building trades.[40] Moreover, as Whiteman has argued, the instrumental use of drawing has continued to gain greater currency because of the effects of modern criticism, which, like drawing, usually has its greatest impact prior to construction, but relies on the drawing, rather than the built artifact, to make its judgments—judgments made not only by professional peers but also by clients and other interest groups which can influence precisely what gets built. As Whiteman has pointed out, the problem lies in the fact that modern criticism seeks objectivity and remains suspicious of alternative symbolic systems of interpretation.[41] Subsequently: "We get scared of the artistic power of architecture and distrust our capacity to notate and represent artistic intentions to ourselves. We are made nervous by the possibility that a commitment in symbolic form might be rendered naïve. So we turn aside from a way of architecture which can reshape things to make meanings immediate and present to us. Instead we run to ideas and conceptions which seem to have automatic justification for us."[42] Furthermore, Whiteman has observed that: "Under the influence of pure criticism we have confused the separate purposes of representation and notation, and have inculcated an aesthetic in which simultaneity, immediacy and impact are the prized values. This involves a refutation of mimesis, and an attack on the notion of depth, by giving a rendering of the world in the flat."[43]

While modern criticism may perhaps promote a more objective and unambiguous form of landscape and architectural depiction, other forms of criticism, such as deconstruction, for instance, or even contemporary art criticism, promote the other extreme of drawing described in the preceding paragraph, the mystical, "artistic" drawing. The problem in both the instrumental and the ethereal drawing is that the drawing itself becomes the focus of attention for criticism. Furthermore, as the critical view also tends to place distance between the critic and the object, in this case the drawing, the distance from the actual landscape is effectively doubled. Not only does an illusory picture plane stand between critic and landscape, but so too does a screen of "critical" schemata—a screen which is often just as sterile or obscure as the drawings to which it refers. Nothing could be more remote from the lived experience of landscape space. The motivations behind either form of drawing and criticism seem antithetical to the work of landscape architecture, inevitably constructing false ground for the justification of such work.[44] Both the mystical "artist" and the pragmatic "technician" effectively sever any authentic dialogue the drawing may have with built experience and the material world, significantly misunderstanding the function of the drawing and building. In effect, the landscape medium becomes "contaminated" by the drawing; that is to say, the innate richness of the landscape itself is suppressed or suffocated by another medium which is either excessively privileged or significantly undervalued.

The source of this dichotomy lies in the fact that both the excessive and repressive uses of drawing are linked to drawing's apparent incongruity, or indirectness, in relation to landscape architecture; one camp revels in drawing's abstractness, while the other is repelled by the same level of abstraction.[45] On the one side are those who insist on an irreducible expressiveness, on the other are those insisting on an objective "realism." As Robin Evans has observed: "The two options, one emphasizing the corporeal properties of things made, the other concentrating on the disembodied qualities in the drawing, are diametrically opposed: in the one corner, involvement, substantiality, tangibility, presence, immediacy, direct action: in the other, disengagement, obliqueness, abstraction, mediation, and action at a distance."[46]

However, neither camp recognizes that landscape architectural drawing gains its potency precisely from its directness of application to landscape, on the one had, *and* its disengaged, abstract qualities on the other. After all, it is just as erroneous to suggest that the designer's free imagination is the source of inventive form as it is to discuss drawing as the sole generator of formal creation. Rather, both play off one another, as in an engaging and probing conversation. How else are the leaps and abridgments between ideas and their embodiment in form made? Drawing is an eidetic medium, and to use it simply as a means to an end, or as a means of self-indulgence in the name of "artistic expression," is irresponsible with respect to the real work of landscape architecture. This suggests a difference between drawings used merely as tools of composition and communication, and drawings which act as vehicles of creativity.[47] The emphasis shifts from drawing as image to drawing as *work* or process, a creative act which is somehow analogous to the actual construing and constructing of built landscapes.[48]

## THE METAPHORICITY OF DRAWING

This essay began by describing drawing as a translatory medium which enabled the figuration of an imaginary *idea* into a visual/spatial corporeality embodied in the built fabric of the landscape. While the essay so far may have stressed the differences between the medium of drawing and the medium that constitutes the landscape, highlighting the limits of drawing in representing (and therefore designing for) landscape experience, there still remain properties of drawing that make it an extraordinarily powerful medium in relation to the production of landscapes. The dilemma of both the ethereal and instrumental drawing, so prevalent today can be resolved when drawing is understood at the *locus* of reconciliation between construal and construction, or between symbolic and instrumental representations.[49] For example, the original Vitruvian "ideas" as embodied in drawing suggest that drawings hold the possibility of being both projective, notational, and representational at the same time. Neither images nor pictures, such drawings are analogical demonstrations of both construal and construction. They are the architecture, embodying the symbolic intentions of the building and demonstrating its construction.

A more significant type of drawing in landscape architectural design might arise from a twofold use of the graphic medium: one is the speculative function, and the other is the demonstrative function. In the first, drawing is used as a vehicle of creativity, and in the second, drawing is used as a vehicle of realization. Both types of drawing work by analogy and occur alongside one another simultaneously.

As a vehicle of creativity, drawing is a highly imaginative and speculative activity, entailing both spontaneity and reflection. It first involves the making of marks and the "seeing" of possibilities. Such work is both imaginal and theoretical, making images and recording spatial and tactile qualities through a process of association, akin to what was said earlier about Kandinsky and the power of synesthesia. For example, in the Chinese and Japanese technique of "flung-ink" painting, originating as early as the fourteenth and fifteenth centuries, ink is first thrown onto the canvas in an energetically random manner to form a visual field. The painter then improvises through immediate response to the thrown image and beings to construct a landscape through the working of the brush. Alexander Cozens developed a similar approach of responsive drawing during the eighteenth century in England. In such improvisational, rapid-response work, the graphic field is deeply inhabited by all the visceral and imaginative capacities of the artist striving to see, to draw out and to bring-into-being.

The flung-ink (although it could be any graphic medium, some much richer such as tempera or oil paints) begins the process by opening up a synesthetic "field," a metaphorically suggestive realm that prompts an imaginative seeing. Leonardo da Vinci had once said that one first truly learns to see by allowing one's attention to become absorbed in streaks of dried spittle or the surface of an old stained wall until the imagination is able to distinguish an *alternative* world.[50] Seventeenth-century artists Johann Konig and Antonio Carracci used the suggestive fields of veined marbles and agates as the basis for highly imaginative paintings of landscapes and other representations. Figures and images were literally drawn out and metamorphosed from the surfaces of stone and minerals.[51] Similarly, the making of graphic and collage fields "irritate" the mental faculties to such a degree that fountains of possibilities emerge before the percipient; one becomes so engaged with the wealth of images that new worlds are disclosed, as if in a dream or hallucination. Like the luminous collages of Schwitters or Ernst, these fields of interpretation make impressions on the receptive mind and, in turn, the imagination impresses itself into the field. Fresh images might be conjured up as one "sees" things in new associations. As the Surrealists have already shown the power of a physically inhabited and synesthetic realm can re-enchant the ordinary and make the everyday world magical once again.[52]

The tactics of appropriation, collage, abstraction, imaginative projection, and so on, are strategies used to prompt free association, providing liberatory mechanisms of construal. However, such work first requires that the drawing be theoretically and critically motivated by the maker. Collage, for example, is not a random and unfocused activity, but demands a highly disciplined and reflective mind. It is not simply a matter of "anything goes." Any creative transformation that results from human intellection will always entail special vocabularies, procedures and modes of demonstration specific to a particular theorem and motive. The game is complex, elusive, unsystematic, and ever subject to modification. It is important to remember that these types of drawing are only strategies; their primary work is in critical response to something. They are neither automatic divination screens, yielding up ideas of their own making, nor are they grounds of justification, falsely legitimizing the project simply because of their perceived magic. The function of abstraction in drawing is simply to discover new ground, to gain insight, not to obfuscate, nor to justify a project.

The difficulty in such drawing lies in distinguishing the culturally and architecturally relevant from the limits of personal fancy or those of more transient value. The percipient must be able to distinguish between weak, fanciful ideas and the more potent images and symbolic structures relevant to landscape architectural experience. Ideas such as archetype, deep structure, and the constancy of the primary or typical human condition, belie the fact that there are universally significant situations peculiar to the human condition.[53] Essentially, a significant "seeing" is about re-cognition, and remains the outcome of productive and meaningful poetic activity. Drawing can best function in this capacity if two tenets are first upheld: first, drawings are eidetic phenomena which work through symbols and analogues, not through likeness of representation. This point is illustrated by Frascari, who equates graphic and constructed angles with "angels." In describing the journeys of the early Mediterranean sailors, Frascari has written:

> The imagining of angels, building essences, was a way of finding the angles necessary to determine the direction for reaching land safely. In architecture this traditional charisma of angels and angles is recorded, in an oblique way, by Vitruvius. In his explanation of the planning of the angles of cities, Vitruvius cites as an example the Tower of Winds in Athens. This hellenistic edifice incorporates both representations of the winds as figures of angels and as the angles of direction.[54]

Later, he concludes: "the objects of architecture should not be given to public knowledge in a rigid, finished state, in their naked 'as suchness.' Rather, they should be presented as demonstrations in such a way that each angle should be dressed up as an angel."[55]

Figure 16. Sesshu, *Water and Mountain,*
1490–1497. Ink on parchment paper,
70 x 34 cm.

For Frascari then, the instrumental and the symbolic (or visible and the invisible), are united through analogies between the signifier and the signified. The degree of reciprocity between both the signifier and the signified thus forms a second tenet of drawing. John Whiteman has referred to this correspondence as a "qualitative precision" between the symbols used in representation and the ideas they embody in built landscape form. He has written: "(An understanding of the terms qualitative precision) means admitting that the logics of formal manipulation cannot be purely autonomous, that judgements in architectural design are guided not by the autonomous reasons of form alone but rather by a coupled sense of the physical and the symbolized, the visible and the invisible."[56]

A more laconic and accurate form of drawing might best be realized by the individual with time and experience, as one can only properly understand the interrelationships between the symbolic and the material worlds more through sensible observation than by secondary constructs such as concepts and analytical matrices. However, the qualitative precision of angles and angels is not simply a case of observational clarity (which is something always susceptible to scientific prescription and duplication), but more properly derives from imaginative construal. The paradox inherent in the term "qualitative precision" is that accuracy of observation belongs not to scientific certainty but to the realm of myth and poetry wherein things make sense and ring true without necessarily being explicit or accountable. It is in this way that symbols retain their open-endedness and are subject to ever richer association.

Speculation through drawing is, however, only part of drawings full function with respect to landscape architectural production. A necessary complement lies in drawings' capacity to demonstrate intention and construction—the drawing as a vehicle of realization. This type of drawing goes beyond speculative fields (and the emergence of ideas), and instead it begins to demonstrate the project in practical terms. In describing the drawings of two contemporary architects, Carlo Scarpa and Mario Ridolfi, Fascari has written:

> Scarpa works out his strata of architectural mediations on pieces of Bristol board with overlays of light pieces of tracing paper, using drafting and colored pencils, diluted inks and applying the painterly technique of *pentimenti*. Ridolfi utilizes layers of heavy tracing paper for his analogical thinking, employing a fountain pen, and editing the final drawing with a skilful use of scissors and transparent adhesive tape. Scarpa's and Ridolfi's drawings . . . are visual descriptions of processes that are not visible. They are conceived not to be read by the public, but to carry out a demonstration of intent. On the other hand, conventional working drawings are scientific tools for presenting a future reality within an appearance of continuous and uniform order; *they show a result, not the intent.*[57]

The dynamic drawings of Scarpa and Ridolfi are "productive representations of an eidetic process,"[58] the result of analogically working the medium of drawing with the medium of building. Scarpa, for example, scores his paper with a plan delineation of the particular site and its physical context. Layers are then added and subtracted orthographically, as if alternately building and partly demolishing foundations. Scales are shifted and overlaid as parts and details are played alongside the construal of the whole. The drawings are made neither for construction nor presentation, but rather for the disciplined *work* found in these ideational drawings, enabling the ideas to be translated into built form. The representation of space is not separated from the space of representation, just as the function of representation is not separated from the representation of function.

A common aspect of both the speculative and the demonstrative drawing is that they each act as vehicles for creativity, as intermediary catalysts that are used to *generate* a landscape architectural project. Never are they merely descriptive on the one hand, nor decorative and fetishistic on the other. Rather, they both belong to a kind of work called *deixis*. In describing deixis, Norman Bryson has explained how the term originally derives from *deikononei*, meaning "to show," to make evident, and that in linguistics the term *deictic* is

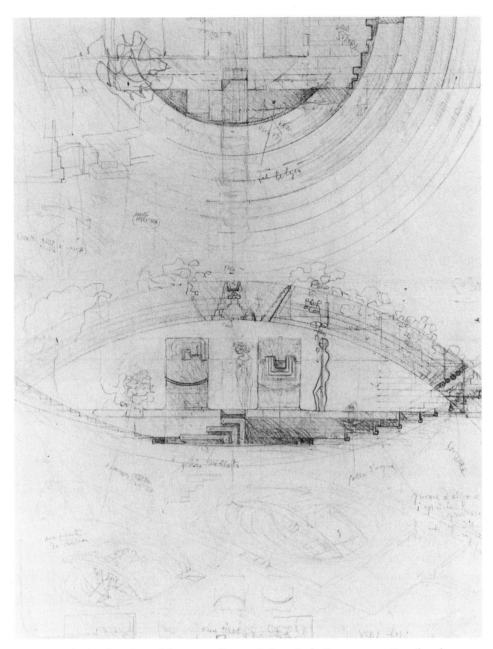

Figure 17. Plan and section of the Arcosolium at Brion, Carlo Scarpa, 1969. Pencil and crayon on brownline copy, 50 x 40 cm.

applied to utterances that supply information regarding the source of utterance. Deictic tenses are always compounds of the present, the here and now, and stand in contrast to aoristic tenses which are past and imperfect, and belong characteristically to the historian, "reciting the events of the past impersonally and without reference to his/her own position."[59] In further describing deixis, Norman Bryson has written: "The wider class of deixis there-

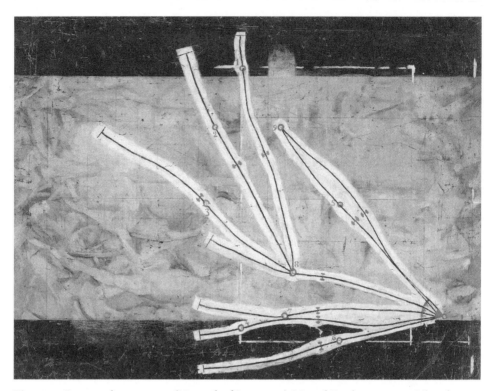

Figure 18. *Reseaux des stoppages (Network of Stoppages),* Marcel Duchamp, 1914. Oil and pencil on canvas, 148.9 x 197.7 cm (The Museum of Modern Art, New York). © Marcel Duchamp, 1914/ADAGP. Licensed by VISCOPY, Sydney, 2002.

fore includes all those particles and forms of speech where the utterance incorporates into itself information about its own spatial position relative to its content (here, there, near, far), and to its own relative temporality (yesterday, today, tomorrow, sooner, later, long ago). Deixis is utterance in carnal form and speaks back directly to the body of the speaker."[60]

In relationship to painting, Bryson has elaborated on deixis by discussing the making of Chinese and Japanese flung-ink paintings. While landscape is clearly the focus of attention in these canvases, equally so is the spontaneous work of the brush in "real," or processual, time. Bryson has written: "The work of production is constantly displayed in the wake of its traces; in this tradition the body of labor is on constant display, just as it is judged in terms which, in the West, would only apply to a *performing* art."[61]

The imaginal is both enacted and constructed in a radically temporal and dynamic sequence of painterly responses. The action of seeing and marking does not attempt to conceal its own evolvement, mistaken attempts and all. Instead, the paintings deictically play out and express their own construal, like a performance which maps out its own body. This is in contrast to "the image that suppresses deixis," the image that "has no interest in its own genesis or past, except to bury it in a palimpsest in which only the final versions show through above an interminable debris of revisions. . . . (Here) the existence of the image in its own time, of duration, of practice, of the body, is negated by never referring the marks on canvas to their place in the vanished sequence of local aspirations." The deictic[62] drawing, meanwhile, records and traces its own evolution, and refers back to an entire corpus of prior thoughts, ideas, and associations. Deixis both marks and realizes the moment at which construal becomes construction.

## CONCLUSION

Research into the development of projection, notation, and representation vis-à-vis the effective and artful construal, construction, and sustenance of built landscape form has still yet to occur in a vibrant and imaginative way.[63] This research might begin through an increased understanding of the mechanisms of analogy and metaphor in both speculative and demonstrative drawing. Analogical drawing looks for some form of interaction and dialogue between the symbolic realms of ideas and meaning and the structures of projection and embodiment. In this way, the drawing is an integral part of the landscape "project," holding within its deictic traces the symbolic and instrumental intentions of the scheme. Such drawings might not only tell us what things might be but also what they are *like*, suggesting, without necessarily prescribing quite specific settings and topologies. Plans, sections, notation scores, scale shifts, light and texture studies, and so on, are drawn alongside the speculative play of the collagic field, actively plotting landscape relationships between the idea and construction. While the focus of attention shifts from normative modes of perception to a more liberating discovery of intertextuality between things, a precision of intent and demonstration thereof is still demanded. Analogical thinking is both intuitive and rational, and must play subjective sensibilities off and against systems of order and measure.[64]

Metaphorical/analogical drawing is thus radically different from analytical drawing, which is more instrumental and calculative than it is poetic and imaginative. The generative free-play of metaphorical and deictic drawing, in dialogue with the discipline of notation and projection, is a critical and speculative practice that demonstrates the chiasm of a landscape's construal and construction. Rich with significance and interpretative ambiguity, landscape architectural drawing as a synesthetic and commutative medium might better afford a richer realization of ideas within the built environment. Such a drawing is less a finished "work of art," and even less a tool for communicating instrumental ideas, than it is itself a catalytic locale of inventive subterfuges for the making of poetic landscapes. In essence, the drawing is a plot, necessarily strategic, map-like, and acted out.

# LANDSCAPE AS CULTURAL PRODUCT (1984)

## DENIS COSGROVE

[The key to the modern landscape idea and its development lies in the] dual significance of land during the struggles to redefine it. In a natural economy the relationship between human beings and land is dominantly that of the insider, an unalienated relationship based on use values and interpreted analogically. In a capitalist economy it is a relationship between owner and commodity, an alienated relationship wherein man stands as outsider and interprets nature causally. Culturally, a degree of alienation is achieved by compositional techniques—particularly linear perspective, the formal structure of the pastoral in poetry and drama and the conventional language of landscape appreciation. The idea of landscape holds both types of relationship in an unstable unity, forever threatening to lapse into either the unreflexive subjectivism of the insider where the feeling for the land is incommunicable through the artificial languages of art; or the objectification of land as property pure and simple, the outsider's view, where alienation is complete and a statistical weighting can be placed upon the "landscape value" of a piece of land which can be entered into a cost/benefit analysis against the value that the land might have as an industrial site. The origin of the landscape idea in the West and its artistic expressions have served in part to promote ideologically an acceptance of the property relationship while sustaining the image of an unalienated one, of land as use. The history of the landscape idea is one of artistic and literary exploration of the tensions within it until, with the hegemonic establishment of urban industrial capitalism and the bourgeois culture of property, landscape lost its artistic and moral force and became a residual in cultural production regarded either as an element of purely individual subjectivity or the scientifically defined object of academic study, particularly in geography. The ambiguity in landscape between individual and social meaning may be understood as an alternative way of articulating the same tensions, but at the level of human relationships, of self and community, rather than human life and land. . . .

As an active force in cultural production landscape atrophied in the late nineteenth century. With the secure establishment of industrial capitalism the relationship it had long posited of a separation of individual from land and its private, personal consumption through sight, had become a way of being, experienced in urban life, intellectually defended in science and promoted in education while endlessly reinforced by the stream of visual images set before our eyes. Landscape, for all its appeal, cannot mediate the experience of the active insider and the passive outsider, as Ruskin discovered. Geographers who proclaim a human landscape concept need to recognize this as a point of departure, not a problem to be overcome, but a contradiction to be explored in its various contexts. Commenting on the writing of one of England's greatest landscape novelists, Thomas Hardy—amateur landscape painter and creator of the enduring image of Wessex—John Barrell[1] has stressed the impossibility of capturing "the simultaneous *presence* of someone within the centre of knowledge . . . and his *absence* from it, in a position from which he observes but does not participate." Such a feat is doubly impossible with the landscape idea: it originated as the outsider's perspective, it remains a controlling composition of the land rather than its mirror. Therefore, *Landscapes can be deceptive.*

*Sometimes a landscape seems to be less a setting for the life of its inhabitants than a curtain behind which their struggles, achievements and accidents take place. For those who, with the inhabitants, are behind the curtains, landmarks are no longer geographic but also biographical and personal.*[2]

# THE EXPANDED FIELD OF LANDSCAPE ARCHITECTURE (1997)

ELIZABETH MEYER

I am particularly interested in defining and establishing a theory for the built landscape between the dominant binary categories of many texts on modern design. In particular, I realize that we must alter the marginal role landscape architecture has been assigned in the histories of modernity. As a field that built physical critiques of, and in, the American city that embodied broader society's unquestioning acceptance of industrialization and technological progress, landscape architecture has not fit within the descriptive, evaluative, and interpretive categories of mainstream modernism—historical or theoretical. As such, its contributions to culture and society have either not been recognized or have been misinterpreted and maligned. Landscape architects are only now coming to terms with this deficit and its implications for designers and planners.

My research methods and interpretive strategies for theory-making as a feminist landscape architect can be characterized as follows:

1. Interpretations of built works and treatises should be based on primary experiences that are mediated through the knowledge of historical situations. This primary experience has two forms—visiting a site; and studying historical plans, maps, treatises, journals, letters, photographs, and the like.

For example, to understand the topographic form and hydrologic systems that structure the Emerald Necklace park system, a student of the Olmsted firm's project must study more than the 1894 plan. That engraving depicts streets, water bodies, plantations of trees, and meadows, but no topography. The site appears flat. The shapes and locations of the various "beads" along the Necklace seem arbitrary—or informal and unstructured. After studying the landforms of the park system through grading plans of the period and contemporary U.S. Geological Survey (USGS) maps of Boston, one discerns repeated landforms, such as drumlins and eskers, that characterized this glaciated terrain. The alignment of the Necklace is not irregular; it maximizes the diversity of landscape types that characterize New England. The alignment of the Necklace and the undulations of the land within its boundaries speak of the structure of the land.

A walk along the seven-mile transect from Franklin Park, the country park, to the Public Garden and the Boston Common is an excellent way to assemble the information found in nineteenth-century maps, plans, and reports into a coherent spatial narrative. This walk, too, must be mediated by comparing historic photographs with contemporary appearances, because the growth and decline of vegetation, and the modification of adjacent roadways, have altered the connections between the "beads."

2. We should be suspect of the generalizations that "transcend the boundaries of culture and region."[1] Instead, theoretical work should be contingent, particular, and situated. Grounding in the immediate, the particular, and the circumstantial—the attributes of situational criticism—is an essential characteristic of landscape architectural design and theory. Landscape theory must rely on the specific, not the general; and like situational and feminist criticism landscape architectural design and theory must be based on observation, on what is known through experience, on the immediate and sensory—what is known by

all the senses, not only the eye. Thus, landscape architectural theory is situational; it is explicitly historical, contingent, pragmatic, and ad hoc.[2] It is not about idealist or absolute universals. It finds meaning, form, and structure in the site as it is. The landscape does not sit silent awaiting the arrival of an architectural subject. The site—and land—speaks prior to the act of design.

Earlier I described Prospect Park as a landscape design that applied the abstract conceptual language of nineteenth-century aesthetic theory—the Beautiful or Pastoral, the Picturesque, and the Sublime—to the particular conditions of a tract of land in Brooklyn. The circumstances of the site—its location at the boundary between glaciated and nonglaciated landforms—suggested the most fitting place for each of the aesthetic characters to be developed.

Bos Park in Amsterdam provides another example of how built landscapes should be situated prior to, and through, theoretical interpretation. The location of Bos Park on a polder encourages us to look closely at the section of the park. Height above sea level is the critical dimension in the design; the section, not the plan, is key in describing the structure of the existing land and the design response to it.

3. We should be skeptical of discourses that assign a gender affiliation to the landscape—implicitly or explicitly. The implicit affiliations are manifest as "female"—the "other" who is seen but not heard. Hitchcock's writing on the modern garden, noted earlier, is an example of this. The ideal modern house is surrounded by sylvan nature that merely frames the building. Nature is the neutral backdrop. The explicit affiliations are manifest as "feminine"—that which is irrational, wild, chaotic, emotional, natural. The site descriptions of Duany and Plater-Zyberk are examples of this, as any landscape element that alters the town plan grid is considered awkward or distorting. There are not two structures on the site, only one—that of Euclidean geometry.

4. While the deconstruction of the discourses that relegate landscape to a silent female or irrational feminine role in modernism is necessary, it is not enough. We need to reconstruct the unheard languages of the modern landscape as a means to reinvigorate contemporary design practice. The work of a feminist design critic is reconstructive, not destructive. This reconstruction assumes a multilayered fabric that weaves together threads from primary sources and documents written by landscape architects and about landscape architecture with the concurrent history of ecological ideas, cultural and historical geography, design and planning criticism, and site interpretation.[3]

We must do more than note how badly served landscape architecture is by descriptions that rely solely on architectural categories and concepts. Scholars' research into the history of modern landscape architecture must question what has been lost when landscape design components are overlooked. As noted in the earlier interpretation of Radburn, by ignoring the project's planting plan and the contributions of Cautley, the social spaces of the neighborhood were misunderstood by historians and practitioners. The role of trees and hedges as spatial subdivisions between the public and private realms was ignored, and the result was that the many projects that supposedly emulated Radburn were characterized by amorphous open space. Contemporary residential life, as well as an accurate history, suffered from this incomplete reading.

5. Finally, landscape architectural history has been, for the most part, a masculine discourse focusing on the works of great landscape architects—mostly men. The history of modernity has especially concentrated on the autonomy of these artistic works, their formal attributes, and their plan configurations. This historiography must be enhanced and challenged, for it denies the conditions of practice, conceptualization, and experience. This chal-

lenge exposes landscape history as a fiction that has been written through a particular lens or sensibility that has ideological implications.[4] By challenging the "formulation of the crucial questions of the discipline as a whole," I am following in the footsteps of scholars such as Griselda Pollock and Linda Nochlin, whose writings have enriched the histories of modern art.[5] To paraphrase Pollock, a dual role for feminist landscape architectural history and theory—"recovery of women producers" and "deconstruction of the discourses and practices of [architectural] history itself"—is a positive act of construction, not destruction.[6]

For landscape architectural history and theory, this translates into more than research on the many women designers whose careers were ignored by such scholars as landscape historian Norman Newton. Scholars must also reconsider the methodologies of prior histories to ascertain whether or not they precluded some works from entering into the canon. Scholars and students must determine whether a history comprised of monographs on individual designers and their works allows for the consideration of the complexity of collaborative work in a corporate practice. How does one chronicle the works of Sasaki Associates, the SWA Group, or EDAW, for instance—three firms whose employees move in and out of the practice over time? We must discuss whether landscape architecture's quest for status as a profession and discipline on par with that of architecture resulted in the repression of more horticulturally focused designs and designers. We should wonder about the lack of contextual site plans and urban plans in our histories, which limit our ability to interpret built landscapes as more than great works or objects. Shouldn't landscape architectural history and theory attempt to uncover the interrelationships between a project and its surroundings? If we believe it is important for students to know something about the history of architecture as well as landscape architecture, shouldn't they also know something about the emergence of ecological thinking, especially during the nineteenth and early twentieth centuries?

One goal of scholarship, therefore, is to construct legitimate alternatives to the limiting binary terms that modern society has adopted to describe relationships between landscape and architecture, nature and culture, female and male, nature and man. In place of such oppositional binaries, we need conceptual quaternary fields such as those I have proposed for figure and field, man and nature. These expanded fields are defined by concepts—such as the figured ground, articulated space, the minimal garden, and landscapes for architecture—with complex, not simple, relationships to one another. The scholar can develop theories for site description and interpretation that occupy the space between nature and culture, landscape and architecture, man-made and natural, and that are along the spatial continuum that unites, not the solid line that divides, concepts in binary opposites.

This realm of inclusions will reposition the landscape from "other" to "ground." Andreas Huyssen's essay "Mapping the Postmodern" may offer direction here. He proposes that "in an important section of our culture there has been an important shift in sensibilities, practices and discourse formations which distinguishes a postmodern set of assumptions, experiences and propositions from that of the preceding period." He continues by arguing that postmodernism has not "generated genuinely new aesthetic forms," but rather has continued to employ modernity's forms "reinscrib[ing] them into an altered cultural context." Huyssen lists the environment and ecology—along with the culture of women, minorities, and non-Westerners—as the grounds upon which modernity's forms are reinscribed.[7] Huyssen's procedure for reinscription connotes an image of intersections, overlaps, hybrids, and cyborgs that are created only by acknowledging that two terms of elements can relate to one another without implied hierarchies or dominances—without

## Sculpture in the Expanded Field - Rosalind Krauss

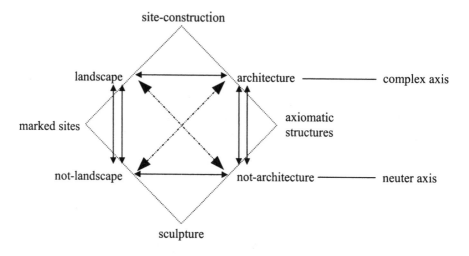

## An Expanded Field for Landscape Architecture 2 - Elizabeth Meyer

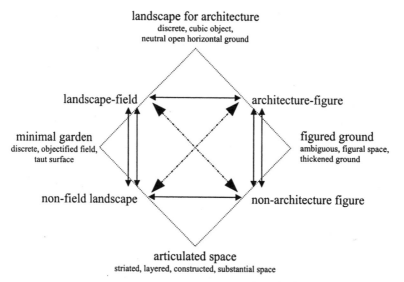

Figure 19. An alternative version of an expanded field for landscape architecture, derived from Krauss's "Sculpture in the Expanded Field" (after Rosalind Krauss and Elizabeth Meyer).

"others." Instead of a static, visual landscape that is out there, irrational, irregular, and open, we have a spatial, temporal, and ecological site that is present before an artist or a designer begins to work. The designer, then, allows the site to speak more clearly through the design interventions he or she makes. The site and the designer are collaborators.

# PART V

# Ecological Design and the Aesthetics of Sustainability

One of the most significant shifts in the theoretical orientation of the discipline over the past fifty years has been the development of concepts of "ecological" and "sustainable" design. This in turn has raised questions about the aesthetic basis for ecological design. In particular, there has been a sustained critique of the way that picturesque conventions have disguised ecological processes within modern landscapes. In Part V, a series of readings sets out a framework of ecological design and alternative approaches to its aesthetic expression. Proposals for a new ecological aesthetic for urbanism have been integral to these developments. The theme that links the readings is best expressed in the title of John T. Lyle's (1991) article "Can Floating Seeds Make Deep Forms?" That is, how can identification and expression of the underlying ecological and cultural processes of a project and site provide the basis for configuration of landscape as "deep" rather than shallow form? The different formulations of an ecological aesthetic in Part V all articulate aspects of this fundamental question.

Ian McHarg's presentation of an "ecological method" for regional planning and design has already been included under Part II, Design Process. In this section, a short extract from *Design with Nature* (1969) expresses something of the aesthetic motivation underlying the method. It is followed by an extract from Anne Whiston Spirn's reconceptualization of the city as *The Granite Garden* (1984), which argued for an ecology of urbanism. Much of the impetus for urban "ecological design" drew upon European, particularly Dutch, work. Alan Ruff was a translator and advocate of this approach in the United Kingdom throughout the 1970s and 1980s, and an extract from his essay "An Ecological Approach to Landscape Design" (1982) succinctly summarizes many of the principles that have subsequently become widely adopted. All three adopt a normative stance.

While McHarg advocated "design *with* nature," John T. Lyle's *Design for Human Ecosystems* is a powerful expression of a more *adaptive* ecological approach. An extensive extract sets out the conceptual basis and main process elements of Lyle's method. It is followed by a short extract from "Can Floating Seeds Make Deep Forms?" (1991) which starts to explore the aesthetic consequences of creating human ecosystems.

The final two readings provide contrasting responses to the development of an "ecological" aesthetic. The first is a series of extracts from Robert Thayer's *Gray World, Green Heart* (1994). In these, Thayer articulates his belief that ecosystem function should be made explicit through landscape form, blemishes and all, in order that people learn the ecological consequences of their actions and behavior, and that sustainable practices gain visibility and acceptance within culture. In *Messy Ecosystems, Orderly Frames* (1995) Joan Iverson Nassauer proposes a somewhat different strategy, by which ecological restoration is "framed" within more familiar cultural forms and patterns, for example "cues for care" such as mown strips, on the basis that this will facilitate wider acceptance of change.

# DESIGN WITH NATURE (1969)

## IAN MCHARG

We need nature as much in the city as in the countryside. In order to endure we must maintain the bounty of that great cornucopia which is our inheritance. It is clear that we must look deep to the values which we hold. These must be transformed if we are to reap the bounty and create that fine visage for the home of the brave and the land of the free. We need, not only a better view of man and nature, but a working method by which the least of us can ensure that the product of his works is not more despoliation.

It is not a choice of either the city or the countryside: both are essential, but today it is nature, beleaguered in the country, too scarce in the city which has become precious. I sit at home overlooking the lovely Cresheim Valley, the heart of the city only twenty minutes away, alert to see a deer, familiar with the red-tailed hawk who rules the scene, enamored of the red squirrels, the titmouse and chickadees, the purple finches, nuthatches and cardinals. Yet each year, responding to a deeper need, I leave this urban idyll for the remoter lands of lake and forest to be found in northern Canada or the other wilderness of the sea, rocks, and beaches where the osprey patrols.

This book [*Design with Nature*] is a personal testament to the power and importance of sun, moon, and stars, the changing seasons, seedtime and harvest, clouds, rain and rivers, the oceans and forests, the creatures and the herbs. They are with us now, co-tenants of the phenomenal universe, participating in that timeless yearning that is evolution, vivid expression of time past, essential partners in survival and with us now involved in the creation of the future.

Our eyes do not divide us from the world, but unite us with it. Let this be known to be true. Let us then abandon the simplicity of separation and give unity its due. Let us abandon the self-mutilation which has been our way and give expression to the potential harmony of man-nature. The world is abundant, we require only a defense born of understanding to fulfill man's promise. Man is that uniquely conscious creature who can perceive and express. He must become the steward of biosphere. To do this he must design with nature.

# THE GRANITE GARDEN (1984)

## ANN WHISTON SPIRN

Seen from space, the earth is a garden world, a planet of life, a sphere of blues and greens sheathed in a moist atmosphere. At night, lights of the cities twinkle far below, forming constellations as distinct and varied as those of the heavens beyond. The dark spaces that their arcs embrace, however, are not the voids of space, but are replete with forests and farms, prairies and deserts. As the new day breaks, the city lights fade, overpowered by the light of the sun; blue seas and green forests and grasslands emerge, surrounding and penetrating the vast urban constellations. Even from this great distance above the earth, the cities are a gray mosaic permeated by tendrils and specks of green, the large rivers and great parks within them.

Homing in on a single constellation from hundreds of miles up, one cannot yet discern the buildings. But the fingers and patches of green—stream valleys, steep hillsides, parks, and fields—swell and multiply. The suburban forest surrounds the city; large lakes and ponds catch the sunlight and shimmer. Swinging in, now only a few miles up, the view is filled by a single city. Tall buildings spring up toward the sky, outcrops of rock and steel, and smaller homes poke up out of the suburban forest. Greens differentiate themselves into many hues. Silver ribbons of roadway flash across the landscape, and stream meanders interrupt and soften the edges of the city's angular grid.

Flying low, one skims over a city teeming with life. The amount of green in the densest part of the city is astonishing; trees and gardens grow atop buildings and in tiny plots of soil. On the ground, a tree-of-heaven sapling is thriving in the crack between pavement and building, and a hardy weed thrusts itself up between curb and sidewalk. Its roots fan out beneath the soil in search of nutrients and water. Beneath the pavement, underground rivers roar through the sewers.

The city is a granite garden, composed of many smaller gardens, set in a garden world. Parts of the granite garden are cultivated intensively, but the greater part is unrecognized and neglected.

To the idle eye, trees and parks are the sole remnants of nature in the city. But nature in the city is far more than trees and gardens, and weeds in sidewalk cracks and vacant lots. It is the air we breathe, the earth we stand on, the water we drink and excrete, and organisms with which we share our habitat. Nature in the city is the powerful force that can shake the earth and cause it to slide, heave, or crumple. It is a broad flash of exposed rock strata on a hillside, the overgrown outcrops in an abandoned quarry, the millions of organisms cemented in fossiliferous limestone of a downtown building. It is rain and the rushing sound of underground rivers buried in storm sewers. It is water from a faucet, delivered by pipes from some outlying river or reservoir, then used and washed away into the sewer, returned to the waters or river and sea. Nature in the city is an evening breeze, a corkscrew eddy swirling down the face of a building, the sun and sky. Nature in the city is dogs and cats, rats in the basement, pigeons on the sidewalks, raccoons in culverts, and falcons crouched on skyscrapers. It is the consequence of a complex interaction between the multiple purposes and activities of human beings and other living creatures and the natural processes that govern the transfer of energy, the movement of air, the erosion of the earth, and the hydrologic cycle. The city is part of nature.

Nature is a continuum, with wilderness at one pole and the city at the other. The same natural processes operate in the wilderness and in the city. Air, however contaminated, is always a mixture of gasses and suspended particles. Paving and building stone are composed of rock, and they affect heat gain and water runoff just as exposed rock surfaces do anywhere. Plants, whether exotic or native, invariably seek a combination of light, water, and air to survive. The city is neither wholly natural nor wholly contrived. It is not "unnatural" but, rather, a transformation of "wild" nature by humankind to serve its own needs, just as agricultural fields are managed for food production and forests for timber. Scarcely a spot on the earth, however remote, is free from the impact of human activity. The human needs and the environmental issues that arise from them are thousands of years old, as old as the oldest city, repeated in every generation, in cities on every continent.

The realization that nature is ubiquitous, a whole that embraces the city, has powerful implications for how the city is built and maintained and for the health, safety, and welfare of every resident. Unfortunately, tradition has set the city against nature, and nature against the city. The belief that the city is an entity apart from nature and even antithetical to it has dominated the way in which the city is perceived and continues to affect how it is built. This attitude has aggravated and even created many of the city's environmental problems: poisoned air and water; depleted or irretrievable resources; more frequent and more destructive floods; increased energy demands and higher construction and maintenance costs than existed prior to urbanization; and in many cities, a pervasive ugliness. Modern urban problems are no different, in essence, from those that plagued ancient cities, except in degree, in the toxicity and persistence of new contaminants, and in the extent of the earth that is now urbanized. As cities grow, these issues have become more pressing. Yet they continue to be treated as isolated phenomena, rather than a related phenomena arising from common human activities, exacerbated by a disregard for the processes of nature. Nature has been seen as a superficial embellishment, as a luxury, rather than as an essential force that permeates the city. Even those who have sought to introduce nature to the city in the form of parks and gardens have frequently viewed the city as something foreign to nature, have seen themselves as bringing a piece of nature to the city.

To seize the opportunities inherent in the city's natural environment, to see beyond short-term costs and benefits, to perceive the consequences of the myriad, seemingly unrelated actions that make up daily city life, and to coordinate thousands of incremental improvements, a fresh attitude to the city and the molding of its form is necessary. The city must be recognized as part of nature and designed accordingly. The city, the suburbs, and countryside must be viewed as a single, evolving system within nature, as must every individual park and building within that larger whole. The social value of nature must be recognized and its power harnessed, rather than resisted. Nature in the city must be cultivated, like a garden, rather than ignored or subdued.

# AN ECOLOGICAL APPROACH (1982)

ALAN RUFF

It has been increasingly appreciated that, in spite of all the efforts in the past thirty years, the quality of life for many people in the city has not been greatly increased. Houses, roads, factories, and traffic all obscure the individual's development of any awareness of the composition and function of the natural ecosystem. The open spaces are bleak and barren, playgrounds are limited, natural phenomena are scarce, food comes from somewhere, usually a factory. In addition, the built environment is constructed for individuals by people who they do not know. All these fundamental aspects of life have become abstract.

In the 1970s a new attitude emerged in European thinking which, according to Max Nicholson, amounted to an environmental revolution.[1] This arose not so much out of any changing attitude toward the environment, but from the failings of human technology. More especially, a shift occurred in the science that underpinned it, as biology developed and matured into the science of ecology. Through the writings of Carson, Commoner, Erlich, and others it became possible to realize the finite nature of the planet and the interdependence and interrelationship between its component living and nonliving parts. It could be appreciated that future survival would depend not so much on the inventiveness of human technology, but upon Man's capacity to work within the natural limits of the environment. In this respect, Man, like all other organisms, was dependent upon the natural bases of life—air, water, soil, climate, flora, and fauna—factors which had largely been overlooked in the postwar planning. Since the 1970s there has been a scientific explosion seeking to describe environmental relationships. An average month of popular television programs, for example, will include the ecology of lions in the African bush, or underwater coral reefs, and, most important, the interrelationships within the domestic back garden.

If we accept that the current level of ecological consciousness is part of the beginning of a long-lasting, fundamental change in attitudes and environmental values (and any optimistic person must, as it is a question of survival for the human race), then landscape architecture must bear a large measure of responsibility for making aesthetic sense out of this attitudinal metamorphosis. Yet the reality of the many urban landscapes referred to earlier shows no relationship or relevance to these changing attitudes. By not responding in design terms, the landscape architect is not only sacrificing all the goodwill and free publicity that is being generated by the media and environmental education program in schools and elsewhere, but is abdicating responsibility for aesthetic form of the urban environment. In future, designed landscapes must convey more than just function and symbolism but serve potentially as visual indicators of a healthy environmental ethic. The persuasive power of the landscape is well known; in the past, the aesthetic interpretation of the physical landscape through paint, poetry, writing, and music has served to heighten our cultural imagery of the land. Today the communicative power of the natural landscape has never been greater, but its real message is largely being obscured. Nature is being harnessed to the selling of material products and life-styles that indirectly bring about its own ultimate and perhaps final destruction. Environmental designers should stop to consider the fact that dwindling habitats, animals and plants are used to demonstrate all that is assumed to be good or desirable in our society; whilst the results of our efforts over the past thirty years are held up as examples of all that is worst in our society. All is not lost, however, for if landscape imagery can sell cars, houses, cigarettes, soft drinks, etc., then, as David Bellamy has said, it can express and promote concern for the optimal relationship between man and the other components of the natural environment. The landscape architect must assume a considerable responsibility for making this possible through the design of the urban landscape.

## THE ECOLOGICALLY INSPIRED LANDSCAPE

If we are to create ecologically inspired landscapes that are to contain the characteristics of spontaneous landscapes, the following points should be observed:

*1. Working with nature.* The physical and biological factors of the site should determine the ultimate design rather than man and his technical muscle. There must be a deliberate attempt not to disturb the natural processes and cycles existing on site, or to restore them where they are absent. Artificial materials like fertilizers and herbicides should be strictly limited, if used at all. Intervention should be restricted to the elimination of destructive conflict.

*2. Enrichment through complexity.* A very varied topography and biological structure should be sought in order to avoid monocultures and uniformity. This can be brought about by artificially creating an irregular surface, or tipping extraneous material, such as building rubble, whilst a diverse structure should be developed, with ecotones, edges, and appropriate layers, so as to encourage a wide variety of plants and animals to the various habitats and microclimates. It is important that open space is not dominated by the visual aesthetic which in the past has been an ecological robber, denying enjoyment of the senses—taste, smell, touch, and hearing—that are so much a part of the natural world.

*3. The landscape as process.* There should be no preconceived idea of the final solution but instead a structure which is capable of responding to changing social needs and biological requirements. The landscape should slowly evolve just as the great cathedrals developed over many centuries, so that instead of using maintenance techniques to retain a specific situation, creative management should ensure that the landscape remains flexible, open to new developments.

*4. Creativity on site.* It is important to restore the designer to a position of real creativity. Ideas come as work is being carried out, not solely at the drawing board, so the designer should be physically as well as intellectually involved with the work. By being on the site and in direct contact with the soil and the plant material, the designer can spontaneously respond to the surroundings, on-site vegetation, and chance events.

*5. Involvement of the users.* The open space should not be the sole responsibility of an individual designer, but the result of joint discussion with the public who will use it. In the absence of a fixed plan there is a greater opportunity for real creativity with future users contributing ideas and requirements of their own. In this way people can identify with the work, and the landscape designer becomes a social catalyst and adviser rather than an all-knowing professional.

*6. Minimal energy consumption.* This can be achieved initially by using locally available soils, regional building materials and recycling local waste materials. Subsequently, after the initial labor-intensive establishment period, maintenance should be reduced, reaching a stage of minimal human intervention. In future, increasing attention must also be given to use of coppice biomass systems for heating and forest farming for food production.

*7. The natural landscape outside the front door.* The natural landscape can serve a whole range of important functions in the home environment—creation of privacy, physical comfort, etc.—and can stand up to robust children's play and make conventional playgrounds superfluous. Natural areas near schools can provide valuable education facilities.

## Conclusion

A landscape developed along these ecological lines will serve to create a powerful aesthetic form that can both reflect and affect positive environmental change. Recognition of this fact can make landscape design more vital, the profession of landscape design more useful and the management of durable and dwindling resources and fragile ecosystems more publicly important. Only in this way will landscape design reflect humanity's dependence upon the land ethic.

# DESIGN FOR HUMAN ECOSYSTEMS (1985)

JOHN T. LYLE

## How Human Ecosystems Work

Eugene Odum has proposed compartmentalization of the total landscape into areas divided according to basic ecological roles. He argues that we need both successionally young ecosystems for their productive qualities and older natural ones for their protective qualities. According to Odum, "the most pleasant and certainly the safest landscape to live in is the one containing a variety of crops, forests, lakes, streams, roadsides, marshes, seashores, and waste-places—in other words, a mixture of communities of different ecological ages."[1] He might well have added houses, gardens, parks, playing fields, offices, and shops. In the interest of achieving or maintaining such a mix, Odum would classify all land in one of four categories:

1. The productive areas, where succession is continually retarded by human controls to maintain high levels of productivity.
2. The protective, or natural, areas, where succession is allowed or encouraged to proceed into the mature, and thus stable if not highly productive, stages.
3. The compromise areas, where some combination of the first two stages exists.
4. The urban industrial, or biologically nonvital, areas.

If we accept this schema a great many of the most pressing, most challenging, and probably even most important landscape issues fall into the third category. "Compromise areas," however, is hardly an adequate term for those places in which human beings and nature might be brought together again after a very long and dangerous period of estrangement. I prefer to call such places "human ecosystems."

Since some might find a hint of humanist arrogance in the whole notion of designing ecosystems, I will hasten to elaborate on my meaning. The truth is that human beings have been designing ecosystems for some twelve thousand years now, ever since they first learned how to cultivate plants. Through all these millennia, they have been habitually, even compulsively, changing the world's landscape. If we are to fulfill our human potential, we will find it necessary to continue doing so. In the present era, we will have to continue to do so merely to provide the basic necessities for burgeoning populations. The ecosystems shaped by our changes of the landscape will invariably be different in structure and function from the previously existing natural ones, but they will continue to respond to exactly the same natural forces even though they may be more or less diverse, more or less stable, more or less productive, or have more or less of any number of other qualities. Our creation of new ecosystems has almost always been unintentional—that is, without conscious understanding of how natural processes work and therefore without any way of predicting how the new ecosystem would work, even without any comprehension of the fact that it was actually a system. Not surprisingly then, without conscious control, new systems usually do not work very well. In the [example of the] San Elijo [lagoon in San Diego] we might call the railroad, the freeway, and the sewage treatment plant all examples of unintentional ecosystem design, and we have seen the results. The developers' and the preservationists' proposals fall into the same general category because, although they do consider some aspects of the lagoon environment, they do not take into account its ecological processes and its interacting, systematic nature.

The point is that if we are going to design ecosystems (and we continually do so whether we want to face all of the implications or not) then it will be best to design them intentionally, making use of all the ecological understanding we can bring to bear. Only then can we shape ecosystems that manage to fulfill all their inherent potentials for contributing to human purposes, that are sustainable, and that support nonhuman communities as well. Not every landscape can fully accomplish all three of these goals, of course, and thus Odum's term, "compromise." There will always be conflict to be resolved and priorities to be assigned. Intentional design means carrying out conscious choices. What we are trying to do, then, is to gain a measure of control, not in order to dominate nature but to participate creatively in its processes.

Ecosystem design is undoubtedly a difficult undertaking. Nature rarely reveals herself unequivocally, and there is always the risk that we will end up agreeing with Spinoza that "the attempt to show that nature does nothing in vain . . . seems to end in showing that nature, the gods, and man are alike mad." We have to begin by admitting that our tools are still crude, and we do not know enough to do the job with absolute confidence, recognizing at the same time that we will have to do it anyway.

To participate creatively in natural processes and to do so with reasonable hope of success, we need to include as subjects of design not only the visible form of the landscape but its inner workings, the systems that motivate and maintain it. Natural systems are continuously self-organizing (there being nobody available to organize them), and we can draw upon the principles by which they work to make human ecosystems more sustainable. Such an aim requires a knowledge of these systems. Fortunately, the sciences provide a great deal of information, which, while far from complete, is yet enough to get us started.

Generally speaking, we can divide this scientific knowledge into two types. First, there are facts or data concerning the situation at hand. For any given landscape, a great many of these may be available, or very few, depending on how much research has been done. For San Elijo, considerable data were available because of the investigations of marine biologists and earth scientists at several nearby universities. Species populations were fairly well known, for example, as were the compositions of rock formations around the edges of the lagoon. Even the shellfish species that had been present in the lagoon's natural state were known—the result of analyses of shell middens left by the Indians. More general facts could be extrapolated from research done on similar lagoons along the California coast. Although all this information would obviously be useful in dealing with specific parts of the design, it was far from complete. In practice, of course, it is impossible to have all the facts needed to describe completely even a very small landscape. We have to work with what we can get.

The second type of scientific knowledge might be loosely categorized under the heading of "concepts," a word the dictionary defines as general notions, ideas, or principles conceived in the mind. The science of ecology has developed a number of basic concepts—such as productivity, trophic levels, succession, and energy flow—that help unify and give coherence to the masses of otherwise unrelated facts produced by research. These concepts are large and inclusive and fit the known facts, but since they are conceived in the mind, it is virtually impossible to prove that any of them actually exist in nature. Although research is continuously accumulating new information that furthers our understanding of the interactions that cause succession, the actual existence of succession, for example, remains beyond experimental proof. This discrepancy causes occasional debate among scientists, who sometimes question concepts like succession or believe that science should deal only with theories that can be experimentally proven and thus turned into facts.[2] For purposes of design, however, concepts are indispensable because they can be put to general use. In fact, utility is the criterion of value for a scientific concept[3] but is rarely considered with respect to scientific facts or theories.

For purposes of design, concepts are useful because they provide access to the mechanisms that join all of the facts. They make it possible to work with the forest before the trees. They make it possible to gain a working understanding of an ecosystem even though many of the facts may be unknown. They give us handles with which to grasp the unseeable. They provide us with a basis for developing theories of ecosystems design that allow us to reach into and reshape the inner workings of the landscape. . . .

## THE ECOSYSTEM CONCEPT

The first concept is that of the ecosystem itself. It is a rather new concept, having been first advanced by A. G. Tansley in 1935, but an important one, having become since that time the fundamental principle of all ecological study. Simply defined, an ecosystem is the interacting assemblage of living things and their nonliving environment. Among living things are human beings themselves, although ecologists usually choose to study ecosystems that exclude man, and human beings usually choose to think of themselves as somehow set apart from ecosystems. This is an important point, and one that is implicit in everything that follows: We human beings are integral, interacting components of ecosystems at every level, and in order to deal adequately with these systems, we have to recognize that simple fact. In most situations, even at the level of the biosphere, we may be an overriding, controlling component, but we are a component nonetheless.

Another important characteristic of the ecosystem is that it can be of any size. That we can consider any landscape of any size is a great convenience for designers, but there are rules to be followed. No ecosystem stands alone. "All ranks of ecosystems are open systems, not closed ones."[4] This implies that ecosystems are connected by flows of energy and materials. Each system draws in energy and materials from the systems around it and in turn exports to them. In drawing the boundaries of an ecosystem, therefore, we need to consider the flows that link it with its neighbors. Ignoring these connections—these imports and exports of energy and materials—has caused a great many of the disasters of unintentional ecosystem design.

In the shaping of ecosystems, three organizational concepts are of fundamental importance. The first is *scale,* or the relative size of the landscape in question and its connections with larger and smaller system and ultimately with the whole. It is scale that provides us with an encompassing frame of reference. The second is *design process,* the pattern of thought that we follow in dealing with this frame of reference. The third is the underlying *order* that binds ecosystems together and makes them work.

### Scale

We need to recognize that every ecosystem is a part—or subsystem—of a larger system and that it in turn includes a number of yet smaller subsystems. It also has necessary linkages to both the larger and smaller units. San Elijo Lagoon, for example, is at the same time a component of a larger watershed unit and a component of an even larger oceanic unit. The water that runs off the land in this eighty-square-mile watershed eventually reaches the lagoon, bringing along everything it has picked up in the interim. This may include silts from eroding slopes, nitrates from fertilized agricultural lands, oil from roads, and any number of other substances that can seriously affect the life of the lagoon. If the lagoon is to operate as a healthy ecosystem, therefore, some control over land use in the watershed will be required. By the same token, all these materials finally flow from the lagoon into the Pacific Ocean, establishing yet another linkage. The lagoon is also linked to the San Diego urban region, even the entire Southern California region, because of all the people who come there for recreation. On a still larger scale, it is tied to Alaska and Central America by the Pacific Flyway. Events in San Elijo can thus seriously affect animal populations thousands of miles away.

Despite all these connections, San Elijo Lagoon is a limited unit of landscape, one of a certain size with definite boundaries, which means that we can deal with it only at a certain scale. The concerns that we can address in detail are likewise limited to those that are appropriate to that scale. Nevertheless, we need to work within the context, or framework, of the larger-scale unit, in this case the watershed, and we need to consider the proposed development projects as smaller-scale units within the framework of the lagoon. Our range of design scales forms a hierarchy that corresponds to the concept of levels of integration in nature or in any other organized system. Certain principles of organization link the levels of this hierarchy and provide guidance for design at any given level.

*Design Processes*

The ways in which we go about design will naturally vary according to the scale of concern and the situation at hand.

At this point I will have to digress briefly in order to clear up a semantic difficulty. The activity of "design," as I am using the term here, means giving form to physical phenomena, and I will use it to represent such activity at every scale. The challenges we face require some broadening and redefinition of the activity of design. According to Erich Jantsch, "Design attempts to find, formalize, and bring optimally into play the innate forms of a process . . . (and) . . . focuses on finding and emphasizing internal factors in evolution, on making them conscious and effective."[5]

This is a departure from the convention of using the term "planning" for landscape shaping at scales larger than that of construction detail. I believe the departure is justified by the very broad, rather indefinite inclusiveness of the term "planning," by the confusion that results from its use, and by the increasing tendency in the environmental design disciplines to associate planning with administrative activity rather than physical form-shaping. This book is about making physical changes in the landscape and not about administrative, legal, or policy-making activity, although, needless to say, it will usually take a great deal of the latter to bring about these changes. Planning and design are thus closely linked and work in tandem, sometimes to the point of being indistinguishable.

In using the term "design" in this sense, I believe I am following, not trying to initiate, a trend. More and more, we hear of "site design" rather than "site planning." Carl Steinitz refers to "regional landscape design" and justifies the usage of his term by defining design as "intentional change . . . the landscape and its social patterns are altered by design."[6] And

Ian McHarg, of course, entitled his famous work *Design with Nature*.[7] In any event, the term "design" carries the connotations of intention, precision, and control that befit the approach I am describing. It also suggests emotional involvement. Jantsch speaks of design as being planning plus love. Consequently, I shall use the term with all these overtones in mind, although with apologies for any confusion it may cause. Likewise I shall use the term "planning" to refer to more strictly administrative and institutional activities, such as the articulation and implementation of policy.

Combining as it does two different modes of thought—analytical use of scientific information and creative exploration (or the left and right sides of the brain, if you will)—ecosystem design can get very complicated. The two modes can work together, but only if the roles of each are clearly established. Especially at the larger scales, design processes are further complicated by the involvement of considerable numbers of people—in some cases, as we shall see, huge numbers. To deal with this complexity in a rational manner, we shall break these processes down into component themes that are more or less common to all of them: formulation, information, models, possibilities, plan evaluation, and management. Then we will examine each of these themes with respect to its content and the analytical or creative orientation associated with it.

The inclusion of management is particularly important in ecosystem design because of the variable future that is a fact of life for any organic entity. The design of ecosystems is probabilistic in that we cannot say what will definitely happen in the future but only what will probably happen. Management deals with this uncertainty in the cybernetic manner, by observing what actually does happen and redesigning as necessary. Thus, being an essential continuation of design by other means, to paraphrase the famous statement on war and politics, management assumes a more creative role than has usually been expected. To repeat, the interlocking relationship between design and management is a *particularly* important feature of any ecosystematic design process.

*Order*

In the midst of complexity, with its many opportunities for diversion, we need to keep reminding ourselves that the purpose of creating order in human ecosystems is to enable them to fulfill the needs of both their human and other components. But how do we define "order"? There are a great many kinds and degrees of order, although in landscape design, we are most used to thinking in terms of visual order. Ecosystematic order is something else again, although it is usually reflected in what we see.

Here, to return to the concepts of ecology, we can identify three modes of order, each of which provides a key to one aspect of the inner workings of ecosystems. The three modes are structure, function, and location.

Odum defines structure as "the composition of the biological community, including species, their biomass, life histories and spatial distribution, the quantity and distribution of abiotic materials, and the range of conditions like light and climate."[8] Margalef is more succinct: "If we consider the elements and the relations between the elements, we have the structure."[9]

The number and types of the elements present and the ways in which they interact are fundamental to the character of an ecosystem. For analytical purposes, structure can be broken down into substructures. The composition of trophic levels is an example of a substructure, one which, as we have seen, plays an especially important role in San Elijo

Lagoon. The relationship of the marshgrasses to the decomposing bacteria and through them to mollusks is unique to coastal inlets and is at the very core of their structure. The birds, though far more visible and more interesting to human beings, are less essential to the ecological structure, and are ultimately dependent on the health of the marshgrasses. In this particular situation, the elements are the species of marshgrass, bacteria, mollusks, shorebirds, and waterfowl, and the relations are their predatory interactions. These we can see as the building blocks and the mortar of the lagoon ecosystem.

The second mode of order, function, or the flow of energy and materials, is closely intertwined with structure. According to Odum, the "complex biomass structure is maintained by the total community respiration which continually pumps out disorder."[10] Respiration is fueled by the flow of energy, and keeping this flow going, distributing energy to all the members of the community, is a basic purpose of ecosystem function. At San Elijo, the tides add their force to the "pumping," thus speeding up the flow and increasing the rate of productivity. Every ecosystem has a characteristic pattern of energy flow that corresponds with its structure. The flow begins as solar radiation imparts energy through photosynthesis and goes on from there to reach every living creature in the system. Every individual and the ecosystem as a whole has the ability to maintain a state of high internal order, or low entropy, as long as it is continuously supplied with its energy needs. As energy flows through the system, in keeping with the second law of thermodynamics, it is degraded to a more dispersed form with each transformation. Thus as it flows from marshgrass to mollusks to fish and birds, energy is lost. It happens that the marshgrass Spartina and the mollusks are particularly efficient converters of energy into biomass. The Spartina has a uniquely efficient cellular structure, whereas the mollusks, thanks to the tides, are in the privileged position of not having to forage for food. Most animals spend most of their energy searching for something to eat, but the detritus food of the mollusks is served up to them by waters propelled by tidal energy—hence the enormous productive value of the tidal subsidy. Even so, more energy is lost to unusable heat at each stage than is actually fixed. Consequently, the lagoon system needs continuous energy inputs from sun and tides to maintain itself.

Also essential to ecosystem function are the flows of water and the chemical elements essential to life. In contrast with energy, these are not continuously dissipated but circulate intact along more or less consistent pathways through storage to environment to organisms and back. Thus, the material flows, or biogeochemical cycles, as they are usually called, provide each organism with its needed chemicals and nutrients.

At San Elijo, as in most unintentionally designed manmade ecosystems, the material flows have long been in a state of perpetual dysfunction, not for lack of materials, but because they are directed to the wrong places. During the long period when primarily treated sewage effluent was dumped into the lagoon, the enormous concentration of nutrients from the sewage brought about rapid growth of algae, which used enormous quantities of oxygen from the water, thus denying it to fish and mollusks and depleting their populations. When the algae died at a faster rate than the waters could absorb them or the tides move them out, they decayed on the surface, causing unsightly masses of green scum and unpleasant odors. This is an example of a very common difficulty created by unintentional design. The solution eventually implemented for the "water pollution problem" was the four-mile-long ocean outfall. Now there are only a few occasional algae blooms on the lagoon's surface, mostly caused by fertilizer nitrates in runoff water. But it is not only the nutrients that have been lost for human purpose; with the freshwater infusions from the sewage cut off as well, the surface level of the lagoon has dropped, leaving dried-up stretches of mudflat around some of its edges. The natural fresh water supply through Escondido Creek was long ago drastically reduced by upstream impoundments.

What we have here, then, is a classic example of the type of once-through flow that has become characteristic of single-purpose, unintentional human ecosystems. Most of the water that flows in over two hundred miles from the Colorado River is used once, mostly for flushing toilets, and then flows out into the ocean. Nutrients flow in, mostly in the form of food from far-flung sources, are used once, and then join the water in household toilets to flow out into the ocean with it. Such a system makes a dramatic contrast with natural systems in which both inputs and outputs are minimal, flows are much slower, and water and nutrients are used and reused over and again to support a diversity of organisms.

The alternative that we propose would redirect the flows to reuse both water and nutrients through biological sewage treatment. Thus, by feeding the primarily treated effluent into a series of ponds in which water hyacinths and other aquatic plants will take up the nutrients, the water will eventually reach a level of purity that will permit its use for irrigating recreational areas and its eventual return to the lagoon. The hyacinths can be harvested for cattle feed and thus eventually be returned to the system as well. Such a pattern of water and nutrient flow is more like that of a natural ecosystem, more efficient and economical. The outfall, incidentally, would still be needed for overflows and emergencies.

One major consideration remains, however, at least for the predicable future. Such a system will not operate itself. Management will have to take the place of the self-regulating mechanisms of a natural estuarine system, which means that a high level of ongoing, creative management of the sort mentioned earlier will be needed.

The third mode of ecosystematic order—locational patterns—usually receives far more attention in design than the other two, although it is less explored in the scientific literature. Usually, the proposed pattern of locations is considered *the* plan. Although this practice follows historical precedent and fits established decision-making patterns, it often results in the less visible aspects of structure and function being ignored. Ideally, the three modes would be considered equally important, so interrelated indeed, that one could not consider one mode without considering the others. Location, nevertheless, remains the most visible of the three, and "the plan" will probably remain the vehicle on which the design of ecosystem structure and function will ride.

The ideal pattern of locations is determined mostly by what is already there. The processes and organisms that we have described are distributed over the landscape in relation to climate and topography. If our purpose is to build on these to develop the sort of human ecosystem we have discussed, then that pattern will have to be respected. At San Elijo, the tidal areas where marshgrasses grow to support the food chain are essential parts of the picture, as are the mudflats where the shorebirds feed and the shallow waters and matted islands where they find cover for nesting.

These, however, are only a few pieces of the puzzle. Other patterns have been superimposed on the natural ones by human beings. The berms that support the railroad, the coastal highway, and the freeway divide the lagoon into three distinct parts. There is also an existing development pattern that includes commercial uses along the highway and residential uses on the upper slopes. There is also a pattern of demand for more open breaches and for more protected, lagoon-side play areas.

Perhaps most difficult to deal with is the pattern of private ownerships, which makes it necessary to show how the land can be used profitably. Whenever public acquisition is recommended, strong justification will be needed.

The most useful tool for sorting out the competing patterns is the *suitability model,* which consists of an analytically derived map showing the relative suitabilities of land increments for given human activities. In the case of San Elijo Lagoon, the complexity of the data made it convenient to use a computer-mapping technique for defining suitabilities. Whether it is produced by hand or by computer, however, there is nothing magical or definitive about a suitability model. The hand or the computer simply combines and aggregates the information that is given in the ways it is told to and produces a graphic expression of the results.

For example, a computer-generated map can show relative residential suitability. Each of the little symbols, or grid cells, represents an area approximately 111 feet square and gives the estimated level of suitability for the given activity in that area. In each map, the darkest symbol indicates the lowest level of suitability and the lightest, and highest.

These estimates of suitability are based on predictions of future economic costs and environmental impacts. For the first model, that concerned with residential development, the most suitable locations were hypothesized to be those where development costs are likely to be lower, erosion rates less, landsliding improbable, and wildlife populations left undisturbed. Any number of other criteria might have been used, of course, but these were the ones judged most important in this particular case. The dark areas, then, assuming the technical reliability of the models, are those where some combination of high development costs, rapid erosion rates, probable landsliding, and wildlife disruption renders the land unsuitable for residential development.

The series of models that follow shows the relative suitability for various recreational and residential uses. The criteria for each model are different, but in each case the most and least suitable locations are defined.

Suitability models play a pivotal role in ecosystem design, providing a bridge between the consideration of processes and their location on the land. The aggregate complex collections of information concerning natural, social, and economic functions into usable forms. They disclose new patterns that are extremely difficult, if not impossible, to discern in any other way.

It sometimes happens that a model is used not as a basis for planning, but as a plan in itself. This is a serious mistake. Models are simply expressions of the interactions of clearly stated facts and values. Once they are made, there is sill a creative leap to be taken to shape a plan. The models provide a firm footing for this leap, but in the end, the plan will look quite different from the models.

## FROM MODELS TO PLAN TO MANAGEMENT

Witness the plan for San Elijo that emerged from the long process we have been describing here. It divides the lagoon and its watershed into seven distinct categories of land use. These generally follow the patterns of suitability models, but the actual configurations are quite different. Moreover, the seven uses bear no resemblance to the traditional zoning categories, because the purpose of the zoning is quite different from that of traditional zoning. Here, we are not trying to promote uniformity of use, but to encourage the greatest diversity that

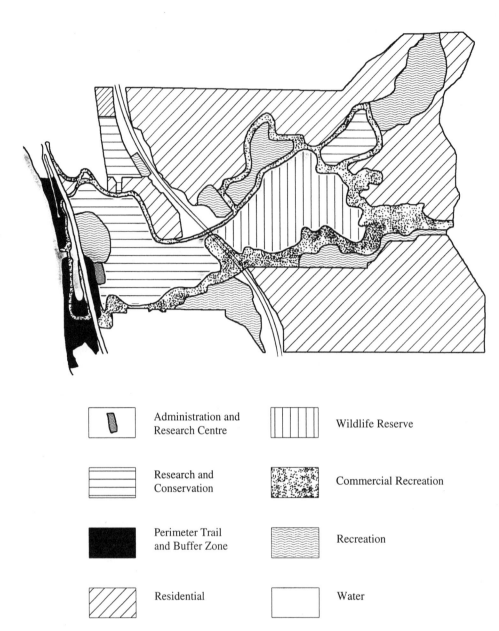

| | | | |
|---|---|---|---|
| Administration and Research Centre | | Wildlife Reserve | |
| Research and Conservation | | Commercial Recreation | |
| Perimeter Trail and Buffer Zone | | Recreation | |
| Residential | | Water | |

Figure 20. Plan for San Elijo Lagoon (based on John T. Lyle, *Design for Human Ecosystems* [New York: Van Nostrand Reinhold, 1985]).

is consistent with the healthy and productive functioning of lagoon processes. Consequently, the definition of uses is as general and as open to ideas as it can reasonably be.

The wetlands themselves are divided into three distinct zones, following the divisions already established by the railroad and the freeway. The inner zone east of the freeway—already the richest, most diverse habitat and the birds' favorite feeding and nesting place—becomes a wildlife preserve. The zone between the freeway and the railroad—where the water is deeper and wildlife far less abundant—will be devoted to biotic production and research. Areas in both natural, or protective, and productive landscape are thus important parts of the plan. The productive area is largely a manmade landscape, but one that is biologically very much alive. Some dredging and shoreline alteration may be needed here to develop the best environment for raising fish and mollusks. The old sewage treatment plant on the lagoon's edge will be refurbished as a biological treatment facility to provide an inflow of fresh water.

The westerly zone—between the railroad and the ocean, already heavily altered—will become an intensive recreation area, with some commercial development. Buildings will rest on piers over the waters of the lagoon so that marine processes can go on undisturbed beneath.

Surrounding the wetlands is a protective buffer zone with a hiking trail, screened from the more sensitive wildlife habitats, and outside that, on the flatter lands, will be several passive recreation areas. Although urban development will be encouraged on the slopes overlooking the lagoon, it will be subject to design controls that limit grading, maintain natural drainage courses and levels of runoff, and require planting for erosion. With such controls, development of these slopes will be entirely compatible with a productive lagoon.

Such a system, however, will continue to work well only if it is managed—man aged—well. Once the system begins to take shape, ongoing management is to be instituted as one of its essential components. Only management can control the feedback loops needed to augment those that have evolved as internally functioning mechanisms in natural systems. Certain kinds of control are needed to prevent foreign and potentially damaging materials like fertilizers, pesticides, oil residues, or phosphates from entering the lagoon. Human activities can be regulated in such a way as to prevent their interfering with sensitive lagoon processes or populations. Critical indicators of environmental quality, especially water quality, in the lagoon need to be monitored to maintain the stability of the system. When an imbalance appears, or if there is evidence of deterioration or conflict somewhere, some corrective action can be taken. In the absence of such a program, however carefully the initial design may be conceived, the lagoon will eventually return to its present sorry state or worse.

This intentionally designed and managed ecosystem represents a symbiosis of urban and natural processes. Food production, wildlife habitats, recreation, dwelling, resource conservation, water and nutrient recycling, and visual amenity are joined in a network of interdependence. The composition as a whole is very different from the estuarine ecosystem that would still exist at San Elijo had man never arrived on the scene, being more varied in its forms and more intense in its activities. Although it is dependent on human energy and ingenuity for its stability, the reverse is also, to some degree, true. If all goes well, if our models are correct and our design works as it should, and if the management is both imaginative and sound, then human and natural processes will merge indistinguishably into an organic whole, a human ecosystem in the best sense of the term. That, hard as it may be to achieve, is the ideal.

# CAN FLOATING SEEDS MAKE DEEP FORMS? (1991)

## JOHN T. LYLE

In natural landscapes, [the] three basic modes of ecosystematic order combine to generate form. Thus what we see in a natural landscape is the direct expression of its structural, functional, and locational order as they exist at that particular moment. Form is the visible manifestation of underlying organization. In fact, the order is so complex that only an observer who is knowledgeable in the ecology of landscape will perceive it within the form. Natural order is not designed for human perception or understanding. One understands the order of a natural landscape only by meeting it on its own terms.

In the designed landscape, form is a somewhat different matter. Ecological order is as much there as in a natural landscape, but it meets and merges with human activity and with aesthetic order as perceived by the human mind. We can know nature only through perception and intellect. Where the merging is harmonious, where ecological and aesthetic order are congruent, we have a human ecosystem.

A human ecosystem embodies ecological order, including the whole physical, emotional, and cultural realm of humanity, in human terms. Such a landscape has deep form, because underlying its surface and giving it deeper substance is this cohesive fundamental order. Thus deep form is shaped by the interactions of inner ecological process and human vision, which can make the underlying order visible and meaningful in human terms. Such deep form stands in contrast to shallow form, which has only the surface perceptual order and lacks the solidity of coherent process beneath the surface. In deep form is a meeting of appearance and reality, mind and nature, art and science.

To generate deep form requires a rational understanding of natural systems in combination with intuitive imagery, and thus a design process that combines high levels of both analytical and creative thinking. The right and left sides of the brain come into alternating play, each feeding the other.

This interplay of creativity and rationality is the passageway to deep form. As in nature, form is the expression of process.[1] In the process of design, we merge human creativity with the ongoing rhythm and harmonies of nature's evolving order.

What I propose then is that we take the underlying complex and elegant ecosystematic order of nature as the essential and fundamental inspiration for design. Too often, landscape architects have ignored the inspiration for creativity offered by natural processes and have chosen instead to view "ecological factors" as constraints on creativity. Too often, too, they have responded to nature by shaping pale limitations of her forms in the picturesque tradition and in so doing have produced shallow form.

# GRAY WORLD, GREEN HEART (1994)

ROBERT THAYER

## How Important Are Sustainable Landscapes?

Can a few conspicuous solar houses, constructed wetlands, bike paths, recycling industries, wildlife habitat corridors, organic agriculture plots, and wind farms really be the key to saving the world? Isn't a much greater transformation needed in global economic, political, and social institutions? The answer to the last question is, of course, yes. But the new institutions needed for a transition to a sustainable world must ultimately be based upon the perception and comprehension of the ordinary people who will create them. In turn, *their* ultimate reality is in the land and spaces around them. The small steps taken to build sustainability into the local landscape in discreet, manageable chunks which people can observe, try out, experience, and improve are actually large steps for humankind. In the eighteen years I have lived in my current house in our solar neighborhood, there have been countless bus loads of visitors from many states and foreign countries passing through, asking questions, and taking pictures. I have given innumerable house tours and minilectures on the solar, water, and open space features of the neighborhood myself. In spite of the frequent interruptions, I realize that this is the way it should be; a critical purpose of the sustainable landscape is the demonstration and diffusion of environmentally and socially sustaining principles into common usage in the everyday world.

This kind of direct experiential role for sustainable landscapes can not be overemphasized. An *acceptance of sustainable techniques and technologies into our concept of nature and human nature* is an essential part of the process toward remaking global institutions....

*Landscapes that create an illusion of a better world while depriving us of the actual means of achieving it are not sustainable.* If the *perceptual* function of a technology is to convince us the world is a more pleasant place, while the *practical* dimensions of the technology functionally contribute to making the world worse, something is critically out of balance. Air conditioners powered by fossil fuels create the illusion of coolness in one place by making the entire planet hotter through their contribution to global warming. Sustainable landscapes, therefore, are an essential grounding element in the transition to a new philosophical framework—the antidote to a runaway world of consumption and fantasy where technology is destroying nature and making a lifeless replica....

## Transparency: Expressing the Unseen

Transparency—the ability to see into and understand the inner workings of a landscape—is an absolutely essential ingredient to sustainability. In a world where more and more of the technology controlling our lives is not only beyond our individual control but is also invisible and incomprehensible to the average person, the landscape serves not only as the foundation for our only genuine "tangible" reality, but as the only mechanism by which we can really know *where* we are—and *how* and *why* as well. It can be argued that as humans we have a *right* to know where we are, how we are connected, and *how we are doing*....

## Visual Ecology

Without being able to see into the workings of our own landscapes, we may be unable to make necessary adjustments to changing environmental conditions. The feedback of experience between habitat and organism which guides environmental behavior is a cornerstone of ecology. In transparent landscapes, a *visual ecology*, where we are able to assess the conditions affecting us and make cogent environmental decisions, is both possible and necessary.[1] Since humans are symbolic animals who interpret the world through abstraction, deduction, and discourse, the feedback we receive from the environment is, of course, laden with symbolic meaning. But positive meanings (and hence constructive action) accrue more steadfastly to things that can be seen and experienced. That which is not seen is often viewed with fear and exaggeration. The first step toward building a sustainable world then is to open up our landscapes to view, such that we may learn from them where we are, how we are doing, and what we need to do to make the world better. Opacity and fakery in the landscape ultimately only serve to perpetuate the unsustainable status quo. . . .

## Congruency: Complexity *Without* Contradiction

While occasional surprise, contradiction, feint, and whimsy are ingredients of humor (and humor makes life worth living), by and large people strive for *congruency* between various departments of their daily lives and between their various emotional, behavioral, and cognitive states. I have already discussed cognitive dissonance as the emotional state where an individual's beliefs, feelings, and actions are incongruous and uncomfortable. The natural tendency of humans is toward consistency between emotions, thoughts, and actions. This should be the natural, normal tendency in our landscapes as well. When—as in the landscapes of today—the opposite tendency toward surprise, contradiction, simulation, and irony moves beyond the boundaries of art and entertainment into the absolute mainstream of human existence, something is fundamentally wrong.

The second major point regarding the experience of sustainable landscapes is that once made transparent, sustainable landscapes must ultimately be *congruent*. In other words, the emotional state provoked by the landscape's *surfaces* should be congruent with and not contradictory to the manner in which the *core* properties of the same landscape provide for our functional needs and well-being. If an air-conditioned building that allows one group of people to feel like spring in the middle of summer simultaneously contributes to the painful death of others, the various levels of meaning and experience represented by the building cannot be congruent. On the other hand, if a constructed wetland not only safely processes the human wastes it receives but also provides safe habitat for birds and a recreational venue for humans, it is most certainly a congruent and sustainable landscape.

There is, of course, a natural relationship between transparency and congruency. Congruency is often prevented by opaqueness—if we can't see how a landscape functions, we are unable to detect the possible incongruities. Merely by an increase in landscape transparency, the natural human tendency toward congruity between thought, feeling, and action, or between surface and core, will foster the remaking of a more sustainable environment. . . .

## FANTASY IS NECESSARY, BUT SO IS THE BOUNDARY BETWEEN IT AND REALITY

The sustainable landscape should not herald an era devoid of fun, fantasy, or imagination. Fantasy and imagination are necessary for human survival. In today's world saturated by entertainment and illusion, the danger is not as much in the *amount* of fantasy itself but in the *blurring of the line between fantasy and reality*.[2] Sustainable landscapes need not be austere, solemn, dictatorial x-rays of ecological processes blaring across our consciousness. On the other had, Baudrillard's *reality principle* should be kept in mind; landscapes should give strong cues when one is leaving reality and entering the realm of fantasy and entertainment. Much has been written about "entertaining ourselves to death,"[3] but entertainment and death are fundamentally in opposition. When landscapes contribute to the excessive blurring of reality and fantasy, they are contributing to unsustainable conditions for human life. . . .

## BEYOND AESTHETIC: THE STYLE OF NO STYLE

The postmodern preoccupation with simulation, fantasy, irony, contradiction, vague historical reference, boundary warping, and lack of guiding principles will not last long, simply because "postmodern" style attempts to "deconstruct" or make a mockery of all former, form-giving influences and assumptions. It has given up seeking an underlying "truth." I argue, however, that an underlying truth is rapidly revealing itself to us in the birth of the notion of sustainability, however "trendy" the world has become. A need to put flesh (in the form of physical landscapes) on the skeletal philosophy of sustainability has become too powerful to resist.

Yet even when sustainable and regenerative values can be embodied in landscape form, they are unlikely to collectively result in any one particular "style." Instead, sustainable landscapes are likely to express a unique sense of visual and spatial pluralism. Sustainable landscapes can vary from humanized farm country to rough-looking wetlands to precisely ordered arrays of wind turbines. Some sustainable landscapes are those in which people live, while others are relatively devoid of human presence. Because of the infinite relationships possible between humans, ecosystems, and natural resources, no two sustainable landscapes are apt to look alike, particularly if they occur in different regions or evolve with different baseline ecosystems or cultures. The movement toward bioregionalism deliberately attempts to exploit the *uniqueness* of local cultures and landscapes in creating a sustainable future, and runs counter to the idea of a widely dispersed, externally imposed aesthetic style.

In some sense, new forms of the sustainable landscape will have certain commonalties with modernism, but with several key differences. There may be a partial return to a version of "form follows function," but this time the "function" is not mechanistic (in the narrow, modernist sense) but *ecological* (in the *post*-postmodern sense). Form will follow a highly complex, evolving notion of the core interrelationships of nature, and will be expressed uniquely in the surfaces of local landscapes as experienced by local cultures. Sustainable landscape form and content will seek to reveal this ecological order through an interplay of surface and core *unique* to both place and culture. Consequently, there may be no distinct style, since "style" itself necessarily separates surface from core. . . .

## ART AND CREATIVITY ARE CRITICAL

The unlikeliness of a common "style," of course, does not imply the lack of a role for art and creativity. Artful interpretation is necessary to offer alternative visions and to explore and make sense out of the unseen. Bringing core ecologies to the surface will be an important role of landscape artists and designers. The continually unfolding complexity of the natural world and the inability of traditional forms to represent these changes will result in the evolution of new, unfamiliar surface-core relationships. A critical function of landscape architecture and environmental art will be to continually interpret the relationship of human beings to their environment in spatial, visual terms. Since the change in relationship between people and nature is accelerating, new formal interpretations are required at an ever-increasing rate. Here is where artistic creation plays a key role. Art has the ability to anticipate society. Genuinely artful interpretation offers a range of possible futures by which sustainable landscapes can be identified, emphasized, evaluated, and made visible. . . .

## CONSPICUOUS EXPERIENTIAL QUALITY SPEEDS ACCEPTANCE

There may be two or more groups of actors relating to any sustainable landscape: those "within" the landscape itself and those who observe it from without. As such, different sets of meanings may evolve for the same landscape. But for either the internal "players" or the external observers, the visibility of the sustainable landscape and its ability to form images in the human mind is critical to its experiential impact and the rate at which it will be adopted by society and emulated in common use. Theory on the diffusion of innovations[4] suggests that *complexity* impedes the rate of adoption of an innovation (like sustainable technologies or landscape processes), whereas *observability* speeds the adoption rate. Since they represent a higher level of system complexity than "cosmetic" landscapes and incorporate ecological relationships that may be invisible or difficult to observe, sustainable landscapes present obstacles to their own acceptance. However, making sustainable landscapes *observable* can help to counteract this problem. Fourteen years ago I argued that solar energy systems should never be regulated out of sight because their high visibility—however controversial by contemporaneous aesthetic standards—was crucial to their widespread adoption by society. Sustainable technologies and landscape features like natural storm drainage and visible solar collector systems symbolize "conspicuous nonconsumption" and are essential markers along the road to a more sustainable world. . . .[5]

## SUSTAINABILITY, CULTURE, AND COMMUNITY

Ultimately, the goal of sustainable landscapes is the transformation of *culture*—the taming of technology, the emergence of a new environmental ethic, a new measure of life quality, and a substantially broadened sense of *community* including not only humans, but all life. If this sounds like a manifesto or a grandiose political wish, I suppose it is. What I have written in this book implies the need for "*not* business as usual," and I believe more decision makers and social critics are accepting this implication each day. Therefore, it is important to look at sustainable landscapes in terms of the nature and degree of social change they imply.

In the search for prototypes for sustainable landscapes we often focus on established,

Figure 21. The experience of sustainable design: an earth-sheltered home in its vineyard, with maximized energy efficiency. Designed and built by Jim Zaretto (Robert Thayer).

nonindustrial cultures that have practiced regenerative agricultural or other resource-harvesting techniques over a long period of time.[6] A potential criticism leveled at the movement toward a sustainable landscape is that it appears to depend upon human labor rather than energy inputs, coupled with the obvious limitation and reluctance of modern society to revert to labor-intensive agricultural and industrial practices.[7] Although we admire and often romanticize the Amish culture of Pennsylvania and the nine-hundred-year-old productivity of the Hopi mesa landscapes in Arizona, for example, it is naïve to assume that the majority of Americans would intentionally adopt the austere social structure and involvement with the land implicit in both of these cultures. However, sustainable landscapes need not be heavily peopled nor labor intensive. Wind farms generally lack human dwellers, and multipurpose constructed wetlands can and do exist a stone's throw away from places like the Los Angeles International Airport.[8] While a sustainable world will not be able to support the excessive resource consumption levels of our western societies, it will depend a great deal upon renewable energy sources and laborsaving devices we recognize today.

There will, however, be limits. In fact, recognizing the limits of our technological lifestyles and landscapes is what the book [*Gray World, Green Heart*] and many others are all about.[9] However, both the landscape venues and the cultures that animate them will evolve gradually toward sustainability in concert, each influencing the other in mutual cause and effect. We created the conflict between nature and technology slowly over a long period of time, and we are likely to climb out of it steadily and incrementally as well. To some extent, sustainable culture will *evolve,* but if we are to make a more sustainable world, we must do so by *intentional design.* This implies that we will not usually have the advantage of an existing culture or subculture upon which to build. We may, quite literally, need to design and build the cultural elements necessary to accompany and actualize new sustainable landscapes as we build the landscapes themselves. . . .

## LIVING WITH INCONSISTENCY AND MANAGING LANDSCAPE GUILT

While sustainable subcultures and their corresponding landscapes are evolving together, there is still much in the dominant culture which seems inconsistent, unreal, and out of control. By and large, landscapes are getting more opaque as society entangles itself further in the veil of technologically aided simulation, avoidance, and fantasy. As a consequence, our sense of what is real is becoming as fragmented as the landscape itself. In this state of affairs, we will have to learn to live with inconsistency for a quite a long while. Environmental guilt, the sense of dissonance we feel about technology's impact on the land, will likely increase as we struggle to reinvent a more regenerative landscape in the face of cultural momentum to the contrary. The colliding tendencies toward simulation on the one had and sustainability on the other will be the dominant tension affecting the landscape for some years to come. . . .

Ultimately, we must accept the fact that guilt over the impacts of technology on nature may never completely disappear, and manifestations of this guilt will be revealed in the landscape well into the future. Perhaps it is just as well, for our intuitive adverse reaction to technology is a baseline check against its autonomy. However, when guilt over technology results in a landscape of opacity, concealment, and illusion, it is not constructive. To arrive at a more sustainable world, we will need to make clear choices in favor of certain technologies and against others. The choice to employ and express a more sustainable technology in place of a less sustainable one should not be paralyzed by technophobia, but only guided by it. . . .

## TAMING THE TECHNOLOGICAL TYRANT

The evolution of nature, technology, and their conflicting interrelationship demands movement toward resolution. We created the dilemma of topophilia, technophilia, and technophobia, and we must strive to resolve it. The sustainable landscape is a natural step in the transformation toward resolution; we cannot kill the technological tyrant, only tame it. There is a parallel here between the evolution of sustainable landscapes and David Rains Wallace's metaphor of the Klamath giants. Mythical or not, the Klamath giants symbolize a nontechnological, peaceful, human-like animal capable of complete and totally nondestructive integration with nature. Likewise, sustainable landscapes represent a turnabout in the direction of fundamental human tinkering away from dominance of nature toward reverence for the subservience to it. Like the Klamath giants, if sustainable landscapes had not begun to emerge, it would have been necessary for us to invent them. We may never actually see the Klamath giants, but we can certainly *build* sustainable landscapes. In essence, to tame the technological tyrant, it has become extremely necessary to reinvent both culture and environment—to reconfigure both our landscapes and ourselves. . . .

## TAKING ACTION

So far, I have aimed the discussion in this chapter at the unique role of sustainable landscapes in relation to human experience; we create them and they create us. By far the most critical aspect in our experience of sustainable landscapes is *taking action* to bring about their existence. It is easy to talk about sustainable landscapes, and although frustrating at times, it is still relatively easy to write books about them. What is most difficult is *making* them. Sustainable landscapes imply a different set of ground rules, yet the game must go on in order for the rules to change, like a child's sandlot baseball game where players share the role of umpire and argue over the calls. We must *make* sustainable landscapes to know *how* to make them, and we must make them in order to know *what* they really are. Taking action will involve considerable commitment to change in "business as usual," faith that viable alternatives to the status quo are possible and effective, and resiliency to put up with inevitable and innumerable failures. Above all, action requires unbridled optimism and enthusiasm.

I recommend that citizen activists, planners, and designers of sustainable landscapes set a limited number of achievable goals within the scope of each project, and try to reach at least one or two of them. Learning will take place in the attempt, even if all goals are not reached. In one recent hundred-acre neighborhood design project, for example, my consulting partners and I were successful in providing solar access, calming a major auto street, structuring an open space network with pedestrian and bicycle linkages, providing a natural storm drainage system, and designing a water-efficient landscape. We were unable to persuade our clients to provide a community garden, common areas, cohousing, a critical wildlife habitat connection, or dense, mixed-use neighborhood/commercial area which might have reduced auto use even further. However, we accepted these limited accomplishments and moved on.

Each concrete action to make a specific landscape more functionally sustainable will involve several outward, symbolic dimensions: reinforcement of personal values; maintenance of a sense of self, place, and community; influence on the attitudes and behaviors of one's immediate peer group; and evidence of political feasibility or economic viability. For the next several years, every planning or landscape architectural project intended to move toward sustainability will necessarily be a "demonstration," or "pilot" project. As in the case of Laguna West, the potential is great for each of these projects to achieve too little in the way of measurable reduction in the impact of consumptive technology, and too much in the way of media exposure and superficial success. While the *experiential* qualities of sustainable landscapes are critical, without *functionally* contributing to actual environmental solutions, supposedly sustainable landscapes degenerate into mere simulations.[10] Continual effort must be made to ensure that the actions taken toward more sustainable design be concrete and measurable at the core as well as informative and meaningful on the surface. . . .

## Small Victories and Large Question

Finally, we must learn the *joy* of working on the solution—not to be consumed by despair over the immensity of the task—but enriched by the steps to be taken, one at a time. In the words of Gandhi, "What you do may seem unimportant, but it is terribly important that you do it."[11] Each additional piece of the sustainable landscape is a small victory, and should be celebrated as such. Fundamental change in the relationship between nature, technology, and landscape will come from the incremental experiences of thousands of individuals in the actual places where they live, work, play, and touch. . . .

Ultimately, the conflict between nature and technology—the triangular tension of topophilia, technophilia, and technophobia—is a dilemma of *love*. Humans have an immense capacity for love, but as any lover knows, affection and commitment often require painful prioritization. Hidden behind the layers of our profligate material culture, between extravagant gardens and electronic gadgets, beyond wilderness areas and theme-park shopping malls, is the paramount dilemma of our very most fundamental, emotional priorities. Is our *deepest* attachment to technological culture, or is it to Earth? We might ask: Which could we ultimately not do without?

The earth existed before the explosion of human technology, and it will remain afterward. Our infatuation with technology is a brief, distracting affair, but we are webbed to the earth for life. Sustainability asks not for the banishment of technology from the landscape, but only for its servitude on behalf of a more fundamental, paramount, ecological ethic. Through a constant and unfolding process of experiment and experience, we may finally come to place our love of nature and our affection for technology in the right order upon the land.

# MESSY ECOSYSTEMS, ORDERLY FRAMES (1995)

## JOAN IVERSON NASSAUER

> . . . A continuous reframing of the phenomenon as (a) whole becomes a part serves to overcome the inertia of certainty.
>
> —Sidney K. Robinson, *Inquiry in the Picturesque*

## Ecological Function, Cultural Perception

Ecological quality tends to look messy, and this poses problems for those who imagine and construct new landscapes to enhance ecological quality. What *is* good may not *look* good, and what looks good may not be good. The distinction between function and appearance may distress idealists who regard presentation as dissembling, but it is intrinsic to the concept of design, in which each landscape is recognized as one of any number of possible designs for a particular place. Landscape architects may consult the genius of the place, but they do not expect the genius of the place to design it.

However, even designers may become strangely submissive in the face of nature's genius, sharing in a common popular delusion that nature will speak for itself—if only human beings will quit interrupting. A belief that nature needs no presentation and that presentation is essentially sinister in its intent leaves ecosystems highly susceptible to misunderstanding. Decades ago, Lowenthal and Prince[1] instructed that people "see their terrain through preferred and accustomed spectacles." As much as our affection for the cultural concept of nature would lead us to believe otherwise, people do not know how to see ecological quality directly. We know how to see ecological quality only through our cultural lenses, and through those lenses, it may or may not look like nature.[2] Nature has come to be identified with pictorial conventions of the picturesque,[3] a cultural not ecological concept. More significantly, picturesque conventions have become so integral to landscape perception that we no longer are able to accept their origin in culture.[4] Picturesque conventions seem so intrinsic to nature that they are mistaken for ecological quality.

The difference between the scientific concept of ecology and the cultural concept of ecology and the cultural concept of nature, the difference between function and appearance, demonstrates that applied landscape ecology is essentially a design problem. It is not a straightforward problem of attending to scientific knowledge of ecosystem relationships or an artistic problem of expressing ecological function, but a public landscape problem of addressing cultural expectations that only tangentially relate to ecological function or high art. It requires the translation of ecological patterns into cultural language.[5] It requires placing unfamiliar and frequently undesirable forms inside familiar, attractive packages. It requires designing orderly frames for messy ecosystems.

Some might see culture as an unnecessary barrier between science and popular public attitudes that are increasingly, even cloyingly, green. When the public is highly receptive to doing the right thing for the environment, scientific answers about what is ecologically correct should be sufficient. But in fact social conventions keep the same people who dress in green slogans dressing their homes and cities in homogenous plant communities where enormous species diversity once existed, appreciating robins where once they were warblers, and recycling plastic while depleting aquifers.

Once we begin talking about the landscapes where we live everyday—about specific changes in the way the landscape will look even for the purposes of protecting or improving ecological quality—we encounter fear, anger, rejection. Why? There is a clue in an example from Minneapolis, where a goal had been established to improve water quality in the lakes that form the heart of the public park system and some of the most desirable neighborhoods in the city.

Storm sewers in the watersheds surrounding the lakes emptied directly into the lakes, and the construction of upstream wetlands to act as settling basins for pollutants had been identified as the most efficient means of improving water quality. *Here is the clue:* City council, park board and task force members, and the engineers who were involved in the process that recommended construction referred to the new features as *wetlands*. Citizens who lived near the grassy open spaces that were the proposed construction sites referred to them as *swamps*. The citizens are not self-serving or arbitrary; their perceptions fit within the centre of the cultural mainstream. People may care about improving ecological quality but not at the expense of the proper appearance of their own landscapes.

## Proper Appearance: Neatness and Ecological Function

It may be time to add a new acronym to the planning lexicon. "Not in my back yard" (NIMBY) resists the sitting of controversial land uses. The sentiment expressed here is *not in my yard* (NIMY). It resists changes in the way my landscape looks because of the way it may reflect on me. Aldo Leopold poetically expressed the powerful social identification of the landowner with the look of the land in 1939: "The landscape of any farm is the owner's portrait of himself."[6]

We need to recognize that the landscapes of city dwellers' homes, neighborhoods, parks, roadsides, and businesses are public portraits of themselves. The expectation that I represent myself as a citizen in the landscape of my home is etched deeply into popular culture. In the United States it dates at least from the early nineteenth century.[7] Like all highly public speech, the language of landscape does not lend itself to colloquialism. It is adaptable, taking varied forms in different eras, but it is highly attuned to propriety and resistant to fundamental change.

The dominant culture in much of North America reads a neat, orderly landscape as a sign of neighborliness, hard work, and pride. Typically, people want to achieve or know they are expected to achieve this landscape appearance and all that is signifies about themselves. At the same time, a neat, orderly landscape seldom enhances the ecological function of the landscape.

## Human Intention and Design

When we conceive of popular perceptions in this way, we think of the role of design differently as well. If I create my landscape in order to communicate with my neighbors and maintain their approval, then the language of form that I believe that my neighbor understands is of paramount importance. *I may like* the idea of living in a landscape that provides wildlife cover, but I am unlikely to change my own yard or advocate that the neighborhood park take on this look if I believe that *people won't like it.*

Human inhabited landscapes operate as ecological systems, but they also operate as communication systems,[8] and above all other information, *people seek information about other people* when they experience the landscape. For designers who wish to affect the pervasive landscape pattern that landscape ecology has demonstrated to be fundamental to ecological quality, knowing the everyday language for making and interpreting landscapes will be a necessity.

Special places or preserves may be presented in more arcane scientific or privately expressive language. In the everyday landscape, rather than simply designing to enhance ecological quality or even to express ecological function as form, we must design to *frame ecological function within a recognizable system of form.*

In the everyday landscape of North America, the recognizable system of form typically is characterized by neatness and order. While many observers have associated neatness and order with the human desire to control or dominate the landscape,[9] these characteristics are more validly interpreted as signs of sociable human intention.[10] Neatness cannot be mistaken for untended nature; it means a person has been in a place and returns frequently. It means a place is under the care of a person.

In settled landscapes, urban or countryside, people expect to see the look of human intention. Where people intend indigenous plant communities or habitats to exist as gardens or preserves, and where the landscape communicates this intention by the way it looks, people are likely to understand that this is "nature" and find it aesthetically pleasing. Where those same plant communities or habitats exist without obvious signs of human intention, they may be mistaken for neglected land or be readily compromised as land awaiting development. Perception of human intention may be the difference between a nature preserve and a dumping ground, or the difference between a wetland and a slough. Designing ecosystems so that people will recognize their beauty and maintain it appropriately may depend upon including design cues of human intention.

## NATURALNESS AND CARE

While a neat landscape is the unmistakable product of human intention, a natural looking landscape is more likely to be misinterpreted. Nature is a cultural concept that is frequently mistaken as an indication of ecological quality. It has no specific appearance in form and may be as readily applied to a canopied urban plaza[11] or cultivated field[12] as to a wilderness.

While naturalness frequently has been described on a continuum from the pristine to "the most humanly degraded end of the ecological scale,"[13] this intuitively appealing continuum can lead us to significant errors of ecological perception, which have been described earlier.[14] For example, we might assume that a nature preserve represents the absence of human influence when in fact the existence of intact remnants of indigenous ecosystems depends upon human protection and management. We also might assume that design of landscapes to look natural is a form of deceit about the *real* and destructive effects of human influence. Equating design with deceit leaves no room to acknowledge how design is necessary to represent and maintain ecological function. Finally, we might assume that people know how to see ecological function, that ecosystems speak for themselves. Consequently, we might live in the landscape without knowledge of critical but invisible ecological functions. In fact, invisible ecological function must be actively represented for human experience if human beings are to maintain ecological quality.

The fact that apparent naturalness can lead to such perceptual mistakes about ecological function underscores the power of the cultural concept of naturalness. It we acknowledge the distinction between ecological function and natural appearance, we can begin to critically analyze the cultural language of naturalness and use it as a language to intentionally communicate ecological function.

A large body of landscape perception research suggests some elements of landscape language that communicate naturalness. The elements that are repeated in the conclusions of study after study are vegetation, especially canopy trees, and water.[15] Furthermore, this body of research leaves no doubt that people prefer to see landscapes that they perceive as natural.

At the same time, perception of even the most fundamental elements of a natural appearance, vegetation and water, is highly contingent on cultural interpretation. Not all vegetation is equally preferred. For example, a case study of Minnesota owners of rare ecosystems found that owners of oak woodlands tend to appreciate and manage these ecosystems to maintain them, but owners of wetlands or prairies are far less likely to appreciate them. In fact they are likely to change wetlands or prairies in order to "improve" them.[16] Preference for woodlands is also subject to cultural interpretations. For example, woodlands with dense understory or very dense canopy woodlands may not be attractive.[17]

Even within the context of appreciating nature, "too much nature" or nature that falls outside cultural expectations is unappealing. In an effort to remake nature to fit cultural expectations, people care for the landscape to the detriment of indigenous ecosystems. Wetlands are mown and planted with exotic species, prairies are planted with trees, and woodlands are mown and cleared of dead wood.[18]

The naturalness that Americans appreciate today is more closely related to an eighteenth-century concept of the picturesque and the beautiful than it is to the understanding of ecological function.[19] Whether one accounts for the love of a picturesque mix of a neat open ground plane with well-spaced canopy trees on rolling terrain as a consequence of evolution[20] or taste,[21] the cultural concept of picturesque nature produces a landscape that looks tended, not wild. It enters the recognizable system of landscape form with powerful symbols that work beside neatness to represent human intention.

How we show we are good citizens and good neighbors by the way we care for the landscape to make it look neat or picturesque, safe or inviting, how we use the landscape to express power or wealth—these will establish the framework within which ecosystems are manipulated on a planet dominated by human beings. In an urban or countryside context, people tend to perceive landscapes that exhibit biodiversity as messy, weedy, and unkempt. A central problem in introducing greater biodiversity and heterogeneity to the urban landscape is that these characteristics tend to be mistaken for a lack of care.

### ORDERLY FRAMES: CULTURAL SYMBOLS OF NEATNESS AND NATURALNESS

When ecological function is framed by cultural language, it is not obliterated or covered up or compromised. It is set up for viewing, so that people can see it in a new way, much in the same way as Joseph Cornell set up everyday objects in his boxes. Describing Cornell's boxes as descendants of slot machines, Harold Rosenberg asserted that in comparison with the objects they displayed, the boxes were the artist's "most inclusive symbol," and represented the artist's "means of participation in the common life holding himself strictly apart from it. (The artist) becomes a member of the crowd by making anonymous use of its games."[22]

Landscape architects need to strike a relationship with vernacular design traditions much like that struck by Cornell: being both "a member of the crowd" and "holding himself strictly apart from it," using its symbols for a different purpose. Cues to human care, expressions of neatness and tended nature, are inclusive symbols by which ecologically rich landscapes can be presented to people and can enter vernacular culture. Working from vernacular culture is necessary to infiltrating everyday acts of landscape change and ultimately achieving radically innovative pervasive landscape structure. This paper summarizes several projects that help to develop the argument for this concept and demonstrate its implications by constructing orderly frames for messy ecosystems.

### HUMAN INTENTION: THE LOOK OF CARE—FARM FIELDS AND SUBURBAN YARDS

We grossly underestimate the power of landscape appearance when we fix our attention on characteristics of scenic landscapes. If we invest only the scenic with aesthetic quality,

| | | CARE | | | |
|---|---|---|---|---|---|
| **Neatness** | | **Stewardship** | | **Naturalness** | |
| Attractive | Unattractive | Attractive | Unattractive | Attractive | Unattractive |
| **Apparent yard care** | **Dead or rotten** | **Good con- servation** | **Poor con- servation** | **Apparent naturalness** | **Too formal** |
| Fences | | | | | Too formal |
| Flowers or shrubs | Dead or rotten | Conservation | All planted to corn | Development blends in | |
| Home | **Lack of yard care** | Contour plowing | | | Too much concrete |
| Landscaped | | | Effluent from feedlots— | Habitat | |
| Lawn orna- ments or architectural details | No flowers | No erosion | poor quality | Native vegetation | Too open |
| | No shade | | | | Bare |
| | Not landscaped | Pasture | Erodible land plowed | | |
| Trees in rows | Not mown | Stripcropping | | Natural | Flat |
| **Big yard** | | Terraces | No conservation practices being used | Trees | Monotonous |
| Big yard | **Messy** | Windbreak | | Wildlife | No trees |
| **Clean and neat** | Cluttered | | | | |
| Clean | Construction going on | | Pastures are overgrazed | | |
| Neat | Junk | | | | |
| No junk | Messy | | Plowing up the hills | | |
| Put away | **Poor care** | | | | |
| **Good care** | Abandoned | | Runoff | | |
| Cared for | Neglected | | | | |
| Maintained | No house on a farmstead site | | Slimy-looking water | | |
| Well kept | | | | | |
| **Mown** | | | | | |
| Mown | **Weedy** | | | | |
| **New** | Weedy | | | | |
| New | | | | | |
| **No weeds** | | | | | |
| No weeds | | | | | |
| **White** | | | | | |

Figure 22. Cues for care: content analysis of descriptive terms organized under the concept of landscape care (after Joan Iverson Nassauer).

we construct a very coarse filter that leaves only rare places for our examination and fails to capture the aesthetic experiences and aesthetic conventions that shape the larger land-scape matrix. In the United States, most of the countryside, suburbia, and city neighbor-hoods have been the detritus of this fixation on the scenic. What could possibly make a flat Illinois cornfield without fencerow or farmstead or distant grove beautiful? Farmers see beauty in the straightness of the rows, uninterrupted by weeds or water, their even green color, and the neatly mown roadside that surrounds the field.[23] These characteristics con-stitute a recognizable image of care so powerful that it is a stereotype that has been successfully used to violate its own original meaning—for example as a device for advertising pesticides.

In two projects in which Midwestern farmers described rural landscapes,[24] the look of care was highly associated with landscapes that farmers found attractive. While terms that were used to describe care spanned a range from the neat and tidy aesthetic of "yard care" to the cultural interpretation of "naturalness," all of the terms were summarized under the global concept of care.

That terms like "landscaped," as applied to yard care, and "habitat," as applied to naturalness, could be organized under the look of care points to a possible means of resolving perceptual conflicts across this spectrum. Any of these perceived qualities can be the consequence of human intention to care for the land.

In the second rural landscape project,[25] people who lived in the countryside but were not farmers were also interviewed. Both these people and the farmers tended to use some of the same words and the same global concept, care, to describe what made home landscapes, i.e., yards, attractive as they did to describe what made fields attractive. Not surprisingly, two projects that focused on a suburban landscape matrix dominated by yards returned similar results.

In the first suburban project,[26] 234 residents of a third-tier Twin Cities suburb rated video imaging simulations of seven alternative treatments of home landscapes on five dimensions: attractiveness, care, neatness, naturalness, and apparent need for maintenance. The seven alternative treatments of home landscapes demonstrated a range of six increasingly ecological rich landscapes designed within vernacular expectations: the first treatment was entirely conventional, and the succeeding five framed gardens of indigenous plant communities with cues to human intention. The seventh alternative showed the conventional landscape grown to weeds, untended. While suburban residents generally preferred the immediately recognizable, conventional landscape treatment to all others, they rated the treatment in which half of the mown lawn had been replaced with a garden of plants indigenous to the oak savanna almost equally attractive. The weedy lawn was rated far less attractive than all other treatments, including the ecologically rich design.

More instructive for designers of human inhabited ecosystems was the association among the five characteristics. In the conventional treatment and the alternative treatments that maintained a strong resemblance to the conventional, care and neatness scores were associated with attractiveness. Naturalness joined that association where half the lawn was replaced by the indigenous garden. The characteristics were associated in the same way for the weedy lawn, but on opposite ends of the scale. The weedy lawn looked unattractive, uncared for, and messy, but it did look natural and as if it required little maintenance. Where more than half the lawn was replaced by the indigenous garden or where the garden was composed entirely of dense indigenous shrubs, the clustering of characteristics was different. Neatness was no longer associated with care and attractiveness. For designers the results suggest that novel suburban landscapes are more likely to be attractive if they look neat and well cared for.

The second suburban landscape project was designed to learn about how people perceived wildlife habitat in their own neighborhoods.[27] Ethnographic interviews and, later, a complete population survey where conducted in suburban neighborhoods adjacent to the largest urban national wildlife refuge in the United States, the Minnesota River Valley National Wildlife Refuge. Suburban residents said that people who had an attractive yard were neat, cared about the appearance of the neighborhood or about the environment, and took pride in their home or their neighborhood. People who had unattractive yards were believed to not care, to have negative personality traits (to be "different," to have no taste, etc.), or to lack resources to care for their yard. They were also described as not being good neighbors.[28] In a factor analysis of the 258 terms that suburban residents used to describe attractive and unattractive landscapes in the neighborhoods, four of the eight most powerful factors (cumulative percent of variance = 32.6 percent) related to care and "landscaping." The other four factors related to attractiveness and naturalness. In these suburban neighborhoods, terms like "park-like, a blend of the natural and unnatural," were associated with naturalness. While people found "bare, severe, or unnatural" landscapes unattractive. "Wildlife habitat" was a term used by some people to describe what made a landscape attractive and by others to describe what made it unattractive.

Both of the suburban projects support the conclusion that "neatness" labels a landscape as well cared for, and that "naturalness" is defined by cultural expectations. Trees, shrubs, flowers, and grasses look attractive unless there is "too much." Then the immediate cues to care, the presence of human intention, are lost.

## Cues to Care

*. . . Words are never our own . . . language is one strategic part of the total social fact.*[29]
Cues that indicate human intention are cultural symbols that can be used to frame more novel ecosystems in inhabited landscapes. Using cues to care in design is not a means of maintaining traditional landscape forms but rather a means of adapting cultural expectations to recognize new landscape forms that include greater biodiversity. Cues to care make the novel familiar and associate ecosystems that may look messy with unmistakable indications that the landscape is a part of a larger intended pattern. The cues may vary from region to region and among ethnic groups, but an underlying principle across cultures and regions is that these cues express care of the landscape. For example, care may be apparent in straight, weed-free rows of corn on a farm in the Midwest, but it may also be apparent in an intricate pattern of gourd vines intercropped with corn planted in mounds in dryland farming by the Acoma people in New Mexico. In some places, care will not look neat in the way we might recognize it in a North American suburb. However, cues to care can be observed in the vernacular landscapes of many communities. To identify them, ask yourself the same question that people ask when they are appraising their own yards and neighborhoods: Does it look like they're taking care of it? Then, study the landscape. What makes it look well cared for?

Cues that emerged in the Midwestern studies cited here are:

*Mowing.* While the omnipresent, large, continuous lawn is not necessary to communicate care, mowing a strip along human paths (streets, walkways) frames patches of greater biodiversity with clear signs of human intention.

*Flowering Plants and Trees.* Wetland and prairie plants with small flowers tend to be misunderstood for weeds. If restorations or gardens include an "unnaturally high" proportion with larger, brighter flowers, at least in the first few seasons, people are more likely to find them attractive. Compared with shrubs or grasses, people are more likely to immediately appreciate trees, especially those they themselves can maintain in some way.

*Wildlife Feeders and Houses.* People widely appreciated songbirds, and while people may not be able to identify the necessary habitat for the birds they enjoy, and they may not find the "brushy" quality of the habitat attractive, they do associate bird houses and feeders with the birds they enjoy. The feeders and houses are structural cues to care for wildlife and habitat.

*Bold Patterns.* The rural landscape studies described above strongly suggested that the bold, clearly visible patterns of soil conservation practices like strip cropping, grassed waterways, and terracing were vivid cues to care, even for people who are not farmers or know little about agriculture. These patterns indicate human intention by their crisp edges and landscape scale. Similar patterns can be adapted to urban land uses.

*Trimmed Shrubs, Plants in Rows, Linear Planting Designs.* At a smaller scale, obvious trimming and pruning of shrubs and linear planting clearly indicate human presence and the intention to care for a landscape.

*Fences, Architectural Details, Lawn Ornaments, Painting.* These are all structural cues to the care of the adjacent landscape. Where a fence is well-maintained, or especially freshly painted, where nearby buildings are well maintained and painted, where lawn ornaments or architectural details like window boxes or shutters indicate human attention to a place, the landscape nearby is more likely to appear to be well cared for. In the Midwest, the color white used to paint buildings and fences is particularly associated with care.

*Foundation Planting.* The suburban studies described above indicate that foundation plantings are a nearly unassailable cultural expectation for the home landscape. They should cover the foundation of the house but they should not obscure its window or doors to fit within the vernacular.

## DESIGNS TO FRAME MESSY ECOSYSTEMS

Two projects that incorporated cues to care are briefly described below. In the first project, cues to care were used to frame habitat patches that were established as part of the USDA Conservation Reserve Program (CRP). Since 1986, 36.4 million acres of formerly cultivated farmland has been enrolled in the CRP. Despite the enormous habitat and soil conservation benefits that were immediately achieved by the program, people in rural communities were critical of the "weedy, messy" appearance of land in the program.[30] To address these criticisms, aesthetic conservation to "communicate the appearance of good stewardship" was added to technical guidelines for implementing the CRP after 1990. Cues to care were used to design model landscapes that communicate the appearance of good stewardship for the USDA Soil Conservation Service. Mow strips, bold strip patterns of perennial cover at the recognizable scale of strip cropping, and the use of seed mixes heavily loaded with native forbes all helped to maintain habitat and soil conservation goals, but did so within the familiar language of care for the agricultural landscape.

A second project used cues to care to frame a created wetland in an urban park. The Phalen Wetland Amenity Park is retrofitted on a site that is currently a shopping center (and was a wetland forty years ago) in a stable working-class neighborhood of St. Paul, Minnesota. The plan for the park frames the proposed wetland with bold, crisp bands of wet meadow plants that will drift with time but initially will introduce local people to the appearance of a wetland garden. Prairie grasses and forbes pour down an enormous south facing lawn from which people will view the wetland. While the conventional appearance of the lawn establishes that the wetland park is well maintained for people, the prairie grasses filter runoff from lawn and road chemicals before water reaches the wetland.

Figure 23. Nassauer's design for Phalen Wetland Park in St. Paul, Minnesota, employs a peninsula of turf ringed by a boardwalk to bring visitors to the wetland edge and indicate human intention. Wetland, wet meadow, prairie, and oak savannah plants comprise a broad band that provides habitat elsewhere throughout the site (Joan Iverson Nassauer).

## CONCLUSIONS

For new forms of ecologically rich landscapes to be sustained, the forms must be recognized and perpetuated by people in everyday situations, maintaining the landscape and creating their own landscapes. Designing orderly frames is one way of using the vernacular language of landscape to create greater ecological quality. Orderly frames bring novel landscape structures into highly stable social conventions just as Joseph Cornell's boxes allowed the artist to "participate in common life" and "become a member of the crowd" while using the symbols of the common life for a different purpose.[31] Orderly frames show that design with ecology can be motivated and perpetuated by the most ordinary human desires and habits.

This way of incorporating human nature into a concept of ecological responsibility is very different from requiring human beings to be confronted with ecologically destructive behavior. An "in your face" approach to displaying ecological function would logically extend to exposed septic systems, a landfill in every yard, corporate headquarters sited at chemical dumps, and a sense of ecological justice about natural disasters like flooding and drought. It requires people to accept what they regard as ugly or uncomfortable in exchange for what is attractive and familiar.

Using vernacular language to present unfamiliar ecosystems is also very different from purists' rejection of resource-consuming patches within the larger landscape matrix. Rather it strategically positions small pieces of the old landscape matrix of turf and annual flowers as signposts along an evolving popular landscape aesthetic. It also protects even the most pristine landscapes by clearly labeling them under human care.

Neither penance nor purism are likely substitutes for the pride and pleasure that people take in familiar landscape patterns. Over the decades of the life of any designed landscape, penance or purism is unlikely to work. What will work is to acknowledge that cultural expectations and human pleasure will continue to be measures of ecological function, at least in everyday experience. Orderly frames are not a means of dominating ecological phenomena for the sake of human pleasure. Orderly frames can be used to construct a widely recognizable cultural framework for ecological quality.

# PART VI

# Integrating Site, Place, and Region

Much of the theoretical debate in landscape architecture revolves around how best to resolve several fundamental tensions. There are tensions between the different ways of knowing the world expressed within the various bodies of knowledge and theoretical frameworks upon which the discipline draws. There are tensions between knowledge and representation of the general and the particular, of abstract space and lived place. And there are tensions across the multiple scales of site, city and region, and global system. The preceding readings have each adopted an implicit or explicit position upon how these relationships should or could be integrated within design. Geoffrey and Susan Jellicoe, for example, argued for a search for a "single big idea" of humanity. Edward Relph and Elizabeth Meyer, on the other hand, argued against the search for the universal, in favor of the specificity of place and site. In this final section, the role of the region as a framework for design thinking is explored. In a sense, the idea of region corresponds to the Jellicoes' "middle distance," between the individual and infinity. Richard Forman[1] has noted the paradox that whereas our ability to act is greater at the "landscape" (and site) scale, the probability of long-term success in pursuing a goal of sustainability is greater at the regional level. In the following readings, several authors argue that site and landscape design should be undertaken within a regional design context.

The reemergence of the region as a focus of interest is not unique to landscape architecture. One of the effects of the increasing rate of globalization[2] of economies and technologies during the latter part of the twentieth century has been renewed attention to regions as centers of both strategic investment and cultural and political resistance.[3] In landscape architecture, the region gains additional potency through its expression of ecological process, both in an analytical sense,[4] and as a framework for conservation, for example through the concept of bio-regionalism.[5]

In the first reading, Michael Hough draws on these different strands of regional thinking as a focus for design and planning integration. In his book *Out of Place: Restoring Identity to the Regional Landscape* (1990) he illustrates his argument with examples from the Toronto region. The extracts here summarize essential principles of his approach, in which cumulative action at site level contributes to an enhanced sense of regional identity. However, the region can also inform the site. Terry Harkness's *Gardens from Region* (1990) shows how individual site designs can be based upon a distillation of regional characteristics. Next, Joan Woodward uses the idea of *signature-based design* (drawing on the linguistic metaphors explored in Part IV) to express the interrelationship between region and site.

The conceptual link between the "middle distance" of the region and the contemporary interest in the creative potential of technological infrastructure was noted in Part III. The final reading, from *Infrastructure as Landscape* (1996) by Gary Strang, provides a succinct summary of the idea and its potential as an integrating focus within the discipline. He presents infrastructure as a regionally based approach by which to assert design leadership. This contemporary attempt to adopt infrastructure as a core concept for the discipline[6] is therefore both a critical and an instrumental strategy. It also reflects a growing interest of other disciplines in landscape as a theoretical concept and area of practice, and sets an agenda for the first part of the twenty-first century.

# PRINCIPLES FOR REGIONAL DESIGN (1990)

## MICHAEL HOUGH

### PRINCIPLES FOR REGIONAL DESIGN

What role does design play in the development of a contemporary regional landscape? A historical perspective suggests that the differences between one place and another have arisen, not from efforts to create long-range visions and grand designs, but from vernacular responses to the practical problems of everyday life. Indeed, it can be argued that purposeful design has done more to generate placelessness than to promote a sense of place. The new forces shaping the landscape are no longer small and local in scope but are great in scale and consequence. The technological and economic impact of these forces on the environment has never before had such profound potential for the destruction of life systems. As a discipline dedicated to fitting man to the land and to giving it form, contemporary design is faced with solving problems that have traditionally not been a part of the agenda in the creation of vernacular places.

In the past, there were limits to what one was able to do and the extent to which one could modify the natural environment. The constraints of environment and society created an undisputed sense of being rooted to the place, but they were, nonetheless, limitations to be overcome, not inherent motivations to be at one with nature. In today's landscape the heterogeneity of the past is giving way to a more homogeneous, information-based society. In design terms, therefore, it becomes as much romantic nonsense to force the old regional differences upon this new landscape as it is to expect people to give up cars, washing machines, and television in the interests of a better environment. We are locked into our times and ways of doing things.

Yet, there is a dilemma for designers in the new and evolving landscape. The determinants that shaped the settlements and countryside of pre-industrial society and that gave rise to the physical forms which we now admire are now no longer those of environmental limitation but of choice. Creating a sense of place involves a conscious decision to do so. At the same time, the need to invest in the protection of nature has never been so urgent. The connections between regional identity and the sustainability of the land are essential and fundamental. A valid design philosophy, therefore, is tied to ecological values and principles; to the notions of environmental and social health; to the essential bond of people to nature, and to the biological sustainability of life itself. This is the new necessity that will counterbalance and bring some sanity to a world whose goals are focused on helping us "live in a society of abundance and leisure."[1] Yet values that espouse a truly sustainable future will only emerge when it is perceived that there are no alternatives. It is possible that over time the fragility of earth's life systems will create an imperative for survival on which a new ethic can flourish. The international agreement to protect the earth's ozone layer, signed in 1987, may be one indication of this trend. And it is only on this basis that regionalism can become an imperative—a fundamental platform for understanding and shaping the future landscape. . . .

## KNOWING THE PLACE

Recognizing how people use different places to fulfill the practical needs of living is one of the building blocks on which a distinctive sense of place can be enhanced in the urban landscape. Regional identity is connected with the peculiar characteristics of a location that tell us something about its physical and social environment. It is what a place has when it somehow belongs to its location and nowhere else. It has to do, therefore, with two fundamental criteria: first, with the natural processes of the region or locality—what nature has put there; second, with social processes—what people have put there. It has to do with the way people adapt to their living environment; how they change it to suit their needs in the process of living; how they make it their own. In effect, regional identity is the collective reaction of people to the environment over time. . . .

## MAINTAINING A SENSE OF HISTORY

Rarely does the designer have the luxury, or more appropriately, the misfortune, to create a place from scratch. Something is always there before he begins: a history, a peculiar character, a meeting place. Design inevitably involves building on what's there in the process of change.

The protection of natural and cultural history—the reuse and integration of the old into the new without fanfare while avoiding the temptation to turn everything into a museum because it's old—lies at the heart of maintaining a continuing link with the past and with a place's identity. Our overwhelming desire to eliminate our past is nowhere more evident than in the destruction of nature that we find in every corner of the globe in large or small measure. Similarly, the tendency for the new in urban development to destroy the old in the interests of economics is one of the major reasons for placelessness in the changing urban landscape. There are no longer any historical reference points by which one understands where one has come from in the process of building the new. The remnant native plant communities that still survive in protected parts of the city—in cemeteries, valley lands, older residential area—also link us with the past, with the pre-development landscape, and with the historic interactions of man and environment. Evolving and fortuitous naturalizing plant communities in the city's forgotten places—railway corridors, abandoned lands, industrial properties, the corner spaces found in every city lot tell us more about the dynamics of natural processes and the sustainability of nature in urban areas than those that have been imposed, in aesthetic, or horticultural terms, on the environment. . . .

## ENVIRONMENTAL LEARNING AND DIRECT EXPERIENCE

Environmental literacy lies at the heart of understanding the places with which we are familiar, and thus at the heart of the issue of identity. It is necessary for people who live in and use urban places, indeed places of any kind, to know the environment around them. An awareness of place can only be enhanced when it becomes a part of people's everyday lives. Formal school programs, like the once-a-year visit to the country to "educate" urban children in nature lore, do little to engender or deepen knowledge of the environment, or more importantly, to encourage environmental values. These are more likely to come from understanding the places that are close to home. The same principle applies to the interpretive programs provided for the enlightenment of adult campers in provincial parks, that explain the workings of unspoiled nature out in the woods, but totally ignore the problems of water pollution, deterioration of vegetation, garbage dumps, and disruption to wildlife from human presence that occurs in the campgrounds themselves. . . .

## DOING AS LITTLE AS POSSIBLE

Kevin Lynch remarks, "A hunger for the control of large-scale form is all the more dangerous because it coincides with strong contemporary trends towards large-scale investment."[2] The pressures (that come from educational conditioning) to do as much as possible in making changes to places often appears endemic to the land design disciplines. In the absence of a basic ecological foundation on which design can rest, this is to be expected. Doing as little as possible, or economy of means, involves the idea that from minimum resources and energy, maximum environmental and social benefits are available. The greatest diversity and identity in a place, whether a regenerating field or urban wetland, or a cohesive neighborhood community, often comes from minimum, not maximum interference. This does not mean that planning and design are irrelevant or unnecessary to a world that if left alone would take care of itself. It implies, rather, that change can be brought about by giving direction, by capitalizing on the opportunities that site or social trends reveal, or by setting a framework from which people can create their own social and physical environments and where landscapes can flourish with health, diversity, and beauty. . . .

## SUSTAINABILITY

Sustainable landscapes are central to the regional imperative. Sustainability involves, among other things, the notion that human activity and technological systems can contribute to the health of the environments and natural systems from which they draw benefit. This involves a fundamental acceptance of investment in the productivity and diversity of natural systems. Conflicting points of view over the priorities of development versus the preservation of natural wealth have been the focus of discussion and argument for a very long time, particularly as it affects the Third World. The World Commission on Environment and Development, established by the United Nations in 1983, and whose report appeared in 1987, has examined and proposed ways in which economic development initiatives and environmental conservation might be reconciled. For this to be workable would require the development of an environmental ethic far different from current attitudes and perceptions that see nature as "resources for the benefit of mankind." Such a notion would seem practically to be unattainable. However, Maurice Strong, the Canadian member of the commission, has commented on the need for countries to shed their narrow concepts of self interest, parochialism and, in the economic field, protectionism.[3] Although he recognizes the odds against the emergence of such a world view, he sees no alternative: "The principle basis for optimism that the kind of changes I foresee as necessary will occur is, very simply, that they are necessary and therefore must occur."[4]

Irrespective of such a world view, however, the principle of investment in nature, where change and technological development are seen as positive forces to sustain and enhance the environment, must be the basis for an environmental design philosophy. Its principles

Figure 24. The Don River corridor, Toronto: restoration of site and regional identity, promoted by the community organization Task Force to Bring Back the Don (Michael Hough).

of energy and nutrient flows, common to all ecosystems when applied to the design of the human environment, provide the only ethical and pragmatic alternative to the future health of the emerging regional landscape. And this leads naturally to the last principle.

## STARTING WHERE IT'S EASIEST

This principle, borrowed from Jane Jacobs,[5] is fundamental to achieving anything in a world where the statistics of global environmental disaster are at once horrifying and numbing. Through the media, the visibility of environmental issues everywhere in the world is immediate, vivid, and emotionally involving. At the same time, these media reports have two things in common. First, they are almost inevitably out of town. They are somewhere else: in the diminishing rain forests of Brazil; in the burgeoning population and desperate poverty of Africa; in the dying northern lakes of Canada and Sweden that are succumbing to acid rain generated by polluting industries a thousand miles away. We have the paradox that in a world increasingly concerned with deteriorating environments and explosive urban growth, there is a marked propensity to ignore the very places where most people live. Second, the issues are so enormously complicated and of such magnitude that most concerned people feel helpless to do much about them.

Beginning where it's easiest, therefore, has to do with where most people are and where one can be reasonably certain of a measure of success from efforts made, not matter how small. Successes in small things can be used to make connections to other larger and more significant ones. This is, consequently, an encouraging environmental principle to follow in bringing about change. It is, in fact, the only practical basis for doing so. In design terms, the regional imperative is about the need for environmental ideals that are firmly rooted in pragmatic reality. It is about focusing on things that work and that are achievable at any one point in time. It is about a concerned and environmentally literate community prepared to insure that the health and quality of the places where they live are made a reality; where the role of technology is integrated with people, urbanism, and nature in ways that are biologically and socially self-sustaining and mutually supportive of life systems. These are the goals for shaping a new landscape based on fundamental environmental values.

# SIGNATURE-BASED LANDSCAPE DESIGN (1997)

## JOAN WOODWARD

Look at the landscape around you: You see relationships. As I write, I look from my studio window in Sierra Madre, California, and see an acacia tree in full bloom, a brilliant yellow, explaining my recent bout with allergies and the dominant wind directions. I see lush green plants orbiting a nearby irrigation head, indicating the connection there between plants and water. Remnants of an old orange grove and an enclosing stone wall attest to the former agricultural estate that once stood here, linking me to a previous place in time. Recognizing relationships in landscapes grounds me in place, prods me to alertness, and brings an enthusiasm and zest to everyday life.

The science of ecology informs us about many landscape relationships. It explains, in part, why landscapes look and function the way they do, why they have changed, and how they may change in the future. Designers and planners use this information to understand landscapes because design and planning involve change. The information helps to shape goals and objectives that facilitate beneficial landscape interventions; it drives the models that predict impacts of future change, and eventually it assists the public and the client, as well as the designer and planner, in selecting a course of action. Ecological design recognizes complex relationships between people, the land, and a place, and it shapes decisions that may affect both positive site function and positive human response to that site.

Signature-based design grows out of a fascination with relationships. We can begin to characterize a place by seeing repeated relationships in a particular region. For example, trees that respond to additional moisture in an irrigation channel or along a stream are seen repeatedly throughout semiarid and arid regions of the High Plains and the American West. Old homesteads and farms in the Middle West still reveal the protective sheath of trees planted to provide shade and protection from wind and soil erosion. Grids of pecan trees in the Deep South and southern New Mexico reflect efficiency and display a resulting beauty in agricultural production. These relationships are both of nature and of culture. They cumulatively characterize an area or region and advance a sense of recognition that potentially can lead to human attachment and vested interest in a place. These characterizations are crafted to a place, become familiar, and are missed when they are gone. They are signatures of a place.

The patterns sensed are not isolated objects, but are inextricably linked to the ecological, cultural, and economic processes that shape them. Thus, signature-based design is the art of understanding the signatures of a region or a site in terms of the processes that shape them and then applying these patterns to design and planning. Why? So we can understand what comprises the indicative relationships of a region, so we can determine which relationships best meet our current goals, and finally, so we can artfully and sensibly use these to create inspired, conscientious designs and plans.

## DETERMINING PATTERNS

According to Diane Ackerman: "Once is an instance. Twice may be an accident. But three or more times makes a pattern."[1] We enjoy identifying patterns since they help us to derive order and meaning from chaos. Understanding a region's vegetation patterns is at first a dizzying task, but by reviewing research studies and photographs, and by carefully observing vegetation, soils, water, and landforms, repeated patterns emerge at varying scales. For example, in the Denver, Colorado, area the rocky, forested Front Range slopes that rise abruptly from the grassy plains are among the most prevalent patterns in that region. When driving, rock outcrops on the nearby Great Plains grasslands are repeatedly seen, accompanied by islands of trees and shrubs, repeating the same shift as seen from the air. Finally, when walking, seeing perennial flowers bloom in rock crevices where additional moisture is available lends a sense of connectedness in scale to observations.

In addition to spatial patterns, temporal patterns are evident within a region. Plants are telling markers of disturbance and succession. For example, shifts in forest composition can announce the presence or absence of fire in open space areas. Shifts in plant composition can also indicate disturbance succession in urban areas. Mae Theilgaard Watts once described the evolution of a house and its garden plants over time: "There has been a definite succession of these plants, and the major ecological force in determining this succession has been *style.*"[2]

Planting design eras can be described, based on the predominant ethos, as well as plant and resource availability. In many western communities, which developed after the 1840s, street tree plantings and flower-spotted parks proliferated following the 1893 Columbian Exposition's widespread influence; Victory Gardens emerged in neighborhoods during World War II; a competitive suburban lawn craze followed in the 1950s and 1960s; Xeriscape plants and principles appeared in gardens during the 1980s; and plants interbedded among recycled materials, such as reused concrete sidewalk pieces, designate the 1990s. In unraveling design eras and resultant plant arrangements, designers look for those that meet goals of creating positive site function and human response. In this way, they enlarge their vocabulary of regionally characteristic forms from which to choose when creating site designs.

## DETERMINING REGIONAL PROCESSES

Seeing repeated patterns linked in spatial and temporal scale is a satisfying first step in understanding a region's signatures. Simply identifying repeated visual expressions and recreating them in design situations, however, is an inadequate approach to meeting overall goals of positive site function and human response. According to William Marsh: "When we describe the forms and features of a landscape, we are actually observing the artifacts and fingerprints of the formative processes."[3]

Geomorphic, climatic, biotic, and cultural processes are largely responsible for shaping the landscape as we see it. Therefore, understanding these four interacting, formative processes is an essential part of deriving patterns from a place. Geomorphic processes are those activities determining underlying parent material and landforms. Climatic processes include precipitation, wind speeds, radiation, temperatures, lightning strikes and fire frequency, evaporation rates, and overall periods of climatic change. Studying biotic processes yields information about species colonization, adaptations, and succession. Wildlife and insect responses to plant growth also influence plant patterns. Finally, cultural processes include three driving motivators behind creating, shaping, or affecting vegetation patterns: The human need for protection, production, and meaning. Protective processes include efforts to provide protection from sun, wind, cold temperatures, and intruders. Productive strategies involve economics and making a living; thus, efficiency, domestication, technology, and transportation create distinctive forms of settlements, agriculture, and industry. The desire for beauty, pleasure, and meaning results in color concentrations, focal points and framed views, sensory design, repeated forms, a sense of mystery, drama, and symbolism. Political tools involving ordinances and plans institutionalize these cultural processes and ultimately reinforce or change prominent patterns.

By studying these interacting processes we can note the blurred line between human and nonhuman influences, although relative influence is apparent. For example, much of our urban landscape is primarily influenced by cultural processes: The need for protection, production, and meaning. Geomorphic, climatic, and biotic influences can be overridden with bulldozers, air conditioning, irrigation, and insect spray. Yet the challenge to weave fitted patterns borne of all four processes into an urban setting is tantalizing. Understanding inherent landscape responses to these formative processes can guide us in creating new and retrofitted designs. Specifically, examining landscape responses through the expressive medium of plants is helpful to designers and planners who seek to create distinctive, appropriate designs and plans for a selected region. . . .

# GARDENS FROM REGION (1990)

## TERRY HARKNESS

By sifting through and selecting from regional cultural history and physical landscape, a vocabulary of design—a wellspring of familiar physical elements—might be found to create places of strong visual presence and shared experience. Cultural and physical landscapes might inspire the creation of places that are rooted in the common American landscape, a distillation of the world as experienced every day. Design based on the culture and land patterns can express social as well as physical elements intrinsic to the region. Today, much of our experience of environments is often casual, fragmented, aspatial, and generic. Place-making that grows out of a region's culture and man-made setting might restructure our perception of and response to our contemporary landscape. This design approach explores and reveals the meaning, memory, and power of yesterday's and today's landscape. It is based on the idea that the common cultural-physical landscape is a container and reflector of diverse, diffuse, and often ambiguous cultural meanings.

Focus on the common, everyday American landscape of the Midwest, and central Illinois specifically, is the starting point of my work. The design elements of this garden have been derived from the prominent or enduring characteristics of particular scenes in the midwestern landscape. These form the basic design vocabulary that is used to evoke a sense of the region and its many intrinsic and vivid qualities. These elements are often organized on traditional or recurring patterns that speak of either persistent or remnant relations of the land and its occupants.

### LANDSCAPE THEMES

The gardens that I have created from this regional vocabulary present several landscape themes within their boundaries. The horizon garden focuses on the experience of the open, flat, treeless landscape dominated by the horizon and the changing sky. Two others, the lowland garden and the remnant prairie, relate to two historic but changing landscape types— the river bottomland and the railroad corridor. Both of these settings were important to regional settlement, growth, and consolidation.

## THE HORIZON GARDEN

Through the horizon garden I have recreated the extreme flatness of the Illinois landscape—the strong horizon, the essentially open and treeless scene, the tension between the crispness of edge and the warping of the land plane. The sky is the backdrop for changing light and for objects seen in front of it. Across this regular-irregular pattern, the eye continually tracks the field, road, and ditch. The eye follows the field line to the horizon or it jumps from one field line to another field line to the horizon. Although the eye seeks man-made structures for scale, orientation, and distance, the cumulative visual sense is of profound openness. This visual experience requires movement or shifting of viewpoint and direction to reveal the changing variety of patterns.

The horizon garden is a small bounded space distilled and compressed to the essential expression of the open fields beyond the city. One device for revealing the horizon and sky as background is the mimetic fence of incised *horizontal* lines and neutral hue, used as a foil for light, climate, and vegetation. The other device is the flat or tipped ground plane with incised lines (headers) and patterns of grass and ground cover that mime the fields, fence lines, and roadways beyond. These elements are combined with a false horizon line to provide a scaleless plain with a background/horizon that merges into the sky overhead.

## THE LOWLAND GARDEN

The lowland garden quadrant addresses rain, rivers, and valleys and the bottomlands they have created. Their historic claiming through drainage control is the motif of this garden. The strong artificial geometry of dikes and levees has contained those river bottomlands for use as fields. Their precise boundaries and sloping sides attempt to manage the river and its periodic flooding. The river and the bottomland woods shift and encroach on the manmade structures. The inscribed fields of corn and soybeans are foreground to the long extended dikes, lowland woods, channeled streams, distant bluffs, and riverside. The lowland garden distills and contains these elements in a small quadrangle of land.

## THE PRAIRIE REMNANT GARDEN

The last garden speaks to the economic connection of farm and market—the early transport ties of railroad and later highway. These linear ribbons provided the essential connections for individual farms out on the square-mile section. The highway system later followed directly adjacent to the rail rights of way. Their patterns were distinctive diagonals crossing the original survey grid. The abandonment of many of these rail lines has allowed the reflourishing of native plant communities almost entirely lost by the intensive farming of the dominant cash grain economy—the tall grass prairie. The prairie is reestablishing itself in the narrow margins bordering the rights of way of railroads and adjacent highways. These remnant prairies present a startling seasonal contrast to the cultivated fields adjacent. Each plant community has its own distinctive structure and seasonal sequence highlighted by the changing climate and light. As one travels the roadways, the fields and prairie edges unroll and recede to the horizon.

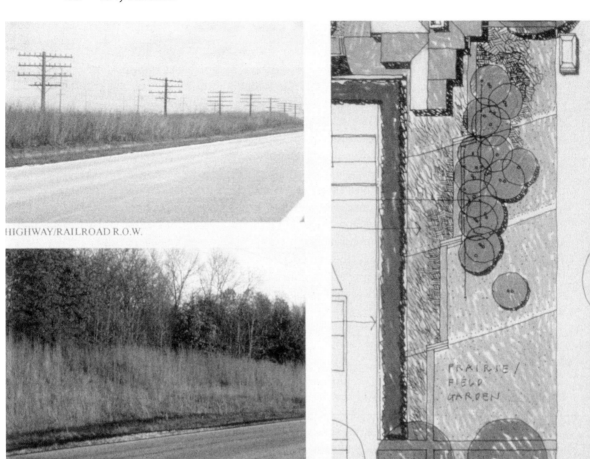

HIGHWAY/RAILROAD R.O.W.

PRAIRIE REMNANT/HIGHWAY R.O.W.

PRAIRIE / FIELD GARDEN

PRAIRIE REMNANT GARDEN

Figure 25. Gardens from Region: the remnant prairie garden (Terry Harkness).

## LANDSCAPE AND BUILT DESIGN ORDER

The house and garden in this design express essential relationships that have determined the landscape at large. Physical garden and house elements relate to the four cardinal directions and the square-mile grid. The house and farmstead in this landscape are inside the square-mile section. The house is one of the centers of the farm economy. The placement and orientation of the house should be symbolically at the intersection point of the quarter sections of the square-mile grid to emphasize the centrality of the house and farm in the organizing sense of the place.

The outward orientation of house and garden is anchored along the lines and edges of the fields and the hedgerows. The house as center is further elaborated in the offset from the quarter-section lines to dramatize the house in the gridded landscape. As one moves through the house, the interior rooms and windows frame and focus the offset and the intersection of the house and the larger landscape.

VISUAL EXPERIENCE AND LANDSCAPE

Another essential issue in the house and garden is the way the larger, everyday landscape is perceived. There are three characteristic visual modes that epitomize the daily landscape in the rural Midwest. Over and over the linear patterns of fence, road, and field line draw one's eye to the horizon. A powerful point of perspective is framed and repeated by the square-mile grid, volunteer tree rows, roadway, fence property line. One's visual sense is focused outward to the horizon.

The second recurring visual experience is related to movement arrested, a view across fields, lines, and ridges parallel to one's position at the moment. This view, which also ends at the horizon, is quieter, almost a momentary equilibrium of long horizontal lines receding into far distance. This experience emphasizes the flatness of the land and the immense expanse of sky.

The particularly powerful third visual experience is one of transition and reorientation resulting from any diagonal movement across the landscape grid. Roads, railroads, and highways form an overlay of pathways across the checkerboard of fields and section lines. As one moves along these linear networks, the field lines, hedgerow, woodlots, buildings, and towns are approached (obliquely), passed (beside), and moved beyond in a continuously changing pattern of triangles, diagonals, and tangents.

These visual experiences are recreated at a walking scale both inside the house looking out (the viewing frame) and outside in the garden by its organization and spatial bisection. The three organizing rules and viewing frames establish the background for how the larger landscape is transformed into a small place that expresses the larger region's characteristics. . . .

What I intend by these gardens is not a personal picturesque notion of garden design but a closely observed reading of context that transforms the common, everyday landscape into a carefully constructed distillation of place. The designed parts of the garden focus one's experience back on the larger setting but in such a way as to reexperience and resee what is so often taken for granted. To treat such everyday landscape patterns and rituals as worthwhile subjects is a matter of conscious decision. Through their use I assert the importance of those objects and places and refer to the history and labor of those who created these landscapes.

When gardens have meant something to a culture or a period of history, they have done so by referring to something shared, understood, and valuable to that culture. My horizon, lowland, and remnant prairie gardens create physical references to a set of shared ideas and themes that created and still exist in a common American landscape. Such regional vocabularies, crafted into regional gardens all over the country, might counter the often-placeless generic gardens too often made in America today.

# INFRASTRUCTURE AS LANDSCAPE (1996)

GARY STRANG

Traditionally, the tools and landscapes that insured human survival were viewed with great reverence. But in contemporary times, they have been replaced with centrally controlled systems that extract the resources necessary for life—food, water, power—and transport them hundreds or thousands of miles to urban centers. The architecture of the city has evolved into a complex mechanism extended deep into the earth and far into the hinterland, beyond any individual's understanding or direct influence.

Infrastructure systems, by virtue of their scale, ubiquity, and inability to be hidden, are an essential visual component of urban settlements. Yet the responsibility for designing this machinery into the landscape is diffused, falling piecemeal to many disciplines—engineering, architecture, landscape architecture, agriculture, planning, and biology.

The potential these infrastructure systems have for performing the additional function of shaping architectural and urban form is largely unrealized. They have an inherent spatial and functional order that can serve as the raw material of architectural design or establish a local identity that has a tangible relationship to the region. They can be designed with a formal clarity that expresses their importance to society, at the same time creating new layers of urban landmarks, spaces, and connections.

## INFRASTRUCTURE AND LANDSCAPE

In 1964, cultural historian Leo Marx wrote *The Machine in the Garden*, which explores an inherent contradiction in the American ideology of space. Free economic competition and technological progress are valued equally with the tradition of landscape pastoralism; thus, Marx observed, in our landscape the machine is accommodated in the garden. Today it is fair to say that the machine is not so much in the garden as it is indistinguishable from the garden; they are inexorably intertwined.

California was once a land of flash floods and drought, but most of the state has been transformed into a huge catchment basin, where water flow is monitored from Lake Shasta to the Mexican border. Most California rivers have been removed from their beds and flow directly into water treatment plants and irrigation canals that constitute the only visible, architectural components of a system that interfaces with every habitable space in the state.

In Los Angeles, the structure of the Los Angeles River is indistinguishable from the urban and residential structure of the city. If Angelenos know their city has a river, it may be because it has been featured in chase scenes in movies like *Grease* and *Terminator Two*. A member of the California assembly actually proposed using the river bed to carry a carpool lane in the dry season.

One needs to know that Los Angeles has 470 miles of concrete-lined channels in order to reclaim the meaning of the term "L.A. basin." The river is a huge storm drain that carries rainwater from the Santa Monica and San Gabriel Mountains to the Pacific Ocean; much of the rainwater never even touches soil. As the Los Angeles basin has been covered with roofs, roads, and parking lots, the land has lost its capacity to absorb water and the increased runoff has overloaded the system.

While the architecture of water systems provides the most easily understood opportunities for architects, there are corollaries for steam, natural gas, electricity, sewage, oil, and telecommunications. Each of these constitutes a network as complex as a river system; each has the unrealized potential to perform multiple uses.

The tendency to engineer for a single purpose is also apparent in horticulture. Genetic engineering and cloning of plant materials has emphasized, primarily, visual characteristics while breeding out desirable qualities such as resistance to disease and drought and tolerance to local soils.

Plants have become unfamiliar to insects and wildlife. Parks and gardens may seem a minor consideration, but taken collectively, we are building large areas of a new habitat that is essentially sterile in terms of its ability to support the biological diversity necessary for human life. This new habitat is a mixed suburban forest that consists of a community of plants assembled from around the world and is guaranteed to confound any indigenous plant or animal that tries to colonize it (African daisies, Japanese maples, Australian tea trees, Canary Island pines, Burmese honeysuckle, and so on). Since the 1950s, the whole thing has been supported by a horticultural heart and lung machine made up of irrigation pop-ups, electric timers, fossil-based fertilizers, and the associated blowers and weed whackers.

If we pulled the plug, much of this landscape would disappear in a few months.

Despite this reliance on the constructed landscape, our culture's response to the disruptions of infrastructure has largely been one of denial, rather than reverence. Designers have most often been charged with hiding, screening and cosmetically mitigating infrastructure, in order to maintain the image of the untouched natural surroundings of an earlier era. They are rarely asked to consider infrastructure as an opportunity, as a fundamental component of urban and regional form.

As early as 1924, social critic Lewis Mumford castigated modern architects for romanticizing new technologies while ignoring the potential for making civil architecture from the important, everyday elements of the city, such as water towers and subways. He attacked the City Beautiful movement for obscuring important structural and social developments saying that beautification was equivalent to "the icing on a birthday cake" that "detracts from the realism needed for the colossal task of the renovation of the city."[1] Today we are still masking a system of infrastructure vastly and impractically expanded beyond the boundaries of the city, multiplying the task of maintenance and renovation beyond comprehension.

## FROM HEROISM TO BIOLOGICAL COMPLEXITY

To regard infrastructure as a legitimate field for regional architecture, it helps to understand the periods of civil engineering which have transpired in the last two centuries.

The first American school of engineering was started at the U.S. Military Academy in 1802. The Army Corps of Engineers, which is responsible for waterway design in the U.S., was founded at that time. The school was started with the aid of French engineers who had helped during the Revolutionary War. From them, we inherited the idea, dating to Louis XIV, that a nation needs an army to direct public works.

Beginning in the 1850s was the heroic period of bridge and dam building which culminated in the great projects of the Works Progress Administration, which integrated engineering, architecture, agriculture, and the arts and was memorialized in Diego Rivera's murals.

To be an engineer between 1850 and 1950 was to participate in a great adventure, to lead the crusade for health and progress that corresponded to the high period of modern architecture in Europe. Plumbers were the pioneers of cleanliness at the end of the pre-industrial age, when people could still remember that the earth was swept by plagues that traveled thousands of miles before their forces were spent. In 1898, Viennese architect Adolph Loos observed that the plumber brings civilization.

As the statue "Mercury, The Genius of Electricity" was being mounted on top of the AT&T headquarters in New York in 1916, the street below told a dramatically different story. Romantic images that depicted the benefits of technology contrasted with the messy process of retrofitting cities to accommodate an overwhelming tangle of pipes and wires—which often laid claim to open space formerly reserved for people. The city was undergoing a fundamental, systemic change as energy formerly produced by human labor was being generated or collected in remote areas and carried into the city from the surrounding region.

In 1947, WPA writer Harry Granick identified the dawn of a new era of biological complexity in engineering. He authored *Underneath New York*, the first book to describe the anatomy of a modern city using the metaphor of the human body. The book conveys his sense of wonder at the hidden structure that converts natural resources into the energy that makes urban culture possible.[2]

Granick's New York rested on a foundation of tangled plumbing as deep as the Chrysler Building is high. On the top lay a three-inch mat of asphalt, beneath that ten inches of concrete. Below that, a few inches of soil soaks up chemicals from the street. In the next three inches are the wires—telephone, electric, street light, and fire alarm. Gas lines lay another foot below, water mains are four feet deep, steam pipes puff away six feet under. Sewer pipes are above the subway vaults, which vary from a few feet to eighteen stories deep. Water tunnels, running between 200 and 800 feet deep, occupy the farthest man-built depths.

There are two ironies about this infrastructure of biological complexity. First, the system is so complicated that it has begun to take on qualities of nature itself and, therefore, presents the same threat of random catastrophe that nature does. Infrastructure, like nature, is resilient and adaptable, but it is also unpredictable and uncontrollable.

It is well known that a simple broken water main in Manhattan can trigger what is known in ecological circles as a "feedback loop." The problem is directed back into the system, resulting in additional and magnified effects. In July 1995, a thirty-six-inch diameter water main carrying three million gallons per day erupted from beneath the asphalt on 34th Street, turning Seventh Avenue into a river that flowed to Greenwich Village. Water drained into subway ventilation grilles, shutting down two lines, forcing pedestrians to the streets, and causing power outages. In extreme cases, technological malfunction can have catastrophic results. In April 1992, the sewers of Guadalajara filled with propane and exploded, leveling twenty-five square city blocks and leaving 15,000 homeless.

The second irony is that the support system occupies so much space that it overwhelms the amenity it was intended to provide. The public realm and natural areas have become repositories for meters, transformers, and zones of access to buried conduit networks. Anyone who has peered into an urban street during construction will need no explanation to comprehend the difficulty of finding an uninterrupted volume of soil large enough to support a tree for the seven to twenty years that now constitutes its average life span.

## INFRASTRUCTURE, ARCHITECTURE, AND LANDSCAPE

Utilitarian intrusions—which often result in disturbed landscapes, defaced retrofitted buildings, and the erasure of nature that we have come to accept as the everyday urban and regional landscape—are actually opportunities. Designers can generate meaningful new architectural, urban, and regional forms by integrating the works of the estranged disciplines of architecture, civil and structural engineering, landscape architecture, and biology.

An examination of pre-industrial cities shows that some of their most profoundly moving landscapes were nothing more than the irrigation, domestic water supply, sanitary sewer, and flood control systems of the time. These landscapes allowed the workings of nature to be revealed in the urban setting.

The technology of a pre-industrial urban fountain maintained, by necessity, a legible connection to a watershed. At a tiny Inca village in Peru, a manmade fountain was the ordering system for the town. Agricultural terraces took their form from a bowl in the topography while an elaborate stair and fountain connected a temple at the top with a compact cluster of houses and storage buildings below. The foundation intercepted the flow of the drainage beyond with a series of stepping water basins, whose volume could be retained or released depending on the seasonal flow. The logic of the watershed was evident within the context of the city.

In contemporary American cities, the hydrology of the place has been largely ignored. Drainage systems have been put underground unnecessarily or channelized with concrete, erasing the visual and spatial logic of the region. Contemporary fountains, which are loops of recirculating chlorinated water that operate independent of rainfall and gravity, need to be replaced with fountains that have nature-driven, seasonal variations.

A place's hydrology should be part of the basic armature of the urban form. Water treatment plants should be designed to accommodate visitors and to demonstrate appropriate site design and water use. Sewage plants are magnificent sources of nutrients, which could be collected and expressed in landscapes that could rival the great gardens of the renaissance.

Significant sources, paths, and transition points of our collectively owned resources should be made legible in the landscape. They can comprise an alternative system of urban and regional landmarks that replace those that glorify the transitory economic prowess of individuals and companies.

In Sunol, California, a water temple marks the place where water piped from San Francisco's Hetch Hetchy Reservoir, more than one hundred miles away, surfaces before passing into Crystal Springs Reservoir, where it is stored for domestic use. This logic could be applied to all the great utilities. Oil, steam, and natural gas lines should be marked at significant locations, such as their source and the point at which they enter the city, with structures that make their functions, and important positions in society, legible. A huge natural gas line could be marked with an eternal flame that announces the number of miles the gas has traveled. Invisible communications technologies could be expressed at transfer points.

The biggest immediate gains can be made in the renovation of single-purpose utilities. The reconstruction of urban drainage systems, for example, can provide networks of open space shared by people and working biological systems at little additional cost. To reduce the loads on drainage systems, many regions (such as Los Angeles, where proposals are already on the table) will eventually require that water be retained on site in basins, gardens, and cisterns, from which it will soak directly back into the earth. Compare this approach to the recently adopted proposal by the Army Corps of Engineers to heighten the walls of the Los Angeles River by four to eight feet and to raise eleven street and railroad bridges.

Architects should be more like farmers, who depend upon the architecture of natural systems for their livelihood. The strict lines of human geometry and production efficiency should be allowed to deform to incorporate, rather than neutralize, biological networks. Good agricultural fields perform more than the single function of producing food; they can also be percolation fields, floodplains, or flyways for migrating geese that fertilize the earth. Buildings, likewise, can be elements of infrastructure that contribute to stable natural ecosystem; they can occupy more than one niche simultaneously.

Horticultural practices also need to be revamped to incorporate the common-sense attitudes of small farmers who use materials at hand to solve complex technical and horticultural problems in an efficient and beautiful manner. Nature is being severely altered and we need new, legible models to illustrate how nature currently works and does not work—intertwined, such as it is, with architecture. We must find ways to allow the natural landscape and the landscape of infrastructure, which occupy the same space, to coexist and perform multiple functions.

In California, this means planting more Monterey cypress in the fog belt, more oaks and grasses in the hot interior. It also means understanding that a western urban landscape is better informed by an Islamic courtyard in Spain than by the green English countryside. This was a principle not lost on Frederick Law Olmsted, who demonstrated his understanding of regional variation with his site plan for the Stanford campus, which included arcaded courtyards and a dry oak woodland landscape. The fragmentation of the building process into so many different disciplines has led to a gross simplification of the issues involved in building.

In the earlier part of the century architects were more optimistic about expressing utilities, buildings and highways as legitimate components of a larger system. Frank Lloyd Wright, raised on a farm and trained as an engineer, demonstrated an uncommon understanding of structure and nature. Taliesin West is sited adjacent to a seasonal desert wash that provided a full range of sands and gravel for his masonry and supplies water for domestic use (stored in a tower) and firefighting (stored in a central garden basin). Russian constructivist Iakov Tchernikov developed a language based on the new spatial possibilities of technological expansion. He produced exuberant architectural compositions from building types we have regretfully given up on—electrical towers, industries, and factories.

More important are developments in architecture and structural engineering, which are being remarried after a hundred-year divorce—a movement that predicts the corresponding and much needed reconciliation between landscape architecture and civil engineering. Renzo Piano and Ove Arup engineers have begun to overcome the barriers to developing integrated architectural systems by combining technological developments with the organic principles of nature. Says Piano, "at the beginning of the century technology was really an adversary to nature. But today you can see that technology and nature are not so far apart."

In San Francisco, Bill Leddy has made a proposal for the renovation of Sutro Baths on the Pacific Coast, which would be enclosed by a water desalinization system driven by a dependable supply of offshore wind. In this instance, infrastructure, serving a multiple

Figure 26. Landscape as infrastructure: Beth Israel Chapel and Memorial Garden, making the regional drainage system present and transparent, using a retention pool as the central design feature of the site (Gary Strang).

purpose, would renovate an existing ruin, reinvigorate a civic landmark, generate power, provide fresh water and relieve pressure in the Hetch Hetchy Reservoir.

In an open chapel and cemetery Dan Solomon and I designed in Houston, the fifty to one hundred inches of rain that fall on the roof each year will be captured in a huge elevated gutter that doubles as a portico. The rainfall will be captured in a pool that retains floodwater as a seasonal site amenity. The pool overflows to walkways that double as drainage structures, and form the geometric lines which structure the site for the ritual of burial. The problem of drainage and flooding in Houston is seen as an opportunity to organize the site and to allow mourners to confront the cycles of nature.

## PROSPECTS FOR REGIONAL INTERVENTION

Acknowledging the potential for appropriating infrastructure as landscape offers pragmatic and immediate advantages. The amount of funding for building and renovating public infrastructure is likely to far exceed the amount that will be available for buildings, parks and open space. These large budgets can be used to produce urban designs that simultaneously solve utilitarian problems and help repair cities and regional landscapes at a scale not dreamed of since the days of the great dams.

Given the magnitude of changes occurring within natural and technological systems worldwide, a position that links human survival to the preservation of pristine nature is increasingly difficult to visualize; nature is a dynamic process that is rarely independent of human interaction. Nevertheless, we must learn to intervene in a way that facilitates, rather than disrupts, natural processes.

The historian of religion Mircea Eliade contends that the Neolithic shift from nomadic to agricultural civilization provoked upheavals and spiritual breakdowns whose magnitude the modern mind finds it impossible to conceive. It is not only imaginable but probable that the current shift to a predominantly technological environment has provoked a similarly profound spiritual crisis—one that can be relieved by reconsidering the relationship between urban settings and natural processes.

Likewise, the total management of nature is a dream that fades farther from view with every Kobe earthquake and Mississippi flood. An architectural method that exploits the unignorable marriage between nature and technology provides an opportunity for new spatial and visual possibilities that result from using infrastructure as a fundamental component of architectural design. Nature and infrastructure, working together, must both be allowed to express themselves as a major determinant of urban and regional form. It is up to architects, landscape architects, engineers, and biologists to show the way.

# CONCLUSION: THE THEORETICAL TERRAIN OF LANDSCAPE ARCHITECTURE

SIMON SWAFFIELD

The theoretical terrain of landscape architecture is undoubtedly contested ground. There are differences in belief about the nature of the world in which the discipline exists, over the forms of knowledge that can tell us about this world, and over the strategies, methods, and tactics that might be used to investigate and then act within the world. Underlying these contests is a search for legitimacy: which ways of knowing and acting serve best as a basis for education and practice in landscape architecture?

Do such differences in approach undermine the proposition that landscape architecture might constitute a viable discipline? On the contrary, theoretical debate signals an active process of knowledge formation. Indeed, while some critics in the 1980s bemoaned a supposed lack of theoretical debate in the preceding decades, the evidence suggests otherwise. Each decade can be characterized in terms of the development of at least one major theoretical issue. During the 1950s and early 1960s much attention focused upon the development of theories of process, as a counter to the previous dominance of formal principles. In the late 1960s and 1970s the impact of the environmental movement became significant, as attention shifted to the development of "ecological" design and planning. This was also the decade of community design, as the design process was opened out to include a wider range of participants. The 1980s were characterized by a renewed search for theories of meaning, drawing both upon existing lines of development such as ecological design, and upon related fields, particularly land or environmental art. During the 1990s there has been exploration of issues of language and representation, the aesthetics of ecological design, regionalism and infrastructure, as well as renewed interest in the nature and role of theory.

There are of course many other theoretical strands in addition to those highlighted above, as well as diverse developments in closely related fields; in landscape ecology, environmental perception, landscape planning, for example, which inform the discipline and enrich the terrain. Indeed, it can be argued that, rather than the "theoretical vacuum" seen by some commentators in the past,[1] the current situation is more reminiscent of feast than famine,[2] in which the main challenge is to choose an appropriate theoretical basis for action from among the many available. Does this suggest a discipline so diverse and widely scattered in its approach that it risks fragmentation into discrete subdisciplines? There is certainly evidence that professional practice is becoming increasingly diverse, to the extent that it must be questioned whether there remains any shared common experience of *being* a landscape architect.[3] However, the themes in this survey demonstrate more commonality of purpose than they do differences. While there are debates over theoretical presumptions and over detailed methods and tactics, there is also an overall pattern to the issues being addressed and the responses to those issues.

First, *design process in landscape architecture is situated, phased, and reflexive*. It focuses upon site, landscape, or region, and has discrete phases. While the precise makeup and sequence of action may be interpreted differently, theories of design process in landscape architecture continue to include: (1) a phase of observation and collation of both site-specific and contextual knowledge; (2) a phase of analytical and interpretive thinking; (3)

a phase of creative exploration of possibilities for the future; and (4) a phase of deliberation and determination of action. There is a rich body of accumulated knowledge and critique upon how each of these phases may be undertaken, their strengths and limitations, and how they interrelate with other phases in addressing the central concerns of the discipline. There is also now a clear expectation that the design process is self-critical, checking its own progress.[4]

Second, *meaning and significance in landscape architecture are determined within fields of potential relationships, which include, but are not limited to, concepts of nature and culture.* An essential theoretical contribution of the past couple of decades has been to explore and clarify the nature of these fields. This is exemplified by Jacobs's reinterpretation, for landscape architecture, of the "expanded field" of sculpture developed by Krauss, which situates landscape in relation to axes such as nature–not nature, and culture–not culture. It is important to note that there is not a *single* defined field. Meyer (1992) provides an equally compelling interpretation of a rather different field, of spatial relationships around landscape and architecture. Most of the contributions in this volume explore particular sets of relationships. It is the recognition that the meaning and significance of landscape form (and process) are defined by relationships, rather than static absolutes, that is significant, as it provides an approach through which alternative formal possibilities can be explored and elaborated. Even the arguments against attempts to "create" meaning in design are based upon the premise that meaning will accrue over time from the relationships between site and use/users.

Third, *the way landscape is represented in plan, image, and text transforms its meaning.* The "linguistic turn" in the discipline has highlighted the way in which the choice of the medium of design, and the language of representation of landscape in design, influences the meanings that are expressed and assigned. Furthermore, recognition of the way that particular forms of landscape representation are associated with particular values, interests, and ideologies highlights the need for continual reflection upon the vocabulary and syntax of design. One sign of the growing maturity of the discipline is the increasing number of theoretical contributions which seek to draw out distinctive features of a design language of landscape architecture.

Fourth, *a central concern of the discipline is how to configure the modified and constructed ecologies of human settlement and production.* One of the strengths of the historical awareness that now underpins much contemporary theory is that it enables us to trace how particular landscape configurations express ideals about nature, and types of ecological system and management process. These two dimensions are not the same, nor are they necessarily congruent. For example, critique of the still-influential Picturesque convention has highlighted how picturesque landscapes typically symbolize a level of "naturalness" which is seldom reflected in the underlying ecology. Much recent theoretical debate has therefore focused upon the emerging tensions between cultural convention, perception, and values on the one hand, and ecological function on the other. There is also increasing focus upon the strategies to be used to address such tensions.

Fifth, *landscape integrity requires active and critical mediation between site, place, and region.* While landscape is practically located in what Jellicoe described as the "middle" distance, it is nonetheless multi-scalar. Embedded within each site are traces, influences, and signs of natural and cultural processes operating at larger and smaller scales, past and present. While design action may principally be at a site scale, design thinking must embrace other relevant scales, from the global to the local. Furthermore, there is growing attention directed toward the strategic need to articulate design thinking and action at a regional scale. So connections between different spatial scales become critical to design integrity. While there continues to be debate as to whether landscape architecture is primarily site design *or* landscape planning, the theoretical contributions of the past decade suggest a convergence of these two perspectives.

As well as multiple scales, landscape embodies multiple experiences. The growing influence of phenomenology within the discipline highlights that every site is also a place: a locus of human experience and meaning. So the interrelationship between dimensional site and experiential place is also now central to theoretical thinking in the discipline.

Sixth, *landscape architectural theory may be instrumental, interpretive, and/or critical to differing degrees in different situations.* Arguments for a singular basis for design significance have been superseded by recognition that "meaning" emerges within a field or fields of relations. In the same way, advocacy for a singular role and definition of theory in the discipline is being superseded by recognition that theorizing is a situated and contingent activity. It is part of the social formation of the discipline, and is interconnected with wider cultural movements and contexts. There is a tendency in recent work, however, that in counterposing *critical* against *instrumental* roles of theory in order to present an argument for greater attention to a critical, reflective perspective, the continuing need for instrumental knowledge becomes downplayed, or even dismissed. Yet landscape architectural practice relies upon and requires continual refinement of a substantive knowledge base for design intervention in the material world.

One of the ironies of contemporary calls for the discipline to adopt infrastructure as a *critically* strategic focus for action is that if successful, this will increase expectations from clients and related professions for landscape architects to demonstrate high levels of technical (i.e., *instrumental*) knowledge and competency. As Strang and Corner point out, infrastructure is strategically important because it is needed by society in order to function. There is no benefit, therefore, in replacing an emphasis upon instrumental theory which ignores its critical role in society, with a critical theory that ignores or abandons systematic investigation of the material world. Landscape intervention relies upon both critique and instrumentality. This in turn requires an understanding of the nature of theory that can embrace current thinking in both the natural and social sciences. While calls for a conceptual reorientation of the discipline toward the fine arts can be persuasive, successful design will continue to rely upon an ability to understand technical possibilities for intervention. This requires us to engage with a range of theoretical traditions, including both "arts" and "science."[5] The challenge of achieving this combination was an important focus of Garrett Eckbo's writing in the 1950s, and it is a testament to his contribution that the issue remains central to the discipline at the beginning of the new millennium. What has changed is our understanding of the possibilities and limitations of the project, and of the strategies through which the challenge may be pursued.

This reader's two objectives were, first, to provide a teaching resource upon theory, which introduces students to a range of concepts and authors and situates them within the discipline, and, second, to explore the proposition that there exists a coherent core body of theory in landscape architecture. The theoretical themes by which the reader has been organized, and the six statements above, which have been distilled from these themes, provide a map of what I see as the essential theoretical terrain of the discipline. The map serves as an initial orientation for students (and teaching faculty), while the individual themes and statements provide markers in the intellectual landscape of the discipline. There is consideration of the nature of that landscape (the discussions on theory), of process, meaning, and representation, of the interface of function (ecology) and aesthetics, and of the dimensional tensions within landscape (site, place, region). While there are many horizons yet to explore, and tangled thickets, barren fields, and perilous areas within the intellectual landscape, there is also, to my mind, an emerging structure. Much interesting exploration awaits us over the next fifty years.

# NOTES

Notes and references that were separate in the original essays have been combined, and references have been converted to notes.

## Preface

1. For example, G. F. Thompson and G. Steiner, eds., *Ecological Design and Planning* (New York: John Wiley and Sons, 1997).

2. G. Eckbo, *Landscape for Living* (New York: Dodge, 1950).

3. E. K. Meyer, *Situating Modern Landscape Architecture—Theory As a Bridging, Mediating and Reconciling Practice*, in *Design + Value: Proceedings of the Council of Educators in Landscape Architecture 1992* annual meeting (CELA, 1992), 167–178.

4. R. Krauss, "Sculpture in the Expanded Field," *October 8* (Spring 1979).

5. P. Jacobs, "DeInRe(form)ing landscape," *Landscape Journal* 19, no. 1 (1991).

6. E. K. Meyer, "The Expanded Field of Landscape Architecture," in G. F. Thompson and G. Steiner, eds., *Ecological Design and Planning* (New York: John Wiley and Sons, 1997).

7. For example, J. Corner, *Recovering Landscape* (Princeton, N.J.: Princeton Architectural Press, 1999).

## Introduction

1. In the following discussion I summarize the main positions that have been articulated within landscape architecture. These positions and the debates within the discipline to which they contribute are of course closely linked to wider debates over the nature of knowledge and theory in contemporary society. It is difficult to strike a balance between the need to acknowledge this wider intellectual context, and the practical limits on the time students have available to become familiar with sources outside the discipline. Inevitably, commentators within the discipline tend to emphasize sources which strengthen their particular arguments. There is, as yet, no comparative critique of the theoretical assumptions underlying the different facets of the discipline. In the following discussion, I adopt a pragmatic classification of theory into three types: instrumental, interpretive and critical. Each of these derives from rich and complex traditions of knowledge, and is vigorously debated in other disciplines.

Most of the key sources used within the discipline appear in the notes, particularly those to Corner, Meyer, Treib, Howett, and Nassauer.

In addition, I have found useful a recent reader edited by Michael Crotty (*The Foundations of Social Research: Meaning and Perspective in the Research Process* [St. Leonards, Australia: Allen and Unwin, 1998]), which succinctly reviews current debates in the social sciences, and in so doing provides an excellent overview of the key debates that influence landscape architecture. Included in this is a very helpful mapping of the debates over postmodernism and poststructuralism. I have also found Andrew Sayer's writing on realism in social science a particularly helpful and relevant guide to issues affecting landscape architecture; see *Method in Social Science: A Realist Approach*, 2nd ed. (London: Routledge, 1992).

2. J. Corner, "A Discourse on Theory I—'Sounding the Depths'—Origins, Theory and Representation," *Landscape Journal* 9, no. 2 (1990), and "A Discourse on Theory II—Three Tyrannies of Contemporary Theory and the Alternative of Hermeneutics," *Landscape Journal* 10, no. 2 (1991).

3. G. Eckbo, *Landscape for Living* (New York: Dodge, 1950).

4. J. I. Nassauer, "Messy Ecosystems, Orderly Frames," *Landscape Journal* 14, no. 2 (1995).

5. K. Lynch, *Site Planning* (Cambridge, Mass.: MIT Press, 1984).

6. J. O. Simonds, *Landscape Architecture* (New York: McGraw-Hill, 1961).

7. E. Meyer, "Landscape Architecture as Modern Other and Postmodern Ground," in H. Edquist and V. Bird, *The Culture of Landscape Architecture* (Melbourne: RMIT, 1994). The term "critical" originates from the Frankfurt school of social research, and refers to the need for social theory to actively critique the society in which it is created. The school is associated with early writers such as Adorno and Horkheimer, and latterly with Jürgen Habermas (J. Habermas, *The Theory of Communicative Action,* vol. 1 [London: Heinemann, 1984]).

8. J. Corner, *Recovering Landscape* (Princeton, N.J.: Princeton Architectural Press, 1999).

9. Commentators such as Terry Eagleton argue that this is the fundamental role of theory. However, it is important to qualify the position, in that Eagleton is referring to literary theory in the first instance (T. Eagleton, *Literary Theory* [Minneapolis: University of Minneapolis Press, 1983]). An alternative view is frequently expressed within the sciences, to the effect that theory "helps us make our way in the world." This expresses the "instrumental" role of theory, in the Baconian tradition.

10. Corner, "A Discourse on Theory II."

11. The "interpretive" tradition has been largely based within the social sciences, and is associated particularly with qualitative and ethnographic methods. "Interpretism" seeks to draw out the meanings and experiences of people and cultures expressed in their own terms, and is based upon understanding (*verstehen*).

12. The tripartite division of theory into instrumental, interpretive, and critical theories derives from Jürgen Habermas.

13. M. Treib, ed., *Modern Landscape Architecture: A Critical Review* (Cambridge, Mass.: MIT Press, 1993).

14. The extent to which theory is historically bounded is one of the fundamental points of tension between traditional views of theory within the natural sciences, and more contemporary social (and natural) science perspectives. In the positivist tradition (upon which most natural sciences continue to be based) there is an assumption of a progression towards better understanding of the world "out there." Thomas Kuhn's contribution was to recognize the way in which paradigms of science are grounded in particular cultural and social settings (T. S. Kuhn, *The Structure of Scientific Revolutions* [Chicago: University of Chicago Press, 1970]). For contemporary realists, the social framing of knowledge is now taken as given, although there is still an assumption that understanding can evolve over time, as knowledge is tested against "real world" experience (Sayer, *Method in Social Science*). In contrast, one of the main destabilizing effects of the more recent post-structural and post-modern critiques of knowledge is its increasingly relativist position, which aims to detach knowledge (and hence theory) from any reference independent of the society which generates that knowledge. One of the challenges for landscape architecture is that while the discipline is clearly a social practice, and hence bounded by society and culture both in its underlying concepts and in its actions, it works at the interface of the social and natural sciences, and is therefore continually encountering and using knowledge that relates to both the social and biophysical world, which may be based upon contrasting assumptions about the nature of theory.

15. J. B. Jackson, "By Way of Conclusion: How to Study Landscape," in *The Necessity for Ruins and Other Topics* (Amherst: University of Massachusetts Press, 1980).

16. Most cogently expressed by Karl Popper, *The Logic of Scientific Discovery* (New York: Basic Books, 1959).

17. See, for example, R. E. Chenoweth, "Research: Hype and Reality," *Landscape Architecture Magazine* (March 1992): 47–48; and R. E. Chenoweth "Much Ado About Nothing," in *Proceedings, CELA 1998. Re:Search: The Generation of Knowledge in Landscape Architecture* (Arlington: University of Texas, 1998).

18. R. Riley, "Editorial Commentary: Some Thoughts on Scholarship and Publication," *Landscape Journal* 9, no. 1 (1990).

19. Meyer, "Landscape Architecture as Modern Other," 30–31. This rejection of universal or metatheory is consistent with some interpretations of post modern thinking.

20. Riley, "Editorial Commentary."

21. Commentary in M. McAvin, "Critical Enquiry in Landscape Architecture," *Landscape Journal* 10, no. 2 (1991): 160.

22. The reasoning for this derives from the point made earlier: landscape architecture is essentially a social practice, dealing with the creation, reproduction, and representation of social and cultural experience and meanings. Its theory must therefore be able to embrace the social construction of meaning. However, the medium in which landscape architecture works includes the biophysical world. The theories of ecology, earth science, hydrology, etc., upon which we draw, typically derive from disciplines which adopt realist positions; that is, while the knowledge they generate is framed socially, it refers to processes which operate, at least in part, independent of human knowledge, even though their "meaning" is entirely human in origin. Some theorists (e.g., A. Giddens, *Modernity and Self Identity: Self and Society in the Late Modern Age* [Stanford: Stanford University Press, 1991]) therefore argue that social and natural knowledge are fundamentally different. Others (e.g., Crotty, *Foundations of Social Research*) place natural science knowledge within a world whose meanings are already constituted socially. In either case, landscape architecture needs to be sensitive to, and able to interpret, knowledge from diverse sources, with differing types of significance for our practice.

23. This is also open to debate, of course. Some commentators will argue that knowledge must always be locally situated, even though the procedures for creating knowledge may span different settings. I take the position that we need to compare settings for two reasons: first, because as noted earlier, knowledge of biophysical processes is typically comparative across situations, and second, there are important social and cultural processes (e.g., globalization) that transcend particular settings, and can best be understood by comparative analysis. In each case, however, the circumstances of the creation and application of knowledge need to be made explicit.

24. The critical point for me here is to distinguish between a "subjectivist" position, which says that meaning is always imposed upon the material world by an individual viewer, and social constructionism, which says that meaning is created from the interplay of society and culture and the material world. This latter form of knowledge is therefore inevitably shaped by the nature of the society or culture, but is not independent of the material world to which it refers.

25. This role and focus has been admirably expressed in the 1998 special issue of *Landscape Journal* on Eco-Revelatory Design, edited by Brenda Brown.

## Part I. The Nature of Theory in Landscape Architecture

1. M. McAvin, "Critical Inquiry in Landscape Architecture," *Landscape Journal* 10, no. 2 (1991).

## Origins of Theory, *James Corner*

1. This essay is closely allied to the work of others, to who I am indebted. Similar arguments and discussion can be found in Dalibor Veseley, "Architecture and the Conflict of Representation," *AA Files* 8 (London: Architectural Association, 1984); Alberto Perez-Gomez, *Architecture and the Crisis of Modern Science* (Cambridge, Mass.: MIT Press, 1983); and Hans-Georg Gadamer, *Reason in the Age of Science* (Cambridge, Mass.: MIT Press, 1981). I am particularly grateful for references and lengthy discussion provided by David Leatherbarrow and Laurie Olin. I am also grateful to Susan Frey, Mohsen Mostafavi, Dan Rose, and Ann Spirn.

2. E. Grassi, *Kunst and Mythos* (Hamburg: Rowohlt, 1957); J. Ellul, *The Technological Society* (New York: Random House, 1964); and Veseley, "Architecture and the Conflict of Representation." Technology has become an increasingly dominating force over the past two centuries. Its purpose has been to control external reality in the interests of efficiency and usefulness. Traditional knowledge and technique, in contrast, were always motivated by the most fundamental existential problems.

### Theory in Crisis, *James Corner*

1. Edmund Husserl, *The Crisis of European Sciences and Transcendental Phenomenology,* trans. D. Carr (Evanston, Ill.: Northwestern University Press, 1970). Martin Heidegger, *Basic Writings* (New York: Harper and Row, 1977). Martin Heidegger, *The Question Concerning Technology* (New York: Harper Torchbooks, 1977). Alberto Perez-Gomez, *Architecture and the Crisis of Modern Science* (Cambridge: MIT Press, 1983).

2. Jean-François Lyotard, *The Postmodern Condition—A Report on Knowledge* (Minneapolis: University of Minnesota Press, 1984).

3. Perez-Gomez, *Architecture and the Crisis of Modern Science.* This tendency to think of theory as objective methodology and technique differs from the traditional conceptions of theory. Unlike the "abstractness," or autonomy, of modern theory's foundations, traditional theory was based in the *Lebenswelt.* The *Lebenswelt* (life-world) is an old German word that means the world-as-lived, the pre-reflective sphere of lived and subjective relations. It implies that human knowledge derives primarily from direct experience and observation. See A. Schutz and T. Luckman, *The Structures of the Lifeworld* (Evanston, Ill.: Northwestern University Press, 1973).

4. Perez-Gomez, *Architecture and the Crisis of Modern Science.*

5. D. Leatherbarrow, *The Roots of Architectural Invention* (Cambridge: Cambridge University Press, 1993), and Corner, "Origins of Theory," this volume. *Theoria* was the original Greek formulation of theory. It emerged as a way to comprehend observed phenomena in the natural world, especially in relation to holy practices. Practice was understood as a theoretical form of reconciliation between humans and their being in the world.

### Situating Modern Landscape Architecture, *Elizabeth Meyer*

1. See chapter 1, "Ecology and History," in Carolyn Merchant, *Ecological Revolutions: Nature, Gender and Science in New England* (Chapel Hill: University of North Carolina, 1989), for an explanation of the interrelationships between environment, culture, and collective consciousness.

2. While I agree with cultural critics such as David Harvey and Andreas Huyssen that the past thirty years have been characterized by a condition that can be called "postmodernism," this paper will not address that aspect of my course.

3. "Contingent: possible; happening by chance; in logic, true only within certain conditions or contexts; not always or necessarily true." *Webster's New Twentieth Century Dictionary, Unabridged.*

4. This position grows out of my own background in historic preservation and landscape history and shares some attributes with situational criticism as defined by Edward Said and hermeneutical interpretation as described by Hans Gadamer and articulated in landscape architectural theory by James Corner.

5. "Mediation is the construction or production of relationships between levels or instances of the various subtexts (economy, technology, politics, religion, legislation, etc.) and the various social subtexts (architecture, painting, literature, historiography, etc.) such that there is the possibility of adapting analyses and findings from one level or instance to another" (Hays, Harvard Graduate School of Design, Arch 3101, topic 3). I am indebted to Michael Hays for introducing me to the literature on this concept. See also Denis Cosgrove, *Social Formation and Symbolic Landscape* (London: Croom Helm, 1984), 58.

6. J. Silvetti, "The Beauty of Shadows," *Oppositions* (Summer 1977), and Corner, "Theory in Crisis," this volume.

7. See Ann Bermingham, *Landscape and Ideology* (Berkeley: University of California Press, 1986), especially the chapters "Theories of the Picturesque" and "Politics of the Picturesque," for a summary of these interrelationships.

8. M. Hays, "Critical Architecture: Between Form and Culture," *Perspecta* 21 (1984).

9. Note that Fletcher Steele and Garrett Eckbo would assign that beginning to the 1920s in France and the 1930s in Cambridge, Massachusetts. Those who expand the time-frame of Picturesque/

modern landscape history and theory back into the eighteenth century include Sidney Robinson (see *Inquiry into the Picturesque* [Chicago: University of Chicago Press, 1991]) and John Dixon Hunt (see *Gardens and the Picturesque: Studies in Landscape Architecture History* [Cambridge, Mass.: MIT Press, 1992]).

10. The original texts are all available in the Loeb Library's Rare Books collection; reprints and photocopies are available as well. A number of secondary sources, including Ann Bermingham, "Theories of the Picturesque" in *Landscape and Ideology* (which has an excellent description of the concept of mediation); R. G. Saisselin, "The French Garden in the Eighteenth Century: 'Belle Nature' and the Landscape of Time," *Journal of Garden History* 5, no. 3 (1985): 284–297; and Rudolf Wittkower, "Classical Theory and Eighteenth Century Sensibility," in his *Palladio and Palladianism* (New York: Braziller, 1974), offer historical background on the period.

11. W. Gilpin, *Remarks on Forest Scenery* (1791; rpt. Richmond: Richmond Publishing Co., 1973).

12. Gilpin, *Remarks on Forest Scenery*, 6–8.

13. See Saisselin, "The French Garden in the Eighteenth Century," 317, for a discussion of the theoretical shift from "belle nature" to specific sites.

14. R. Williams, *Keywords* (London: Fontana, 1983).

15. In *Gardens and the Picturesque*, J. D. Hunt states that the ability to appreciate these rural woodlands for their aesthetic value requires an eye familiar with the overgrown landscapes of both English landscape gardens built in the mid-eighteenth century by designer Kent and Italian villa gardens and boscos. This reading places Gilpin's books in both a bridging and mediating role.

16. Other examples of such treatises include: Dezallier, *The Theory and Practice of Gardening* (London: G. James, 1712); Thomas Mawson, *The Art and Craft of Garden Making* (1900; New York: Scribner's, 1926), and Garrett Eckbo, *Landscape for Living* (F. W. Dodge, 1959).

17. See my previous remarks at the 1990 CELA plenary session in which I invoked Jorge Silvetti's call for a criticism from within the design of architecture. Such critical design practice requires a set of formal codes and conventions which are generally understood by some group, however select, of "readers." Then, the act of combining, recombining, weighting, inverting, and assembling those codes will not only be understood as formally inventive, but more important, as symbolically or semantically significant. See Silvetti, "The Beauty of Shadows."

18. Denis Cosgrove defines a social formation as a mode of production or set of economic conditions--the base or infrastructure--that is modified by a particular cultural and natural geography to suggest new land patterns. Each social formation produces material and cultural products which are not mere epiphenomena of economic production. Rather, these cultural products—for example, art, design, philosophy, religion, education, legal mechanisms—have the status of expression and the ability to effect change in the social formation itself. Landscape architecture and architecture, when understood as cultural products rather than as art objects, are enmeshed in, not detached from, the world.

19. This definition of ideology draws on Bermingham's chapters on Picturesque theory and politics.

20. S. J. Gould, "Church, Humboldt and Darwin: The Tension and Harmony of Art and Science," in *Frederic Edwin Church*, ed. F. Kelly (1989). B. Novak, *Nature and Culture* (New York: Oxford University Press, 1980).

21. Note the land acquisition history of Prospect Park for Vaux's contribution to the reconfiguration of the edge.

22. This is not to deny the import of program requirements in the park design, only to emphasize an aspect of the park's design which has rarely been discussed.

23. See Cosgrove, *Social Formation and Symbolic Landscape*, especially the chapter "America as Landscape" which discusses Crèvecoeur's assessment of the Panorama's significance to early American culture.

24. One need only look at nineteenth-century maps and engravings of the mechanized countryside outside Chicago in the 1870s to persuade students of the artificiality of the suburb of Riverside. William Cronon's *Nature's Metropolis* (New York: W. W. Norton, 1991) has wonderful engravings of the slaughterhouses and cattle yards.

25. "The reconciliatory mission of the architect is poetic. This is necessarily an individual task, encompassing personal expression and reference to totality. There is no meaningful logic without acknowledging the intersubjective world, best revealed in dreams and myths." (Alberto Perez-Gomez, *Architecture and the Crisis of Modern Science* [Cambridge, Mass.: MIT Press, 1983], 325.) Part of our human condition is the inevitable yearning to capture reality through metaphors. Such is true knowledge, ambiguous yet ultimately more relevant than scientific truth. And architecture, no matter how much it resists the idea, cannot renounce its origin in intuition. While construction as a technological process is prosaic—deriving directly from a mathematical equation, a functional diagram, or a rule of formal combinations—architecture is poetic, necessarily an abstract order but in itself a metaphor emerging from a vision of the world and Being" (ibid., 326).

26. Merchant, *Ecological Revolutions*.

27. Merchant, *Ecological Revolutions*, p. 2.

28. By the 1930s when landscape architecture as a profession was establishing itself as an academic discipline, most students knew the Picturesque through textbooks such as Hubbard and Kimball's *Study of Landscape Design*, which petrified the category as a style. Another source of dissemination for the ubiquitous, mass-producible Pastoral and Picturesque was quite different—the polemical books of Le Corbusier: *Towards a New Architecture* and, especially, *City of Tomorrow*. The idealized landscape surrounding and engulfing both urban and rural buildings was the same homogeneous matrix of verdure—a perfect, neutral, formless background for modern architecture's pristine object-buildings.

29. This is not to deny another vein of research that has concurrently revived landscape architecture's awareness of the nonvisual aspects of sites, namely ecological theory and phenomenology.

30. R. Smithson, "Frederick Law Olmsted and the Dialectical Landscape," in *The Writings of Robert Smithson*, ed. N. Holt (New York: New York University Press, 1979).

31. Smithson, "Frederick Law Olmsted," 118.

32. Smithson, "Frederick Law Olmsted," 119.

33. Smithson, "Frederick Law Olmsted," 124.

34. C. Baudelaire, *The Painter of Modern Life, and Other Essays*, ed. J. Mayne (London: Phaidon, 1965).

35. D. Worster, *Nature's Economy: A History of Ecological Ideas* (New York: Cambridge University Press, 1977).

36. As described by Carolyn Merchant in *Ecological Revolutions*: "Ecological thinking constructs nature as an active partner [with human activity]. The 'nature' that science claims to represent is active, unstable, and constantly changing. As parts of the whole, humans have the power to alter the networks in which they are embedded. Nature as an active partner acquiesces to human interventions through resilience and adaptation or 'resists' human actions through mutation and evolution. Nonhuman nature is an actor; human and nonhuman interactions constitute the drama. Viewed as a social construction, nature as it is conceptualized in each social epoch . . . is not some ultimate truth that was gradually discovered through the scientific processes of observation, experiment, and mathematics. Rather, it was a relative changing structure of human representations of 'reality.'"

37. The introduction to Stuart Wrede and William Howard Adam's *Denatured Visions* (New York: Museum of Modern Art, 1991) is an example of this mode of historiography.

38. See Nicholas Green, *The Spectacle of Nature: Landscape and Bourgeois Culture in Nineteenth Century France* (New York: Manchester University Press, 1990) for an excellent analysis of the "environmental gaze" in pre-Haussman Parisians' landscape consciousness.

39. Note Huyssen's contention that poststructuralism is not antimodern; rather, it is an archaeology of the modern. He argues that poststructuralist theory theorizes the modern.

40. J. Burnham, "Systems Aesthetics," in *Esthetics Contemporary*, ed. R. Kostelanetz (Buffalo: Prometheus Books, 1978). A. Huyssen, *After the Great Divide: Modernism, Mass Culture, Postmodernism* (Bloomington: Indiana University Press, 1986). Smithson, "Frederick Law Olmsted."

41. My affiliations with various theoretical and critical schools are contingent relationships—they seem to develop after I struggle with certain issues for a while. Those theories clarify, but have not determined, my analytical and methodological approaches or interpretations. Recently, I have been studying feminist theory as a vehicle for "unpacking" the constraints placed on landscape architectural theory by the dominant theories and practices of art and architectural history and theory. But this is another article.

42. Standard historiographies' failures to address the industrial, aesthetic, and ecological revolutions relegate modern landscape architecture to a subset of architecture or art and explain the impoverished understanding that contemporary landscape architectural practitioners have of their own design tradition. The descriptive and evaluative languages of art and architectural history are only partial tools for deciphering the history of landscape architecture. Here I am also thinking about Norman Newton's *Design on the Land* (Cambridge, Mass.: Belknap Press, 1971), which is of interest for what and who it does not include. Despite his attempt at a structuralist approach (landscape architecture history as the history of space), Newton's spatiality has little range beyond geometric and informal. He rarely describes sites for their topographic structure, plant assumptions, phenomenal characteristics, and so on.

43. I am indebted to Griselda Pollock's "Modernity and the Spaces of Femininity," in *Vision and Difference: Femininity, Feminism and the Histories of Art* (New York: Routledge, 1988) which underscores the necessity of confronting the conceptual framework of a field as well as expanding the list of old masters to include old mistresses.

44. Marshall Berman's *All that Is Solid Melts into Air* (New York: Simon and Schuster, 1982), a study of modern culture, identifies the contradictory forces of destruction and creation inherent in modernization.

45. A. Kolodny, "A Map for Rereading: Gender and the Interpretation of Literary Texts," in *The New Feminist Criticism*, ed. E. Showalter (New York: Pantheon, 1972).

46. Merchant, *Ecological Revolutions*, 22. M. Foucault, "Questions of Geography," in *Power/Knowledge: Selected Interviews and Other Writings, 1972–1977*, ed. C. Gordon (New York: Pantheon Books, 1980).

## Part II. Design Process

1. M. Nicholson, *The Environmental Revolution* (London: Penguin, 1970).

## The Art of Site Planning, *Kevin Lynch and Gary Hack*

1. Nan Fairbrother, *New Lives, New Landscapes* (New York: Knopf, 1970). Gerald Suttles, *The Social Order of the Slum* (Chicago: University of Chicago Press, 1970).

## An Ecological Method, *Ian McHarg*

1. See Ian L. McHarg and David A. Wallace, "Plan for the Valleys vs. Spectre of Uncontrolled Growth," *Landscape Architecture* (April 1965) (Ed.).

2. See Philip H. Lewis Jr., "Quality Corridors for Wisconsin," *Landscape Architecture* (January 1964).

3. Sciences:

| | | |
|---|---|---|
| | Simplicity, complexity; | Robert McArthur |
| | Uniformly, diversity; | Robert McArthur |
| | Independence, interdependence; | Robert McArthur |

| Instability, stability; | Robert McArthur |
| Stability, instability; | Luna Leopard |
| Low or high nature of species; | Ruth Patrick |
| Low or high entropy; | Harold F. Blum |
| Ill health, health; | Ruth Patrick |

## The RSVP Cycles, *Lawrence Halprin*

1. C. G. Jung et al., *Man and His Symbols* (New York: Doubleday, 1964).

2. F. S. Perls, R. F. Hefferline, and P. Goodman, *Gestalt Therapy*, 4th ed. (New York: Julian Press, 1962).

## Community Design, *Randolph Hester, Jr.*

*Editor's note:* All reprint permissions noted here are as acknowledged in the original text.

1. Norman T. Newton, *An Approach to Design* (Cambridge, Mass.: Addison-Wesley, 1951), pp. 100, 109. Reprinted by permission of Norman T. Newton. Copyright 1961 by Addison-Wesley Publishing Company, Inc. p. 81.

2. Jan C. Rowan, "Editorial," *Progressive Architecture* 49, no. 9 (September 1968): 101. Reprinted by permission of Reinhold Publishing Company.

3. Hugh C. Davis, "What We Don't Know About Open Space," *Open Space Action* 1, no. 3 (March-April 1969): 28. Reprinted by permission of Open Space Institute.

4. Samuel Z. Klausner, *On Man in His Environment* (San Francisco: Jossey-Bass, 1971), p. 165. Reprinted by permission of Jossey-Bass, Inc. Copyright 1971 by Jossey-Bass, Inc.

5. Davis, "What We Don't Know About Open Space," p. 28.

6. John Friedmann, *Retracking America: A Theory of Transactional Planning* (Garden City, N.Y.: Doubleday, 1973), pp. xiii-xvi. Reprinted by permission of Doubleday & Company, Inc. Copyright 1973 by John Friedmann.

7. Ibid., pp. xvi-xvii.

8. See William H. Whyte, *Cluster Development* (New York: American Conservation Association, 1964).

9. William A. Caldwell, *How to Save America* (New York: New American Library, 1973), pp. 124–125.

10. Garrett Eckbo, *Urban Landscape Design* (New York: McGraw-Hill, 1964).

11. Simpson F. Lawson, ed., *Workshop on Urban Open Space* (Washington, D.C.: U.S. Department of Housing and Urban Development, ASLA 1), p. 10.

12. *The First Report of the National Policy Task Force*, in MEMO Jan. 1972/Special Issue, p. 3.

13. Randolph T. Hester, Jr., "Institutionalized Team Advocacy Design," in *Eleven Views: Collaborative Design in Community Development*, John Pearce, ed. (Raleigh, N.C.: Student Publication of the School of Design), vol. 20, no. 7, p. 133.

14. Randolph T. Hester, Jr., "What About People?" a paper presented for the North Carolina Chapter of the American Institute of Architects special Landscape Architecture Issue, p. 2.

15. Charles A. Reich, *The Greening of America* (New York: Bantam Books, 1971), p. 13.

16. Lewis Clarke articulated this in 1967. He pointed out that the designer's best alternative when designing for a group unknown to himself is to provide a multichoice potential environment that could be used differently by different users. This is the meaning of potential environment referenced here. It is similar to Herbert Gans' potential environment, which Gans contrasts with the effective environment.

17. See Robert Goodman, *After the Planners* (New York: Simon and Schuster, 1971).

18. Ed Schweitzer, "Whatever Happened to Grass Roots Design?" *Here and Now* (Raleigh, N.C.: Student Publication of the School of Design), vol. 21, no. 2.

19. Goodman, *After the Planners*.

20. Self-help design is a process whereby the user's sweat equity or own labor goes into the build-

ing of an environment to lower the cost. See Guy L. Angster et al., *Human Development Through Housing Rehabilitation,* Urban Affairs and Community Services Center, Raleigh, N.C.

21. Plural planning refers to the process whereby conflicting user groups prepare their own plans for an environment rather than developing a single consensus plan.

22. John Brinckerhoff Jackson, *American Space: The Centennial Years, 1865–1876* (New York: W. W. Norton, 1972), p. 219. Reprinted by permission of W. W. Norton & Company, Inc. Copyright 1972 by W. W. Norton & Company, Inc.

23. Herbert J. Gans, *People and Plans: Essays on Urban Problems and Solutions* (New York: Basic Books, 1968), p. 80. Reprinted by permission of Basic Books, Inc. Copyright 1968 by Basic Books, Inc.

24. Ibid., p. 81.

25. Paul Davidoff, "Advocacy and Pluralism in Planning," *Journal of the American Institute of Planners* 31, no. 4 (November 1965): 332–333. Copyright © 1965 by the Journal of the American Institute of Planners. Reprinted by permission.

26. David Robinson Godschalk, "Collaborative Planning: A Theoretical Framework," in *Eleven Views: Collaborative Design in Community Development* (Raleigh, N.C.: Student Publication of the School of Design), vol. 20, no. 7, p. 19.

27. Friedmann, *Retracking America,* p. 187.

28. Lawson, ed., *Workshop on Urban Open Space,* p. 20.

29. Ibid.

30. J. Christopher Jones, *Design Methods: Seeds of Human Futures* (New York: John Wiley & Sons, Interscience Division, 1972), p. 46.

## Site Design, *Kevin Lynch and Gary Hack*

1. Donald A. Schon, *The Reflective Practitioner* (New York: Basic Books, 1983).

## Creative Risk Taking, *Steven Krog*

1. John Dewey, *Art as Experience* (New York, 1934).

2. John Fowles, *Daniel Martin* (New York, 1977).

3. John Ormsbee Simonds, *Landscape Architecture* (New York, 1961).

4. "Presence" is the intellectual and emotional, perceptual response to the combined temporal and spatial characteristics of a place. "Metaphor" is intended to mean the extent to which a work is "like," or refers to, something outside itself, with or without intent on the part of the artist.

5. Norman Newton, letter to the editor, *Landscape Architecture* (July 1981): 442.

6. Fowles, *Daniel Martin.*

7. Richard Williams, letter to the editor, *Landscape Architecture* (July 1981): 444.

8. James Turrell, *James Turrell light and space* (New York, 1980).

9. "Commentary" is used here, in its broadest sense, to mean an explanatory remark, observation, or elucidation.

10. William Widdowson, "Who Makes Architecture?" (unpublished paper, University of Cincinnati, 1975).

11. Lawrence Weschler, "Profiles: Robert Irwin," *New Yorker* (March 8 and March 15, 1982).

12. Mary Gordon, "The Fate of Women of Genius," *New York Times Book Review* (September 13, 1981): 6–28.

13. Herbert Mitgang, "Barthelme Takes on Task . . .," *New York Times* (February 18, 1982): C15.

14. Ben Shahn, *The Shape of Content* (New Haven, Conn., 1957).

15. See also John Morris Dixon, "Quality vs. Ideology," *Progressive Architecture* (March 1981), and Perry Meisel, "Imitation Modernism," *Atlantic* (March 1982).

## The Obligation of Invention, *Bernard Lassus*

1. *Landscape Journal,* 12, no. 2 (Fall 1993): 103, 181.

2. Heterogeneity is more receptive than homogeneity; Bernard Lassus, *Jeux* (Paris: Galilée, 1977).

3. Bernard Lassus, *Villes, paysages, couleurs en Lorraine* (Paris: Mardaga/Batigère, 1990).

4. Bernard Lassus, *Fluidités*, Urbi VIII (Paris: Mardaga, 1983), 74–75.

5. Bernard Lassus, *Polychromie architecturale*, Cahier 423 (Paris: Centre Scientifique et Technique du Bâtiment, 1961).

6. Bernard Lassus, *Jardins imaginaries*, coll. Les Habitants—Paysagistes (Paris: Presses de la Connaissance/Weber, 1977).

7. Bernard Lassus, "Les Continuités du paysage," *Urbanismes* 250 (September 1991): 64–68; "Le Choix de l'entité paysagère," *Urbanismes* 215 (August-September 1986): 143–145.

8. Bernard Lassus, "Schéma d'ambiances paysagères—Ville nouvelle de Marne-la-Vallée," 1982.

9. Bernard Lassus, "L'Intervention minimale," *Traverses* 26 (October 1982): 148–51; "L'Intervento minimo—Il gardino del passato," *D'Ars* (Milan) 99 (July 1982): 12–23; "L'Intervention minimale," *Archivert* 12 (2d trimester 1982): 28–31; "Minimal Intervention."

10. Lassus, *Jeux*.

11. To extend the expression used by William Gilpin about the characteristics of the landscape in Great Britain.

12. Bernard Lassus, *Le Jardin de Tuileries* (London: Corack Press, 1991); "The Tuileries—A Reinvented Garden" in Bernard Lassus, *The Landscape Approach* (Philadelphia: University of Pennsylvania Press, 1998).

13. "Les Buissons optiques" (Niort, 1993); see "The Optical Bushes," in Lassus, *The Landscape Approach*.

14. Bernard Lassus, "Schéma directeur d'ambiances visuelles du secteur II de la ville nouvelle de Marne-la-Vallée Bernard Lassus," 1975.

## Part III. Form, Meaning, and Experience

1. As noted in the Introduction, the complex cross currents of intellectual debate under the broad headings of (post)modernism and (post)structuralism are of great significance to the way theory is developing in the discipline, but require extensive study. Distilling such literature into a short statement is fraught with risk. Nonetheless, my interpretation of the influence of these two linked movements follows. The shift from modernity to postmodernity is a much debated evolution in the material basis for society, from one in which wealth is created through predominantly industrial activity, to one in which symbols (and symbolic capital) assume the greater prominence (Lash and Urry, *Economies of Signs and Space* [London: Sage, 1994]). A shift from "modern" to "postmodern" *thinking* expresses a move from a generally progressive and essentialist outlook (that is, a better future is possible and can be created through culture); to a much more diffuse and self-questioning position, which doubts both the possibility of salvation, and the likelihood of being able to identify essential qualities.

A shift from structuralism to poststructuralism represents a move from a belief that meaning in the world derives primarily from the structural relationships within language, to a position which rejects the possibility of meaningful structures, or at least the possibility of identifying such structures in an objective way. In place of formal structures and processes of investigation, we have instead a continually changing field of relationships, whose meanings are in constant flux, and which are open to continual interrogation and re-presentation.

The effect of these changes upon a design discipline is profound. A modern, structuralist position creates the possibility of designing landscapes whose meanings can be largely predetermined, and which may be assumed to enhance human life. A postmodern, poststructuralist position (or positions, given that they are always changing) undermines confidence or certainty in any of the points of reference. In our continually changing, unstable, simulated world, meaningful action is elusive. In landscape architecture, a major effect of this has been an intellectual turn toward phenomenology, typically expressed as notions of site, dwelling, and place, in a search for a grounded sense of meaning. Feminist thinking in the discipline occupies an interesting position, critical of the universal tendencies of modernity, but committed to meaningful action in particular places.

2. J. O. Simonds, *Landscape Architecture* (New York: McGraw-Hill, 1961), pp. 224, 225.

3. R. Krauss, "Sculpture in the Expanded Field," *October 8* (Spring 1979), reprinted in H. Foster, *The Anti-Aesthetic* (Port Townsend, Wash.: Bay Press, 1983).

## Form, Meaning, and Expression, *Laurie Olin*

1. Arthur Danto, *Transformation of the Commonplace* (Cambridge, Mass.: Harvard University Press, 1981), pp. 1–32.

## Cubist Space, Volumetric Space, *Patrick Condon*

1. Erno Goldfinger, "The Sensation of Space," *Architectural Review* 90 (November 1941): 129–131.

2. Camillo Sitte, *City Planning According to Artistic Principles*, translation of 1898 original (New York: Random House, 1965).

3. Jusuck Koh, "A Post Modern Design Paradigm of Holistic Philosophy and Evolutionary Ethic," *Landscape Journal* 1, no. 2 (1982): 76–84.

4. John T. Lyle, "The Alternating Current of Design Process," *Landscape Journal* 4, no. 1 (1985): 7–13.

5. Catherine Howett, "Systems, Signs, Sensibilities: Sources for a New Landscape Aesthetic," *Landscape Journal* 6, no. 1 (1987): 1–12.

6. J. Grange, "On the Way Toward Foundational Ecology." *Soundings* 60, no. 2 (1977): 135–49.

## Must Landscapes Mean? *Marc Treib*

1. For example, the fall 1988 issue of *Landscape Journal*, guest edited by Ann Whiston Spirn and called "Nature, Form, and Meaning," was devoted to just this subject. As might be expected, the range of approaches to the subject was broad, and the resulting interpretations broader still.

2. See D. W. Meinig, ed., *The Interpretation of Ordinary Landscapes* (New York: Oxford University Press, 1979). Like anthropologists, cultural geographers read the landscape as a text and are relatively reticent to make judgments about it, much less those of aesthetics. Others, like W. H. Hoskins, however, may decry the modernization of the English landscape and may appraise these residues of culture process on the base of personal values. See also W. H. Hoskins, *The Making of the English Landscape* (Harmondsworth: Penguin Books, 1955) and compare with J. B. Jackson, *Landscapes* (Amherst: University of Massachusetts Press, 1970).

3. Mark Francis and Randolph T. Hester, Jr., *The Meaning of Gardens* (Cambridge, Mass.: MIT Press, 1989). The book, developed from a conference held at the University of California at Davis in 1987, should be distinguished from the previously released typescript and unillustrated proceedings.

4. Robert B. Riley, "From Sacred Grove to Disney World: The Search for Garden Meaning," *Landscape Journal* 7, no. 2 (1988): 149–168, p. 138. Whether Riley's statement encompasses history as well as contemporary life was not spelled out. The author's hesitation to assign meaning to gardens may stem from the pluralistic and multicultural composition of the contemporary American population. One could add, somewhat desperately perhaps, that this admittedly diverse population appears to be bent on expressing its constitution of differing cultural groups, rather than examining the shared characteristics of all human beings.

5. Laurie Olin, "Form, Meaning, and Expression in Landscape Architecture," *Landscape Journal* 7, no. 2 (1988): 136–147, p. 159. The problems that develop from dividing the production of meaning into distinct categories are obvious to the author of the article as well as to its readers. I imagine that Olin would agree that meaning ultimately derives from both categories operating simultaneously.

6. Olin's classifications roughly parallel the two categories I had once proposed in discussing the idea of formalism in the landscape. The first, *trace*, was the unintentioned marking or making of space through use. The second, *intent*, concerned conscious spatial definition and/or construction that considered dimensions beyond that of functions; that is, the semantic as well as the syntactic aspects of landscape design. Marc Treib, "Traces upon the Land: The Formalistic Landscape." *Architectural Association Quarterly* 1, no. 4 (1979): 28–39.

7. The library on meaning in philosophy is vast and makes trying reading. The award for the most provocative title should probably be given to Cambridge dons C. K. Ogden and I. A. Richards, *The Meaning of Meaning* (New York: Harcourt, Brace & World, 1923). If one accepted their definition of meaning in *language* and extended it to *landscape architecture*, one would have to agree that it was indeed possible to design meaning into landscapes: "The meaning of any sentence is what the speaker intends to be understood from it by the listener" (p. 193). The authors, obviously, make no such claim for landscape design, however, nor do they imply that linguistic theory is applicable in any form to the making of landscape.

8. For example, I am told that, like landscape meaning, there remains no clear definition of electricity. This has not hampered our ability to understand, produce, modulate, and utilize the resource, however. Louis Armstrong is supposed to have said that if he had to explain jazz to people, they would never really understand it. This just may be true of meaning as well.

9. That this stance is problematic seems obvious.

10. Tunnard's essays that would constitute his 1938 *Gardens in the Modern Landscape* appeared serially in *Architectural Review,* starting the previous year. About the same time, James Rose contributed a series of articles to *Pencil Points,* the predecessor of today's *Progressive Architecture,* including one essay titled "Plants Dictate Garden Form," written in 1938. The conclusions that Rose reached in this essay closely paralleled those of Tunnard. Both included a list of plant materials suitable for modern conditions.

11. Conversation with the author, June 1988; but he still says it.

12. The notable exception was the work of Roberto Burle Marx, who would frequently be characterized as a "painter in plants" who drew on the shapes of modern, often non objective, art. See Marc Treib, "Axioms for a Modern Landscape Architecture," in *Modern Landscape Architecture: A Critical Review,* ed. Marc Treib (Cambridge, Mass.: MIT Press, 1993).

In a series of articles published in *Architectural Record* at the beginning of the 1940s, Rose, Eckbo, and Dan Kiley linked the physical and social environment from the intimate to regional scales as a prerequisite of responsible landscape architecture. They did not talk of significance, however, but implied that meaning accompanies an intelligent design, or that it was just not an issue. These articles have been republished in Treib, ed., *Modern Landscape Architecture.*

13. In Gideon's eyes, space was the primary quest of modern architecture, the realization of an adventure he traced back to Baroque spatial planning in Rome under Sixtus V and the undulating facades of Francesco Borromini. See Sigfried Gideon, *Space, Time and Architecture* (Cambridge, Mass.: Harvard University Press, 1938).

14. For a representative collection of Greenberg's ideas and writings, see Clement Greenberg, *Art and Culture: Critical Essays* (Boston: Beacon Press, 1961).

15. Garrett Eckbo, *Landscapes for Living* (New York: Reinhold Publishing, 1950). See also Reuben Rainey (1993), "'Organic Form in the Humanized Landscape': Garrett Eckbo's *Landscapes for Living,*" in Treib, ed., *Modern Landscape Architecture,* pp. 180–205.

16. Ian McHarg, *Design with Nature* (New York: Doubleday, 1966). Despite his predominant polemic and pervasive rationale, McHarg admits moments of poetry and suggestions of meaning: "The best symbol of peace might better be the garden than the dove" (p. 5).

17. Olin, "Form, Meaning and Expression in Landscape Architecture," pp. 150–151.

18. To my mind, one of the real burdens of landscape architecture is that two professions are combined under the same name, as if their interests and goals were coincident. Landscape architecture is concerned with forming, as well as planning, a landscape; landscape management or planning, with

its regulation. Obviously, they overlap in their concern with living systems, but landscape architecture requires active, formal intervention in a way that regional planning does not. This is not to say, however, that they both do not have consequences in the form of the landscape.

19. In his 1984 *California Scenario* plaza-garden in Costa Mesa, California, Noguchi appears to have adapted a wedge-shaped fragment of the astronomical observatory for use as a water source. While this element can also be read as a modernist abstraction of a hill, the form bears a striking resemblance to its Indian predecessor. Noguchi's program for the garden encompassed the various ecological zones of California, from mountain meadow to desert: an attempt at evoking the genius loci and creating meaning?

20. Gary Dwyer, "The Power Under Our Feet," *Landscape Architecture* 76, no. 3 (1986): 65–68. The choice of Ogham as the script with which to inscribe the fault line was based on its formal properties alone: it is written as cross marks across a linear spine. Dwyer himself asks the critical question: "How can an ancient Celtic language have anything to do with the San Andreas Fault?" And replies: "Aside from its development by a primitive people who were rhythmically allied with the forces of nature, Ogham began like all languages with the mark, with 'naming the unknowable.'" To my mind, the substantiation remains unconvincing.

21. After an exhaustive search and a telephone call to the author, I have been unable to find the exact source of the quotation, or even whether this was the exact quotation. If not precisely those words, the spirit of Howett's observation is captured by them.

22. Christian Norberg-Schulz determined three ways in which manmade places relate to nature. The first regards rendering the natural structure "more precise"; in the second, construction complements the natural order, while the third symbolizes it: "The purpose of symbolization is to free the meaning from the immediate situation, whereby it becomes a 'cultural object,' which may form part of a more complex situation, or be moved to another place." *Genius Loci* (New York: Rizzoli, 1980), p. 17. Edward Relph's *Place and Placelessness* (London: Pion Limited, 1976) constitutes, in some ways, the complement to Norbert-Schulz's more natural oriented vision. Relph also includes the symbolic as part of the triad of factors that create the sense of place: "The identity of a place is comprised of three inter-related components, each irreducible to the other—physical features or appearance, observable activities and functions, and meanings of symbols" (p. 61).

23. My anecdote is a paraphrase of a citizen reaction I overheard in 1990 when photographing an urban triangle in Washington, D.C., planted by Oehme/Van Sweden. My kibitzer read my taking of the photographs as documenting a deplorable urban condition, presumably as evidence to have the wrong righted as soon as possible. This was in spite of the fact that numerous plaques identified the various grasses and cluing, at a second level, that the wild look was intentional.

24. I realize, of course, that there are far more considerations bearing on these decisions than the aesthetic alone. But at some point in the process, aesthetic questions must be addressed.

25. "If one wishes to work on the cutting edge in either fine art or design," writes Martha Schwartz, "one must be informed of developments in the world of painting and sculpture. Ideas surface more quickly in painting and sculpture than in architecture or landscape architecture, due to many factors including the immediacy of the media and the relative low investment of money required to explore an idea." "Landscape and Common Culture (1993)," in Treib, ed., *Modern Landscape Architecture*, p. 264. As is often the case, however, by the time art ideas are applied to landscape design, they are a bit tired and worn. For a passionate argument for the Neoarchaic in art—one source of landscape architecture in the 1980s—see Lucy Lippard, *Overlay* (New York: E. P. Dutton, 1983).

26. Norma Evenson, *Paris: A Century of Change* (New Haven: Yale University Press, 1978). Or taken at rush hours, as a round and linear parking lot.

27. In fact, one of the slaughterhouses, la Halle aux Boeufs, was renovated into an art space by Reichen and Robert in 1985; a modern recent structure for animal dispatch was heroically recast as the City of Science and Industry by Adrian Fainsilber in 1987 and is the park's principal attraction.

28. The notable exception is Alexandre Chemetoff's Sequence IV or Bamboo Garden. Given its sense of path, its enclosure, and its Didactic revelation of subterranean services, the bamboo gar-

den is both a lesson and respite from the city and the other parts of the park at La Villette. As of June 1993, however, it had become overgrown and is in need of pruning and reformation.

29. Much of what has been written perpetuates the designer's original claims; many of the authors seem never to have visited the actual park, and their writings are discourse about discourse.

30. According the J. B. Jackson, expediency is a hallmark of vernacular building. *Defining the Vernacular Landscape* (New Haven: Yale University Press, 1984).

31. This friend, who happens to be French and writes about modernist French gardens, wishes to remain anonymous.

32. Garreau offers two "laws" that govern the naming of developments. First, there is Jake Page's Law of Severed Continuity: "You name a place for what is no longer there as a result of your actions." Next, the Keith Severin Corollary: "All subdivisions are named after whatever species are first driven out by the construction. E.g.: Quail Trail Estates." J. Garreau, *Edge Cities* (New York: Doubleday, 1991), pp. 461–471.

33. Sir Geoffrey Jellicoe's proposal for the Moody Gardens in Galveston, Texas, was essentially a landscape theme park, evoking (but not copying) historical garden types. *Landscapes of Civilization* (Woodbridge: Garden Art Press, 1989).

34. There is some indication that they do. Particularly in good weather, the less formal areas of the "gardens in movement" are highly utilized, perhaps because they provide some of the only truly private—and shaded—spaces in what is otherwise a highly structured ensemble. In that way, they resemble the country in comparison to the city.

35. I realize that there is quite another school of thought that regards both human experiences and significance as more or less universal. This belief has produced "pattern languages," among other theories, derived from a selective potpourri of peoples and places, with the assumption that the proper blend (selected and structured by the authors) will perfectly suit all of humanity—certainly at least twentieth-century America. My own experience through travel and reading, supported by historical study, suggests quite the opposite; that is, that values are not universal, but are instead particular to a people, place, and time. Perhaps this could be appropriately termed "cultural relativism"—and it probably has been so termed by someone somewhere.

36. Thus Japanese gardens built outside Japan are mere shadows of their referents because they lack their native cultural matrix. They become "Japanesque" and expose physical features as a photograph captures an image but only rarely the essence of subject.

37. "Polite," like the term Monumental or High Style, is used in this essay in (near) opposition to the Vernacular tradition of landscape making and building. It implies neither a rank ordering of one above the other nor any particular character, except that the Polite tradition will normally approach environmental design far more self-consciously than the Vernacular.

38. "It is doubtless a difficult notion to appreciate today, but in the eighteenth century all the fine arts were deemed to have representation at their center, and gardening aspired to *beaux-arts* status." John Dixon Hunt, "The Garden as Cultural Object," in H. Adams and S. Wrede, eds., *Denatured Visions* (New York: Museum of Modern Art, 1991), p. 26.

39. Ibid., p. 28.

40. Ibid.

41. In his or her notes, the reader anonymously reviewing a draft of this essay for *Landscape Journal* wisely noted two categories of meaning: "A. Systems of Signification/Representation in the landscape (metaphysical, narrative, allegorical, symbolic), and B. Circumstances of engagement with the landscape (experiential, sensory, physical)." This might be interpreted broadly as a meaning that accrues perceptually as opposed to meaning that accrues conceptually.

42. Folk cultures have been described as those that are geographically delimited, developing only slowly over time. Mass culture, in contrast, is more broadly ranged and changes rapidly.

43. Or as Robert Riley put it: "Such a lack of shared symbolism does not rule out the garden as a carrier of powerful meaning but it does discount the likelihood of meanings that speak strongly to the whole society." "From Sacred Grove to Disney World," p. 142.

44. J. B. Jackson, among others, has pointed out that the visual-centric garden is a Renaissance development and that during the medieval and earlier ages the correspondences between plant and cosmos were firmly established. The form of the plant or its fragrance or its name suggested its value through associations. A yellow plant might be appropriate for curing jaundice; a round one might assuage headaches. Those who cared about such things—admittedly, a small community—were bound together in a common belief system through Christianity. *The Necessity for Ruins* (Amherst: University of Massachusetts Press, 1980), pp. 37–54.

45. Robert Riley cited Mary Douglas's term "condensed symbols" that "carry not just one meaning but accretions of many meanings, layered upon each other and over time. They are symbols that are commonly agreed upon, not designer-chosen, that connote deep affective meaning, not quick cleverness, and that are integral to a context that is culturally agreed upon as appropriate." "From Sacred Grove to Disney World," p. 142.

46. Does our involvement for publication enter here? While neither meaning nor pleasure can be photographed, there can be pleasure depicted within a photograph; the photograph itself can provide pleasure, of course. Roland Barthes, *The Pleasure of the Text* (New York: Hill and Wang, 1975), p. 6.

47. Ibid.

48. J. W. von Goethe, "The Collector and His Circle," *Propyläen ii* (1799), in *Goethe on Art,* ed. John Gage (Berkeley: University of California Press, 1980), p. 70.

49. My own thoughts on this subject have been greatly augmented by suggestions from Robert Riley, for which I am grateful.

50. Vitruvius, of course, spoke Latin, not English. This particular rendering of the Latin original is by Henry Wotten.

## Place Reclamation, *Edward Relph*

1. J. Fergusson, *History of the Modern Styles of Architecture* (1st ed. 1862; London: John Murray, 1873), p. 499.

2. K. Lynch, *A Theory of Good City Form* (Cambridge, Mass.: MIT Press, 1981).

3. C. Alexander, *A Pattern Language* (New York: Oxford University Press, 1977), and *The Timeless Way of Building* (New York: Oxford University Press, 1979).

## Systems, Signs, and Sensibilities, *Catherine Howett*

1. Albert Fein, "The American City: The Ideal and the Real," in *The Rise of an American Architecture,* ed. Edgar Kaufmann, Jr. (New York: Praeger Publishers and The Metropolitan Museum of Art, 1970), p. 51.

2. Aldo Leopold, *A Sand Country Almanac,* cited in J. Baird Callicott, "The Land Aesthetic," *Environmental Review* 7, no. 4 (Winter 1983): 348.

3. Del Ivan Janik, "D. H. Lawrence and Environmental Consciousness," *Environmental Review* 7, no. 4 (Winter 1983): 359.

4. Callicott, "The Land Aesthetic," p. 346.

5. Nan Fairbrother, *New Lives, New Landscapes: Planning for the Twenty-First Century,* with foreword by Walter Muir Whitehill (New York: Alfred A. Knopf, 1970), p. 364.

6. Ibid., p. 366.

7. "New Directions: Ecological Approaches," introd. Robert Tregay, *Landscape Design* (hereafter *LD*) 138 (May 1982): 30; A. D. Bradshaw and J. F. Handley, "An Ecological Approach to Landscape Design—Principles and Problems," *LD* 138 (May 1982): 30–34; Roland Gustavsson, "New Directions, 2: Nature on Our Doorstep," *LD* 139 (August 1982): 21–23; O. D. Manning, "New Directions. 3: Designing for Man and Nature," *LD* 140 (November 1982): 30–32; Roger Greenwood, "New Directions, 5: Gorse Covert, Warrington—Creating a More Natural Landscape," *LD* 143 (June 1983): 35–38; Lyndis Cole, "New Directions, 6: Design for Environmental Education," *LD* 145 (October 1983): 28–31; O. L. Gilbert, "New Directions, 7: The Urban Common," *LD* 149 (June 1984): 35–36. See also

Allan Ruff and Robert J. Tregay, eds., *An Ecological Approach to Urban Landscape Design,* Occasional Paper, no. 8 (Manchester: Department of Town and Country Planning, University of Manchester, 1982).

8. Manning, "New Directions," p. 30.

9. See Darrel Morrison, "Restoring the Mid-western Landscape," *Landscape Architecture* 65, no. 4 (October 1975): 398–403; also Morrison, "Tall-grass Prairie in the Landscape," *Landscape Architectural Review* 6, no. 2 (May 1985): 5–11.

10. Stephen Rettig, "The Rise of the 'Ecological Approach' to Landscape Design," *Landscape Design* 143 (June 1983): 40.

11. Lucy R. Lippard, *Overlay: Contemporary Art and the Art of Prehistory* (New York: Pantheon Books, 1983), p. 231.

12. Callicott, "The Land Aesthetic," p. 350.

13. For an excellent discussion of the importance of a new conceptual framework for aesthetics, analogous to an embracing ecosphere, see Tom J. Bartuska and Gerald L. Young, "Aesthetics and Ecology: Notes on the Circle and the Sphere," *Journal of Aesthetic Education* 9, no. 3 (July 1975): 78–91. See also Malcolm B. Wells, "The Absolutely Constant Incontestably Stable Architectural Value Scale," *Progressive Architecture* 52, no. 3 (March 1971): 92–95.

14. Charles Jencks, *The Language of Post-Modern Architecture* (New York: Rizzoli, 1977), p. 15.

15. Robert Smithson, "A Sedimentation of Mi Earth Projects," in *The Writings of Robert Smithson: Essays with Illustrations,* ed. Nancy Holt, introd. by Philip Lieder (New York: New York University Press, 1979), p. 85.

16. Joseph Grange, "Radiant Lessons from the Failed Landscape of Desire," *Places* 2, no. 2 (1985): 21.

17. Ibid.

18. Ernest Becker, *The Denial of Death* (1973), cited in Grange, "Radiant Lessons," p. 22.

19. Amos Rapoport and Robert E. Kantor, "Complexity and Ambiguity in Environmental Design," *Journal of the American Institute of Planners* 33, no. 4 (July 1967): 210.

20. See Robert Venturi's seminal study, *Complexity and Contradiction in Architecture,* 2d ed., intro. Vincent Scully, Museum of Modern Art Papers on Architecture (New York: Museum of Modern Art and the Graham Foundation for Advanced Studies in the Visual Arts, 1977).

21. See Craig Campbell, "Seattle's Gas Plant Park," *Landscape Architecture* 63, no. 4 (July 1973): 338–342.

22. Yi-Fu Tuan, *Topophilia: A Study of Environmental Perception, Attitudes, and Values* (Englewood Cliffs, N.J.: Prentice-Hall, 1974).

23. Ibid., p. 96.

24. Martin Heidegger, "Building/Dwelling/Thinking," in *Basic Writings,* ed. Martin Krell (New York: Harper and Row, 1977), pp. 319–339.

25. Heidegger, *Basic Writings,* cited in Neil Evernden, *The Natural Alien: Humankind and Environment* (Toronto: University of Toronto Press, 1985), p. 68.

26. Grange, "On the Way Towards Foundational Ecology," cited in Evernden, *The Natural Alien,* p. 69.

27. Arnold Berleant, "Toward a Phenomenological Aesthetics of Environment," in *Descriptions,* Selected Studies in Phenomenology and Existential Philosophy, no. 11, eds. Don Ihde and High J. Silverman (New York: State University of New York Press, 1985), p. 125.

28. Lawrence Halprin, *The RSVP Cycles: Creative Processes in the Human Environment* (New York: George Braziller, 1969), p. 98.

## De/Re/In[form]ing Landscape, *Peter Jacobs*

1. Rosalind E. Krauss, *The Originality of the Avant-Garde and Other Modernist Myths* (Cambridge, Mass.: MIT Press, 1985), pp. 282–283.

2. Krauss's essay was first published under the title "Sculpture in the Expanded Field" *October 8* (Spring 1979). It is reprinted in H. Foster (ed.), *The Anti-Aesthetic* (Port Townsend, Wash.: Bay Press, 1983), pp. 31–42.

3. Peter Jacobs, "Sustaining Tomorrow: The Role of Environmental Planning and Design," Bradford Sears Lecture, Syracuse, N.Y.: SUNY, 1988.

4. United Nations, *Our Common Future*, Report of the World Commission on Environment and Development, G. H. Brundtland, chairwoman (Oxford: Oxford University Press, 1987).

5. Robert L. Thayer, "The Experience of Sustainable Landscapes," in *Sustainable Landscapes*, CELA Proceedings, Pomona, Calif., 1988, p. 167.

6. Robert A. Benson, "The Sustainable Dune: A Close Look at the Ecology and Environmental Ethics of a Fictional Landscape," in *Sustainable Landscapes*, CELA Proceedings, Pomona, Calif., 1988, p. 445.

7. Christopher D. Stone, *Earth and Other Ethics: The Case for Moral Pluralism* (New York: Harper and Row, 1987).

8. Herbert Simon, *The Science of the Artificial*, Karl Taylor Compton Lectures (Cambridge, Mass.: MIT Press, 1969).

9. Ian Appleton, "Plants, Paths, and Poems," *Landscape Design* (June 1989): 69–72, p. 69.

10. Laurie Olin, "Form, Meaning, and Expression in Landscape Architecture," *Landscape Journal 7*, no. 2 (1988): 149–169, p. 151.

11. Olin, "Form, Meaning, and Expression in Landscape Architecture," 155.

12. C. Norris and Benjamin A. Norris, *What Is Deconstruction?* (London: Academy Editions, St. Martin's Press, 1988), p.31.

13. Michel Foucault, *This Is Not a Pipe; An Art Quantum* (Berkeley: University of California Press, 1983).

14. Jacobs, "Sustaining Tomorrow."

## Part IV. Society, Language, and the Representation of Landscape
## The Language of Landscape, *Ann Whiston Spirn*

1. See, for example, the tablet of Enannatum I, governor of Lagash, which records the delivery of cedar trees to roof a temple, Mesopotamia, ca. 2900 B.C., and other examples in Gyorgy Kepes, ed., *Sign, Image, Symbol* (New York: George Braziller, 1966). For a review of the literature on evolution of human cognition, see M. Donald, *Origins of Modern Mind* (Cambridge, Mass.: Harvard University Press, 1991).

2. Roland Barthes, *Elements of Semiology* (New York: Farrar, Straus and Giroux, 1968), p. 16.

3. G. Lakoff and M. Johnson, *Metaphors We Live By* (Chicago: University of Chicago Press, 1980). Each developed these ideas further in subsequent books: G. Lakoff, *Women, Fire, and Dangerous Things: What Categories Reveal About the Mind* (Chicago: University of Chicago Press, 1987); M. Johnson, *The Body in the Mind* (Chicago: University of Chicago Press, 1987).

4. J. R. Stilgoe, *Shallow-Water Dictionary: A Grounding in Estuary English* (Cambridge, Mass.: Exact Change, 1990); and J. R. Stilgoe, *Alongshore* (New Haven: Yale University Press, 1994). While I admire Stilgoe's work on the language of the estuary, I reject his definition of landscape as including only land, not water, and countryside, not city.

5. Brown (1716–83), Olmsted (1822–1903), Wright (1867–1959), Halprin (b. 1916), Schwartz (b. 1950).

6. Heidegger, "Building Dwelling Thinking," 145–147 in *Poetry, Language, Thought* (New York: Harper and Row, 1975). Some of these implications have been explored by others, including the geographer Edward Relph, *Place and Placelessness* (Pion, 1976), and the architectural theorist Christian Norberg-Schulz, *Concept of Dwelling* (New York: Rizzoli, 1985).

7. Verner Dahlerup, *Ordbog over det Danske Sprog* (Copenhagen: Nordisk, 1931), Jacob Grimm and Wilhelm Grimm, *Deutsches Worterbuch* (Verlag von S. Hirzel, 1885), Arther R. Borden, Jr., *A Com-*

*prehensive Old English Dictionary* (University Press of America, 1982). For a review of the histories of the words *landscape, nature, land,* and *country* in English, German, and Scandinavian languages, see K. Olwig, "Recovering the Substantive Nature of Landscape," *Annals of the Association of American Geographers* 86, no. 4 (December 1996): 630–653. See also J. B. Jackson, "The Word Itself," in *Discovering the Vernacular Landscape* (New Haven: Yale University Press, 1984): 3–8. I am grateful to Andrew Wink for the translation and interpretation of J. Heinsios, *Woordenboek der Nederlandsche Taale* (Martinus Nijhoff, A. W. Sijthoff, 1916).

8. Webster's *New Universal Unabridged Dictionary* (New York: Simon and Schuster, 1983) and *Oxford English Dictionary* (Oxford: Oxford University Press, 1989).

9. Anthony Hecht, "Gardens of the Villa d'Este," in *Hard Hours* (New York: Atheneum, 1967), 95.

10. Lakoff and Johnson, *Metaphors.* See also Ralph Waldo Emerson, "Nature," in *Essays and Lectures* (New York: Library of America, 1983), 7–49.

11. Stilgoe, *Shallow-Water Dictionary,* 23, 28.

12. Many cultures have no single name or notion for *nature.* The singular quality of the English word masks a real multiplicity and implies falsely that there is a single definition. See Raymond Williams, "Ideas of Nature," in *Materialism and Culture* (London: Verso, 1980), 67–85.

13. Jackson, in "The Word Itself," limits the definition of *landscape* to deliberately created, "man-made systems"; J. R. Stilgoe, in *Common Landscape of America* (New Haven: Yale University Press, 1982), narrows the definition further, to human-made, nonurban land.

## The Hermeneutic Landscape, *James Corner*

1. By "marking" I mean to suggest the whole spectrum of ways in which different peoples signify their relationship to the land. More often than not, these signs are physically constructed, but this need not always be the case, as in the aboriginal songlines, for example.

2. I borrow this analogy from David Leatherbarrow, *The Roots of Architectural Invention* (Cambridge: Cambridge University Press, 1990).

## Reading and Writing the Site, *John Dixon Hunt*

1. *De Natura deorum,* II 60, 151–152. For an extensive exposition and discussion of these three natures see *Greater Perfections: The Practice of Garden Theory* (Philadelphia, 2000), chap. 3.

2. J. Bonfadio, *Le lettere e una scrittura burlesca,* ed. A. Greco (Rome, 1978), 96.

3. The two main writers on picturesque were William Gilpin, famous for his tour guides to various parts of Britain (see below in note 5), and the more theoretical Uvedale Price, *Essays on the Picturesque,* 3 vols. (London, 1810). For two modern commentaries on the picturesque cult see Christopher Hussey, *The Picturesque: Studies in a Point of View* (London and New York, 1927) and Malcolm Andrews, *In Search of the Picturesque* (Aldershot, Hants., 1989). For the bearing of the picturesque upon garden design see the relevant sections of the anthology *The Genius of the Place: The English Landscape Garden 1620–1820,* ed. John Dixon Hunt and Peter Willis (Cambridge, Mass., 1989).

4. *The Palm at the End of the Mind* (New York, 1972), 46. That the American poet's jar is less artful than, say, Keats' Grecian urn does not interfere with the argument offered here.

5. Gilpin set out his approach in *Three Essays: On Picturesque Beauty; On Picturesque Travel; and On Sketching Landscape: to which is added a poem on Landscape Painting* (London, 1792). He also produced a series of guides to different parts of Great Britain, for example, *Observations, relative chiefly to Picturesque Beauty, made in the year 1772, on several parts of England, particularly the Mountains, and Lakes of Cumberland, and Westmoreland* (London, 1786). These are reprinted in *The Picturesque: Literary Sources and Documents,* ed. M. Andrews, 3 vols. (Robertsbridge, East Sussex: Helm Information, 1994).

6. See Augustin Berque, *Médiance de milieux en paysages* (Montpellier, 1990).

7. Two recent books have taken that particular enquiry somewhat further than previous writ-

ers: Charles W. Moore, William J. Mitchell, and William Turnbull, Jr., *The Poetics of Gardens* (Cambridge, Mass., 1989), and *The Meaning of Gardens,* ed. Mark Francis and Randolph T. Hester, Jr. (Cambridge, Mass., 1990).

8. See Richard Foster Jones, *Ancients and Moderns: A Study of the Background of the Battle of the Books* (St. Louis, 1936). This theme is set out economically in Thomas Gray's poem *The Progress of Poetry,* first published in 1757.

9. The contemporary spelling *Gothick* is used to indicate eighteenth-century versions of this architectural style.

10. For this information I have drawn upon the *Royal Commission on Historical Manuscripts,* second report, II (1874), 82–84.

11. I have discussed these matters fully in "Verbal versus Visual Meanings in Garden History: The Case of Rousham," in *Garden History: Issues, Approaches, Methods,* ed. John Dixon Hunt, Dumbarton Oaks Colloquium on the History of Landscape Architecture, 13 (Washington, D.C., 1991).

12. The best introduction to this is Jean Hagstrum, *The Sister Arts* (Chicago, 1968).

13. R. Blome, *Gentleman's Recreation* (London, 1686) links both architecture and heraldry under "Ethicks" as forms which display and therefore need proper understanding or reading.

## Landscape Narratives, *Matthew Potteiger and Jamie Purinton*

1. M. Rakatansky, "Spatial Narratives," in J. Whiteman, J. Kipnix, and R. Burdett (eds.), *Strategies in Architectural Thinking* (Chicago and Cambridge, Mass.: Chicago Institute for Architecture and Urbanism and MIT Press, 1992), pp. 201–221.

2. S. Chatman, "What Novels Can Do That Films Can't (And Vice Versa)," in W. J. T. Mitchell (ed.), *On Narrative* (Chicago: University of Chicago Press, 1981), pp. 117–136, p. 124.

3. S. Cohan and L. Shires, *Telling Stories: A Theoretical Analysis of Narrative Fiction* (New York: Routledge, 1988), p. 53.

4. P. Ricoeur, "Narrative Time," in W. J. T. Mitchell (ed.), *On Narrative* (Chicago: University of Chicago Press, 1981), pp. 165–186, pp. 166–167.

5. E. Blake, designer (in collaboration with Andropogon Associates) and former director of the Crosby Arboretum, interview with authors, March 25, 1996.

6. *Pinecote Master Plan: A Guide for Long Range Development* (1994), Picayune: The Crosby Arboretum, p. 6.

7. *Pinecote Master Plan.*

8. Julia Kristeva, cited in N. Ellin, *Postmodern Urbanism* (Cambridge, Mass.: Blackwell, 1996), p. 254.

9. J. S. Duncan and N. G. Duncan, "[Re]Reading the landscape," *Environment and Planning D: Society and Space* 6 (1988): 117–126, p. 120.

10. J. S. Duncan, *The City as Text: The Politics of Landscape Interpretation in the Kandyan Kingdom* (Cambridge: Cambridge University Press, 1990), p. 16.

11. I. Parker, *Discourse Dynamics: Critical Analysis for Social and Individual Psychology* (New York: Routledge, 1992), p. 20.

12. T. Eagleton, *Literary Theory: An Introduction* (Minneapolis: University of Minnesota Press, 1983), p. 135.

13. C. Franklin, "Foster Living Landscapes," in G. F. Thompson and F. R. Steiner (eds.), *Ecological Design and Planning* (New York: John Wiley & Sons), pp. 263–287, p. 273.

14. J. Johnson and F. Frankel, *Modern Landscape Architecture: Redefining the Garden* (New York: Abbeville Press, 1991), p. 179.

15. *Pinecote Master Plan,* p. 9.

16. Johnson and Frankel, *Modern Landscape Architecture.*

17. H. White, *Tropics of Discourse: Essays in Cultural Criticism* (Baltimore: Johns Hopkins University Press, 1978), p. 2.

18. W. Conway and M. Schulte, unpublished design documents for the *De-Code/Re-Code Atlanta* Project, 1996.

## Representation and Landscape, *James Corner*

1. See Donald Meinig (ed.), *The Interpretation of Ordinary Landscapes* (Oxford University Press, 1979). See especially the essays by Meinig, "The Beholding Eye," pp. 33–48; "Reading the Landscape: An appreciation of W. G. Hoskins and J. B. Jackson," pp. 195–244; and Pierce Lewis, "Axioms for Reading the Landscape," pp. 11–32.

2. Meinig, "The Beholding Eye," pp. 33–48, and "Reading the Landscape," pp. 195–244. See also Denis Cosgrove and Stephen Daniels (eds.), *The Iconography of Landscape* (Cambridge University Press, 1988), pp. 1–10: Denis Cosgrove, *Social Formation and the Symbolic Landscape* (London, 1984), pp. 13–38; and Max Oelschlaeger, *The Idea of Wilderness: From Prehistory to the Age of Ecology* (New Haven: Yale University Press, 1991).

3. By "eidetic" I mean that which pertains to the visual formation of ideas, or to the reciprocity between image and idea. That drawing is fundamentally about making images suggests that it might actually *generate* and transform ideas for the percipient rather than simply representing them.

4. See Robin Evans, "Translations from Drawing to Building," *AA Files 12* (London: Architectural Association, 1986), pp. 3–18.

5. See Maurice Merleau-Ponty, *The Primacy of Perception* (Evanston, Ill.: Northwestern University Press, 1964), esp. chs. 2 and 5.

6. See Martin Heidegger, "The Origin of the Work of Art," *Poetry, Language, Thought*, trans. and intro. by Albert Hofstadter (New York: Harper and Row, 1975), pp. 17–87.

7. Evans, "Translations from Drawing to Building."

8. Bachelard uses extracts from books by Baudelaire and Phillippe Diole to further explicate the idea of "intimate immensity." Bachelard quotes from Diole describing "the magical operation that, in deep water, allows the diver to loosen the ordinary ties of time and space and make life resemble an obscure, inner poem . . . Neither in the desert nor on the bottom of the sea does one's spirit remain sealed and indivisible." Imaginative extension and all-surrounding limitlessness are poetic qualities of landscape which enable us to dream. In the dark forest we may enter the closed and veiled forests of ourselves. In the open desert our own spirit may also be sensed as unbounded and infinite. See Gaston Bachelard, *The Poetics of Space* (Boston: Beacon Press, 1974), pp. 183–210.

9. Martin Heidegger, "Building, Dwelling, Thinking," *Poetry, Language, Thought*, trans. and intro. by Alfred Hofstadter (New York: Harper and Row, 1975), p. 154.

10. See Maurice Merleau-Ponty, *Phenomenology of Perception*, trans. by Colin Smith (London: Routledge and Kegan Paul, 1986), p. 243.

11. The notion of landscape spatiality being akin to a layered map of locations, or as situated places perceived through "spacing," can be related to Kevin Lynch's work in his book *The Image of the City*. The thesis of the book is that we know our built environment as a complex structure of nameable locations, as named loci of phenomena. Lynch's layers of analysis—"path, node, landmark, district, edge"—are collectively understood by ordinary citizens who mentally overlay them as a cognitive map—"something is over there in relation to this." Lynch's notion that a densely stratified landscape fabric, of enormous perceptual complexity, can actually be understood and translated into a spoken, written or drawn "map," by most of its inhabitants, is in concurrence with Heidegger's insights into spatiality: the fact that space is situated, connected, spaced, named, and, most important, "thought through," Kevin Lynch, *The Image of the City* (MIT Press, 1964). In relation to the concept of spacing see Jacques Derrida, "Point de Folie—Maintenant l'Architecture," *AA Files 12* (London: Architectural Association, 1986).

12. Heidegger, "Building, Dwelling, Thinking," p. 156.

13. Merleau-Ponty, *Phenomenology of Perception*, p. 412.

14. See J. J. Gibson, *The Ecological Approach to Visual Perception* (Boston: Houghton Mifflin, 1979).

15. Walter Benjamin, *Illuminations,* ed. Hannah Arendt (New York: Schocken Books, 1969), p. 239.

16. See John Whiteman, "Criticism, Representation and Experience in Contemporary Architecture," *Harvard Architecture Review 4* (New York: Rizzoli, 1985), pp. 137–147.

17. Robert Rosenblum, "The Origin of Painting," *Art Bulletin* (December 1957): 279–290.

18. Evans, "Translations from Drawing to Building," pp. 6–7.

19. Vitruvius Pollio, *On Architecture,* ed. From the Harleian manuscript 2767, and trans. by Frank Granger, 2 vols. (Cambridge: Harvard University Press, 1983), vol. 1, bk. 1, ch. 11, pp. 24–25. Also see Claudio Sgarbi, "Speculation on De-sign and *Finito*," 17A 9: *Representation* (New York: Rizzoli for the University of Pennsylvania, 1988), pp. 155–165.

20. See Kenneth Frampton, "The Anthropology of Construction," *Casabella* 251, no. 2 (January 1986): 26–30. Also see Marco Frascari, "A New Angel/Angle in Architectural Research: The Idea of Demonstration," *Journal of Architectural Education* 44, no. 1 (November 1990): 11–19.

21. Daniele Barbaro, *La Practica della Perspettiva* (Sala Bolognese, 1980), pp. 129–130. Referred to by Alberto Perez-Gomez, "Architecture as Drawing," *Journal of Architectural Education* 26, no. 2 (1982), pp. 2–7.

22. Perez-Gomez, "Architecture as Drawing," p. 3. Also see Alberto Perez-Gomez, *Architecture and the Crisis of Modern Science* (Cambridge, Mass.: MIT Press, 1988), esp. ch. IV.

23. Ibid. Also see Frascari, "The Ideas of Demonstration," p. 12.

24. Nelson Goodman, *Languages of Art* (Cambridge: Hackett Publishing, 1964), pp. 127–176.

25. Edward R. Tufte, *Envisioning Information* (Cheshire, Conn.: Graphics Press, 1990), p. 114.

26. See Ann Hutchinson Guest, *Dance Notation* (London, 1984). Also see Albrecht Kunst, *Dictionary of Kinetography Laban (Labanolation)* (Estover, Plymouth, England, 1979).

27. See Lawrence Halprin, *RSVP Cycles* (New York: George Braziller, 1969).

28. See Sergei Eisenstein, *Film Sense,* ed. Jay Leyda (New York: Harcourt, Brace, Jovanovich, 1975), pp. 176–177.

29. See Arthur Danto, *The Transfiguration of the Commonplace* (Cambridge, Mass.: Harvard University Press, 1981), ch. 6. Also see Nelson Goodman, *Language of Art.*

30. This is discussed by Norman Bryson in *Vision and Painting: The Logic of the Gaze* (New Haven: Yale University Press, 1988), pp. 43–44. Also see E. H. Gombrich, *Art and Illusion: A Study in the Psychology of Pictorial Representation* (Oxford: Phaidon, 1977), pp. 29–34, 320–330.

31. Rosalind Krauss, *The Originality of the Avant-Garde and Other Modernist Myths* (Cambridge, Mass.: MIT Press, 1985), p. 166.

32. See Dan Rose, "The Brandywine: A Case Study of an Ecological Strategy," *Landscape Journal* 7, no. 2 (University of Wisconsin Press, Fall 1988), pp. 128–133.

33. The development of landscape as a scene to be "completed" by the action of visitors was most evident in the landscape gardens by William Kent, especially at Rousham. See John Dixon Hunt, *William Kent, Landscape Garden Designer* (London: A. Zwemmer, 1987), pp. 29–40, 60–99.

34. There are two problems with pictorial representation when making landscapes. The first is that the predominance of the picture plane remains an extremely remote aspect of landscape experience, emphasizing the visual over other modes of cognition. The second is that the drawn picture itself begins to accrue a certain value, inevitably ascending to the status of an aesthetic object, and subsequently playing all-too-comfortably into the hands of modern criticism and the consumptive demand of glassy magazines and galleries. See Whiteman, "Criticism, Representation and Experience," pp. 137–147.

35. Nelson Goodman, *Languages of Art,* pp. 111.

36. See Wassily Kandinsky, *The Spirit of Art* (New York: Dover, 1977). Also see E. H. Gombrich, *Art and Illusion,* ch. XI. Gombrich also has described how figures, in addition to forms or colors, can be juxtaposed to create a new message. The "ideogram" of water alongside an eye might signify "to weep," a mouth and a dog might signify "to bark," and so on. The correspondence between matter and idea forms the basis for meaning.

37. See Robin Evans, "In Front of Lines That Leave Nothing Behind," *AA Files* 6 (London: Architectural Association, 1983), pp. 88–96.

38. This division is most clearly identified and explained by Robin Evans. "Translations from Drawing to Building," pp. 3–18.

39. Whiteman, "Criticism, Representation and Experience," p. 145.

40. See Alberto Perez-Gomez, "Drawing and Architecture," pp. 2–7.

41. Criticism has ascended to a primary role in the production of art works since the enlightenment. Its aim is to reflect on the underlying assumptions and premises which constitute a work. In our modern age, there is a deep suspicion that everything must be questioned if it is to be substantiated. It is a skeptical position, but one most prevalent in our work today.

42. Whiteman, "Criticism, Representation and Experience," p. 143.

43. Ibid., p. 144.

44. While it might be naïve simply to ignore the pervasive effects of objective reasoning and modern criticism, this does not mean we must necessarily play into the hands of it. Through a practice of critical resistance one might hope to re-educate designers and critics in the refined perception of subjective and psychic responses when receiving drawings. Indeed, the poetic critic may well accomplish a real service to society by projecting a richness of association and potentiality previously repressed by the narrow confines of logocentric criticism. On the other hand, this is not a call for greater ethereality and mysticism, so prevalent in much of contemporary criticism. See George Steiner, *Real Presences* (Chicago: University of Chicago Press, 1990).

45. This observation is derived from Robin Evans, "Translation from Drawing to Building," p. 5.

46. Ibid., p. 5.

47. The term "drawing as a vehicle of creativity" is derived from Dalibor Veseley, "Representation as a Vehicle of Creativity," *Scroope*, issue 2 (Cambridge University School of Architecture, 1990), pp. 13–17.

48. See Frascari, "The Ideas of Demonstration." One constructs both theoretical schemata as to things and plans. Construal is theoretical whereas construction is instrumental. Thus, "there is no construction without a construing, and no construing without a construction . . . The construing of a cosmological order is constructed in a Renaissance villa," p. 18. Frascari uses the word chiasm to mean "an exchange between the phenomenal body and the 'objective' body, between the perceiving and perceived" (quoted from Merleau-Ponty, *The Visible and the Invisible* [Evanston, Ill.: Northwestern University Press, 1968], p. 215). Frascari's "angel/angle" trope is used to illustrate this union. Drawings are therefore the site, or *locus*, of both construal and construction.

49. Ibid., pp. 11–19. Also see Dalibor Veseley, "Architecture and the Conflict of Representation," *AA Files 8* (London: Architectural Association, 1984), pp. 21–38.

50. See A. Chastel, *Leonard da Vinci par lui-même* (Paris, 1952).

51. See Jurgis Baltrusaitis, *Aberrations: An Essay in the Legend of Forms,* trans. by Richard Miller (Cambridge, Mass.: MIT Press, 1989), pp. 60–105.

52. For an account of the surrealist view toward the re-enchantment of the world, see André Breton, "Artistic Genesis and the Perspective of Surrealism," *Painting and Surrealism* (New York: Harper and Row, 1972), pp. 50–362.

53. See Veseley, "Drawing as Vehicle of Creativity," pp. 13–17.

54. See Frascari, "The Ideas of Demonstration," p. 11.

55. Ibid., p. 17.

56. Whiteman, "Criticism, Representation and Experience," p. 147.

57. Marco Frascari, *Monsters of Architecture* (Lanham, Md.: Rowman and Littlefield, 1991), p. 102.

58. Ibid., p. 104.

59. Bryson, *Vision and Painting,* p. 88.

60. Ibid., p. 88.

61. Ibid., p. 92.

62. Ibid., p. 92.

63. While the preceding paragraphs have described drawings primarily in relationship to buildings, the same arguments still hold true for drawings vis-à-vis the design of landscapes, with minor modifications. The landscape is a different phenomenon from building. It is expressed differently and the procedures for its construction are also different. Landscapes are also dynamic phenomena, living, growing, changing form and eventually dying. Surely management plans and schedules seem integral parts of any landscape project, for example, demonstrating temporal as well as spatial intentions, and demonstrating practical techniques of stewardship.

64. For more on analogical drawing see Dalibor Veseley, *Drawing as a Vehicle of Creativity*, pp. 13–17.

## Landscape as Cultural Product, *Denis Cosgrove*

1. J. Barrell, "Geographies of Hardy's Wessex," *Journal of Historical Geography* 8, no. 4 (1982): 347–361, p. 358.

2. J. Berger, *Ways of Seeing* (Harmondsworth: Penguin Books/BBC, 1972), pp. 13, 15.

## The Expanded Field of Landscape Architecture, *Elizabeth Meyer*

1. Linda Nicholson, "Feminism as Against Epistemology: Introduction," in *Feminism/Postmodernism*, ed. Linda Nicholson (New York: Routledge, 1990), pp. 1–16, p. 5.

2. There are characteristics of postmodern philosophy as exemplified in the writings of Richard Rorty and Jean François Lyotard. See Nicholson, "Feminism as Against Epistemology," and Nancy Fraser and Linda J. Nicholson, "Social Criticism without Philosophy: An Encounter between Feminism and Postmodernism," in *Feminism/Postmodernism*, ed. Linda Nicholson (New York: Routledge, 1990), pp. 19–38.

3. Denis Cosgrove, *Social Formation and Symbolic Landscape* (Totowa, N.J.: Barnes and Noble, 1984), and Donald Worster, *Nature's Economy: A History of Ecological Ideas* (Cambridge: Cambridge University Press, 1977).

4. Annette Kolodny, "Dancing Through the Minefield: Some Observations on the Theory, Practice and Politics of a Feminist Literary Criticism" [1980], in *The New Feminist Criticism*, ed. Elaine Showalter (New York: Pantheon Books, 1985), pp. 144–167, p. 153. She continues: "We must re-examine not only our aesthetics but, as well, the inherent biases and assumptions informing the critical methods which (in part) shape our aesthetic responses" (p. 157).

5. My position here has been influenced by Griselda Pollock, "Feminist Interventions in the Histories of Art: An Introduction," in *Vision and Difference: Femininity, Feminism and Histories of Art* (London: Routledge, 1988), pp. 1–17, p. 2. This particular quote from Pollock refers to a statement made by Linda Nochlin.

6. Griselda Pollock, "Modernity and the Spaces of Femininity," in *Vision and Difference: Femininity, Feminism and Histories of Art* (London: Routledge, 1988), pp. 50–90, p. 55.

7. Andreas Huyssen, "Mapping the Postmodern," in *After the Great Divide: Modernism, Mass Culture, Postmodernism* (Bloomington: Indiana University Press, 1986), pp. 178–221, p. 181.

## Part V. Ecological Design and the Aesthetics of Sustainability
## An Ecological Approach, *Alan Ruff*

1. E. M. Nicholson, *The Environmental Revolution* (London: Penguin, 1972).

## Design for Human Ecosystems, *John T. Lyle*

1. Eugene P. Odum, "Strategy of Ecosystem Development," *Science* 164 (1969).

2. R. H. Rigler, "The Concept of Energy Flow and Nutrient Flow between Trophic Levels," in

*Unifying Concepts in Ecology*, ed. W. H. van Dobben and R. H. Lowe-McConnell (The Hague: Dr. W. Junk B.V. Publishers, 1975).

3. W. H. van Dobben and R. H. Lowe-McConnell, preface, *Unifying Concepts in Ecology*, ed. W. H. van Dobben and R. H. Lowe-McConnell (The Hague: Dr. W. Junk B.V. Publishers, 1975).

4. Francis C. Evans, "Ecosystem as the Basic Unit in Ecology," *Science* 123 (1956).

5. Erich Jantsch, *Design for Evolution* (New York: George Braziller, 1975).

6. Carl Steinitz, "Simulating Alternative Policies for Implementing the Massachusetts Scenic and Recreational Rivers Act: The North River Demonstration Project," *Landscape Planning* 6 (1979).

7. Ian L. McHarg, *Design with Nature* (New York: Natural History Press, 1969).

8. Eugene P. Odum, *Fundamentals of Ecology*, 3rd ed. (Philadelphia: W. B. Saunders, 1971).

9. Ramon Margalef, "On Certain Unifying Principles in Ecology," *American Naturalist* 97 (1963).

10. Odum, *Fundamentals of Ecology*, p. 37.

## Can Floating Seeds Make Deep Forms? *John T. Lyle*

1. John Tillman Lyle, *Design for Human Ecosystems* (New York: Van Nostrand Reinhold, 1985).

## Gray World, Green Heart, *Robert Thayer*

1. R. Thayer, "Visual Ecology: Revitalising the Aesthetics of Landscape Architecture," *Landscape* 20, no. 2 (1976): 37–43.

2. I. Mitroff and W. Bennis, *The Unreality Industry* (New York: Birch Land Press, 1989).

3. N. Postman, *Amusing Ourselves to Death: Public Discourse in the Age of Show Business* (New York: Penguin Books, 1985).

4. E. Rogers and F. Shoemaker *Communication of Innovations* (New York: Macmillan, 1971).

5. R. Thayer, "Conspicuous Non-consumption," in *EDRA Proceedings* 11 (Environmental Design Research Association, 1980), pp. 176–182.

6. W. Jackson, W. Berry, and B. Colman, eds., *Meeting the Expectations of the Land* (San Francisco: North Point Press, 1984).

7. R. Nash, "Problems in Paradise," *Environment* 20, no. 6 (1979): 25–40.

8. *Landscape Architecture* (1988) ASLA, Washington D.C.

9. D. H. Meadows, D. L. Meadows, and J. Randers, *Beyond the Limits* (Post Hills, Vt.: Chelsea Publishing Company, 1992).

10. W. Kahrl, "Ersatz Environmentalism." *Sacramento Bee*, Forum Section, January 10, 1993, p. 4.

11. R. Attenborough, *The Words of Gandhi* (New York: New Market Press, 1982).

## Messy Ecosystems, Orderly Frames, *Joan Iverson Nassauer*

1. D. Lowenthal and H. C. Prince, "English Landscape Tastes," *Geographical Review* 55 (1965): 186–222.

2. J. I. Nassauer, "The Appearance of Ecological Systems as a Matter of Policy," *Landscape Ecology* 6 (1992): 239–250.

3. C. Howett, "Systems, Signs, and Sensibilities: Sources for a New Landscape Aesthetic," *Landscape Journal* 6 (1988): 1–12.

4. G. Crandell, *Nature Pictorialized* (Baltimore: John Hopkins University Press, 1993).

5. M. M. Eaton, *Aesthetics and the Good Life* (London: Farleigh Dickinson University Press, 1990). M. M. Eaton, "Responding to the Call for New Landscape Metaphors," *Landscape Journal* 9, no. 1 (1990): 22–27.

6. A. Leopold, "The Farmer as Conservationist," *American Forests* 45 (1939): 296–297.

7. J. R. Stilgoe, *Borderland* (New Haven: Yale University Press, 1988). E. Pennypacker, "What Is Taste, and Why Should I Care?" *Proceedings of the Council of Educators in Landscape Architecture* 4 (1992): 63–74.

8. K. Lynch, *Site Planning,* 2d. ed. (Cambridge, Mass.: MIT Press, 1971).

9. Y. Tuan, *Dominance and Affection: The Making of Pets* (New Haven: Yale University Press, 1986). Sara Stein, *Noah's Garden* (Boston: Houghton Mifflin, 1993).

10. J. I. Nassauer, "Landscape Care: Perceptions of Local People in Landscape Ecology and Sustainable Development," *Landscape and Land Use Planning* 8 (1988): 27–41.

11. R. Kaplan, "The Role of Nature in the Urban Context," in Altman and Wohlwill, eds., *Behaviour and the Natural Environment* (New York: Plenum Press, 1983).

12. J. I. Nassauer, "Managing for Naturalness in Wildlands and Agricultural Lands," in *Our Natural Landscape,* pp. 447–453. "USDA General Technical Report PSW-35," Berkeley, Calif., Pacific Southwest Forest and Range Experiment Station, 1979.

13. C. Maser, "On the 'Naturalness' of Natural Areas: A Perspective for the Future," *Natural Areas Journal* 10 (1990): 129–133.

14. Nassauer, "The Appearance of Natural Areas."

15. D. Dearden, "Consensus and a Theoretical Framework for Landscape Evaluation," *Journal for Environmental Management* 34 (1987): 267–278; P. R. Herzog, "A Cognitive Analysis of Preference for Urban Nature," *Journal of Environmental Management* 9 (1989): 27–43; Kaplan, "Role of Nature": R. Knopf, "Human Behavior, Cognition, and Affect in the Natural Environment," in Stokols and Altman, eds., *Handbook of Environmental Psychology* (New York: Wiley, 1987); R. C. Smardon, "Perception and Aesthetics of the Urban Environment: Review of the Role of Vegetation," *Landscape and Urban Planning* 15 (1988): 85–106; R. S. Ulrich, "Human Responses to Vegetation and Landscapes." *Landscapes and Urban Planning* 13 (1986): 29–44.

16. S. Buss, "Private Landowner's Values for Rare Species and Natural Communities," unpublished thesis, University of Minnesota, 1994.

17. Kaplan, "Role of Nature"; Knopf, "Human Behavior"; Smardon, "Perception and Aesthetics"; H. W. Schroeder, "Establishing Park Tree Densities to Maximize Landscape Aesthetics," *Journal of Environmental Management* 23 (1986).

18. Buss, "Private Landowner's Values."

19. S. K. Robinson, *Inquiry Into the Picturesque* (Chicago: University of Chicago Press, 1991); R. B. Bonsignore, "Representing the Ecological Function of Midwestern Farm Streams: Price's Picturesque Applied to Stream Corridors," unpublished thesis, University of Minnesota, 1992; Howett, "Systems, Signs, and Sensibilities"; Crandell, *Nature Pictorialized.*

20. J. Appleton, *The Experience of Landscape* (New York: John Wiley and Sons, 1975); J. D. Balling and J. H. Falk "Development of Visual Preferences for Natural Environments," *Environment and Behavior* 14 (1982): 5–28; S. Kaplan and R. Kaplan, *Cognition and Environment: Functioning in an Uncertain World* (New York: Praeger, 1982).

21. Crandell, *Nature Pictorialized*; Pennypacker, "What Is Taste, and Why Should I Care?"; Robinson, *Inquiry Into the Picturesque.*

22. H. Rosenberg, *Artworks and Packages* (New York: Horizon Press, 1969), p. 78.

23. J. I. Nassauer, "The Aesthetics of Horticulture: Neatness as a Form of Care," *HortScience* 23 (1988): 973–977.

24. Nassauer, "Landscape Care"; Nassauer, "The Aesthetics of Horticulture."

25. Nassauer, "The Aesthetics of Horticulture."

26. J. I. Nassauer, "Ecological Function and the Perception of Suburban Residential Landscapes," in P. H. Gobster, ed., *Managing Urban and High Use Recreation Settings* (St. Paul, Minn.: General Technical Report, USDA Forest Service, North Central Forest Experiment Station, 1993), pp. 55–60.

27. R. D. Martin, "Suburban Residents' Perception of Wildlife Habitat Patches and Corridors in Their Neighborhoods," unpublished thesis, University of Minnesota, 1993.

28. Martin, "Suburban Residents' Perception."

29. Ron Silliman quoted in J. Prinz, *Art Discourse/Discourse in Art* (New Brunswick, N.J.: Rutgers University Press, 1991).

30. J. I. Nassauer, "The Aesthetic Benefits of Agricultural Land," *Renewable Resources Journal*

7 (1989): 17–18; J. I. Nassauer, "Aesthetic Objectives for Agricultural Policy," *Journal of Soil and Water Conservation* 44 (1989): 384–387.

31. Rosenberg, *Artworks and Packages.*

## Part VI. Integrating Site, Place, and Region

1. R. Forman, *Land Mosaics: The Ecology of Landscapes and Regions* (Cambridge: Cambridge University Press, 1995).

2. R. Robertson, "Mapping the Global Condition," *Theory, Culture and Society* 7 (1990): 2–3.

3. K. Frampton, "Towards a Critical Regionalism: Six Points Towards an Architecture of Resistance," in H. Foster, *The Anti-Aesthetic* (Port Townsend, Wash.: Bay Press, 1983).

4. R. Forman, M. Godron, *Landscape Ecology* (New York: Wiley, 1986).

5. C. Reiniger, "Bioregional Planning and Ecosystem Protection," in G. F. Thompson and G. Steiner, eds., *Ecological Design and Planning* (New York: John Wiley and Sons, 1997).

6. See particularly J. Corner, *Recovering Landscape* (Princeton, N.J.: Princeton Architectural Press, 1999).

## Principles for Regional Design, *Michael Hough*

1. A. J. Cordell, "The Uneasy Eighties: The Transition to an Information Society," *Alternatives* 14, nos. 3–4 (1987).

2. K. Lynch, *Managing the Sense of the Region* (Cambridge, Mass.: MIT Press, 1976).

3. *Toronto Globe and Mail*, April 18, 1987.

4. Ibid.

5. Jane Jacobs, "Guiding Principles for Streets that Work," Energy Probe Symposium, "The Streetscape: Planning and Retrofitting As if People Mattered," Toronto, June 1936.

## Signature-Based Landscape Design, *Joan Woodward*

1. P. Murphy, W. Neill, and D. Ackerman, *By Nature's Design* (San Francisco: Chronicle Books, 1993), p. 11.

2. M. T. Watts, *Reading the Landscape of America* (New York: Collier Books, 1982), p. 320.

3. W. M. Marsh, *Landscape Planning: Environmental Applications* (New York: John Wiley and Sons, 1991), p. 43.

## Infrastructure as Landscape, *Gary Strang*

1. Lewis Mumford, *Sticks and Stones* (New York: Boni and Liveright, 1924).

2. Harry Granick, *Underneath New York* (New York: Fordham University Press, 1991).

## Conclusion

1. See P. Radmall, "Landscape by Default," *Landscape Design* 159 (1986): 17–29.

2. S. R. Swaffield, "Directions in Diversity," *The Landscape* 45 (1990): 10–13.

3. S. R. Swaffield, "Professionalism in the Twenty-First Century," in *Proceedings of 1999 ASLA Annual Meeting* (Boston: ASLA, 1999).

4. This aspect owes much to Donald Schon's work. See *The Reflective Practitioner* (New York: Basic Books, 1983).

5. To conclude on a positive note, commentators in a range of fields have noted some convergence of thinking between the "two cultures" of art and science. In the arts and social science, there have been a number of attempts to reconcile the role of the individual and the role of society (e.g., Giddens's concept of structuration). In the natural sciences, there is widening recognition of the role society and culture play in "framing" knowledge. The two positions converge in concepts such as "soft systems," which recognize that knowledge is socially and culturally constructed, while avoiding the worst excesses of relativism.

# CREDITS

Garrett Eckbo, "Landscape for Living." From Garrett Eckbo, *Landscape for Living* (New York: Dodge, 1950), 57–60. Reprinted with the kind agreement of Mrs. A. Eckbo.

J. B. Jackson, "How to Study Landscape." From J. B. Jackson, *The Necessity for Ruins and Other Topics* (Amherst: University of Massachusetts Press, 1980), 113–126. © 1980 J. B. Jackson. Reprinted by permission of the University of Massachusetts Press.

James Corner, "Origins of Theory." From James Corner, "A Discourse on Theory I: 'Sounding the Depths'—Origins, Theory, and Representation," *Landscape Journal* 9, no. 2 (1990): 61–62. Reprinted by permission of the University of Wisconsin Press and the author.

James Corner, "Theory in Crisis." From James Corner, "A Discourse on Theory II: Three Tyrannies of Contemporary Theory and the Alternative of Hermeneutics," *Landscape Journal* 10, no. 2 (1991): 115–116, 129. Reprinted by permission of the University of Wisconsin Press and the author.

Elizabeth Meyer, "Situating Modern Landscape Architecture." Elizabeth Meyer, "Situating Modern Landscape Architecture: Theory as Bridging, Mediating, and Reconciling practice," in *Design + Value: Proceedings of the Annual Meeting of CELA*, 1992, 167–178. Reprinted by permission of CELA.

Hideo Sasaki, "Design Process." From Hideo Sasaki, "Thoughts on Education in Landscape Architecture: Some Comments on Today's Methodologies and Purpose." *Landscape Architecture* 40, no. 4 (1950): 158–160. Reprinted with permission from *Landscape Architecture* magazine.

Kevin Lynch and Gary Hack, "The Art of Site Planning." From Kevin Lynch and Gary Hack, *Site Planning*, 3rd ed. (Cambridge, Mass.: MIT Press, 1984), 11–12. © 1984 Massachusetts Institute of Technology.

Ian McHarg, "An Ecological Method." Ian McHarg, "An Ecological Method for Landscape Architecture," *Landscape Architecture* 57, no. 2 (1967): 105–107. Reprinted with permission from *Landscape Architecture* magazine.

Lawrence Halprin, "The RSVP Cycles." Excerpted from Lawrence Halprin, *The RSVP Cycles* (New York: George Braziller, 1969), 1–5. Used with permission.

Randolph Hester, Jr., "Community Design." From Randolph T. Hester, Jr., *Neighborhood Space* (Stroudsburg, Pa.: Dowden Hutchinson and Ross, 1974), 173–176, 180–183. Used with permission.

Kevin Lynch and Gary Hack, "Site Design." From Kevin Lynch and Gary Hack, *Site Planning*, 3rd ed. (Cambridge, Mass.: MIT Press, 1984), 127–129. © 1984 Massachusetts Institute of Technology.

Steven Krog, "Creative Risk Taking." Steven Krog, "Creative Risk Taking," *Landscape Architecture* 73, no. 3 (1983): 70–76. Reprinted with permission from *Landscape Architecture* magazine.

Bernard Lassus, "The Obligation of Invention." From "The Obligation of Invention," pp. 67–77 in *The Landscape Approach* by Bernard Lassus. Text copyright © 1998 University of Pennsylvania Press. Illustrations copyright © Bernard Lassus. Reprinted with permission.

Laurie Olin, "Form, Meaning, and Expression." From Laurie Olin, "Form, Meaning, and Expression in Landscape Architecture," *Landscape Journal* 7, no. 2 (1988): 155–57. Reprinted by permission of the University of Wisconsin Press and the author.

Geoffrey and Susan Jellicoe, "The Landscape of Man." From Geoffrey and Susan Jellicoe, *The Landscape of Man* (London: Thames and Hudson, 1987), 390–391.

Nan Fairbrother, "New Lives, New Landscapes." From Nan Fairbrother, *New Lives New Landscapes* (London: William Clowes and Son, 1970), 6–8. Reprinted by permission of Butterworth Heinemann Publishers, a division of Reed Educational and Professional Publishing Ltd.

# INDEX

# ACKNOWLEDGMENTS

My first and foremost thanks go to the authors and their publishers who have allowed us to reprint their work, and who in many cases have offered practical support and encouragement. I owe particular thanks to Mrs. Arlene Eckbo and Mrs. J. T. Lyle, who have been gracious in their help. I would also like to acknowledge the support of Kenny Helphand as editor of *Landscape Journal*, and the University of Wisconsin Press, for allowing a significant number of reprints from the *Journal*.

This reader had its origins in two theory courses I have been teaching to the B.L.A. program at Lincoln University, and I owe thanks to the students who over the years have become engaged with the courses and made helpful comments and suggestions. John Dixon Hunt initiated the project and has provided practical, intellectual, and moral support throughout. The anonymous readers for the University of Pennsylvania Press made many helpful comments and suggestions. Not all suggestions could be adopted, often for financial reasons, but they were a great help in shaping the final volume. Jo Joslyn and Noreen O'Connor at the University of Pennsylvania Press have guided me through the editorial process that has literally spanned the globe. At Lincoln University, Bron Bennetts, Sheryll Ashton, Linda Halliday, Brenda Kingi, and Alyson Gardner have provided invaluable help in the detailed process of assembling text and gaining permissions.

In my experience, all scholarly projects of any scale overflow into our family lives, and I owe thanks and appreciation to Jenny, Matthew, and Martin for their continuing support.